SHONEN JUMP MANGA

ONE PIECE

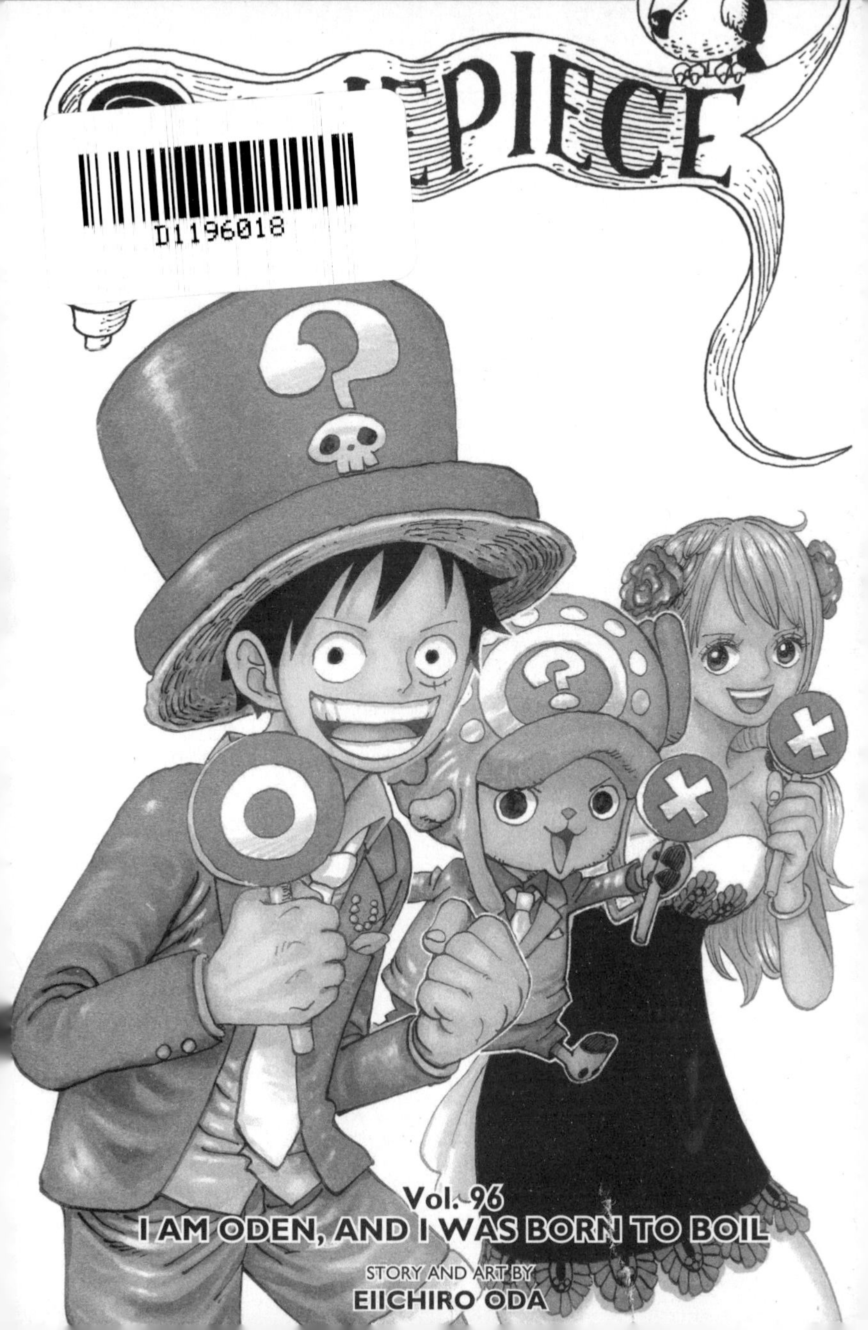

Vol. 96
I AM ODEN, AND I WAS BORN TO BOIL

STORY AND ART BY
EIICHIRO ODA

The Straw Hat Crew

Chopperemon [Ninja]
Tony Tony Chopper

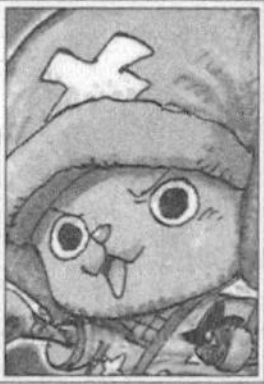

Studied powerful medicines in the Birdie Kingdom as he waited to rejoin the crew.

Ship's Doctor, Bounty: 100 berries

Luffytaro [Ronin]
Monkey D. Luffy

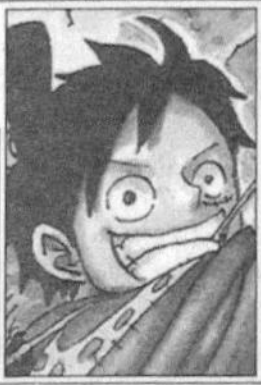

A young man dreaming of being the Pirate King. After two years of training he rejoins his friends in search of the New World!

Captain, Bounty: 1.5 billion berries

Orobi [Geisha]
Nico Robin

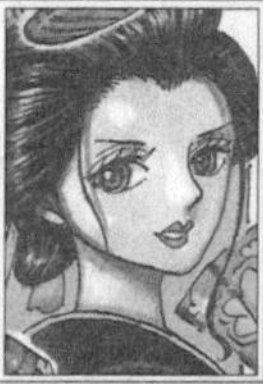

Spent time on the island of Baltigo with Dragon, Luffy's father and leader of the Revolutionary Army.

Archeologist, Bounty: 130 million berries

Zolojuro [Ronin]
Roronoa Zolo

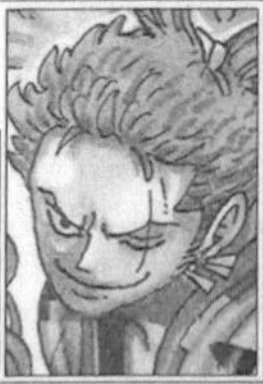

Swallowed his pride on Gloom Island and trained under Mihawk before rejoining Luffy.

Fighter, Bounty: 320 million berries

Franosuke [Carpenter]
Franky

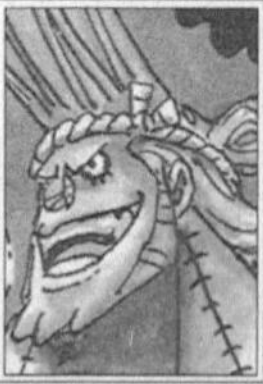

Upgraded himself into "Armored Franky" in the Future Land, Baldimore.

Shipwright, Bounty: 94 million berries

Onami [Kunoichi]
Nami

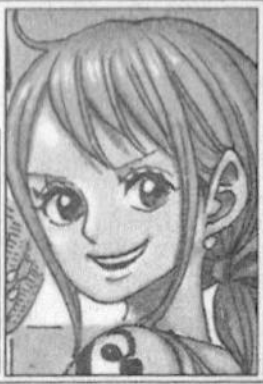

Learned about the climates of the New World on Weatheria, a Sky Island that studies the atmosphere.

Navigator, Bounty: 66 million berries

Bonekichi [Ghost]
Brook

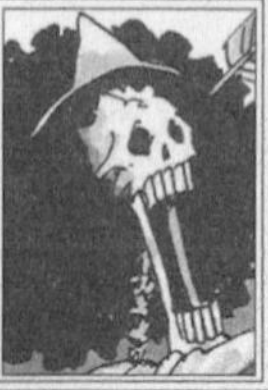

Originally captured by Long-Arm bandits for a freak show, he is now the mega-star "Soul King" Brook.

Musician, Bounty: 83 million berries

Usohachi [Toad Oil Salesman]
Usopp

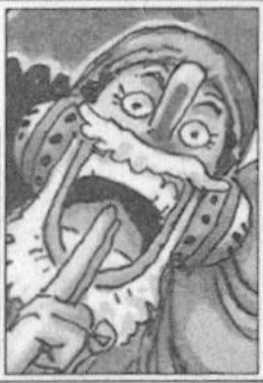

Received Heraclesun's lessons on the Bowin Islands in his quest to be the "king of the snipers."

Sniper, Bounty: 200 million berries

Sangoro [Soba Cook]
Sanji

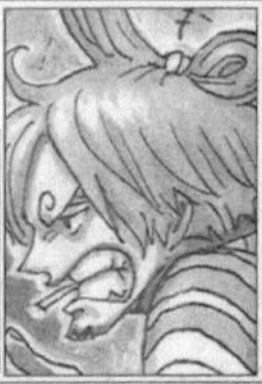

Honed his skills fighting with the masters of Newcomer Kenpo in the Kamabakka Kingdom.

Cook, Bounty: 330 million berries

Shanks

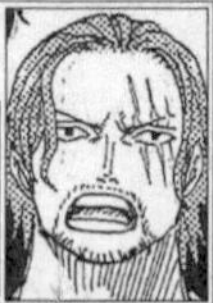

One of the Four Emperors. Waits for Luffy in the "New World," the second half of the Grand Line.

Captain of the Red-Haired Pirates

The story of ONE PIECE 1»96

Land of Wano (Present)

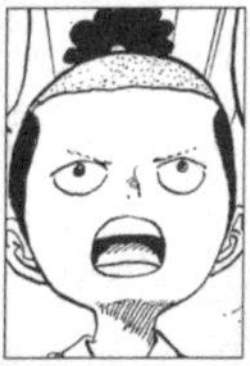
Kozuki Momonosuke
Daimyo (Heir) to Kuri in Wano

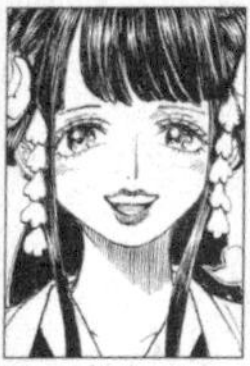
Kozuki Hiyori
Momonosuke's Little Sister

Akazaya Nine

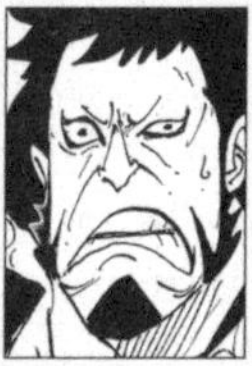
Foxfire Kin'emon
Samurai of Wano

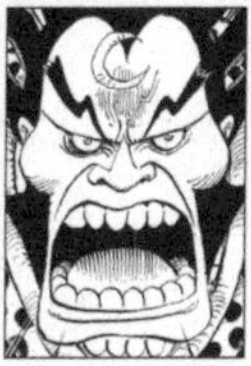
Raizo of the Mist
Ninja of Wano

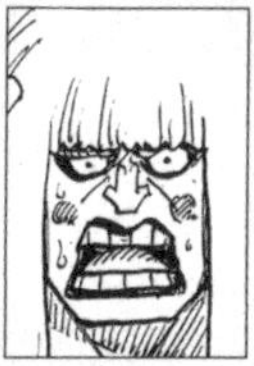
Evening Shower Kanjuro
Samurai of Wano

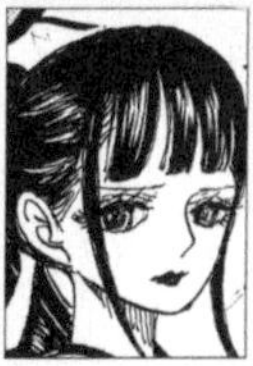
Okiku
Samurai of Wano

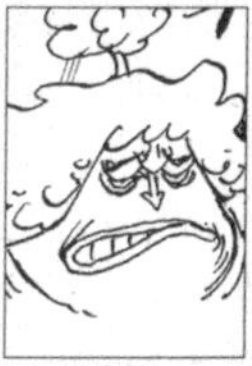
Ashura Doji (Shutenmaru)
Chief, Atamayama Thieves Brigade

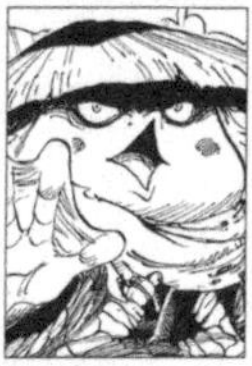
Kawamatsu
Samurai of Wano

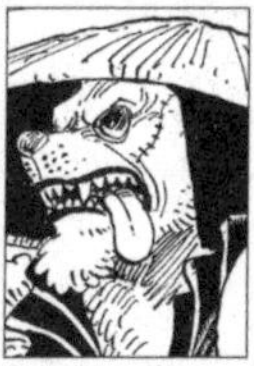
Duke Dogstorm
King of the Day, Mokomo

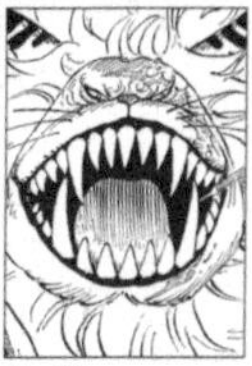
Cat Viper
King of the Night, Mokomo

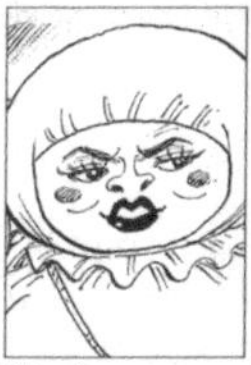
Shinobu
Veteran Kunoichi

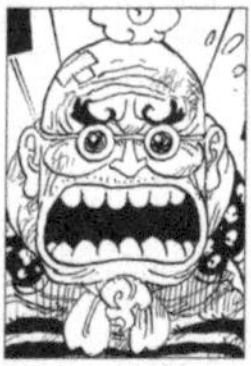
Hyogoro the Flower
Senior Yakuza Boss

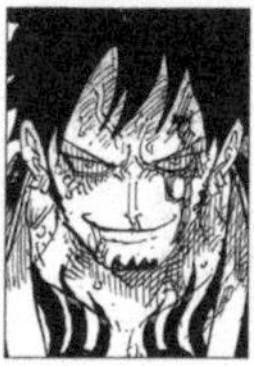
Trafalgar Law
Captain, Heart Pirates

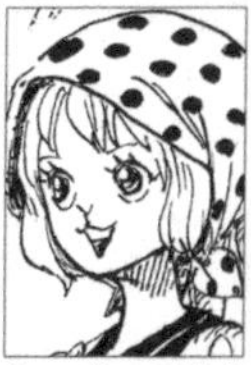
Carrot (Bunny Mink)
Battlebeast Tribe, Kingsbird

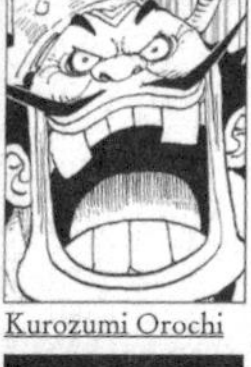
Kurozumi Orochi
Shogun of Wano

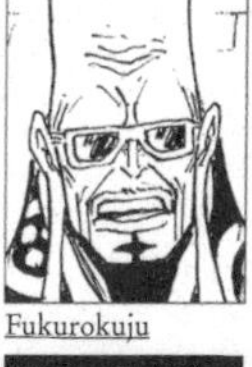
Fukurokuju
Leader, Orochi Oniwabanshu

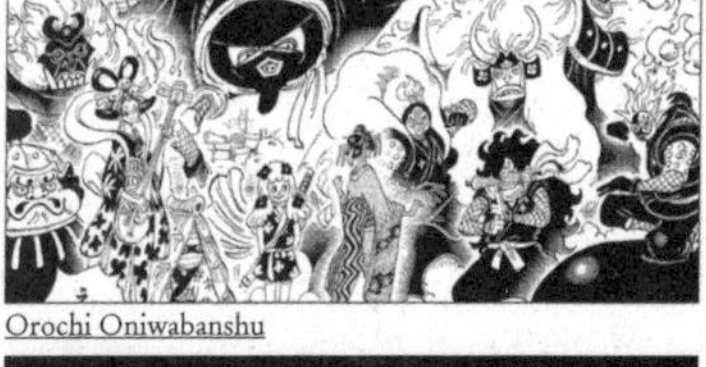
Orochi Oniwabanshu
Shogun of Wano's Private Ninja Squad

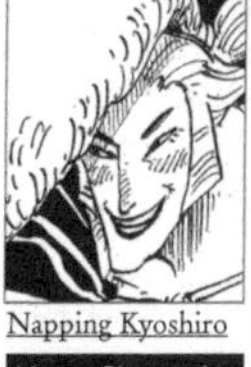
Napping Kyoshiro
Money Changer for the Kurozumi Clan

Animal Kingdom Pirates

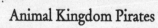

Kaido, King of the Beasts
(Emperor of the Sea)

A pirate known as the "strongest creature alive." Despite numerous tortures and death sentences, none have been able to kill him.

Captain, Animal Kingdom Pirates

Big Mom
(Emperor of the Sea)

One of the Four Emperors. Uses the Soul-Soul Fruit that extracts life span from others.

Captain, Big Mom Pirates

Lead Performers

King the Wildfire

Queen the Plague

Jack the Drought

Tobi Roppo

X. (Diez) Drake

Page One

Headliners

Basil Hawkins

Holdem

Babanuki

Daifugo

Solitaire

Speed

Dobon

Kid Pirates

forms a pirate alliance with Kaido! What effect will this devastating news have on Luffy's group...?

Kin'emon's samurai head to the gathering site on the day of battle, but Orochi's scheming causes the rest of the group to not show up. But the samurai still wish to avenge their lord, Oden. What will happen when they throw themselves into battle regardless?! Then the story travels 41 years into the past...

The story of ONE PIECE 1»96

Land of Wano (Past)

Kozuki Oden

A man of great heroism whose charisma attracts others. Fascinated with the outside world, he goes on a journey with Whitebeard.

Heir to the Shogunate of Wano

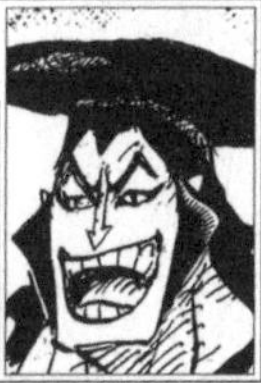

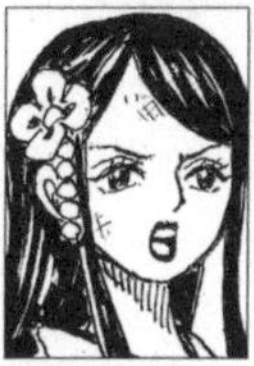

Amatsuki Toki

Wants to get to Wano

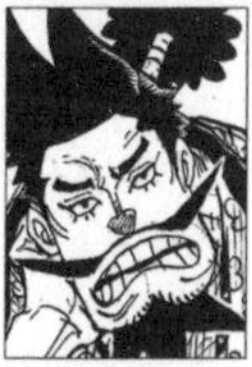

Kozuki Sukiyaki

Shogun of Wano

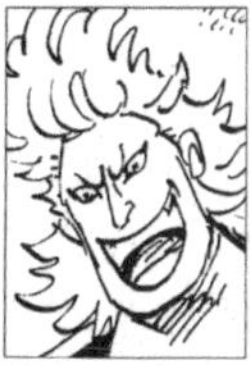

Kin'emon

Thug from the Capital

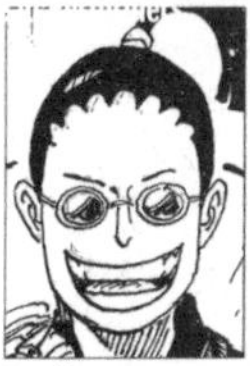

Denjiro

Orphan from the Capital

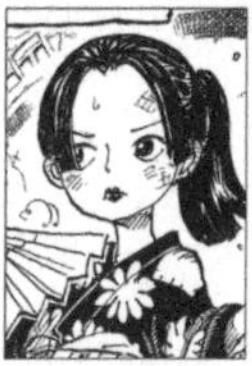

Izo

Son of Former Hanayanagi Dance Master

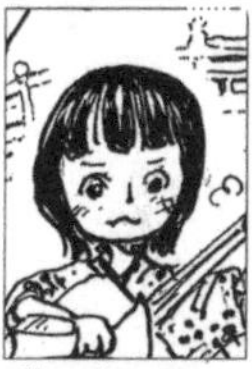

Kikunojo

Izo's Little Brother

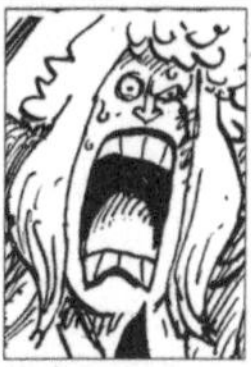

Kanjuro

Goblin of Kibi

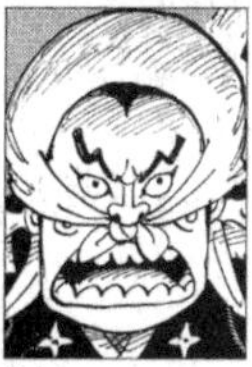

Raizo

Former Kozuki Oniwabanshu

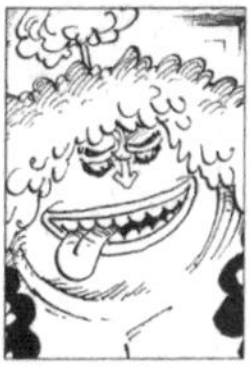

Ashura Doji

Strongest Creature in Kuri

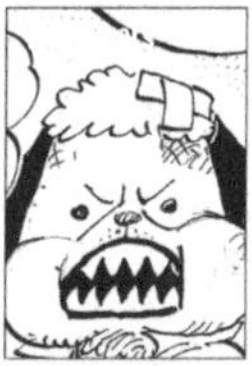

Dogstorm

Mink

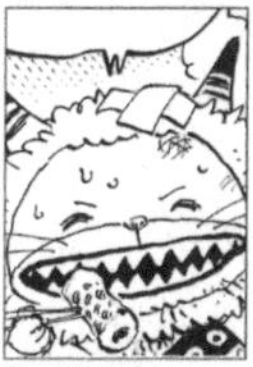

Cat Viper

Mink

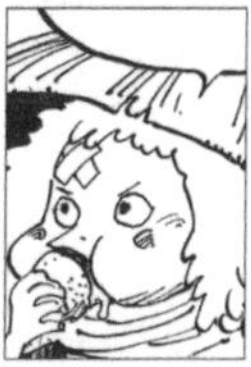

Kawamatsu

Kappa

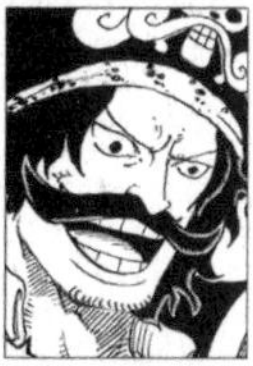

Gold Roger

Great Pirate

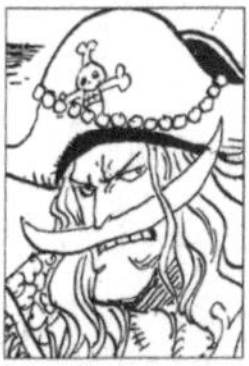

Edward Newgate

Captain, Whitebeard Pirates

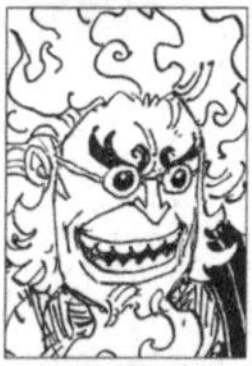

Hyogoro the Flower

Yakuza of the Capital

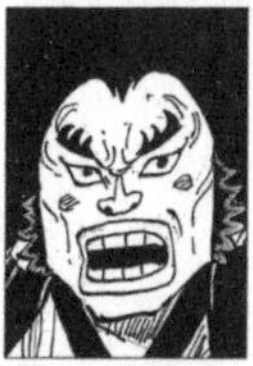

Shimotsuki Yasuie

Daimyo of Hakumai

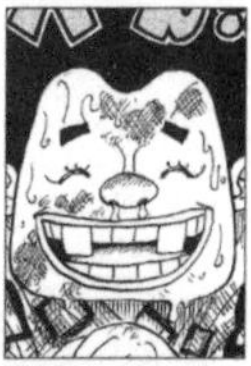

Kurozumi Orochi

Manservant

Story

After two years of hard training, the Straw Hat pirates are back together, first at the Sabaody Archipelago and then through Fish-Man Island to their next stage: the New World!!

Luffy and crew disembark on Wano for the purpose of defeating Kaido, one of the Four Emperors. They begin to recruit allies for a raid in two weeks' time. But Kaido's side finds out, and the plan is in peril. With great effort, the alliance rebounds and gathers members to await the day of the raid. Meanwhile, Big Mom arrives in Wano and

Vol. 96
I AM ODEN, AND I WAS BORN TO BOIL

CONTENTS

Chapter 965:

THE KUROZUMI CLAN'S PLOT

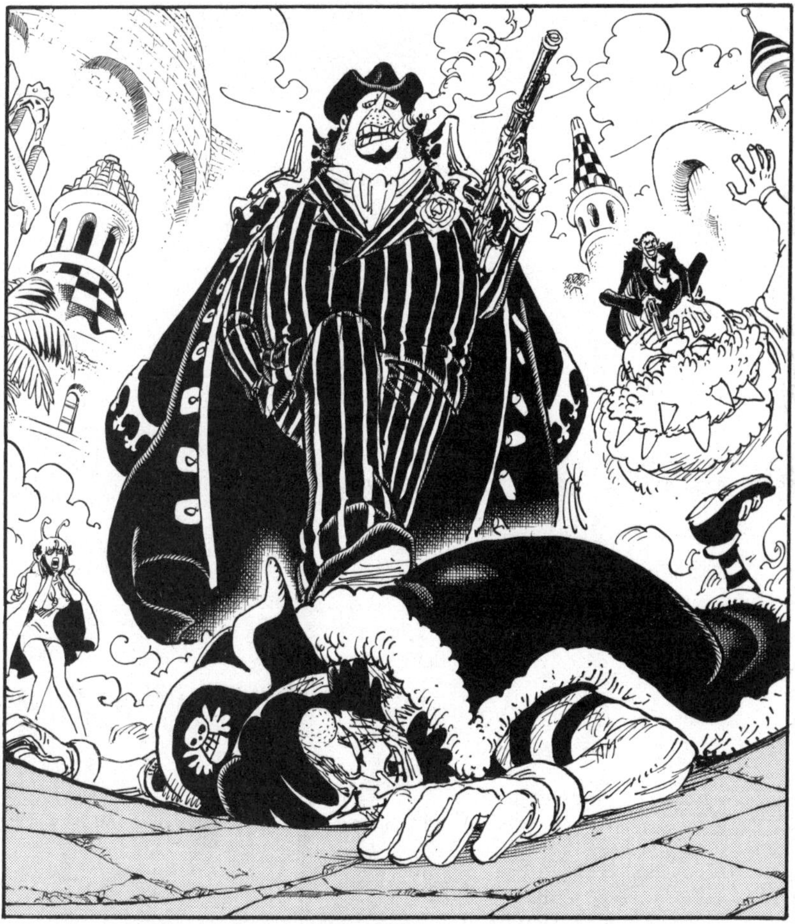

GANG BEGE'S OH MY FAMILY, VOL. 15: "ENOUGH RUCKUS. YOU'RE GONNA GET US SPOTTED TOO"

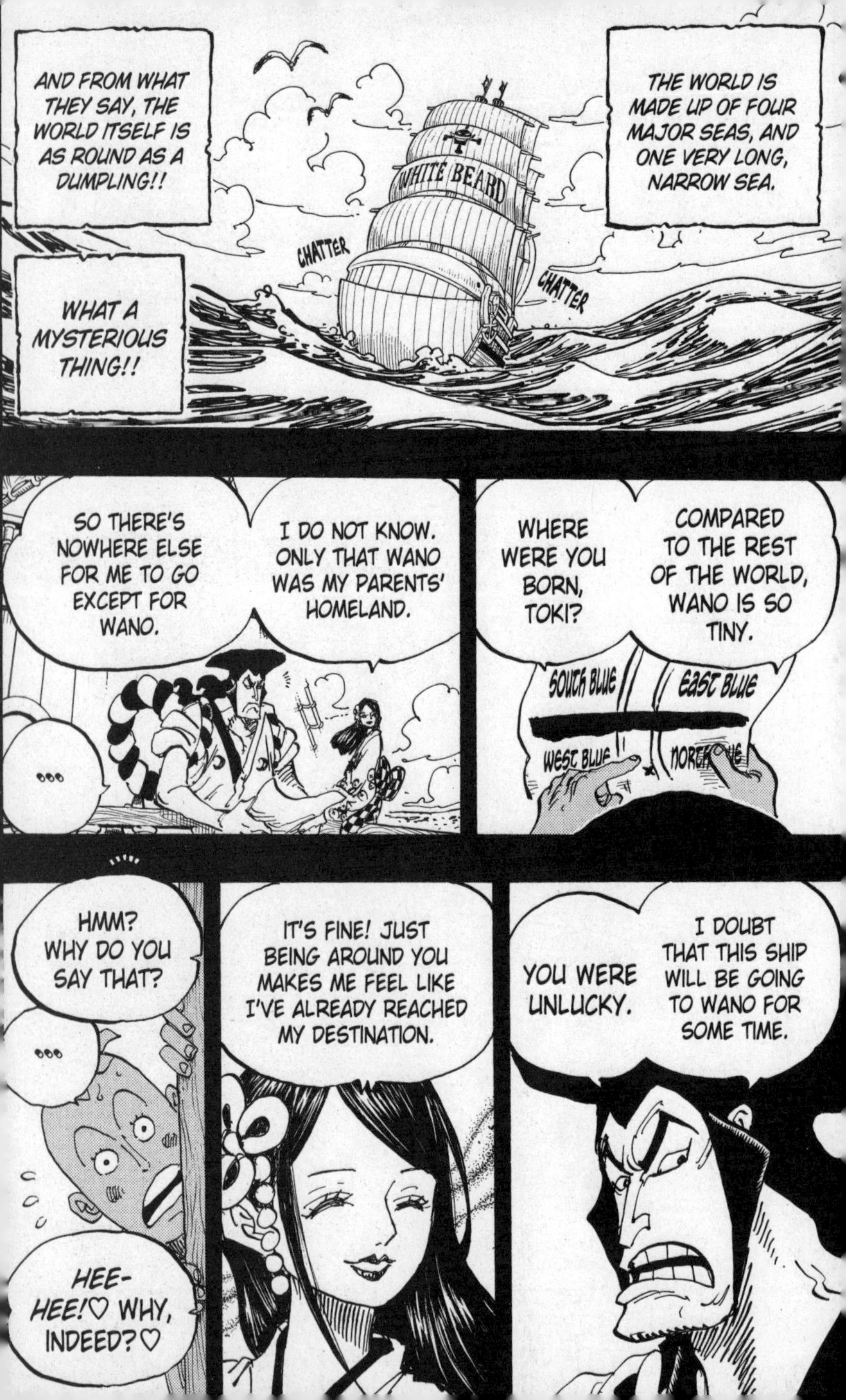
THE WORLD IS MADE UP OF FOUR MAJOR SEAS, AND ONE VERY LONG, NARROW SEA.
WHITE BEARD
CHATTER
CHATTER
AND FROM WHAT THEY SAY, THE WORLD ITSELF IS AS ROUND AS A DUMPLING!!
WHAT A MYSTERIOUS THING!!
COMPARED TO THE REST OF THE WORLD, WANO IS SO TINY.
WHERE WERE YOU BORN, TOKI?
SOUTH BLUE
EAST BLUE
WEST BLUE
I DO NOT KNOW. ONLY THAT WANO WAS MY PARENTS' HOMELAND.
SO THERE'S NOWHERE ELSE FOR ME TO GO EXCEPT FOR WANO.
...
I DOUBT THAT THIS SHIP WILL BE GOING TO WANO FOR SOME TIME.
YOU WERE UNLUCKY.
IT'S FINE! JUST BEING AROUND YOU MAKES ME FEEL LIKE I'VE ALREADY REACHED MY DESTINATION.
HMM? WHY DO YOU SAY THAT?
...
HEE-HEE!♡ WHY, INDEED?♡

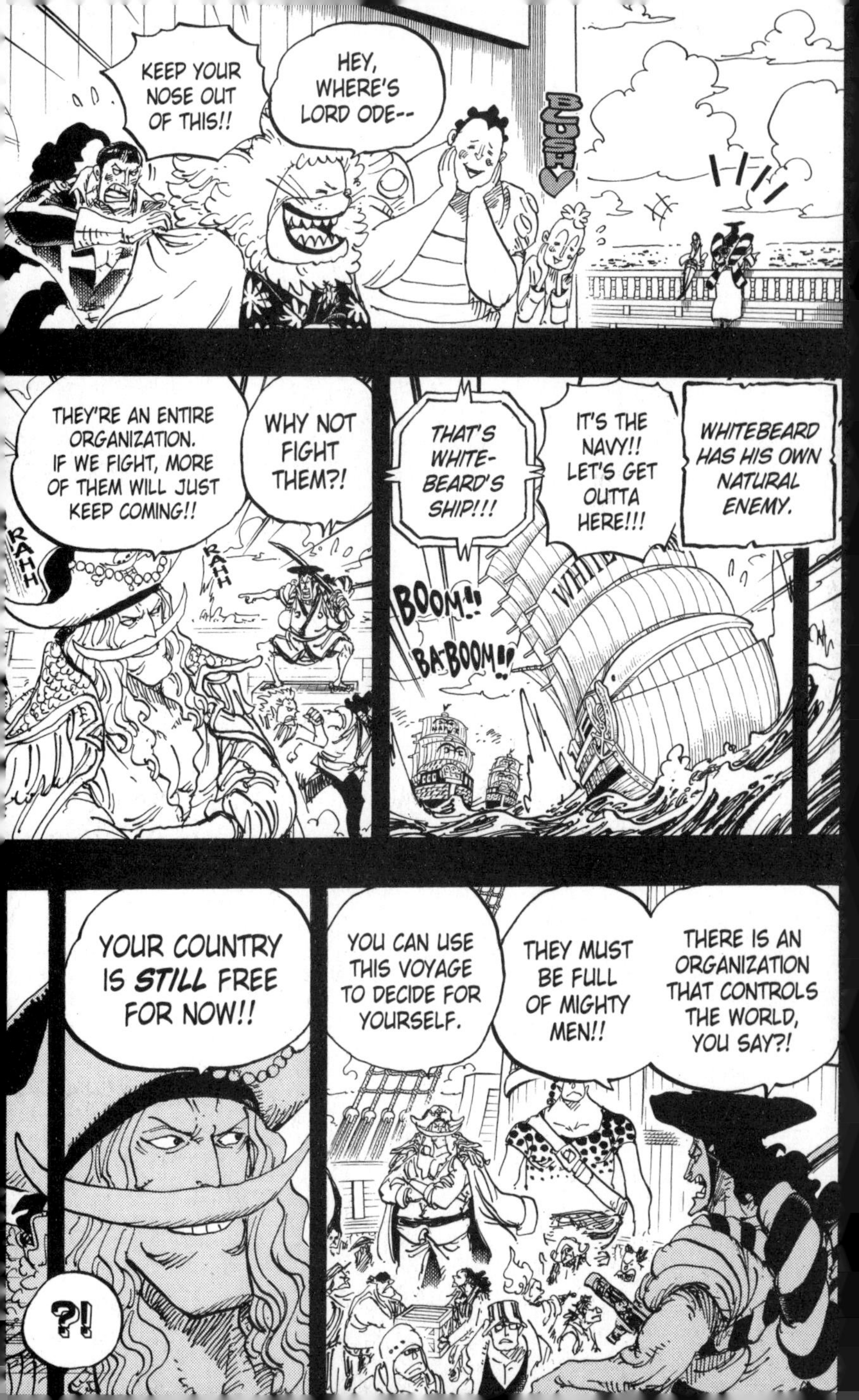
PUSH♥
HEY, WHERE'S LORD ODE--
KEEP YOUR NOSE OUT OF THIS!!
WHITEBEARD HAS HIS OWN NATURAL ENEMY.
IT'S THE NAVY!! LET'S GET OUTTA HERE!!!
THAT'S WHITE-BEARD'S SHIP!!!
BOOM!!
BA-BOOM!!
WHY NOT FIGHT THEM?!
THEY'RE AN ENTIRE ORGANIZATION. IF WE FIGHT, MORE OF THEM WILL JUST KEEP COMING!!
RAHH
RAHH
THERE IS AN ORGANIZATION THAT CONTROLS THE WORLD, YOU SAY?!
THEY MUST BE FULL OF MIGHTY MEN!!
YOU CAN USE THIS VOYAGE TO DECIDE FOR YOURSELF.
YOUR COUNTRY IS ***STILL*** FREE FOR NOW!!
?!

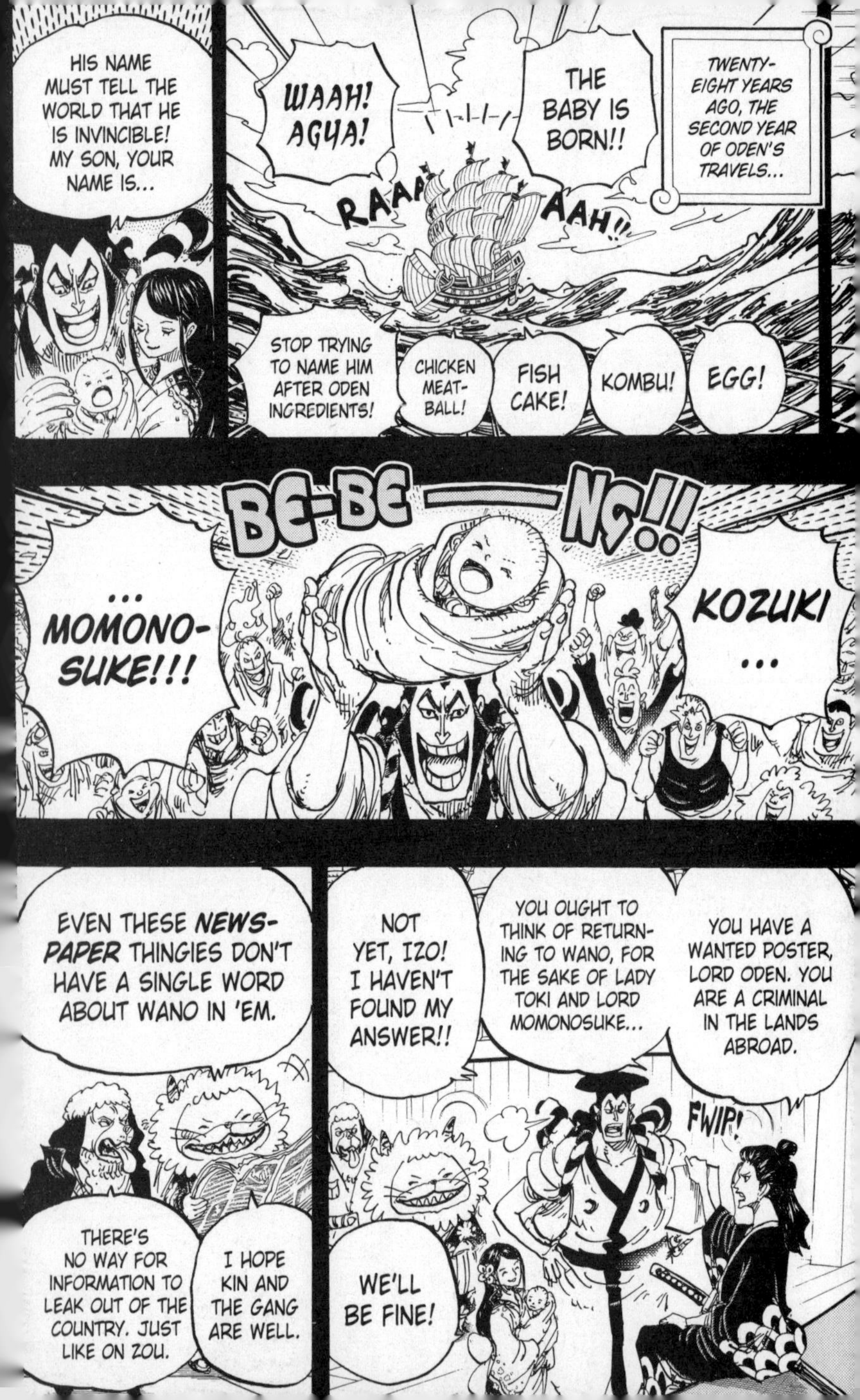
TWENTY-EIGHT YEARS AGO, THE SECOND YEAR OF ODEN'S TRAVELS...
THE BABY IS BORN!!
WAAH! AGUA!
RAAA
AAH!!
EGG!
KOMBU!
FISH CAKE!
CHICKEN MEAT-BALL!
STOP TRYING TO NAME HIM AFTER ODEN INGREDIENTS!
HIS NAME MUST TELL THE WORLD THAT HE IS INVINCIBLE! MY SON, YOUR NAME IS...
BE-BE——NG!!
KOZUKI ...
... MOMONO-SUKE!!!
YOU HAVE A WANTED POSTER, LORD ODEN. YOU ARE A CRIMINAL IN THE LANDS ABROAD.
FWIP!
YOU OUGHT TO THINK OF RETURN-ING TO WANO, FOR THE SAKE OF LADY TOKI AND LORD MOMONOSUKE...
NOT YET, IZO! I HAVEN'T FOUND MY ANSWER!!
WE'LL BE FINE!
EVEN THESE *NEWS-PAPER* THINGIES DON'T HAVE A SINGLE WORD ABOUT WANO IN 'EM.
I HOPE KIN AND THE GANG ARE WELL.
THERE'S NO WAY FOR INFORMATION TO LEAK OUT OF THE COUNTRY. JUST LIKE ON ZOU.

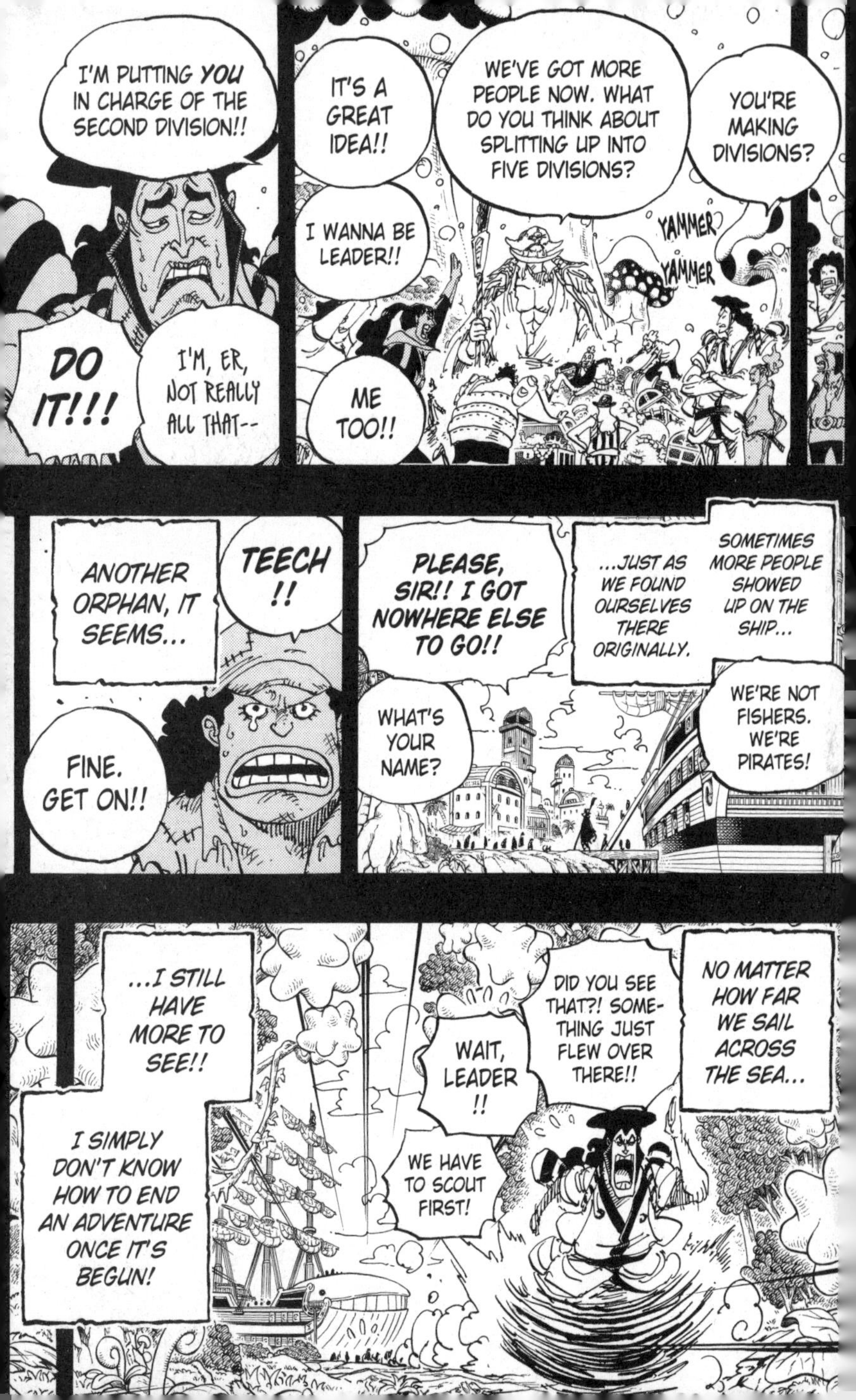
YOU'RE MAKING DIVISIONS?
WE'VE GOT MORE PEOPLE NOW. WHAT DO YOU THINK ABOUT SPLITTING UP INTO FIVE DIVISIONS?
IT'S A GREAT IDEA!!
YAMMER
YAMMER
I WANNA BE LEADER!!
ME TOO!!
I'M PUTTING YOU IN CHARGE OF THE SECOND DIVISION!!
I'M, ER, NOT REALLY ALL THAT--
DO IT!!!
SOMETIMES MORE PEOPLE SHOWED UP ON THE SHIP...
...JUST AS WE FOUND OURSELVES THERE ORIGINALLY.
PLEASE, SIR!! I GOT NOWHERE ELSE TO GO!!
WE'RE NOT FISHERS. WE'RE PIRATES!
WHAT'S YOUR NAME?
TEECH!!
ANOTHER ORPHAN, IT SEEMS...
FINE. GET ON!!
NO MATTER HOW FAR WE SAIL ACROSS THE SEA...
DID YOU SEE THAT?! SOMETHING JUST FLEW OVER THERE!!
WAIT, LEADER!!
WE HAVE TO SCOUT FIRST!
...I STILL HAVE MORE TO SEE!!
I SIMPLY DON'T KNOW HOW TO END AN ADVENTURE ONCE IT'S BEGUN!

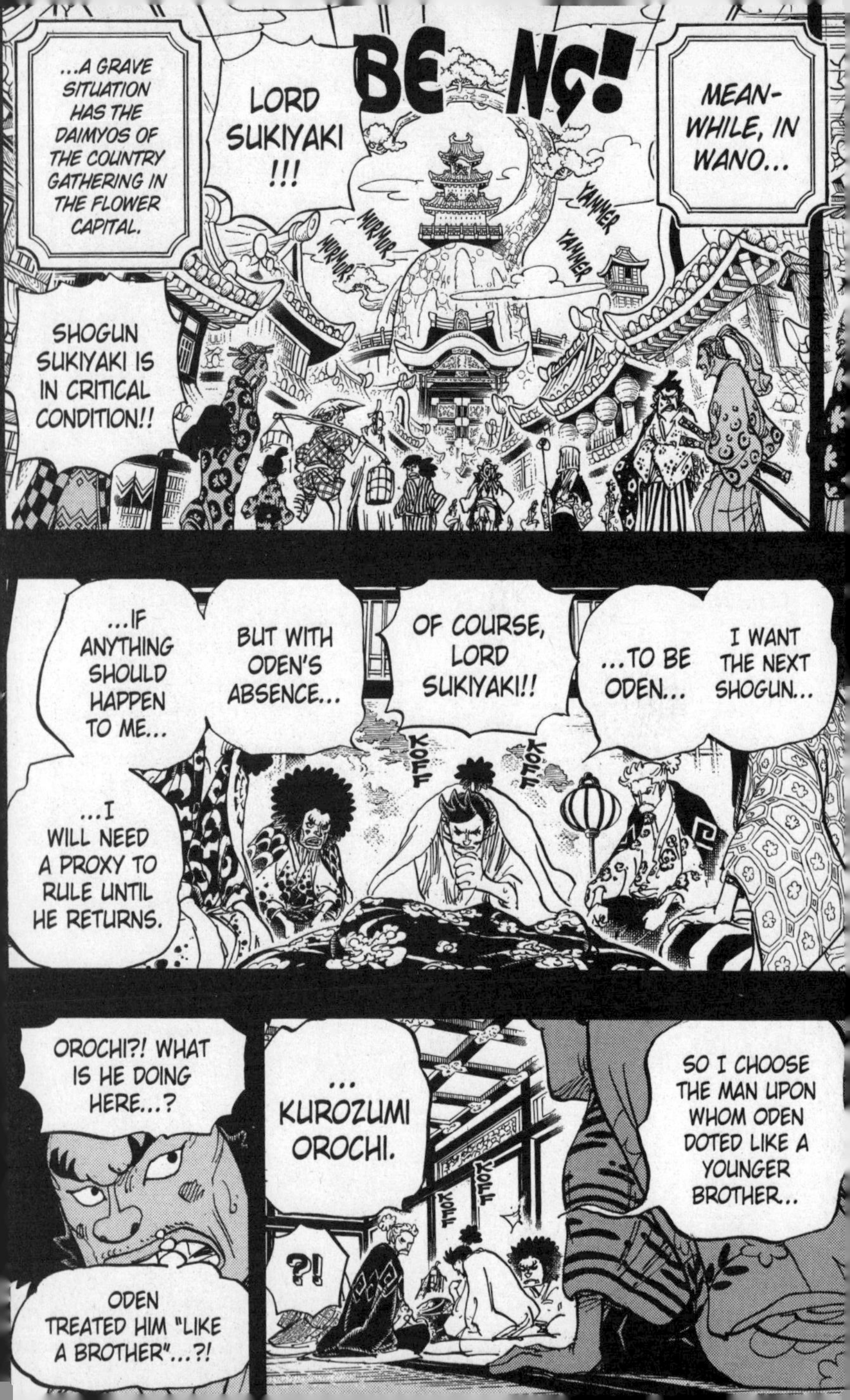
MEAN-WHILE, IN WANO...
BE NG!
LORD SUKIYAKI!!!
...A GRAVE SITUATION HAS THE DAIMYOS OF THE COUNTRY GATHERING IN THE FLOWER CAPITAL.
YAMMER YAMMER
MURMUR MURMUR
SHOGUN SUKIYAKI IS IN CRITICAL CONDITION!!
I WANT THE NEXT SHOGUN...
...TO BE ODEN...
OF COURSE, LORD SUKIYAKI!!
BUT WITH ODEN'S ABSENCE...
...IF ANYTHING SHOULD HAPPEN TO ME...
KOFF KOFF
...I WILL NEED A PROXY TO RULE UNTIL HE RETURNS.
SO I CHOOSE THE MAN UPON WHOM ODEN DOTED LIKE A YOUNGER BROTHER...
... KUROZUMI OROCHI.
KOFF KOFF
?!
OROCHI?! WHAT IS HE DOING HERE...?
ODEN TREATED HIM "LIKE A BROTHER"...?!

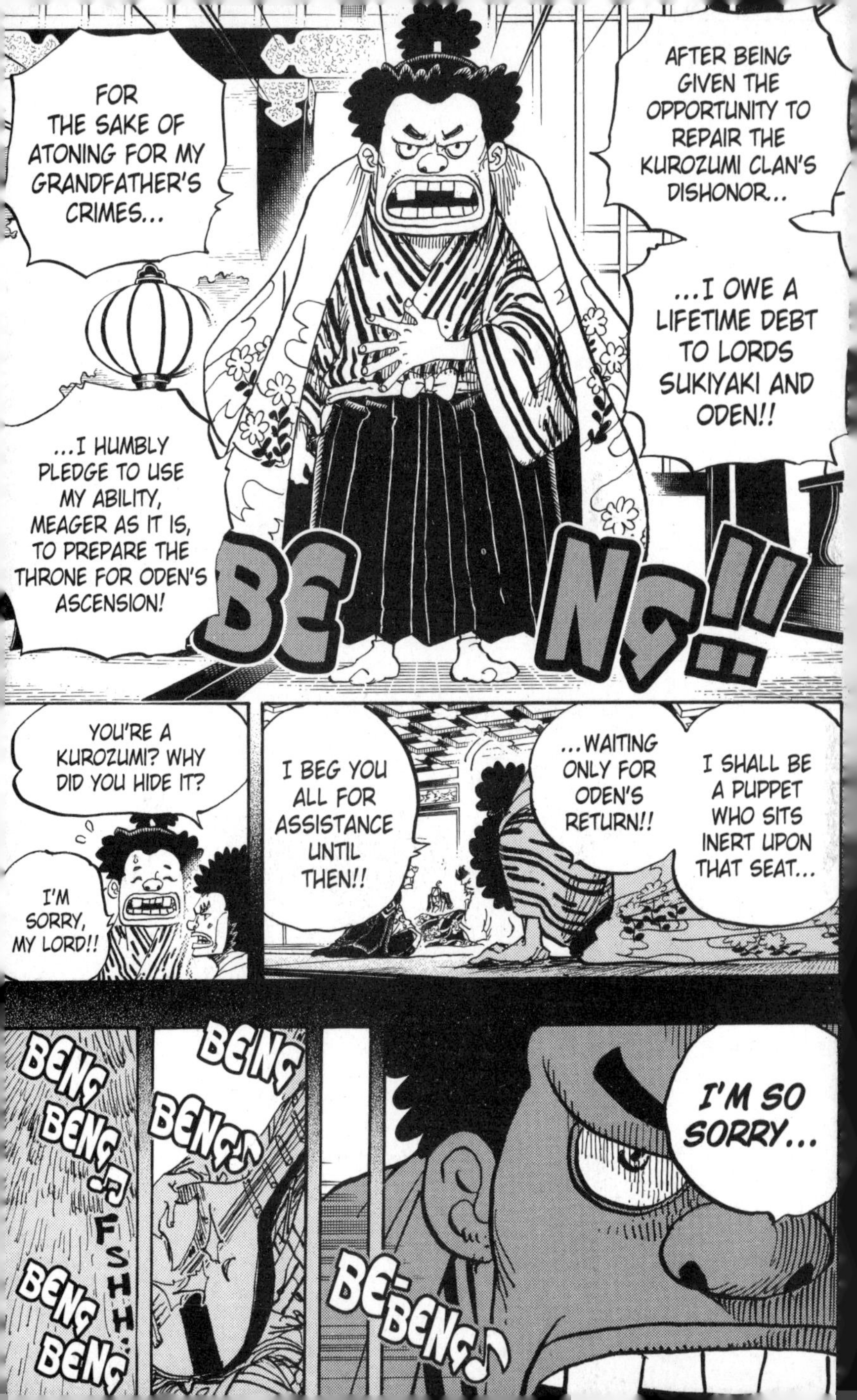
AFTER BEING GIVEN THE OPPORTUNITY TO REPAIR THE KUROZUMI CLAN'S DISHONOR...
...I OWE A LIFETIME DEBT TO LORDS SUKIYAKI AND ODEN!!
FOR THE SAKE OF ATONING FOR MY GRANDFATHER'S CRIMES...
...I HUMBLY PLEDGE TO USE MY ABILITY, MEAGER AS IT IS, TO PREPARE THE THRONE FOR ODEN'S ASCENSION!
BENG!!
I SHALL BE A PUPPET WHO SITS INERT UPON THAT SEAT...
...WAITING ONLY FOR ODEN'S RETURN!!
I BEG YOU ALL FOR ASSISTANCE UNTIL THEN!!
YOU'RE A KUROZUMI? WHY DID YOU HIDE IT?
I'M SORRY, MY LORD!!
I'M SO SORRY...
BE-BENG♪
BENG
BENG♪
FSHH
BENG
BENG♪
BENG
BENG
BENG

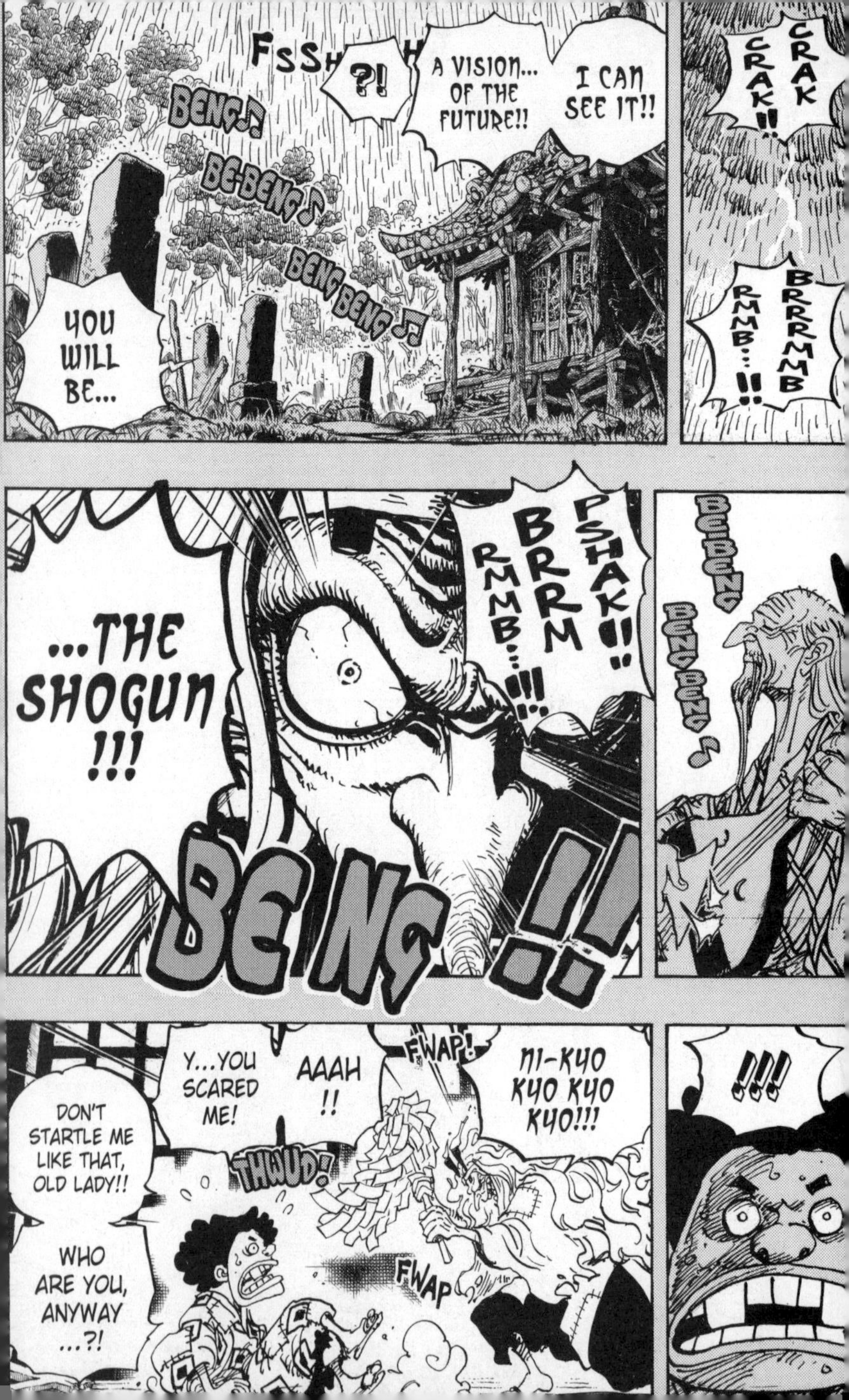

CRAK CRAK!!
BRRRMMB RMMB...!!
I CAN SEE IT!!
A VISION... OF THE FUTURE!!
?!
FSSHH
BENG♫
BE-BENG♫
BENG BENG♫
YOU WILL BE...
BE-BENG
BENG BENG♫
PSHAK!!
BRRRM RMMB...!!
...THE SHOGUN!!!
BENG!!
!!!
NI-KYO KYO KYO KYO!!!
FWAP!
AAAH!!
Y...YOU SCARED ME!
DON'T STARTLE ME LIKE THAT, OLD LADY!!
THWUD!
FWAP
WHO ARE YOU, ANYWAY...?!

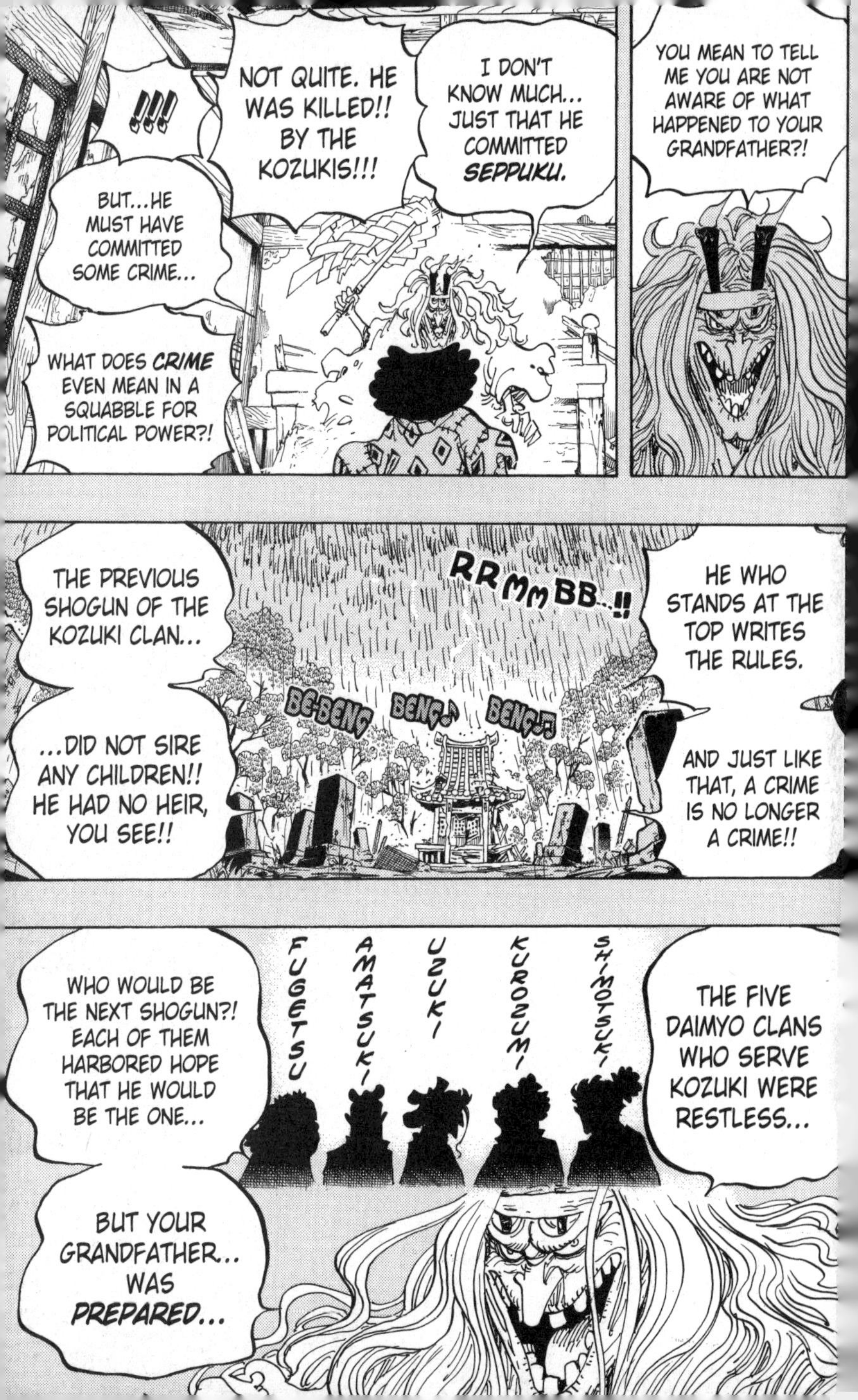
YOU MEAN TO TELL ME YOU ARE NOT AWARE OF WHAT HAPPENED TO YOUR GRANDFATHER?!
I DON'T KNOW MUCH... JUST THAT HE COMMITTED **SEPPUKU.**
NOT QUITE. HE WAS KILLED!! BY THE KOZUKIS!!!
!!!
BUT...HE MUST HAVE COMMITTED SOME CRIME...
WHAT DOES **CRIME** EVEN MEAN IN A SQUABBLE FOR POLITICAL POWER?!
HE WHO STANDS AT THE TOP WRITES THE RULES.
RRMMBB..!!
AND JUST LIKE THAT, A CRIME IS NO LONGER A CRIME!!
THE PREVIOUS SHOGUN OF THE KOZUKI CLAN...
BENG♪
BENG♪
BE-BENG
...DID NOT SIRE ANY CHILDREN!! HE HAD NO HEIR, YOU SEE!!
THE FIVE DAIMYO CLANS WHO SERVE KOZUKI WERE RESTLESS...
SHIMOTSUKI
KUROZUMI
UZUKI
AMATSUKI
FUGETSU
WHO WOULD BE THE NEXT SHOGUN?! EACH OF THEM HARBORED HOPE THAT HE WOULD BE THE ONE...
BUT YOUR GRANDFATHER... WAS **PREPARED...**

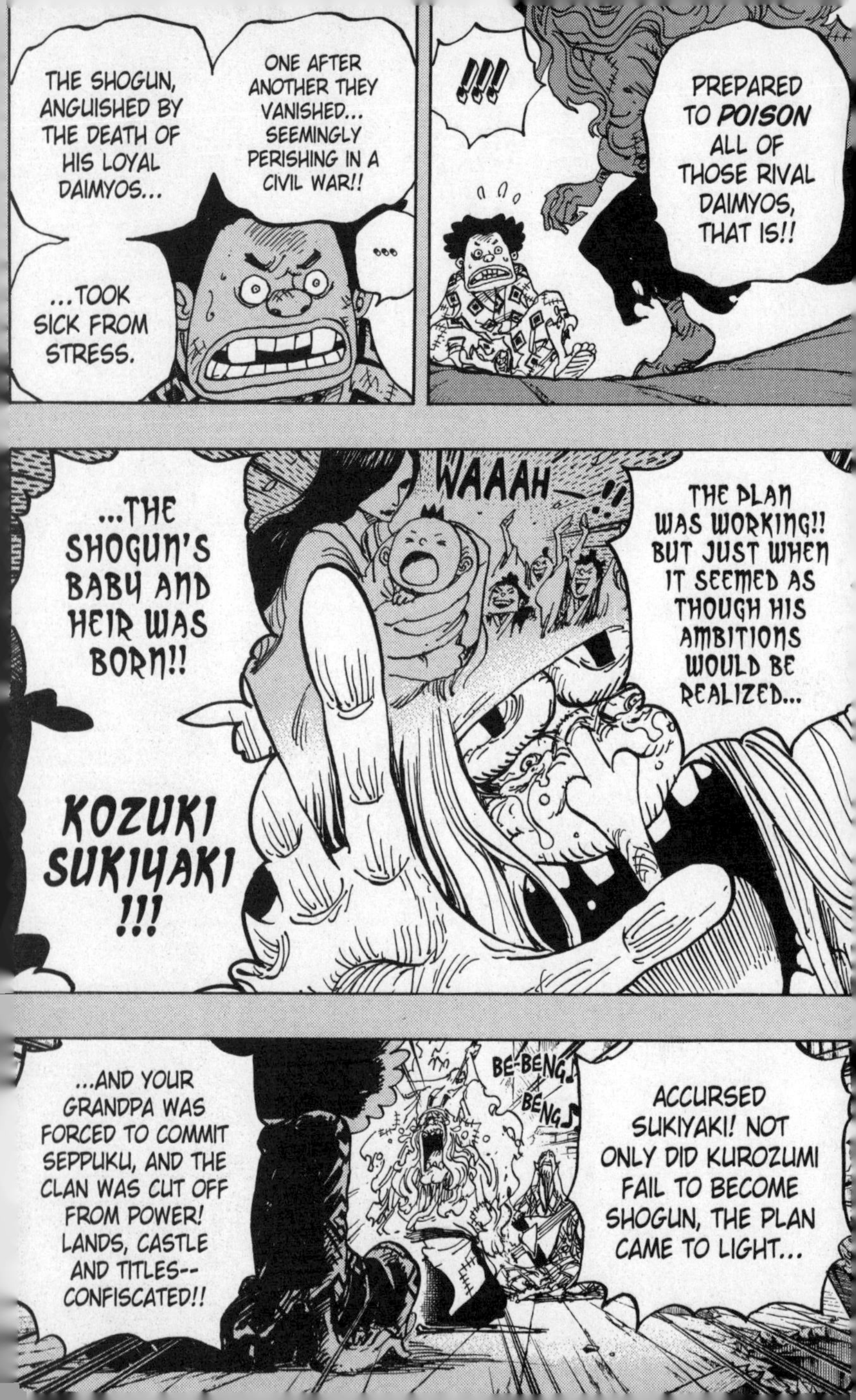
PREPARED TO POISON ALL OF THOSE RIVAL DAIMYOS, THAT IS!!
!!!
ONE AFTER ANOTHER THEY VANISHED... SEEMINGLY PERISHING IN A CIVIL WAR!!
THE SHOGUN, ANGUISHED BY THE DEATH OF HIS LOYAL DAIMYOS...
...
...TOOK SICK FROM STRESS.
THE PLAN WAS WORKING!! BUT JUST WHEN IT SEEMED AS THOUGH HIS AMBITIONS WOULD BE REALIZED...
WAAAH
...THE SHOGUN'S BABY AND HEIR WAS BORN!!
KOZUKI SUKIYAKI !!!
ACCURSED SUKIYAKI! NOT ONLY DID KUROZUMI FAIL TO BECOME SHOGUN, THE PLAN CAME TO LIGHT...
BE-BENG
BENG
...AND YOUR GRANDPA WAS FORCED TO COMMIT SEPPUKU, AND THE CLAN WAS CUT OFF FROM POWER! LANDS, CASTLE AND TITLES--CONFISCATED!!

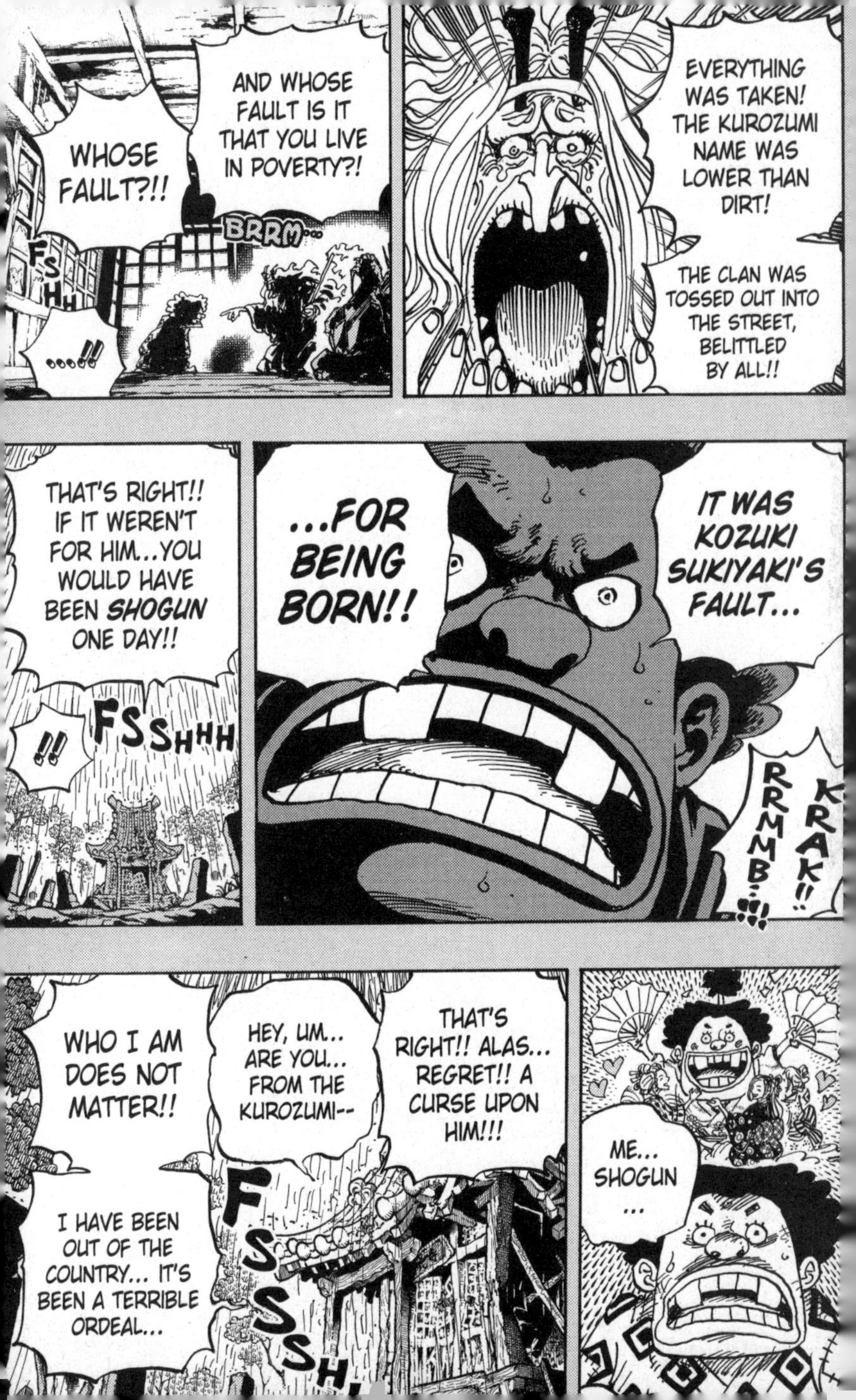
EVERYTHING WAS TAKEN! THE KUROZUMI NAME WAS LOWER THAN DIRT!
THE CLAN WAS TOSSED OUT INTO THE STREET, BELITTLED BY ALL!!
AND WHOSE FAULT IS IT THAT YOU LIVE IN POVERTY?!
BRRM...
WHOSE FAULT?!!
FSHH
....!!
IT WAS KOZUKI SUKIYAKI'S FAULT...
KRAK!!
RRMMB...!!
...FOR BEING BORN!!
THAT'S RIGHT!! IF IT WEREN'T FOR HIM...YOU WOULD HAVE BEEN SHOGUN ONE DAY!!
FSSHHH
!!
ME... SHOGUN ...
THAT'S RIGHT!! ALAS... REGRET!! A CURSE UPON HIM!!!
HEY, UM... ARE YOU... FROM THE KUROZUMI--
WHO I AM DOES NOT MATTER!!
FSSSH
I HAVE BEEN OUT OF THE COUNTRY... IT'S BEEN A TERRIBLE ORDEAL...

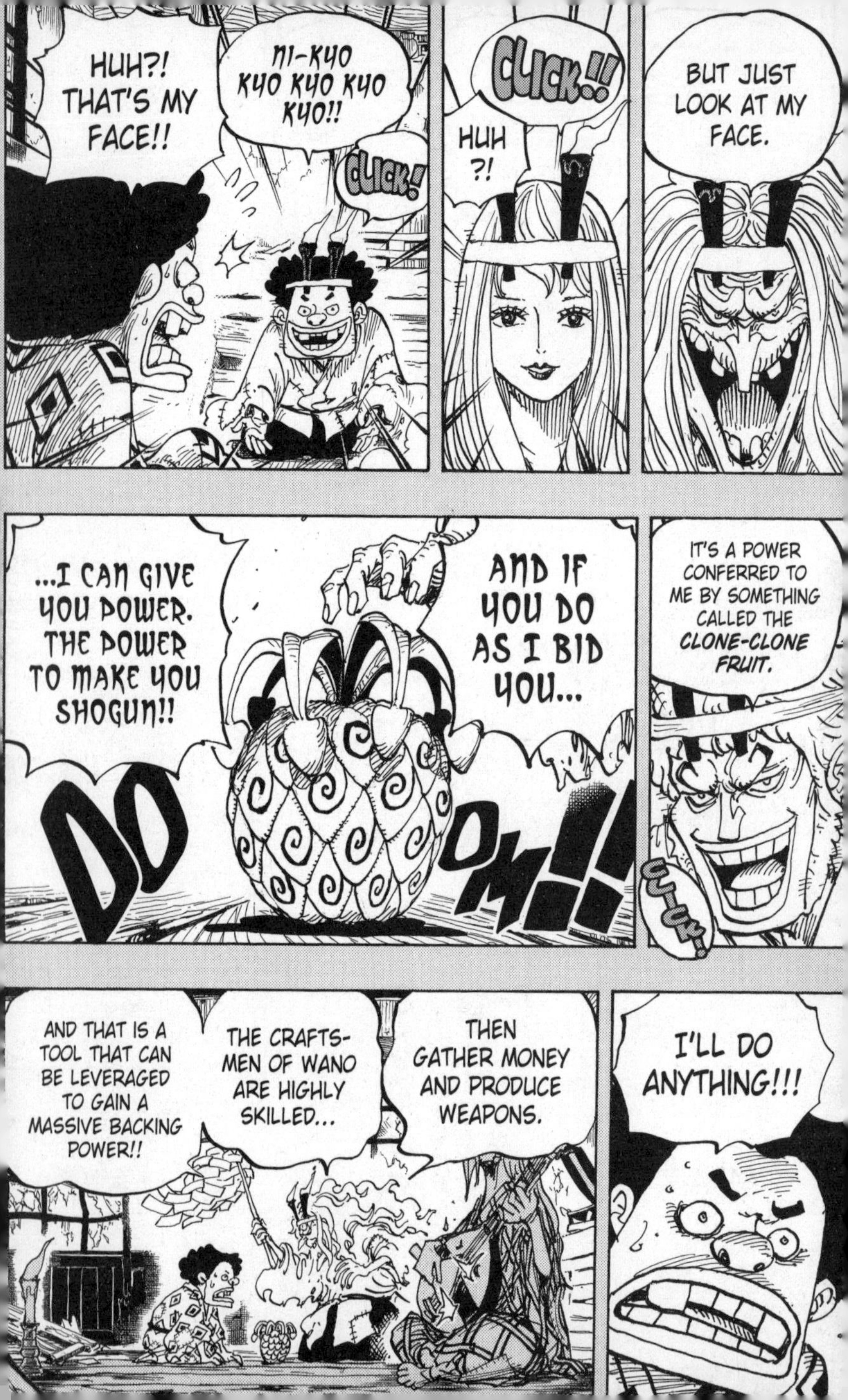
BUT JUST LOOK AT MY FACE.
CLICK!!
HUH ?!
NI-KYO KYO KYO KYO KYO!!
CLICK!
HUH?! THAT'S MY FACE!!
IT'S A POWER CONFERRED TO ME BY SOMETHING CALLED THE CLONE-CLONE FRUIT.
CLICK
AND IF YOU DO AS I BID YOU...
...I CAN GIVE YOU POWER. THE POWER TO MAKE YOU SHOGUN!!
DOOM!!
I'LL DO ANYTHING!!!
THEN GATHER MONEY AND PRODUCE WEAPONS.
THE CRAFTS-MEN OF WANO ARE HIGHLY SKILLED...
AND THAT IS A TOOL THAT CAN BE LEVERAGED TO GAIN A MASSIVE BACKING POWER!!

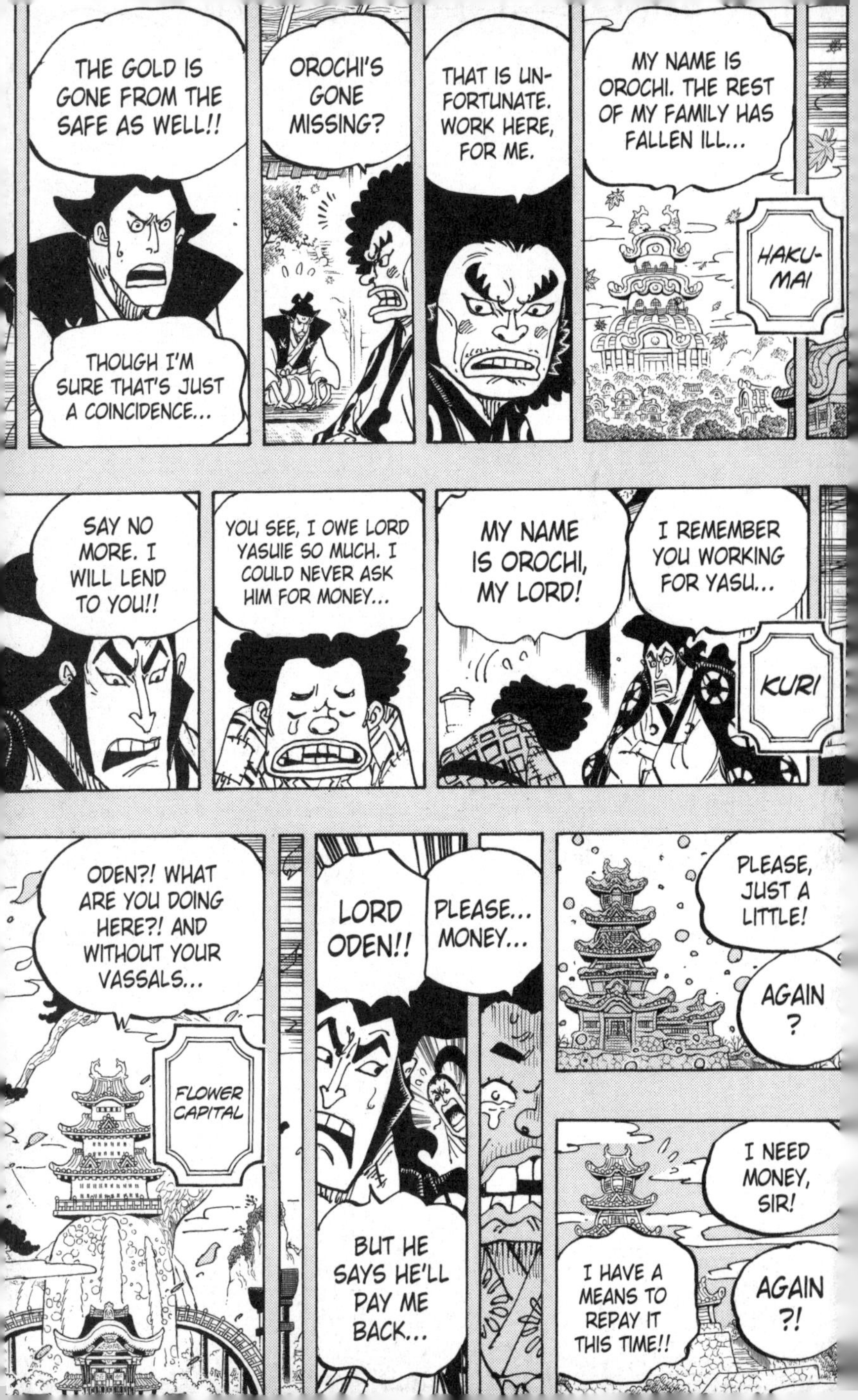
HAKU-MAI
MY NAME IS OROCHI. THE REST OF MY FAMILY HAS FALLEN ILL...
THAT IS UN-FORTUNATE. WORK HERE, FOR ME.
OROCHI'S GONE MISSING?
THE GOLD IS GONE FROM THE SAFE AS WELL!!
THOUGH I'M SURE THAT'S JUST A COINCIDENCE...
KURI
I REMEMBER YOU WORKING FOR YASU...
MY NAME IS OROCHI, MY LORD!
YOU SEE, I OWE LORD YASUIE SO MUCH. I COULD NEVER ASK HIM FOR MONEY...
SAY NO MORE. I WILL LEND TO YOU!!
PLEASE, JUST A LITTLE!
AGAIN?
I NEED MONEY, SIR!
AGAIN?!
I HAVE A MEANS TO REPAY IT THIS TIME!!
PLEASE... MONEY...
LORD ODEN!!
BUT HE SAYS HE'LL PAY ME BACK...
FLOWER CAPITAL
ODEN?! WHAT ARE YOU DOING HERE?! AND WITHOUT YOUR VASSALS...

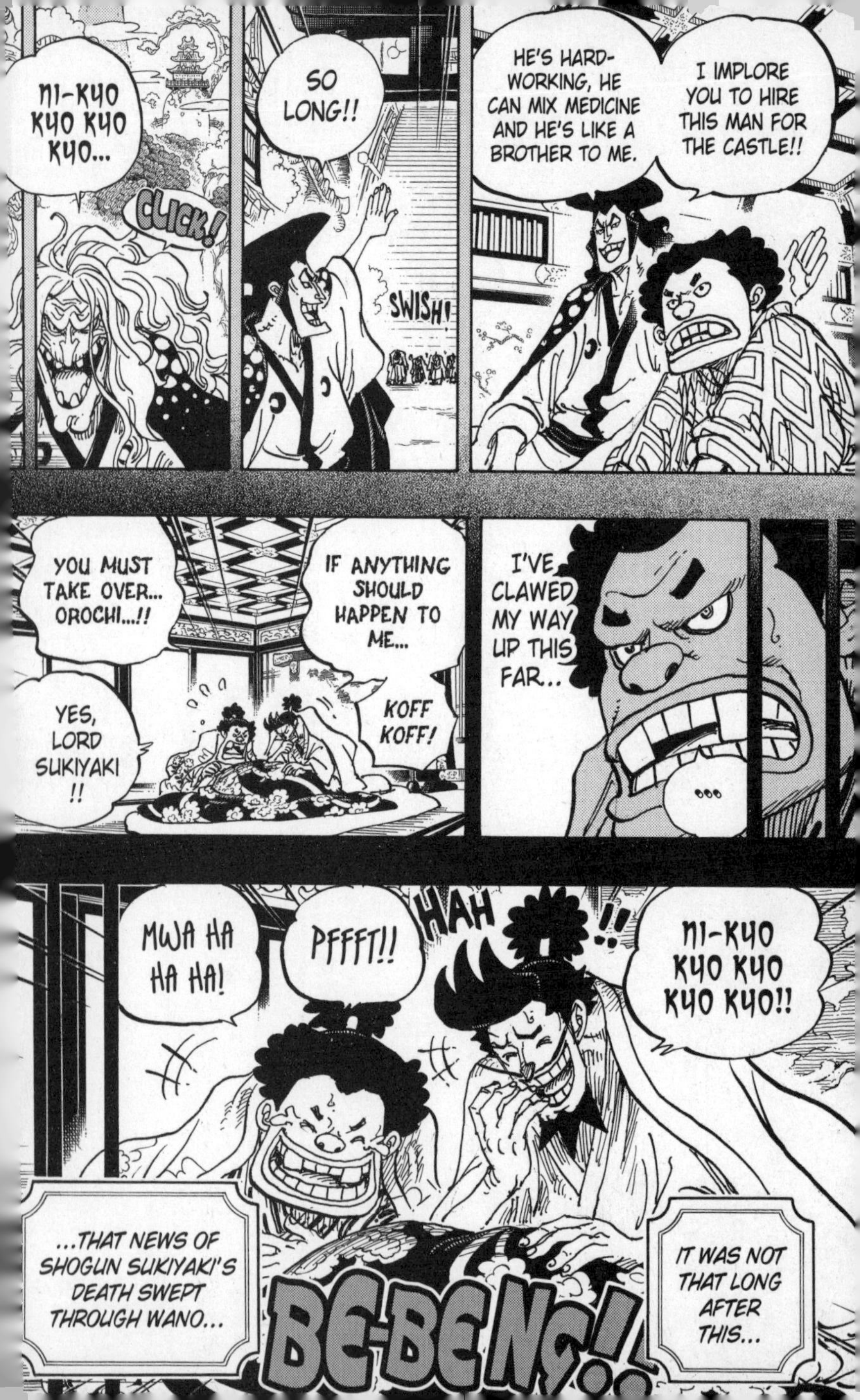
I IMPLORE YOU TO HIRE THIS MAN FOR THE CASTLE!!
HE'S HARD-WORKING, HE CAN MIX MEDICINE AND HE'S LIKE A BROTHER TO ME.
SO LONG!!
SWISH!
NI-KYO KYO KYO KYO...
CLICK!
I'VE CLAWED MY WAY UP THIS FAR...
...
IF ANYTHING SHOULD HAPPEN TO ME...
YOU MUST TAKE OVER... OROCHI...!!
KOFF KOFF!
YES, LORD SUKIYAKI!!
IT WAS NOT THAT LONG AFTER THIS...
NI-KYO KYO KYO KYO KYO!!
HAH!!
PFFFT!!
MWA HA HA HA!
BE-BENG!!
...THAT NEWS OF SHOGUN SUKIYAKI'S DEATH SWEPT THROUGH WANO...

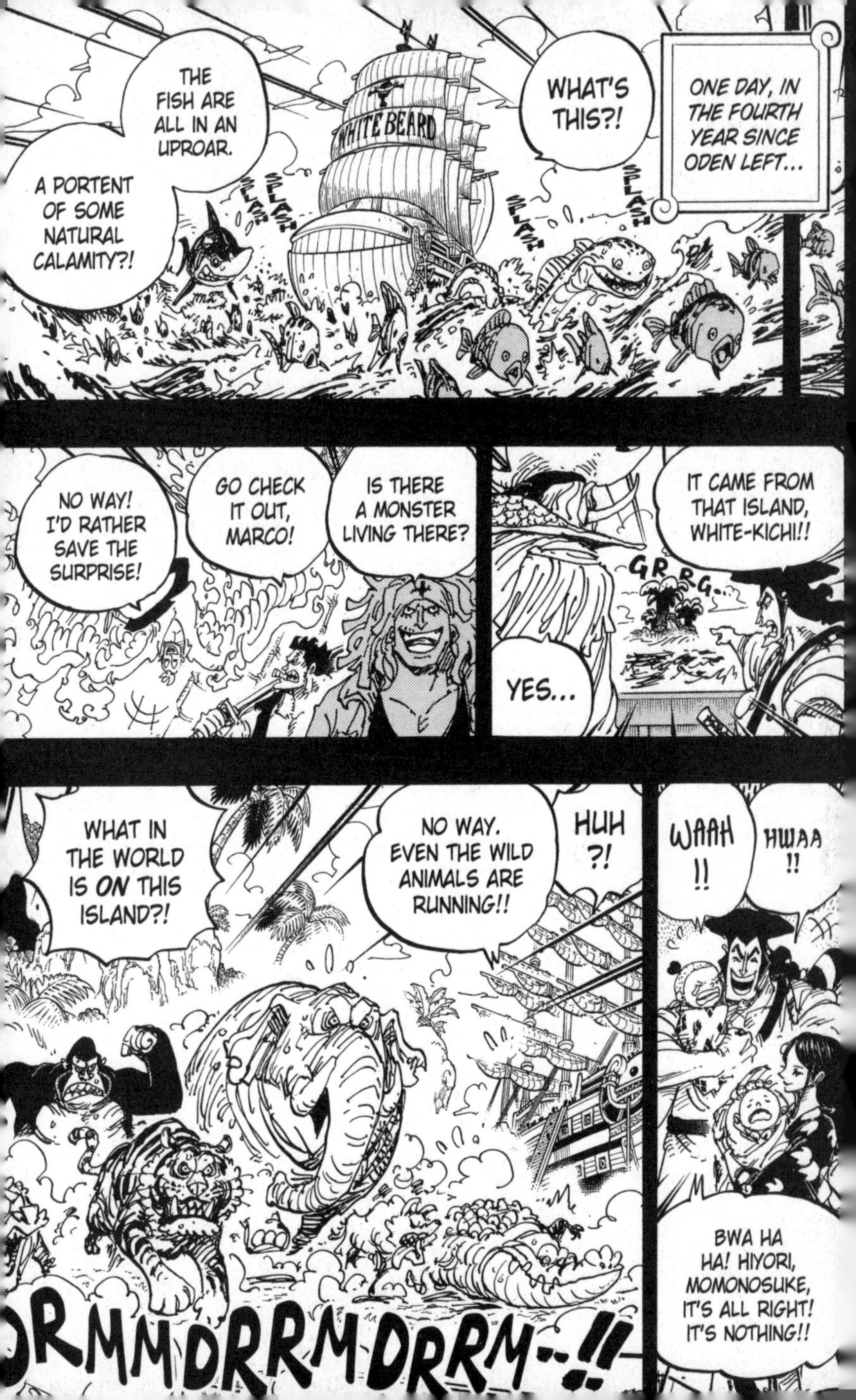
ONE DAY, IN THE FOURTH YEAR SINCE ODEN LEFT...
SPLASH
WHAT'S THIS?!
SPLASH
THE FISH ARE ALL IN AN UPROAR.
A PORTENT OF SOME NATURAL CALAMITY?!
SPLASH SPLASH
IT CAME FROM THAT ISLAND, WHITE-KICHI!!
GRRG...
YES...
IS THERE A MONSTER LIVING THERE?
GO CHECK IT OUT, MARCO!
NO WAY! I'D RATHER SAVE THE SURPRISE!
HWAA!!
WAAH!!
BWA HA HA! HIYORI, MOMONOSUKE, IT'S ALL RIGHT! IT'S NOTHING!!
HUH?!
NO WAY. EVEN THE WILD ANIMALS ARE RUNNING!!
WHAT IN THE WORLD IS ON THIS ISLAND?!
RMMDRRMDRRM--!!

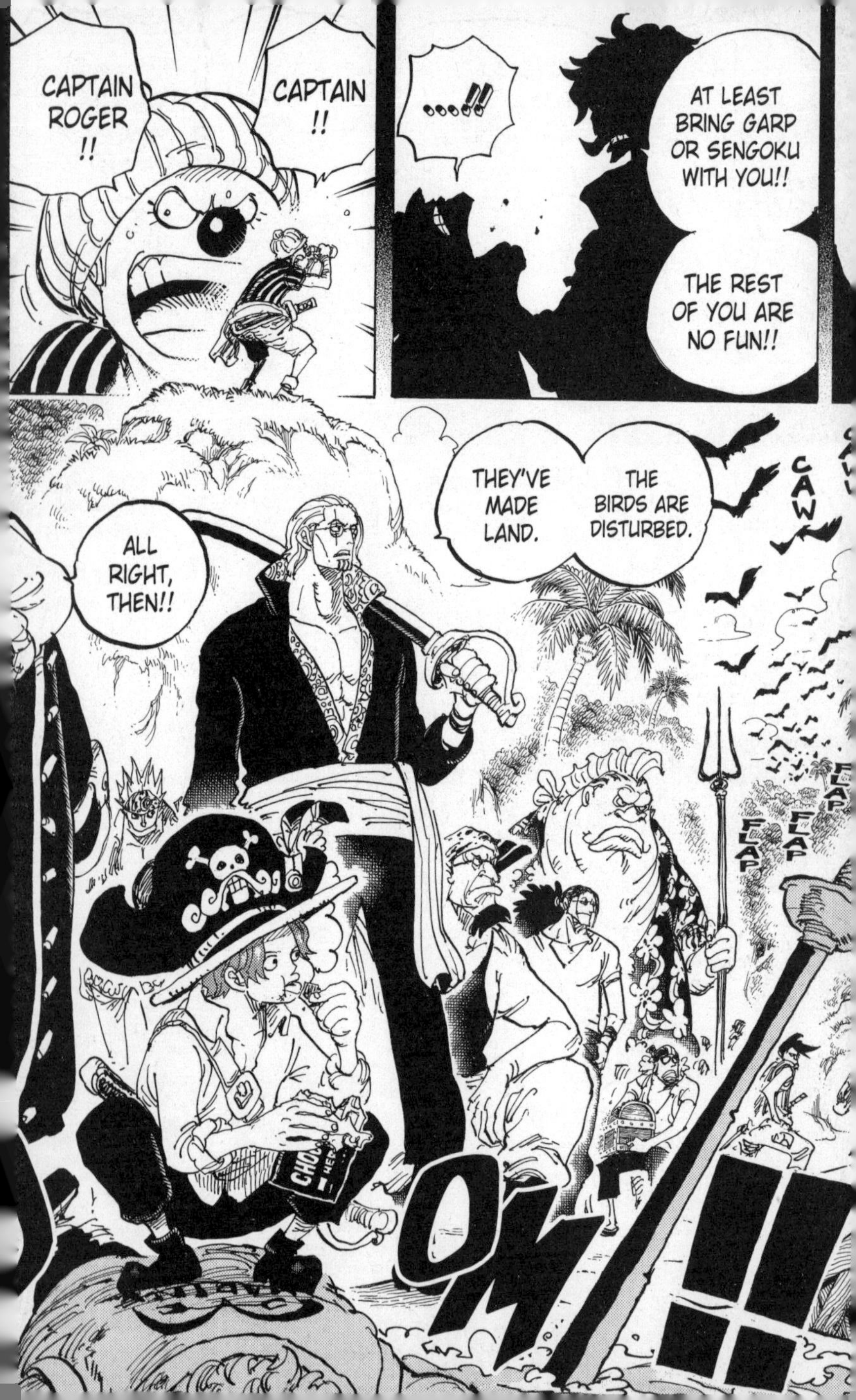
AT LEAST BRING GARP OR SENGOKU WITH YOU!!
THE REST OF YOU ARE NO FUN!!
....!!
CAPTAIN !!
CAPTAIN ROGER !!
CAW
THE BIRDS ARE DISTURBED.
THEY'VE MADE LAND.
FLAP FLAP
FLAP FLAP
ALL RIGHT, THEN!!
OH!!

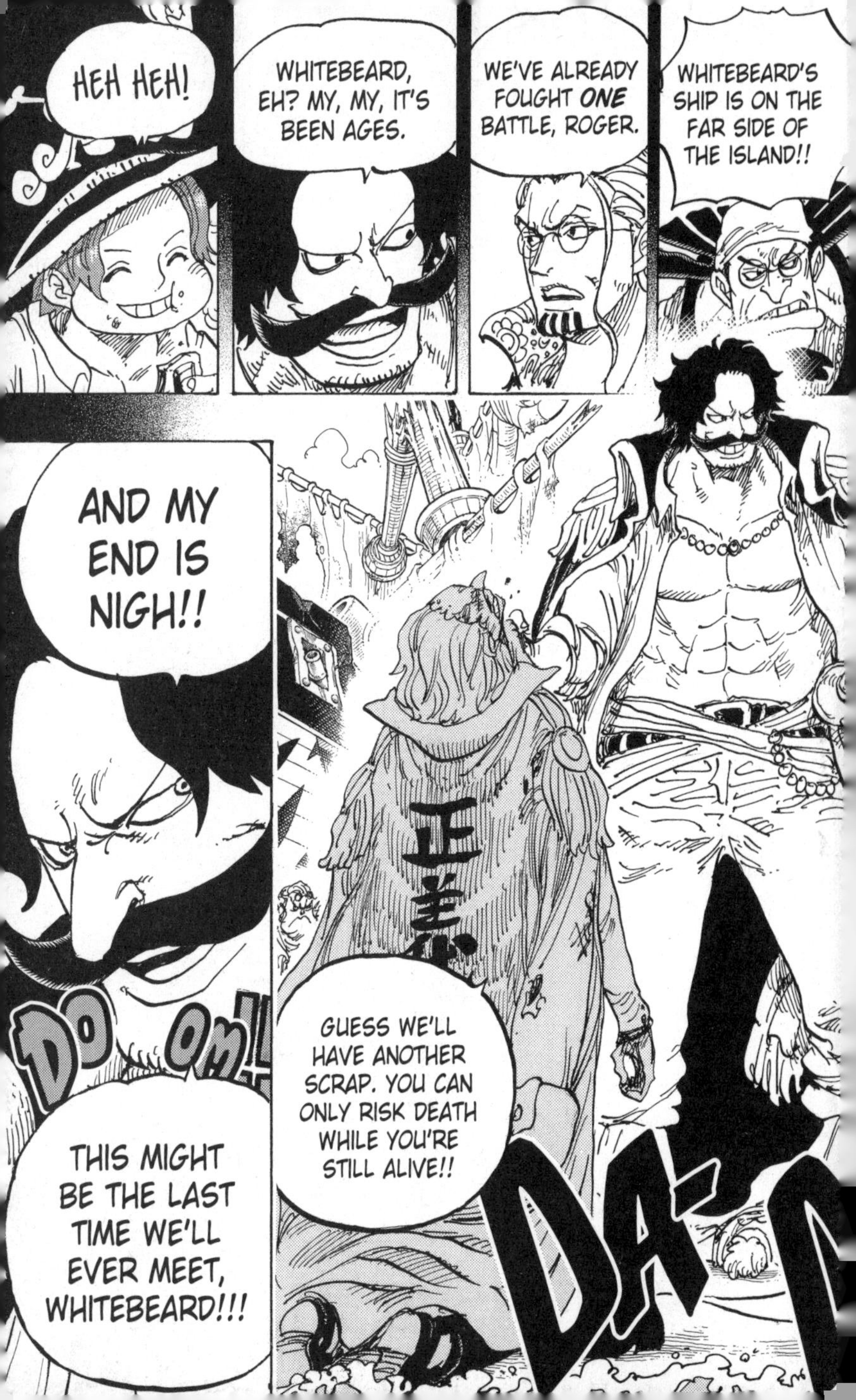

WHITEBEARD'S SHIP IS ON THE FAR SIDE OF THE ISLAND!!
WE'VE ALREADY FOUGHT **ONE** BATTLE, ROGER.
WHITEBEARD, EH? MY, MY, IT'S BEEN AGES.
HEH HEH!
GUESS WE'LL HAVE ANOTHER SCRAP. YOU CAN ONLY RISK DEATH WHILE YOU'RE STILL ALIVE!!
DA-
AND MY END IS NIGH!!
DO OM!!
THIS MIGHT BE THE LAST TIME WE'LL EVER MEET, WHITEBEARD!!!

SBS Question Corner

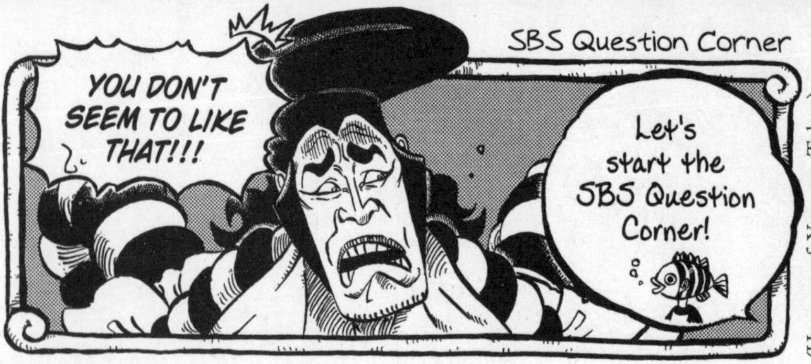
Let's start the SBS Question Corner!
YOU DON'T SEEM TO LIKE THAT!!!

(Hamane of Yamane, Tokyo)

Q: Hi, this is my first time writing to the SBS!
By the way, Odacchi, I saw a dirty mag full of gorgeous women over there.
(Odacchi runs off)
And now, start the SBS!!

--Yuyucchi

A: Hey, wait a second!! You can't just write "Odacchi runs off" like I'd actually do that!! I'm offended!! *Huff, huff...weez...* And there wasn't any magazine back there either!!

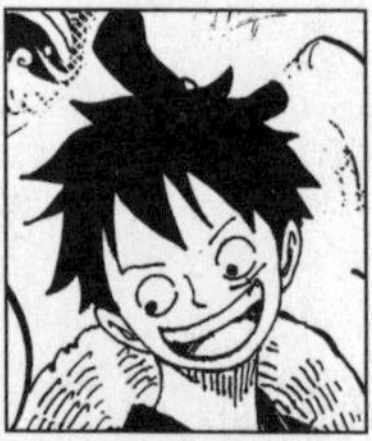

Q: Heso! Here's a question! Luffy gives people all kinds of nicknames, but why doesn't he call the rest of the crew by them?

--Takataka

A: Good question! The thing about Luffy is that he's not interested in learning people's names as a general rule, so he gives them nicknames of his own based only on the impression he gets from them. But when you're on his crew, he will remember. Basically, if he knows your name he'll call you by it. It's as simple as that.

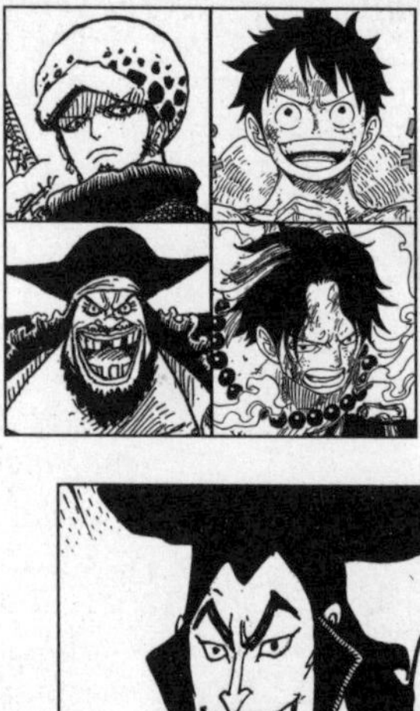

Q: I have a question. I heard that the initial "D" stands for *debeso* (outie bellybutton). Is this true?

--Count Dino

A: Yes! It's true!

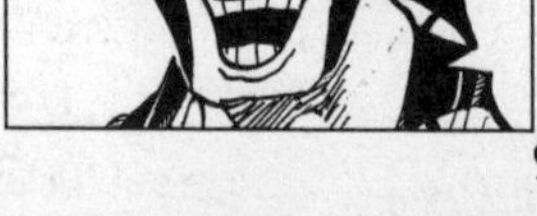

Q: Oda Sensei! Did you know that February 22 is National Oden Day? I was thinking, why don't we make that Kozuki Oden's birthday?!

--Gum-Flame Fruit

A: Okay, listen up...
If you want to just do your own thing and make up a character's birthday like that... Go ahead!!

Chapter 966:

ROGER AND WHITEBEARD

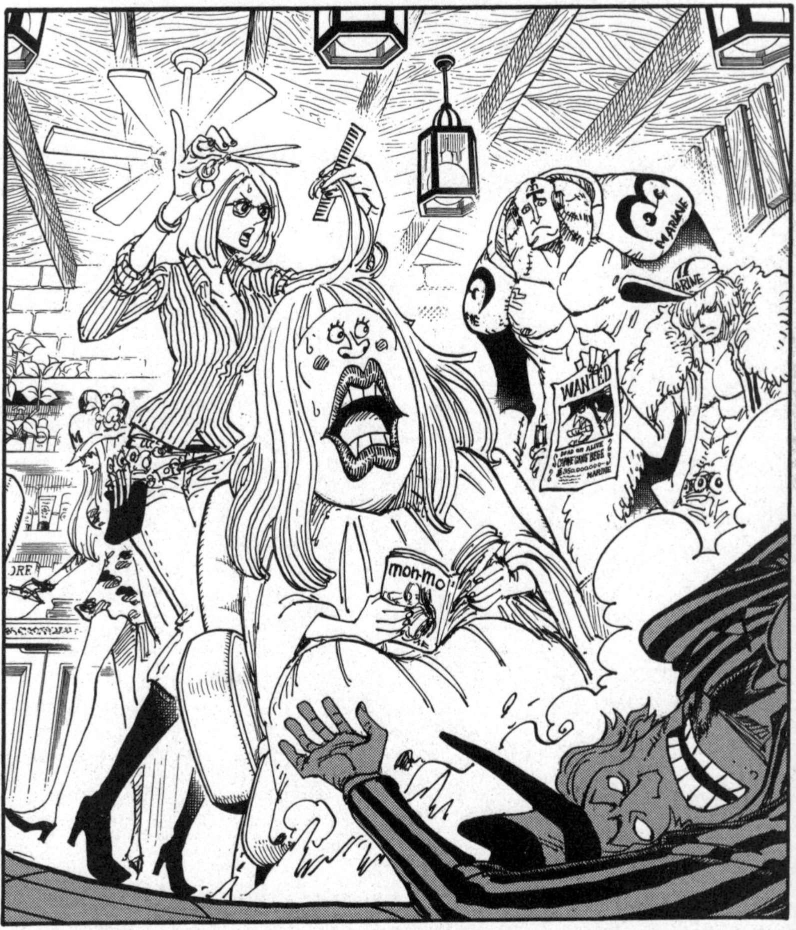

WANTED
mon-mo

GANG BEGE'S OH MY FAMILY, VOL. 16: "BEGE'S WIFE CHIFFON IS ARRESTED BY THE NAVY AT THE SALON!!"

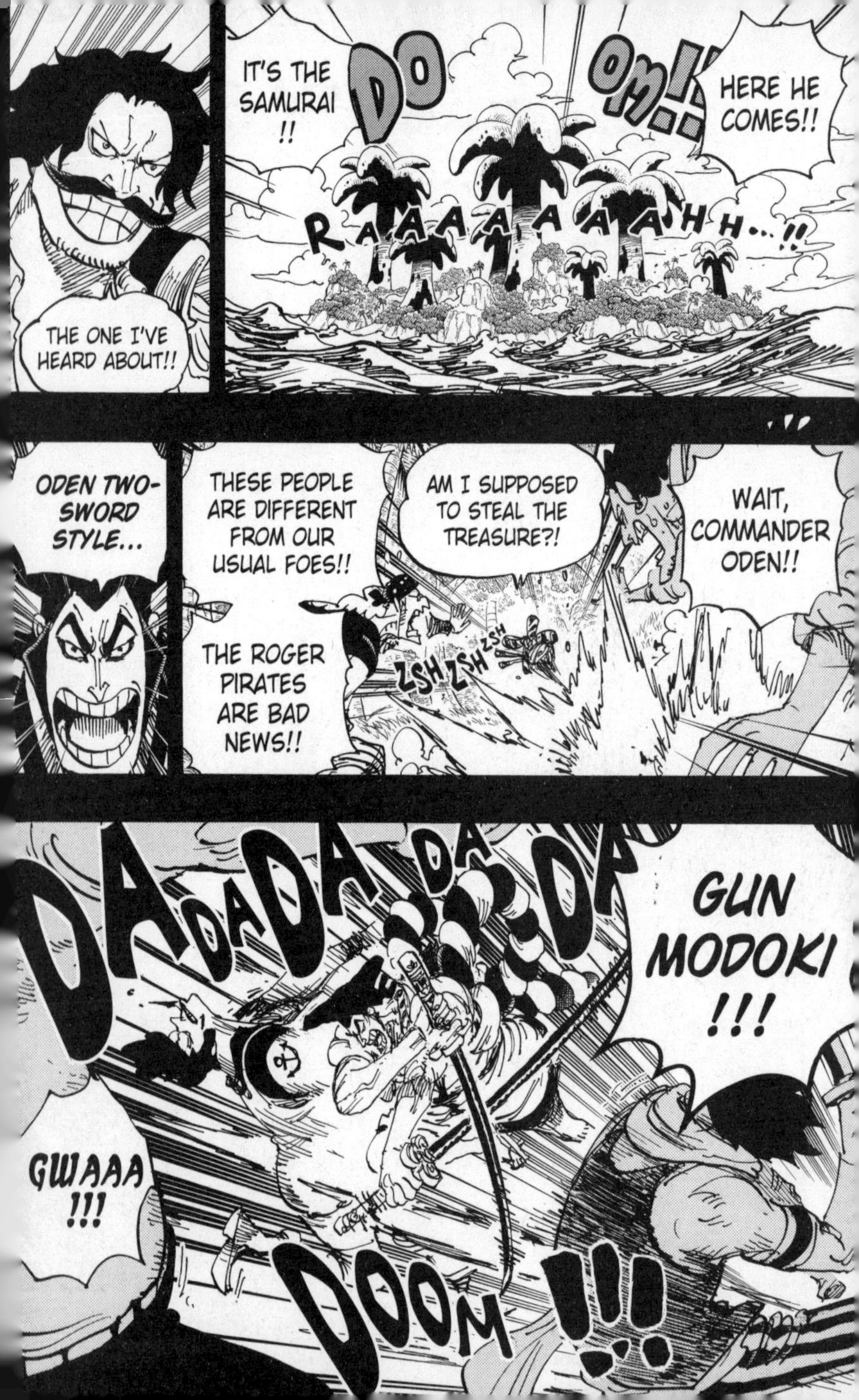
HERE HE COMES!!
DOOM!!
IT'S THE SAMURAI !!
RAAAAAAAHH...!!
THE ONE I'VE HEARD ABOUT!!
WAIT, COMMANDER ODEN!!
AM I SUPPOSED TO STEAL THE TREASURE?!
THESE PEOPLE ARE DIFFERENT FROM OUR USUAL FOES!!
ZSH ZSH ZSH
THE ROGER PIRATES ARE BAD NEWS!!
ODEN TWO-SWORD STYLE...
GUN MODOKI !!!
DADADADADA
GWAAA !!!
DOOM!!!

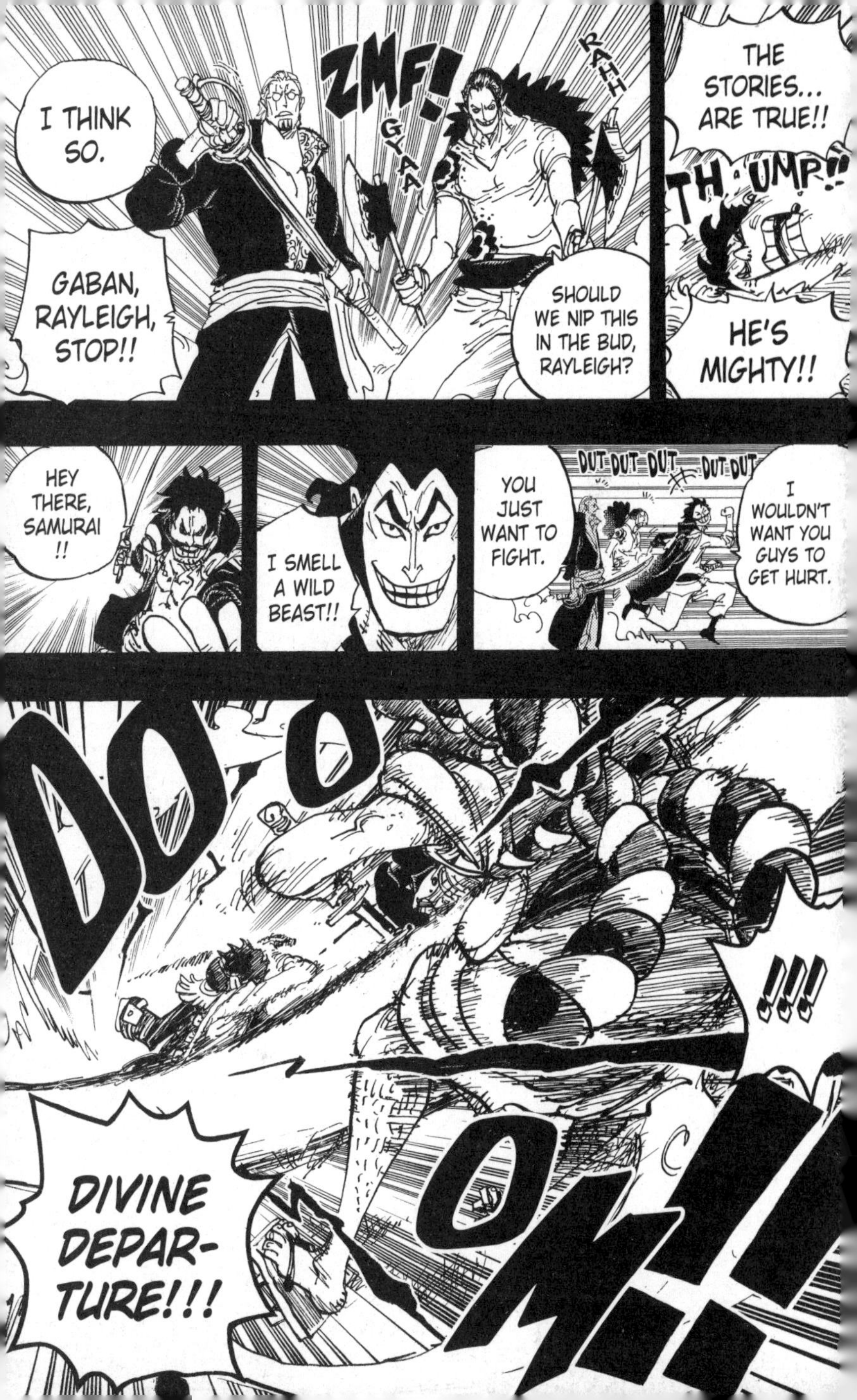
THE STORIES... ARE TRUE!!
TH-UMP!!
HE'S MIGHTY!!
RAHH
ZMF!
GYAA
SHOULD WE NIP THIS IN THE BUD, RAYLEIGH?
I THINK SO.
GABAN, RAYLEIGH, STOP!!
I WOULDN'T WANT YOU GUYS TO GET HURT.
DUT DUT DUT DUT DUT
YOU JUST WANT TO FIGHT.
I SMELL A WILD BEAST!!
HEY THERE, SAMURAI!!
!!!
DOOOH!!
DIVINE DEPARTURE!!!

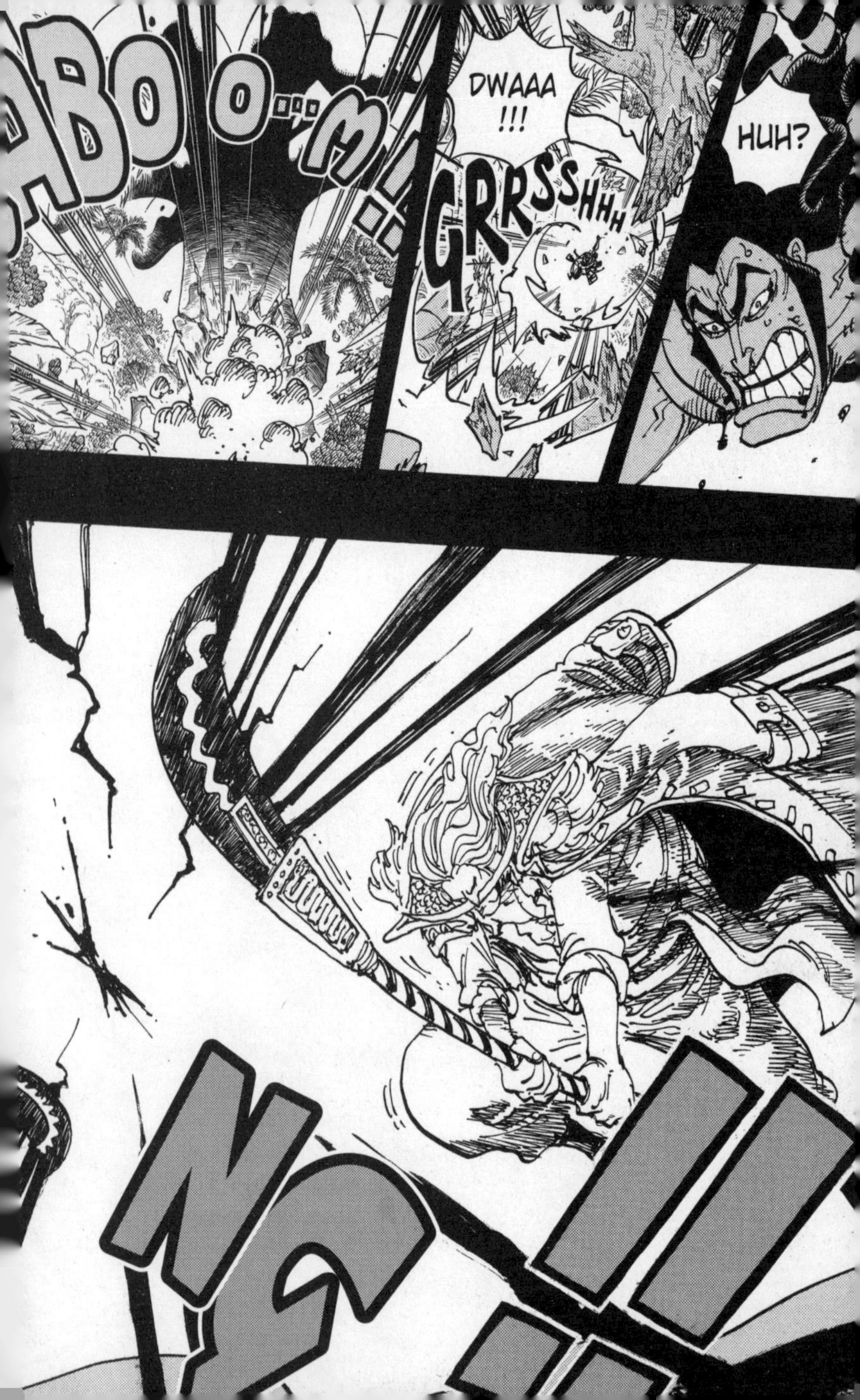
HUH?
DWAAA !!!
GRRSSHHH
BOO...M!!

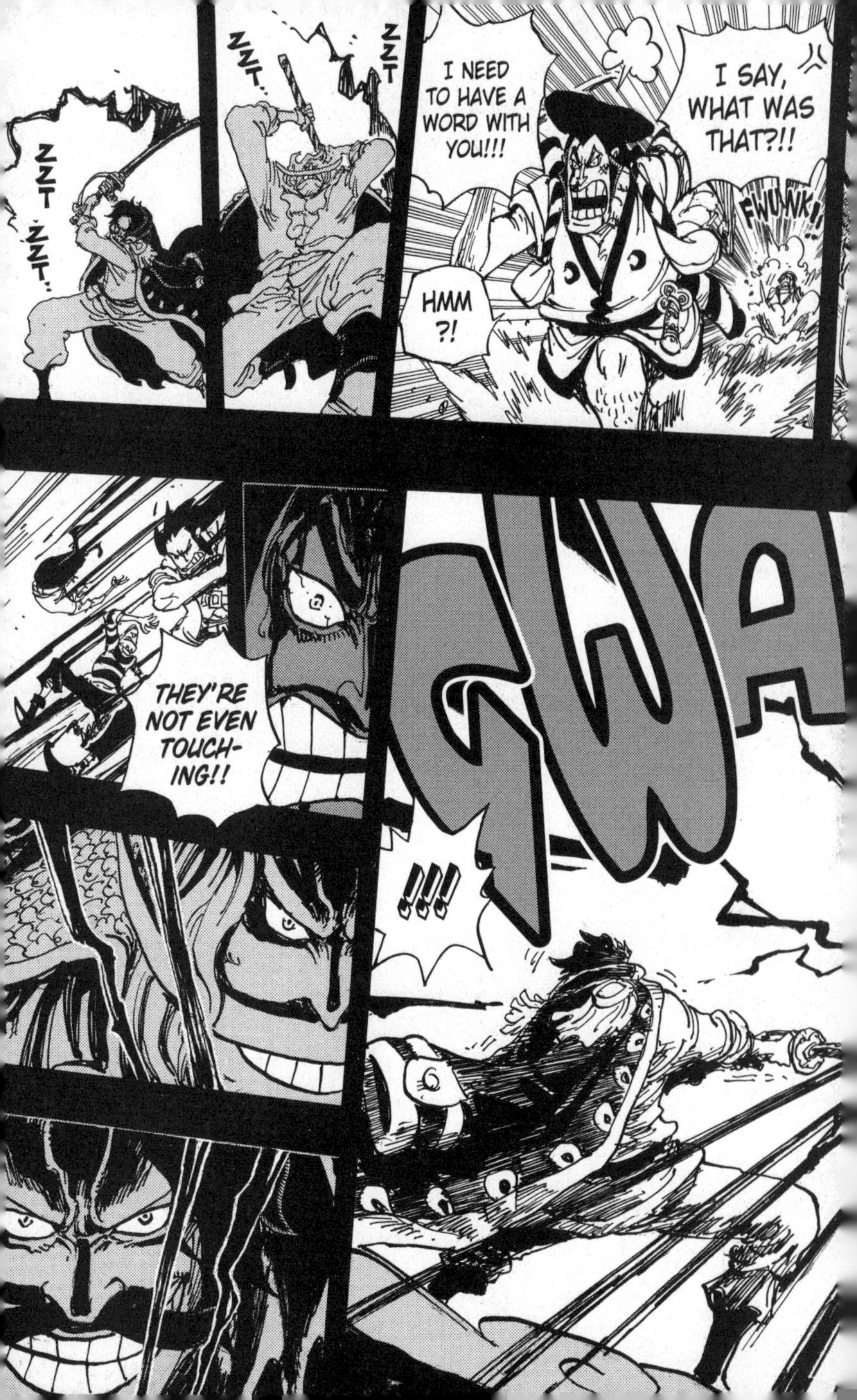
I SAY, WHAT WAS THAT?!!
FWUNK!!
I NEED TO HAVE A WORD WITH YOU!!!
HMM ?!
ZZT
ZZZT..
ZZT
ZZZT..
GWA
!!!
THEY'RE NOT EVEN TOUCH-ING!!

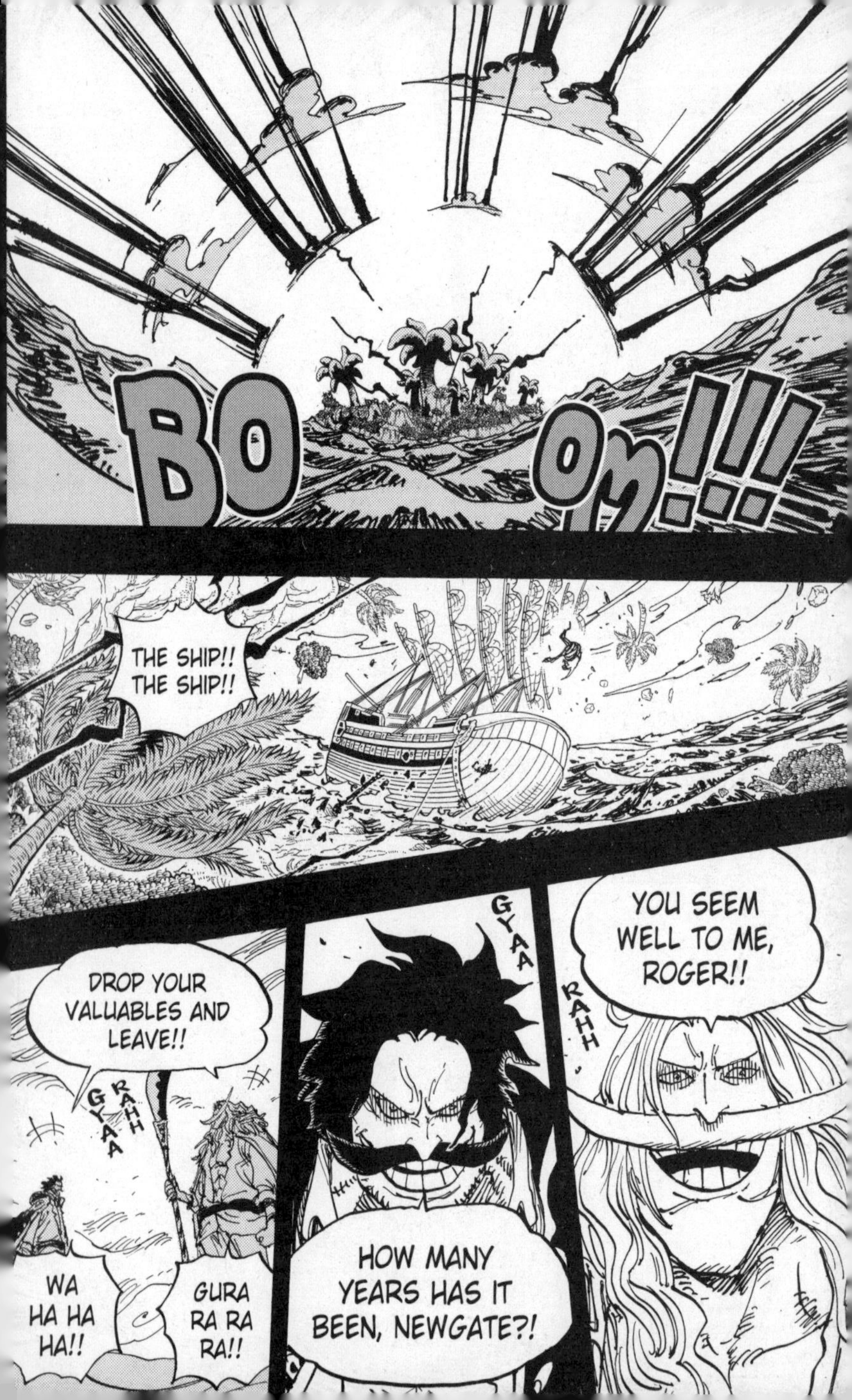

BOOM!!!
THE SHIP!! THE SHIP!!
YOU SEEM WELL TO ME, ROGER!!
GYAA
RAHH
HOW MANY YEARS HAS IT BEEN, NEWGATE?!
DROP YOUR VALUABLES AND LEAVE!!
GYAA
RAHH
GURA RA RA RA!!
WA HA HA HA!!

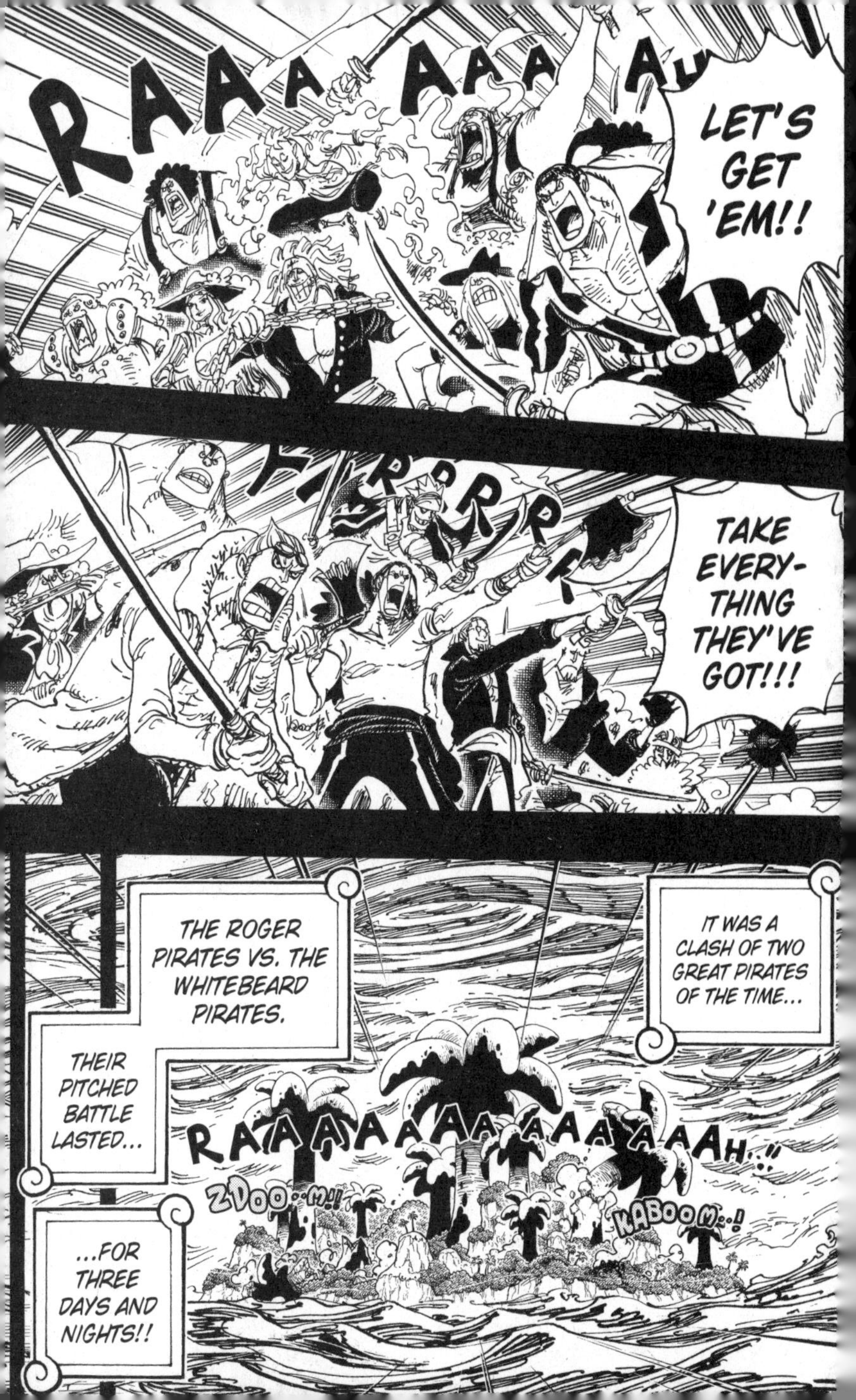
RAAAAAAAA
LET'S GET 'EM!!
YARRRRR
TAKE EVERY-THING THEY'VE GOT!!!
IT WAS A CLASH OF TWO GREAT PIRATES OF THE TIME...
THE ROGER PIRATES VS. THE WHITEBEARD PIRATES.
THEIR PITCHED BATTLE LASTED...
RAAAAAAAAAAAH..!!
KABOOM..!
ZDOOOM..!!
...FOR THREE DAYS AND NIGHTS!!

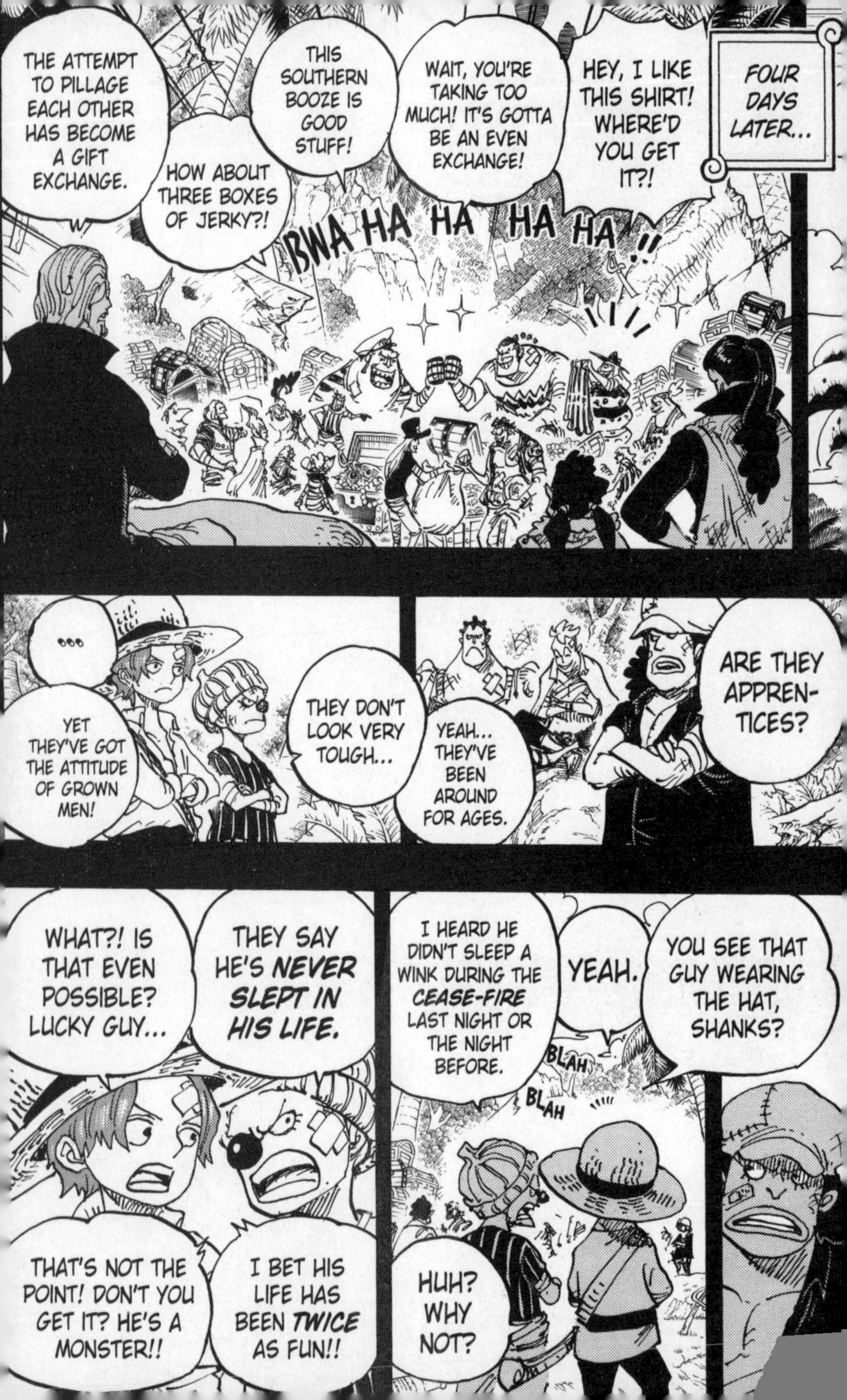
FOUR DAYS LATER...
HEY, I LIKE THIS SHIRT! WHERE'D YOU GET IT?!
WAIT, YOU'RE TAKING TOO MUCH! IT'S GOTTA BE AN EVEN EXCHANGE!
THIS SOUTHERN BOOZE IS GOOD STUFF!
HOW ABOUT THREE BOXES OF JERKY?!
THE ATTEMPT TO PILLAGE EACH OTHER HAS BECOME A GIFT EXCHANGE.
BWA HA HA HA HA!!
ARE THEY APPRENTICES?
YEAH... THEY'VE BEEN AROUND FOR AGES.
THEY DON'T LOOK VERY TOUGH...
...
YET THEY'VE GOT THE ATTITUDE OF GROWN MEN!
YOU SEE THAT GUY WEARING THE HAT, SHANKS?
YEAH.
I HEARD HE DIDN'T SLEEP A WINK DURING THE ***CEASE-FIRE*** LAST NIGHT OR THE NIGHT BEFORE.
BLAH
BLAH
HUH? WHY NOT?
THEY SAY HE'S ***NEVER SLEPT IN HIS LIFE.***
WHAT?! IS THAT EVEN POSSIBLE? LUCKY GUY...
I BET HIS LIFE HAS BEEN ***TWICE*** AS FUN!!
THAT'S NOT THE POINT! DON'T YOU GET IT? HE'S A MONSTER!!

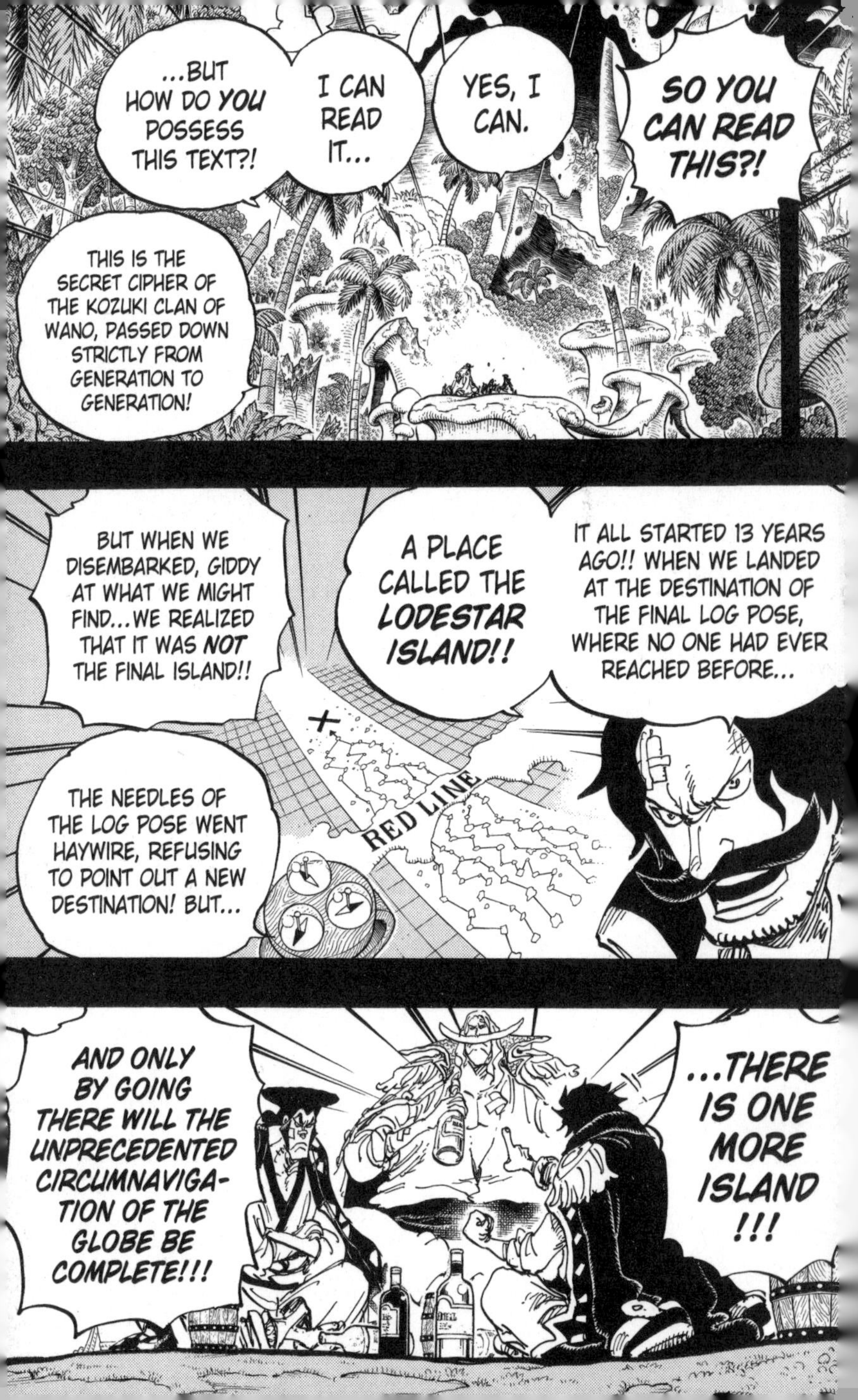
SO YOU CAN READ THIS?!
YES, I CAN.
I CAN READ IT...
...BUT HOW DO YOU POSSESS THIS TEXT?!
THIS IS THE SECRET CIPHER OF THE KOZUKI CLAN OF WANO, PASSED DOWN STRICTLY FROM GENERATION TO GENERATION!
IT ALL STARTED 13 YEARS AGO!! WHEN WE LANDED AT THE DESTINATION OF THE FINAL LOG POSE, WHERE NO ONE HAD EVER REACHED BEFORE...
A PLACE CALLED THE LODESTAR ISLAND!!
BUT WHEN WE DISEMBARKED, GIDDY AT WHAT WE MIGHT FIND...WE REALIZED THAT IT WAS NOT THE FINAL ISLAND!!
RED LINE
THE NEEDLES OF THE LOG POSE WENT HAYWIRE, REFUSING TO POINT OUT A NEW DESTINATION! BUT...
...THERE IS ONE MORE ISLAND!!!
AND ONLY BY GOING THERE WILL THE UNPRECEDENTED CIRCUMNAVIGATION OF THE GLOBE BE COMPLETE!!!

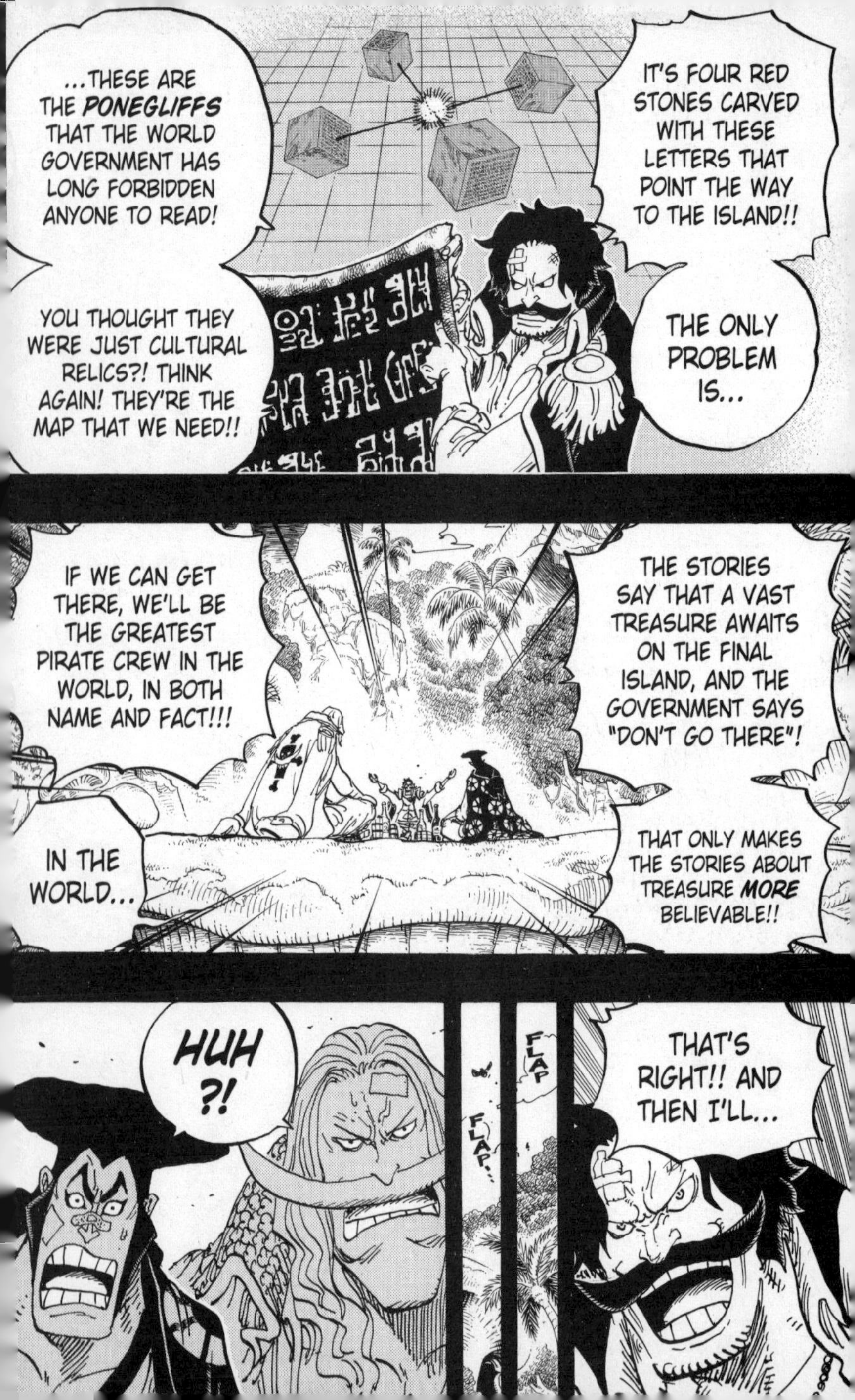
IT'S FOUR RED STONES CARVED WITH THESE LETTERS THAT POINT THE WAY TO THE ISLAND!!
...THESE ARE THE PONEGLIFFS THAT THE WORLD GOVERNMENT HAS LONG FORBIDDEN ANYONE TO READ!
THE ONLY PROBLEM IS...
YOU THOUGHT THEY WERE JUST CULTURAL RELICS?! THINK AGAIN! THEY'RE THE MAP THAT WE NEED!!
THE STORIES SAY THAT A VAST TREASURE AWAITS ON THE FINAL ISLAND, AND THE GOVERNMENT SAYS "DON'T GO THERE"!
IF WE CAN GET THERE, WE'LL BE THE GREATEST PIRATE CREW IN THE WORLD, IN BOTH NAME AND FACT!!!
THAT ONLY MAKES THE STORIES ABOUT TREASURE MORE BELIEVABLE!!
IN THE WORLD...
THAT'S RIGHT!! AND THEN I'LL...
FLAP
FLAP
HUH ?!

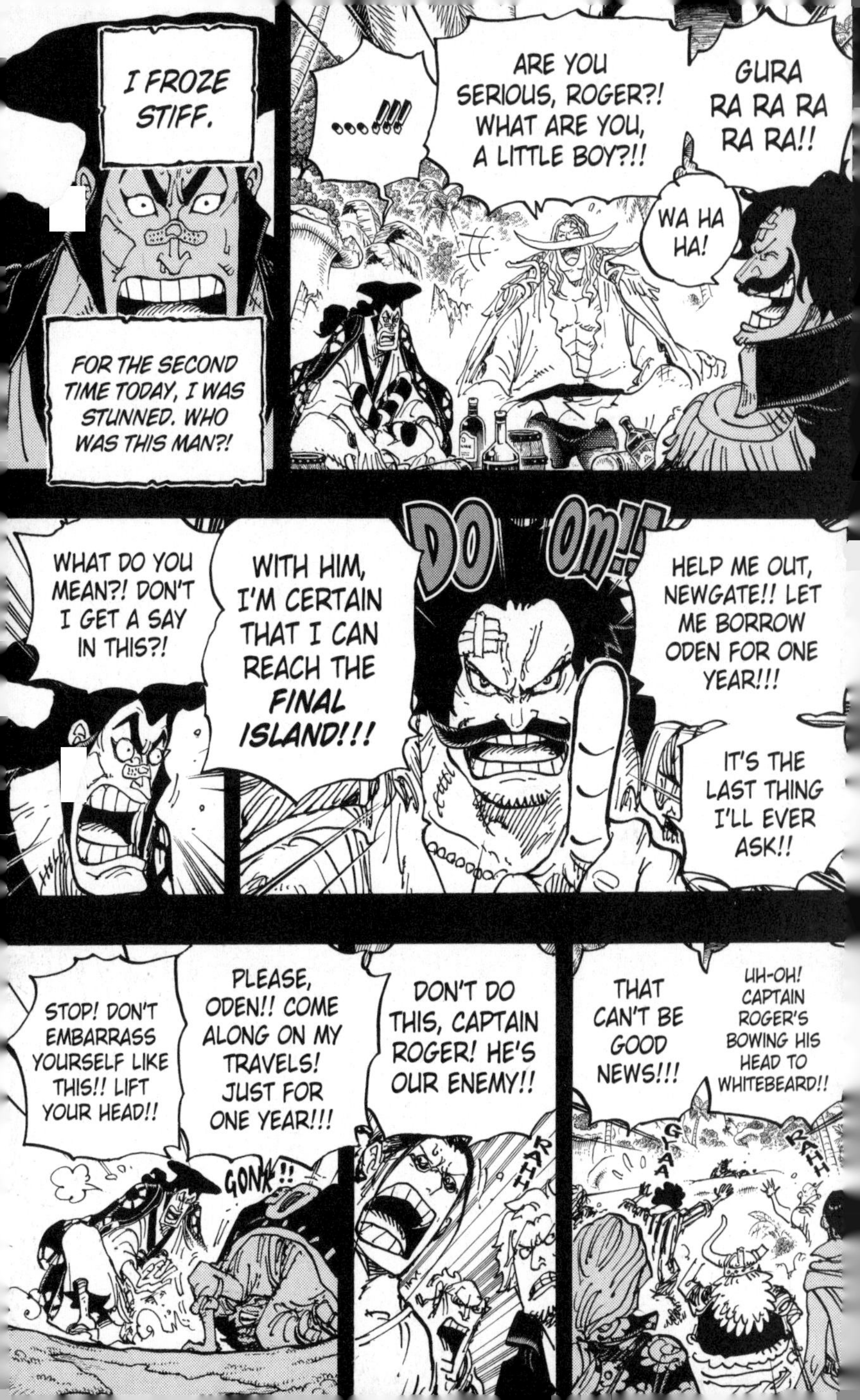
GURA RA RA RA RA RA!!
ARE YOU SERIOUS, ROGER?! WHAT ARE YOU, A LITTLE BOY?!!
WA HA HA!
...!!!
I FROZE STIFF.
FOR THE SECOND TIME TODAY, I WAS STUNNED. WHO WAS THIS MAN?!
DOOM!!
HELP ME OUT, NEWGATE!! LET ME BORROW ODEN FOR ONE YEAR!!!
IT'S THE LAST THING I'LL EVER ASK!!
WITH HIM, I'M CERTAIN THAT I CAN REACH THE FINAL ISLAND!!!
WHAT DO YOU MEAN?! DON'T I GET A SAY IN THIS?!
UH-OH! CAPTAIN ROGER'S BOWING HIS HEAD TO WHITEBEARD!!
THAT CAN'T BE GOOD NEWS!!!
GYAA
RAHH
DON'T DO THIS, CAPTAIN ROGER! HE'S OUR ENEMY!!
RAHH
PLEASE, ODEN!! COME ALONG ON MY TRAVELS! JUST FOR ONE YEAR!!!
STOP! DON'T EMBARRASS YOURSELF LIKE THIS!! LIFT YOUR HEAD!!
GONK!!

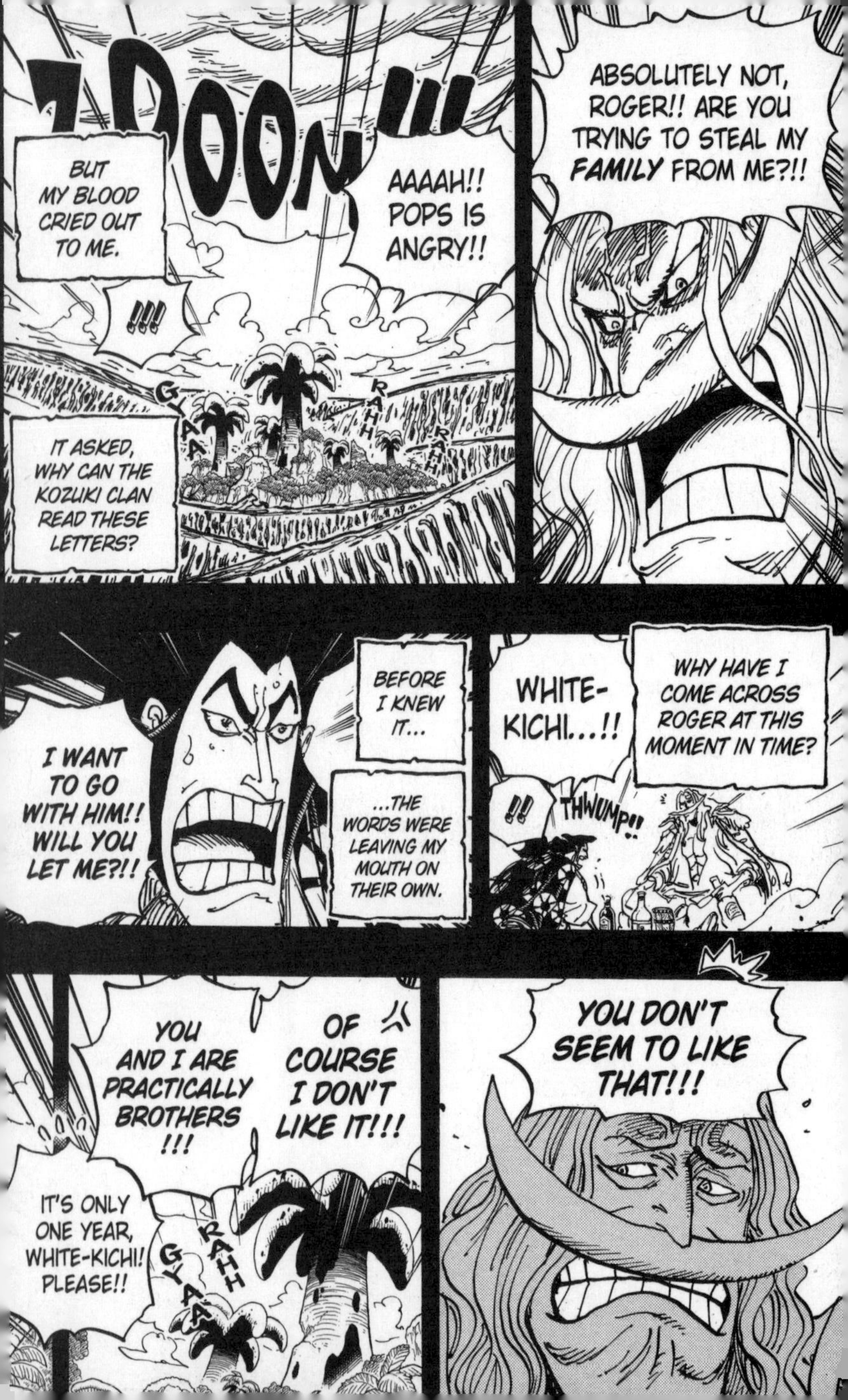
ABSOLUTELY NOT, ROGER!! ARE YOU TRYING TO STEAL MY FAMILY FROM ME?!!
ZDOON!!!
AAAAH!! POPS IS ANGRY!!
BUT MY BLOOD CRIED OUT TO ME.
!!!
RAHH
RAHH
GIAA
IT ASKED, WHY CAN THE KOZUKI CLAN READ THESE LETTERS?
WHY HAVE I COME ACROSS ROGER AT THIS MOMENT IN TIME?
WHITE-KICHI...!!
THWUMP!!
!!
BEFORE I KNEW IT...
...THE WORDS WERE LEAVING MY MOUTH ON THEIR OWN.
I WANT TO GO WITH HIM!! WILL YOU LET ME?!!
YOU DON'T SEEM TO LIKE THAT!!!
OF COURSE I DON'T LIKE IT!!!
YOU AND I ARE PRACTICALLY BROTHERS!!!
RAHH
GYAA
IT'S ONLY ONE YEAR, WHITE-KICHI! PLEASE!!

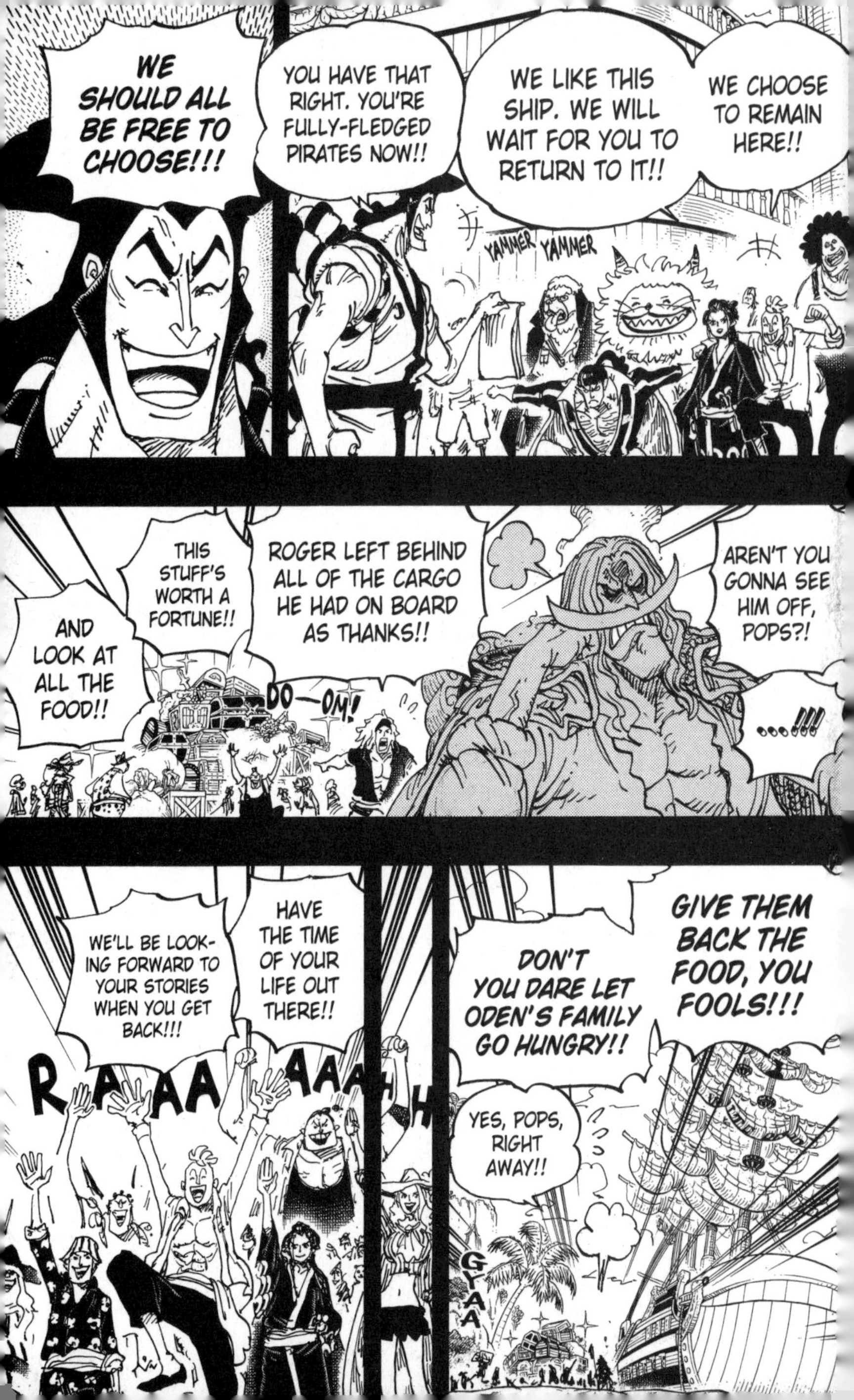
WE CHOOSE TO REMAIN HERE!!
WE LIKE THIS SHIP. WE WILL WAIT FOR YOU TO RETURN TO IT!!
YOU HAVE THAT RIGHT. YOU'RE FULLY-FLEDGED PIRATES NOW!!
YAMMER YAMMER
WE SHOULD ALL BE FREE TO CHOOSE!!!
AREN'T YOU GONNA SEE HIM OFF, POPS?!
ROGER LEFT BEHIND ALL OF THE CARGO HE HAD ON BOARD AS THANKS!!
THIS STUFF'S WORTH A FORTUNE!!
AND LOOK AT ALL THE FOOD!!
DO—OM!
...!!!
GIVE THEM BACK THE FOOD, YOU FOOLS!!!
DON'T YOU DARE LET ODEN'S FAMILY GO HUNGRY!!
YES, POPS, RIGHT AWAY!!
GYAA
HAVE THE TIME OF YOUR LIFE OUT THERE!!
WE'LL BE LOOKING FORWARD TO YOUR STORIES WHEN YOU GET BACK!!!
RAAAAAAAH

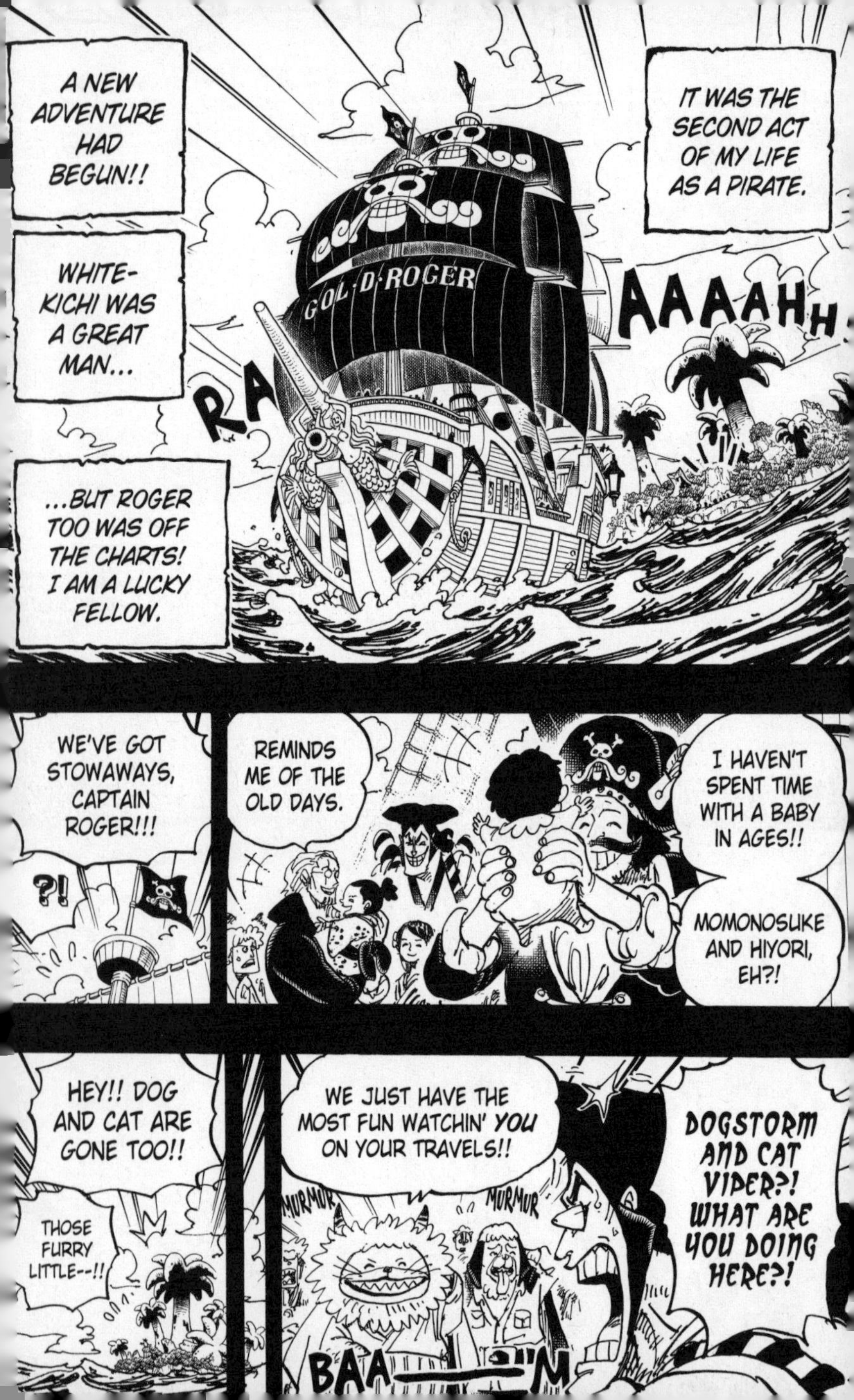
IT WAS THE SECOND ACT OF MY LIFE AS A PIRATE.
AAAAHH
RA
A NEW ADVENTURE HAD BEGUN!!
WHITE-KICHI WAS A GREAT MAN...
...BUT ROGER TOO WAS OFF THE CHARTS! I AM A LUCKY FELLOW.
GOL·D·ROGER
I HAVEN'T SPENT TIME WITH A BABY IN AGES!!
MOMONOSUKE AND HIYORI, EH?!
REMINDS ME OF THE OLD DAYS.
WE'VE GOT STOWAWAYS, CAPTAIN ROGER!!!
?!
DOGSTORM AND CAT VIPER?! WHAT ARE YOU DOING HERE?!
WE JUST HAVE THE MOST FUN WATCHIN' *YOU* ON YOUR TRAVELS!!
MURMUR
MURMUR
BAA——M
HEY!! DOG AND CAT ARE GONE TOO!!
THOSE FURRY LITTLE--!!

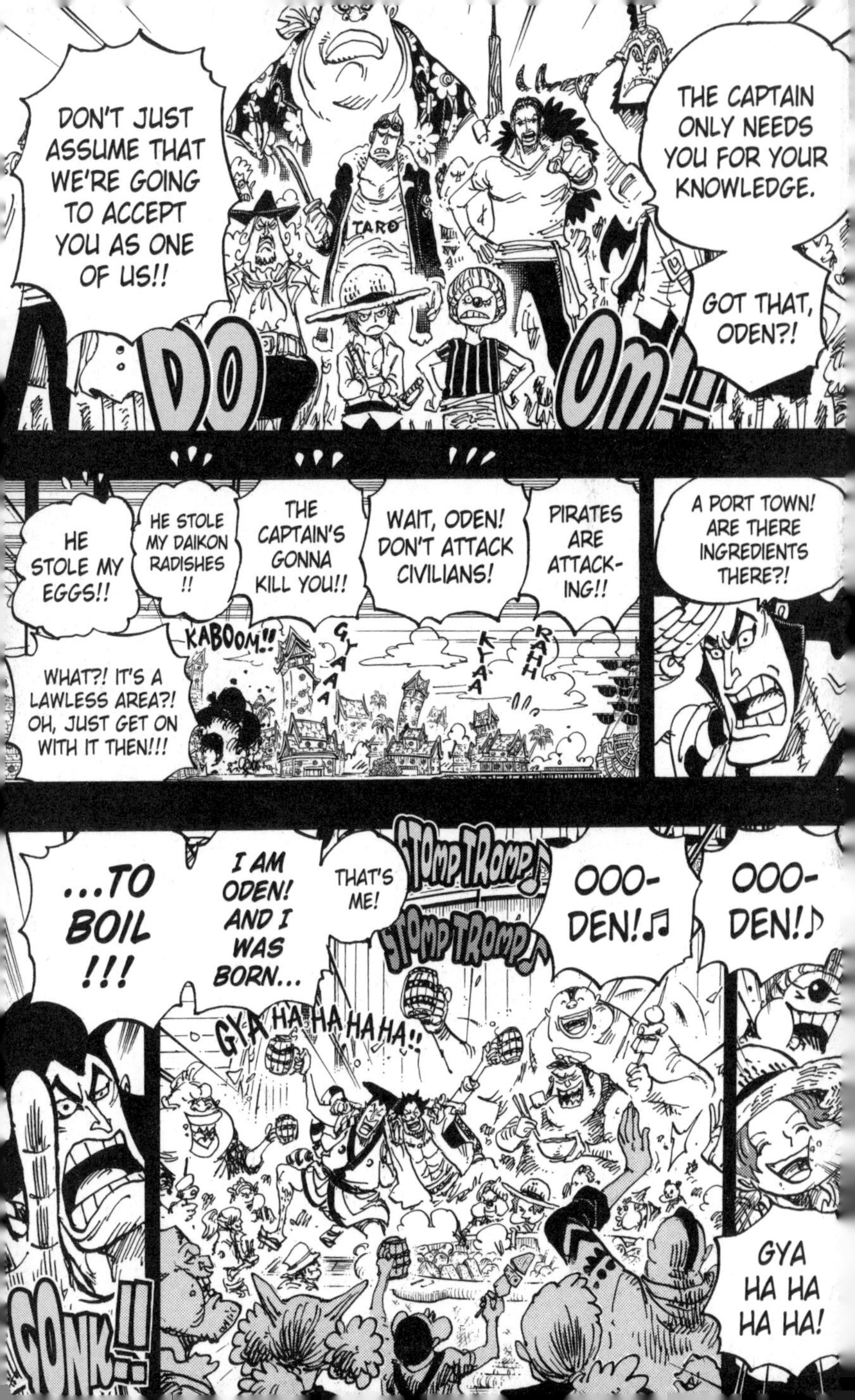
THE CAPTAIN ONLY NEEDS YOU FOR YOUR KNOWLEDGE.
GOT THAT, ODEN?!
DON'T JUST ASSUME THAT WE'RE GOING TO ACCEPT YOU AS ONE OF US!!
DO OM!!
A PORT TOWN! ARE THERE INGREDIENTS THERE?!
PIRATES ARE ATTACK-ING!!
WAIT, ODEN! DON'T ATTACK CIVILIANS!
THE CAPTAIN'S GONNA KILL YOU!!
HE STOLE MY DAIKON RADISHES !!
HE STOLE MY EGGS!!
RAHH
KYAA
GYAAA
KABOOM!!
WHAT?! IT'S A LAWLESS AREA?! OH, JUST GET ON WITH IT THEN!!!
OOO-DEN!♪
GYA HA HA HA HA!
OOO-DEN!♫
STOMP TROMP♪
STOMP TROMP♪
THAT'S ME!
I AM ODEN! AND I WAS BORN...
...TO BOIL!!!
GYA HA HA HA HA!!
GONK!!

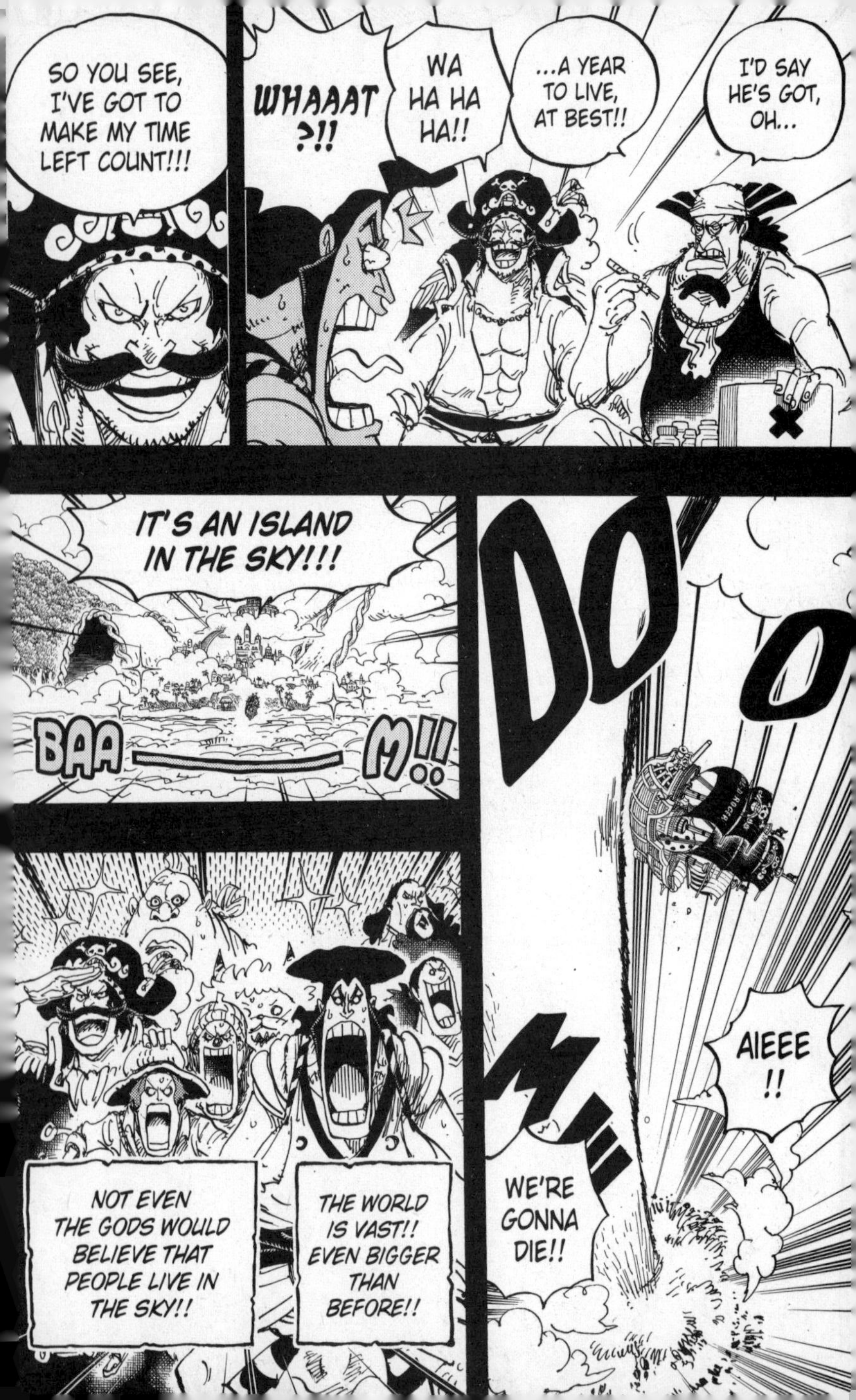
I'D SAY HE'S GOT, OH...
...A YEAR TO LIVE, AT BEST!!
WA HA HA HA!!
WHAAAT ?!!
SO YOU SEE, I'VE GOT TO MAKE MY TIME LEFT COUNT!!!
DOOOM!!
AIEEE !!
WE'RE GONNA DIE!!
IT'S AN ISLAND IN THE SKY!!!
BAA——M!!
THE WORLD IS VAST!! EVEN BIGGER THAN BEFORE!!
NOT EVEN THE GODS WOULD BELIEVE THAT PEOPLE LIVE IN THE SKY!!

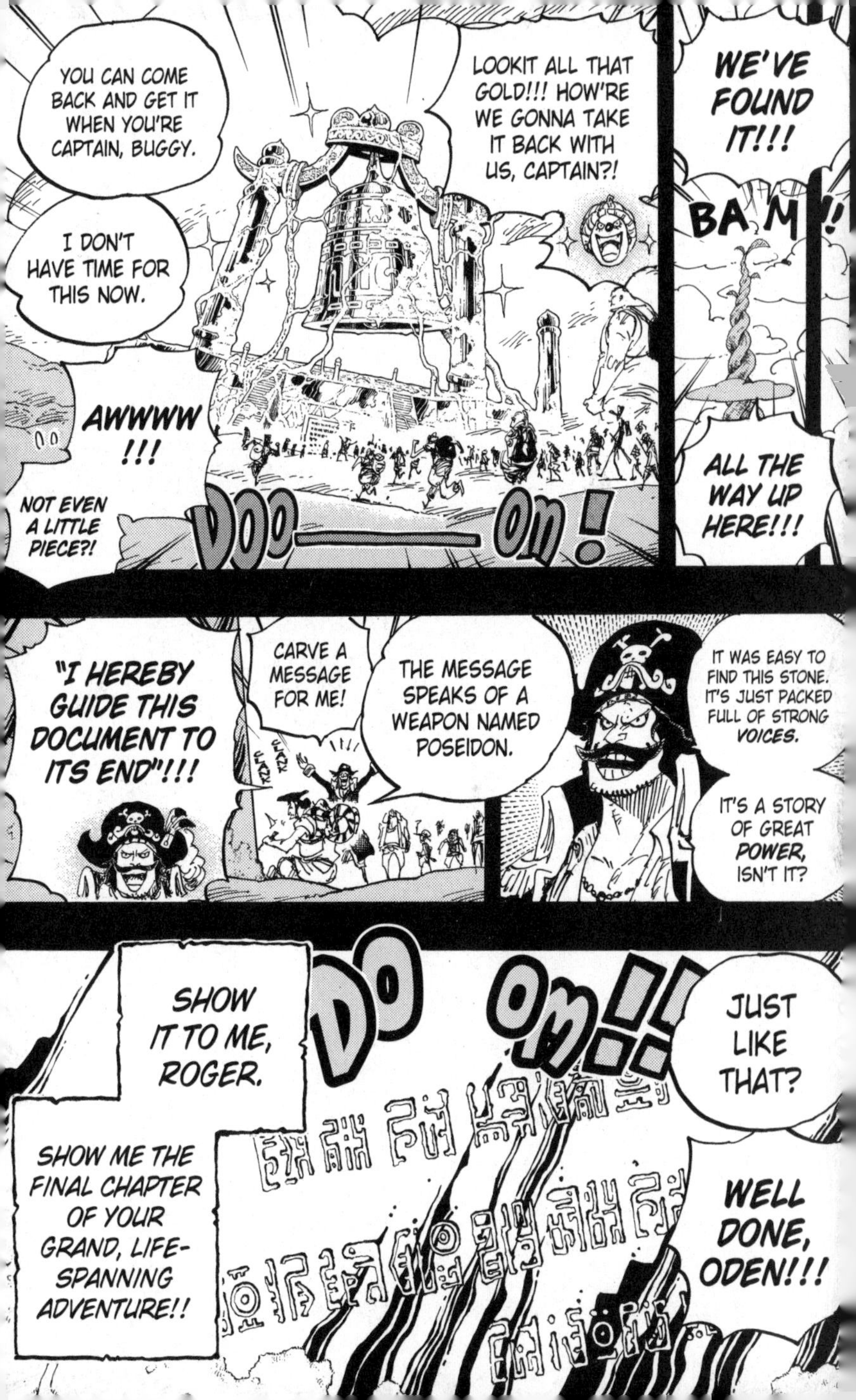
WE'VE FOUND IT!!!
BAM!!
ALL THE WAY UP HERE!!!
LOOKIT ALL THAT GOLD!!! HOW'RE WE GONNA TAKE IT BACK WITH US, CAPTAIN?!
YOU CAN COME BACK AND GET IT WHEN YOU'RE CAPTAIN, BUGGY.
I DON'T HAVE TIME FOR THIS NOW.
AWWWW!!!
NOT EVEN A LITTLE PIECE?!
DOO——OM!
IT WAS EASY TO FIND THIS STONE. IT'S JUST PACKED FULL OF STRONG VOICES.
IT'S A STORY OF GREAT POWER, ISN'T IT?
THE MESSAGE SPEAKS OF A WEAPON NAMED POSEIDON.
CARVE A MESSAGE FOR ME!
CLANK CLANK
"I HEREBY GUIDE THIS DOCUMENT TO ITS END"!!!
JUST LIKE THAT?
DO OM!!
WELL DONE, ODEN!!!
SHOW IT TO ME, ROGER.
SHOW ME THE FINAL CHAPTER OF YOUR GRAND, LIFE-SPANNING ADVENTURE!!

Chapter 967: ROGER'S ADVENTURE

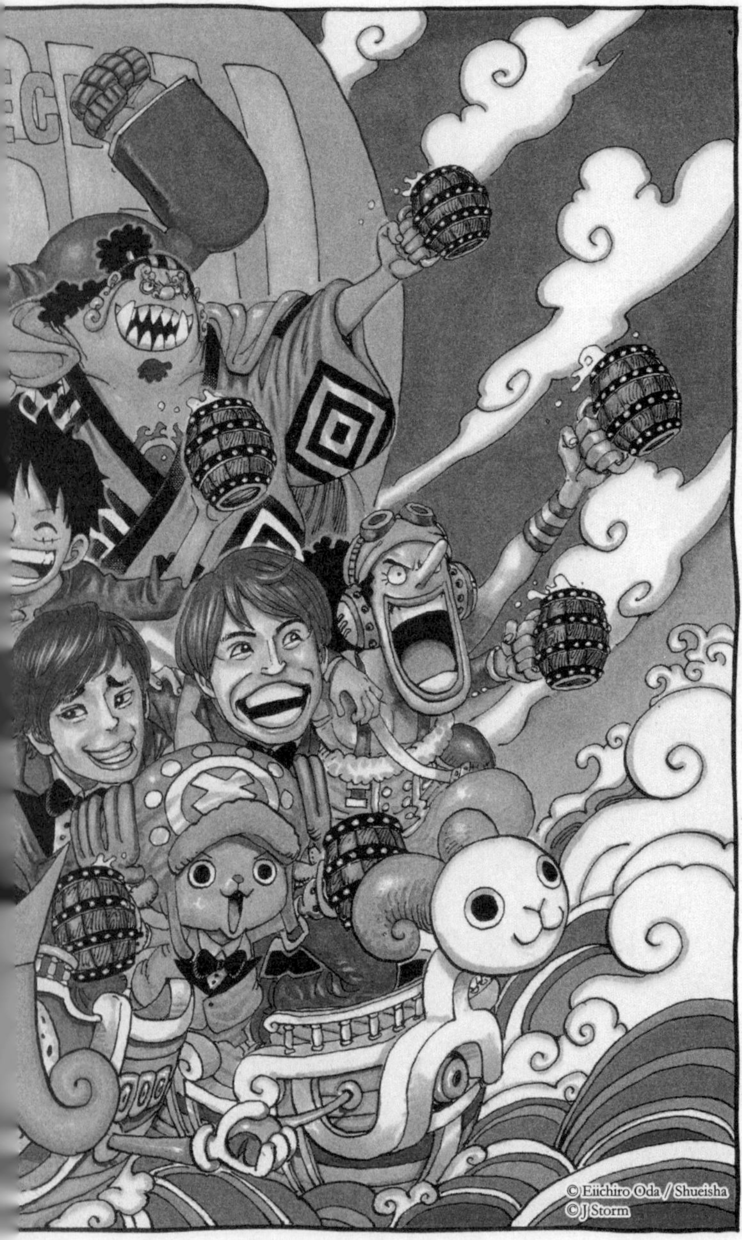

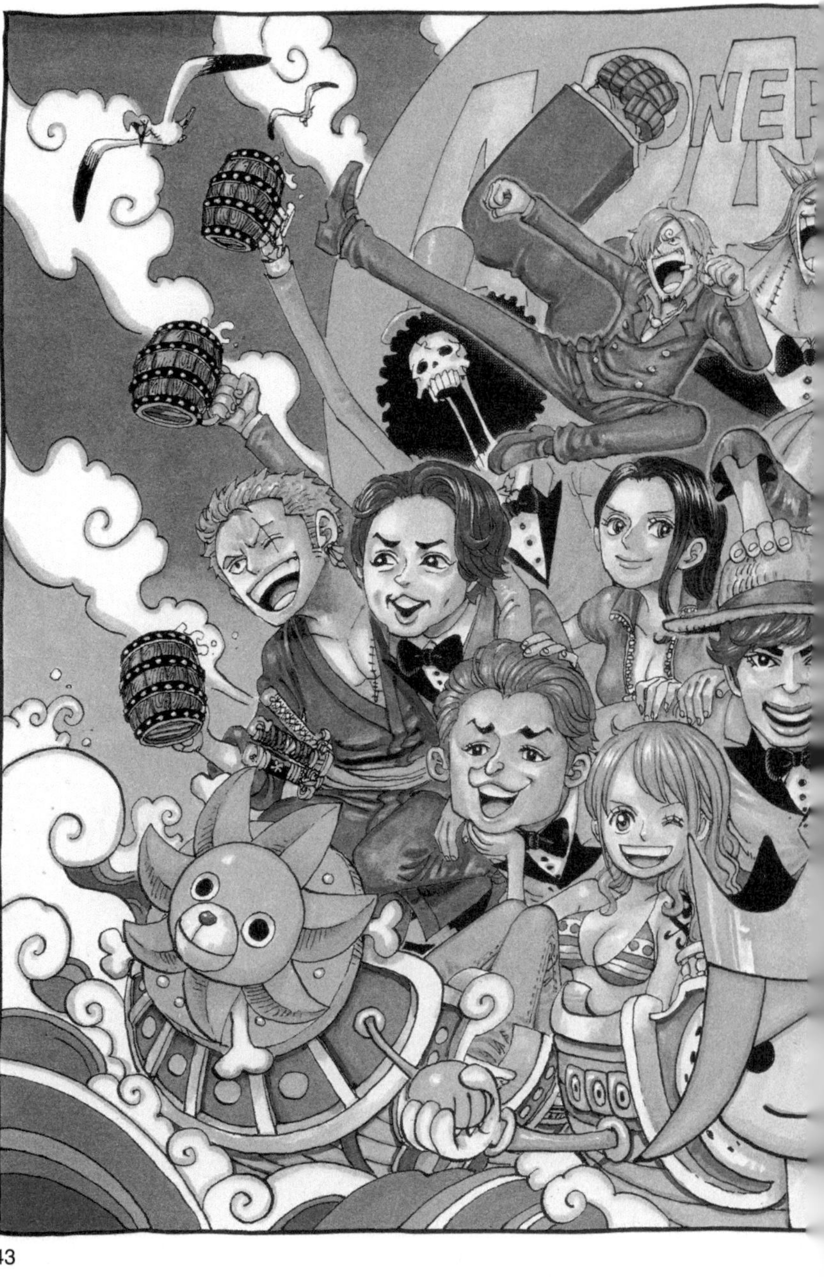

vol.96
ONE PIECE

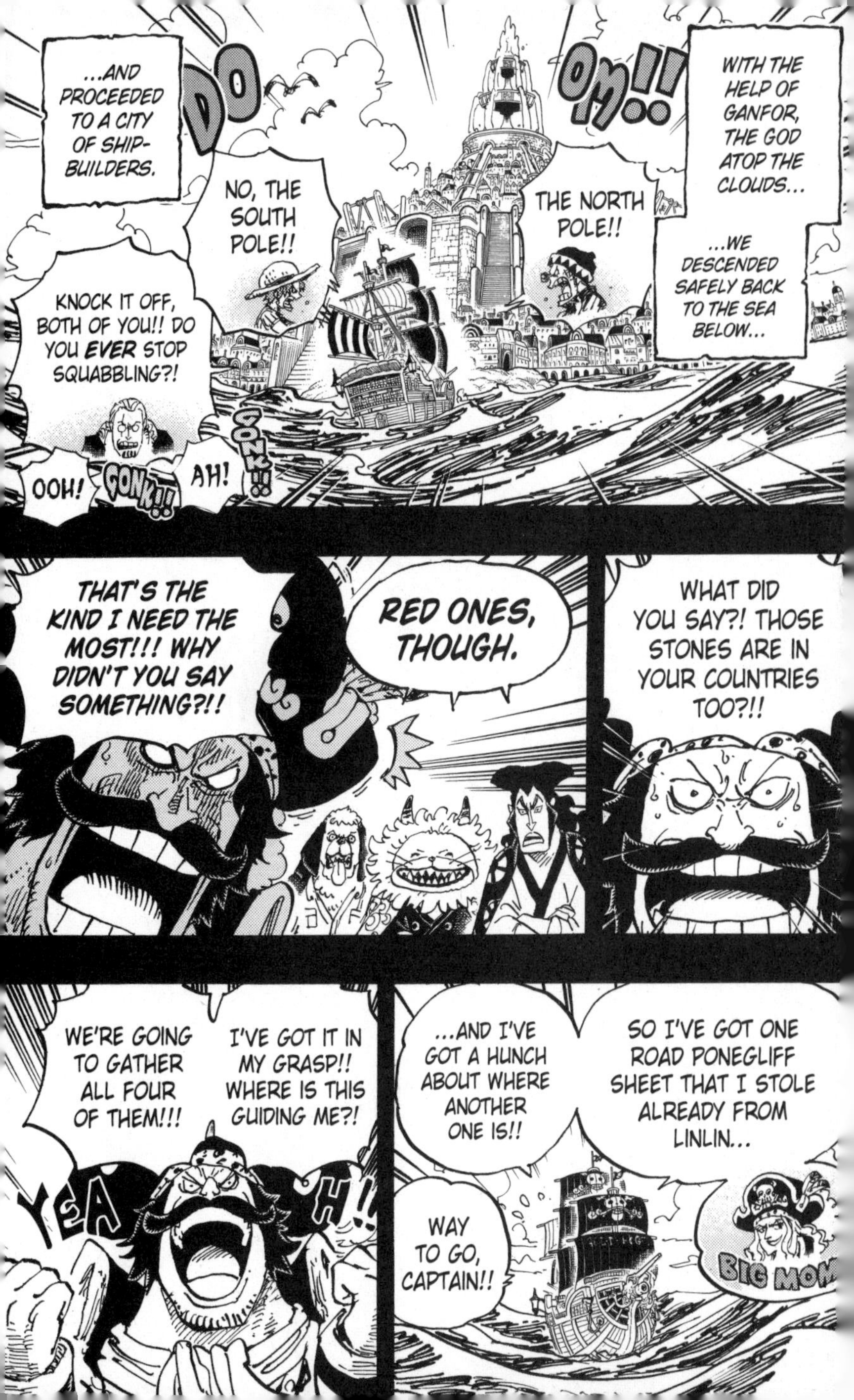
WITH THE HELP OF GANFOR, THE GOD ATOP THE CLOUDS...
...WE DESCENDED SAFELY BACK TO THE SEA BELOW...
OM!!
DO
...AND PROCEEDED TO A CITY OF SHIP-BUILDERS.
THE NORTH POLE!!
NO, THE SOUTH POLE!!
KNOCK IT OFF, BOTH OF YOU!! DO YOU **EVER** STOP SQUABBLING?!
GONK!!
AH!
GONK!!
OOH!
WHAT DID YOU SAY?! THOSE STONES ARE IN YOUR COUNTRIES TOO?!!
RED ONES, THOUGH.
THAT'S THE KIND I NEED THE MOST!!! WHY DIDN'T YOU SAY SOMETHING?!!
SO I'VE GOT ONE ROAD PONEGLIFF SHEET THAT I STOLE ALREADY FROM LINLIN...
BIG MOM
...AND I'VE GOT A HUNCH ABOUT WHERE ANOTHER ONE IS!!
WAY TO GO, CAPTAIN!!
I'VE GOT IT IN MY GRASP!! WHERE IS THIS GUIDING ME?!
WE'RE GOING TO GATHER ALL FOUR OF THEM!!!
H!!
YEA

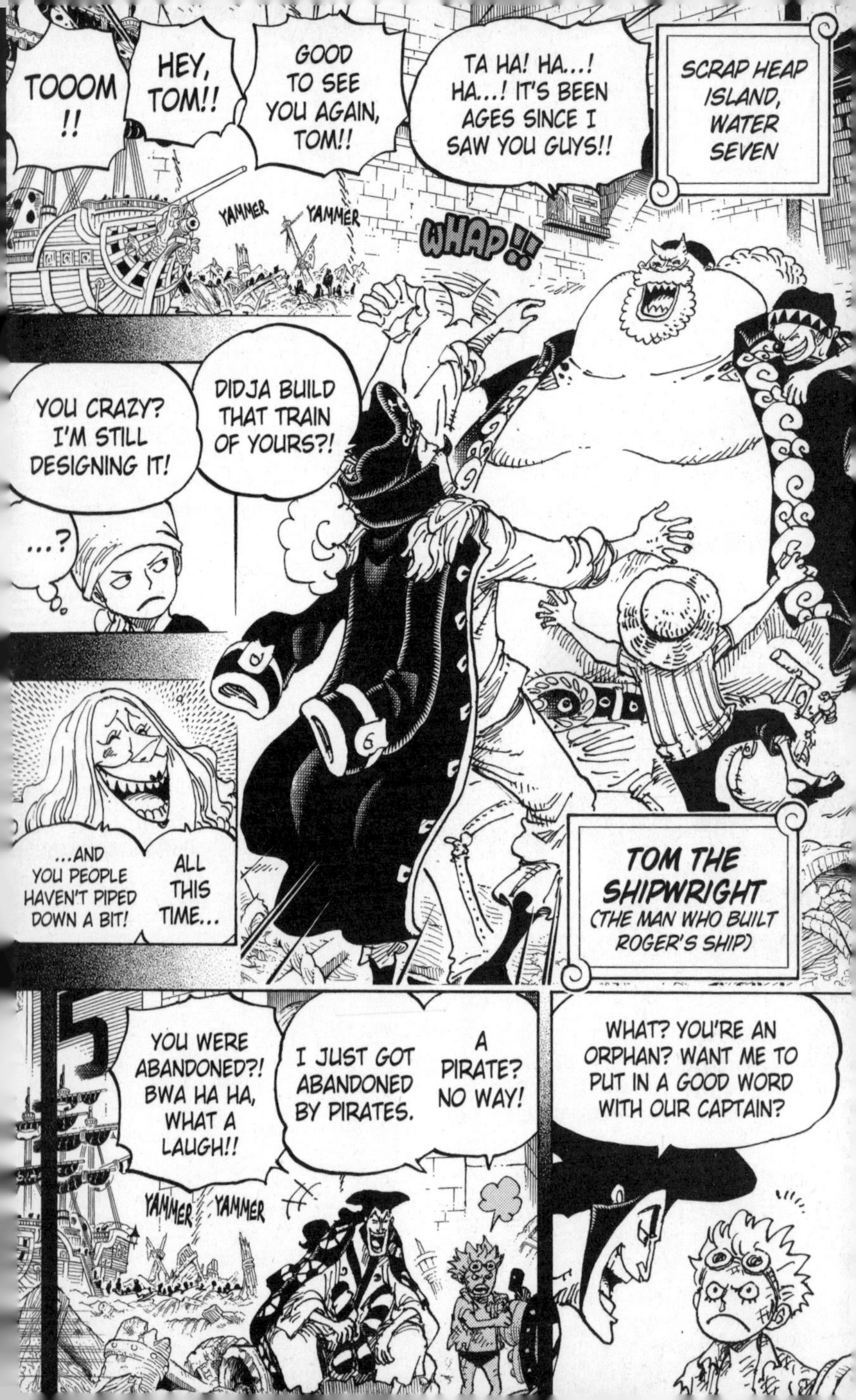
SCRAP HEAP ISLAND, WATER SEVEN
TA HA! HA...! HA...! IT'S BEEN AGES SINCE I SAW YOU GUYS!!
GOOD TO SEE YOU AGAIN, TOM!!
HEY, TOM!!
TOOOM !!
YAMMER
YAMMER
WHAP!!
DIDJA BUILD THAT TRAIN OF YOURS?!
YOU CRAZY? I'M STILL DESIGNING IT!
...?
TOM THE SHIPWRIGHT (THE MAN WHO BUILT ROGER'S SHIP)
ALL THIS TIME...
...AND YOU PEOPLE HAVEN'T PIPED DOWN A BIT!
WHAT? YOU'RE AN ORPHAN? WANT ME TO PUT IN A GOOD WORD WITH OUR CAPTAIN?
A PIRATE? NO WAY!
I JUST GOT ABANDONED BY PIRATES.
YOU WERE ABANDONED?! BWA HA HA, WHAT A LAUGH!!
YAMMER
YAMMER

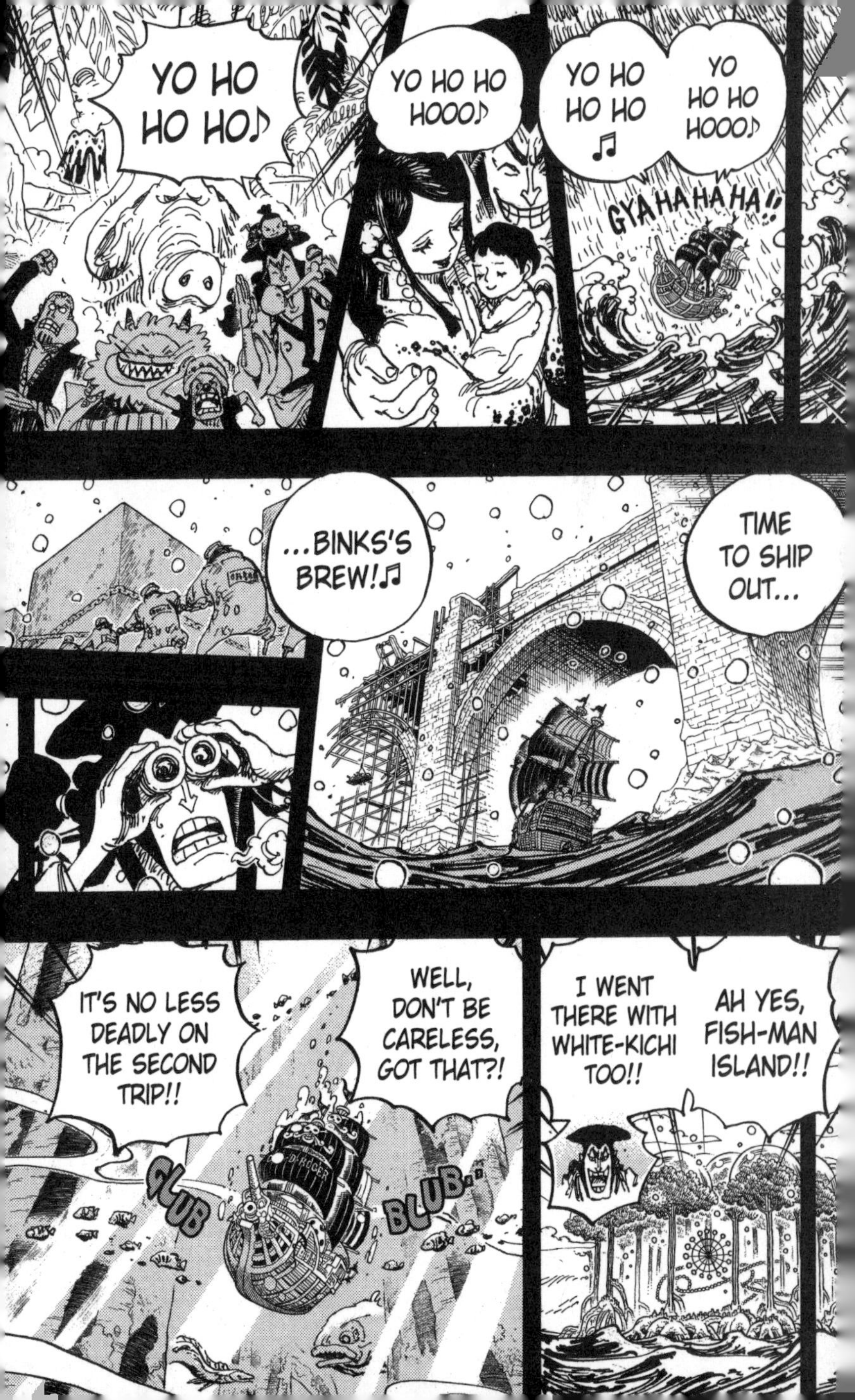
YO HO HO HOOO♪
YO HO HO HO ♫
GYAHAHAHA!!
YO HO HO HOOO♪
YO HO HO HO♪
TIME TO SHIP OUT...
...BINKS'S BREW!♫
AH YES, FISH-MAN ISLAND!!
I WENT THERE WITH WHITE-KICHI TOO!!
WELL, DON'T BE CARELESS, GOT THAT?!
IT'S NO LESS DEADLY ON THE SECOND TRIP!!
BLUB
GLUB

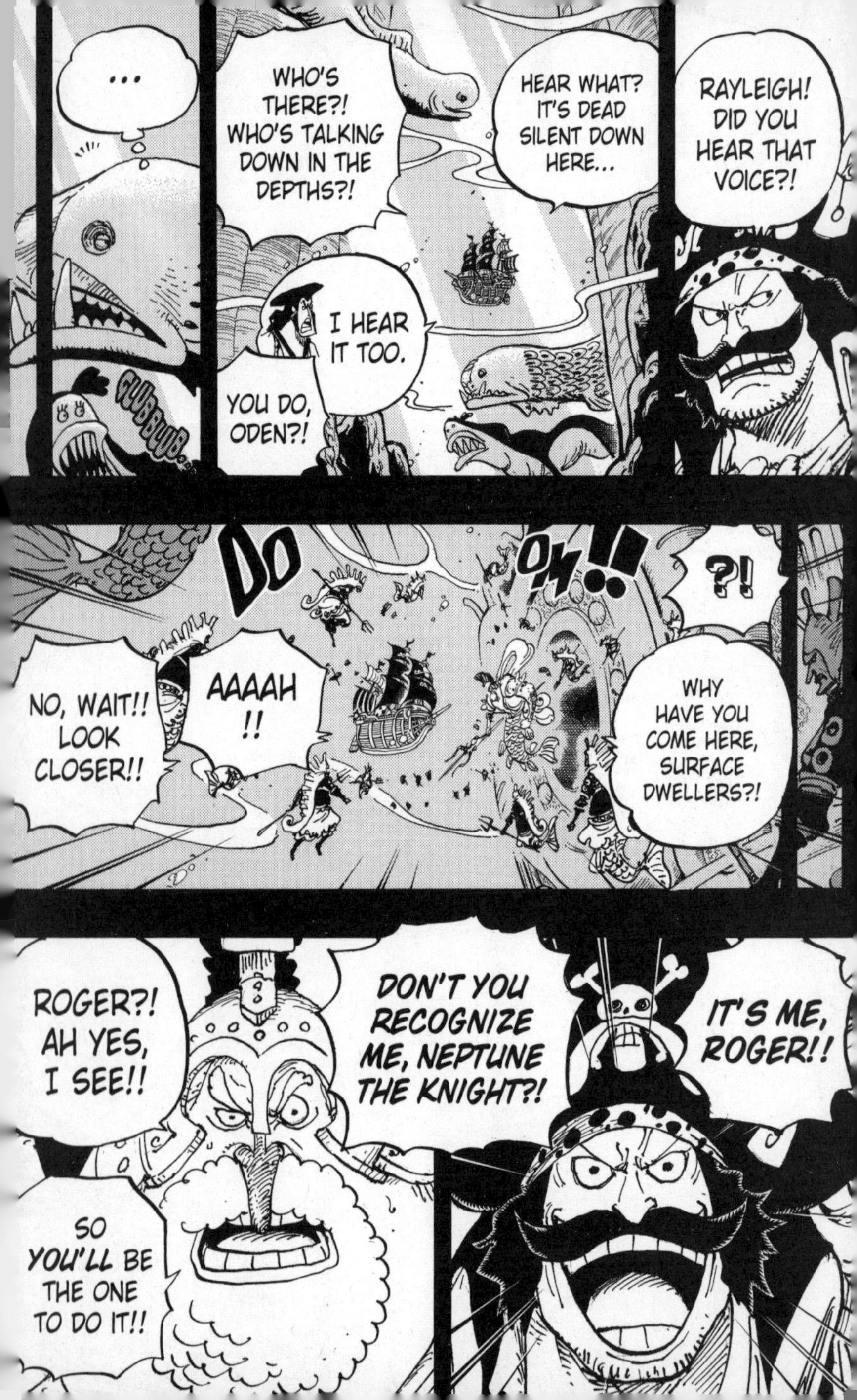
RAYLEIGH! DID YOU HEAR THAT VOICE?!
HEAR WHAT? IT'S DEAD SILENT DOWN HERE...
WHO'S THERE?! WHO'S TALKING DOWN IN THE DEPTHS?!
I HEAR IT TOO.
YOU DO, ODEN?!
...
GLUB BLUB
?!
WHY HAVE YOU COME HERE, SURFACE DWELLERS?!
DO
OM!!
AAAAH !!
NO, WAIT!! LOOK CLOSER!!
IT'S ME, ROGER!!
DON'T YOU RECOGNIZE ME, NEPTUNE THE KNIGHT?!
ROGER?! AH YES, I SEE!!
SO *YOU'LL* BE THE ONE TO DO IT!!

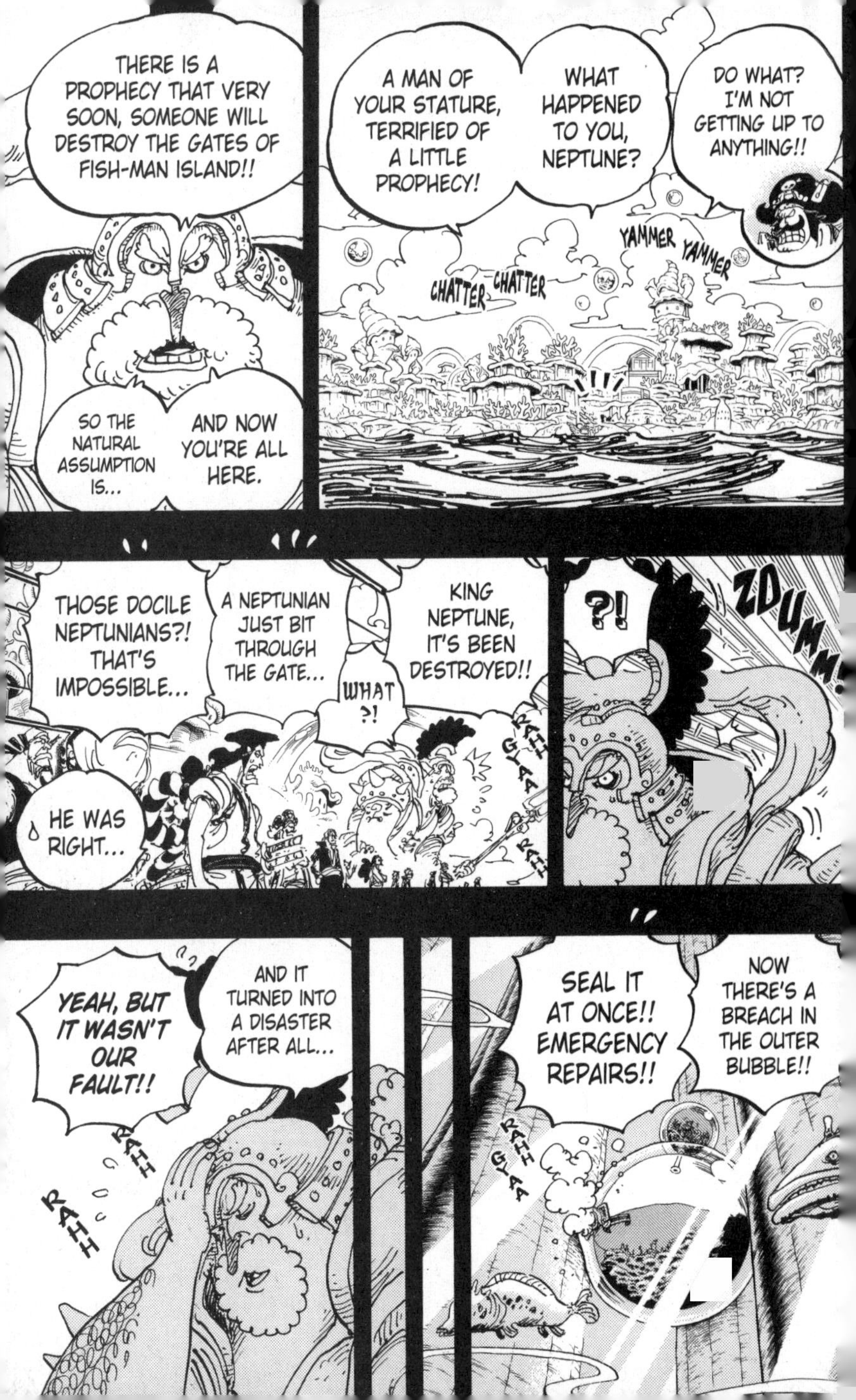

DO WHAT? I'M NOT GETTING UP TO ANYTHING!!
WHAT HAPPENED TO YOU, NEPTUNE?
A MAN OF YOUR STATURE, TERRIFIED OF A LITTLE PROPHECY!
YAMMER YAMMER
CHATTER CHATTER
THERE IS A PROPHECY THAT VERY SOON, SOMEONE WILL DESTROY THE GATES OF FISH-MAN ISLAND!!
AND NOW YOU'RE ALL HERE.
SO THE NATURAL ASSUMPTION IS...
?!
ZDUMM!
KING NEPTUNE, IT'S BEEN DESTROYED!!
WHAT ?!
A NEPTUNIAN JUST BIT THROUGH THE GATE...
THOSE DOCILE NEPTUNIANS?! THAT'S IMPOSSIBLE...
RAHH GYAA
RAHH
HE WAS RIGHT...
NOW THERE'S A BREACH IN THE OUTER BUBBLE!!
SEAL IT AT ONCE!! EMERGENCY REPAIRS!!
RAHH GYAA
AND IT TURNED INTO A DISASTER AFTER ALL...
YEAH, BUT IT WASN'T OUR FAULT!!
RAHH
RAHH

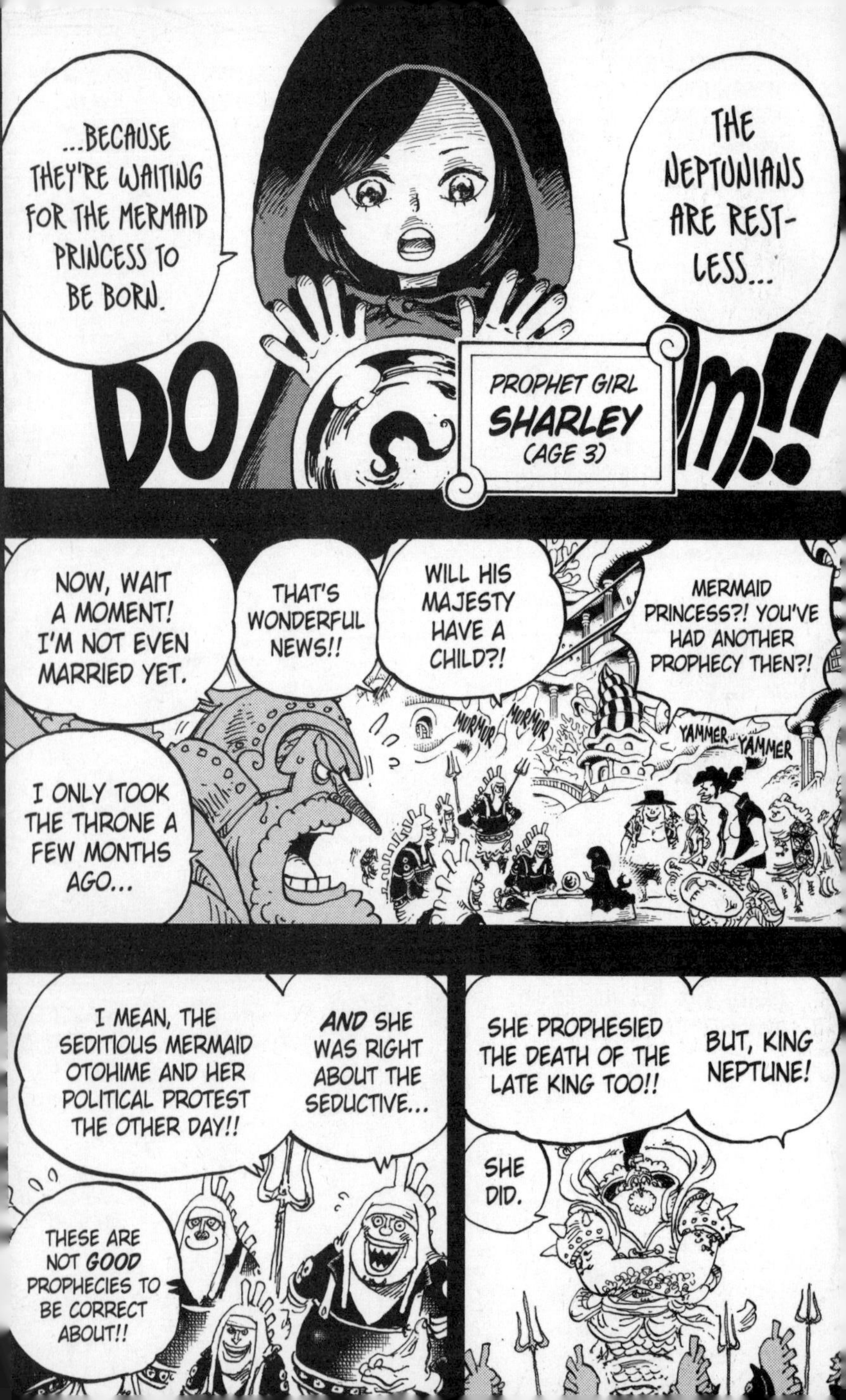
THE NEPTUNIANS ARE REST-LESS...
...BECAUSE THEY'RE WAITING FOR THE MERMAID PRINCESS TO BE BORN.
DO
M!!
PROPHET GIRL SHARLEY (AGE 3)
MERMAID PRINCESS?! YOU'VE HAD ANOTHER PROPHECY THEN?!
WILL HIS MAJESTY HAVE A CHILD?!
THAT'S WONDERFUL NEWS!!
NOW, WAIT A MOMENT! I'M NOT EVEN MARRIED YET.
YAMMER YAMMER
MURMUR
MURMUR
I ONLY TOOK THE THRONE A FEW MONTHS AGO...
BUT, KING NEPTUNE!
SHE PROPHESIED THE DEATH OF THE LATE KING TOO!!
SHE DID.
AND SHE WAS RIGHT ABOUT THE SEDUCTIVE...
I MEAN, THE SEDITIOUS MERMAID OTOHIME AND HER POLITICAL PROTEST THE OTHER DAY!!
THESE ARE NOT *GOOD* PROPHECIES TO BE CORRECT ABOUT!!

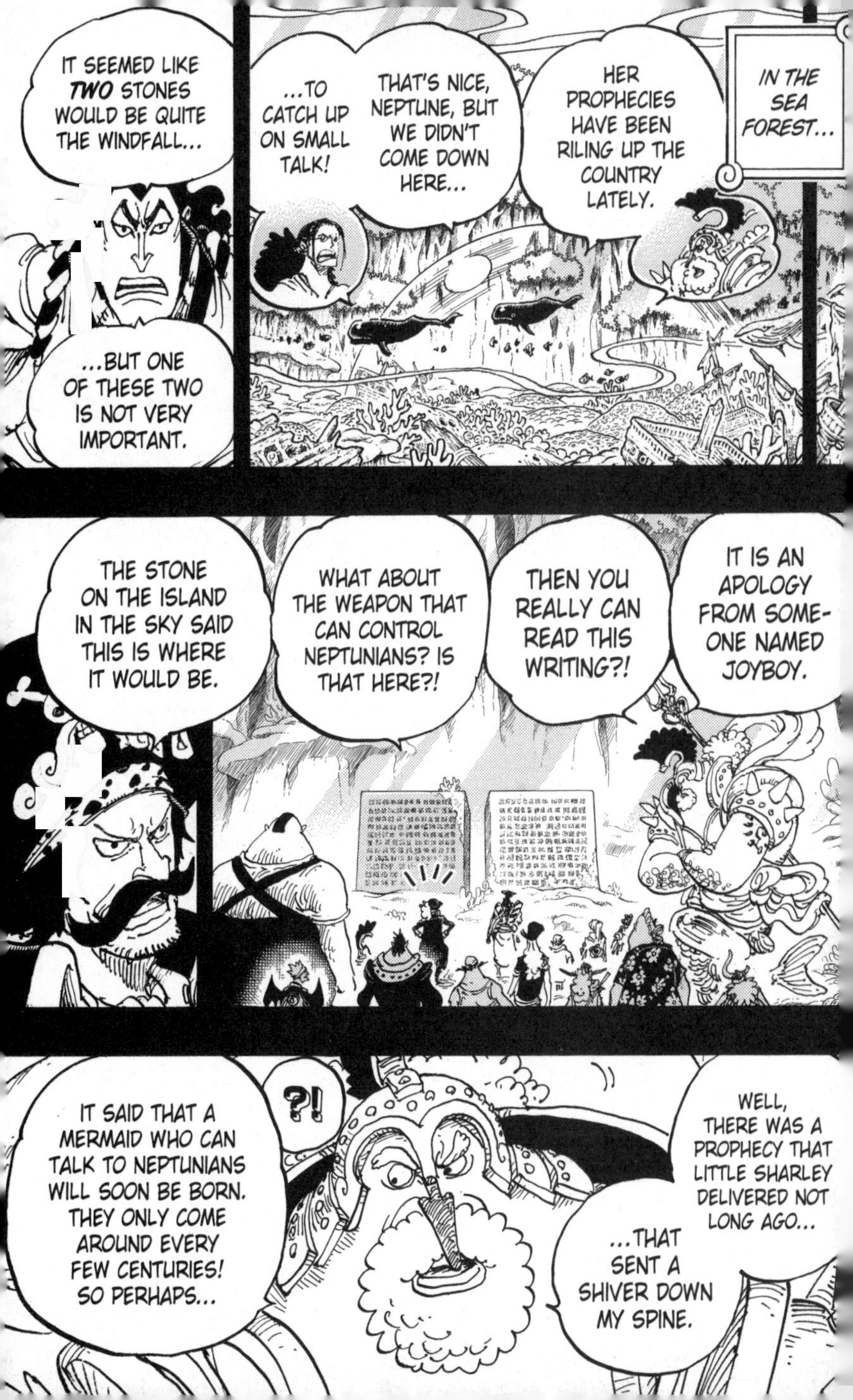
IN THE SEA FOREST...
HER PROPHECIES HAVE BEEN RILING UP THE COUNTRY LATELY.
THAT'S NICE, NEPTUNE, BUT WE DIDN'T COME DOWN HERE...
...TO CATCH UP ON SMALL TALK!
IT SEEMED LIKE TWO STONES WOULD BE QUITE THE WINDFALL...
...BUT ONE OF THESE TWO IS NOT VERY IMPORTANT.
IT IS AN APOLOGY FROM SOME-ONE NAMED JOYBOY.
THEN YOU REALLY CAN READ THIS WRITING?!
WHAT ABOUT THE WEAPON THAT CAN CONTROL NEPTUNIANS? IS THAT HERE?!
THE STONE ON THE ISLAND IN THE SKY SAID THIS IS WHERE IT WOULD BE.
WELL, THERE WAS A PROPHECY THAT LITTLE SHARLEY DELIVERED NOT LONG AGO...
...THAT SENT A SHIVER DOWN MY SPINE.
?!
IT SAID THAT A MERMAID WHO CAN TALK TO NEPTUNIANS WILL SOON BE BORN. THEY ONLY COME AROUND EVERY FEW CENTURIES! SO PERHAPS...

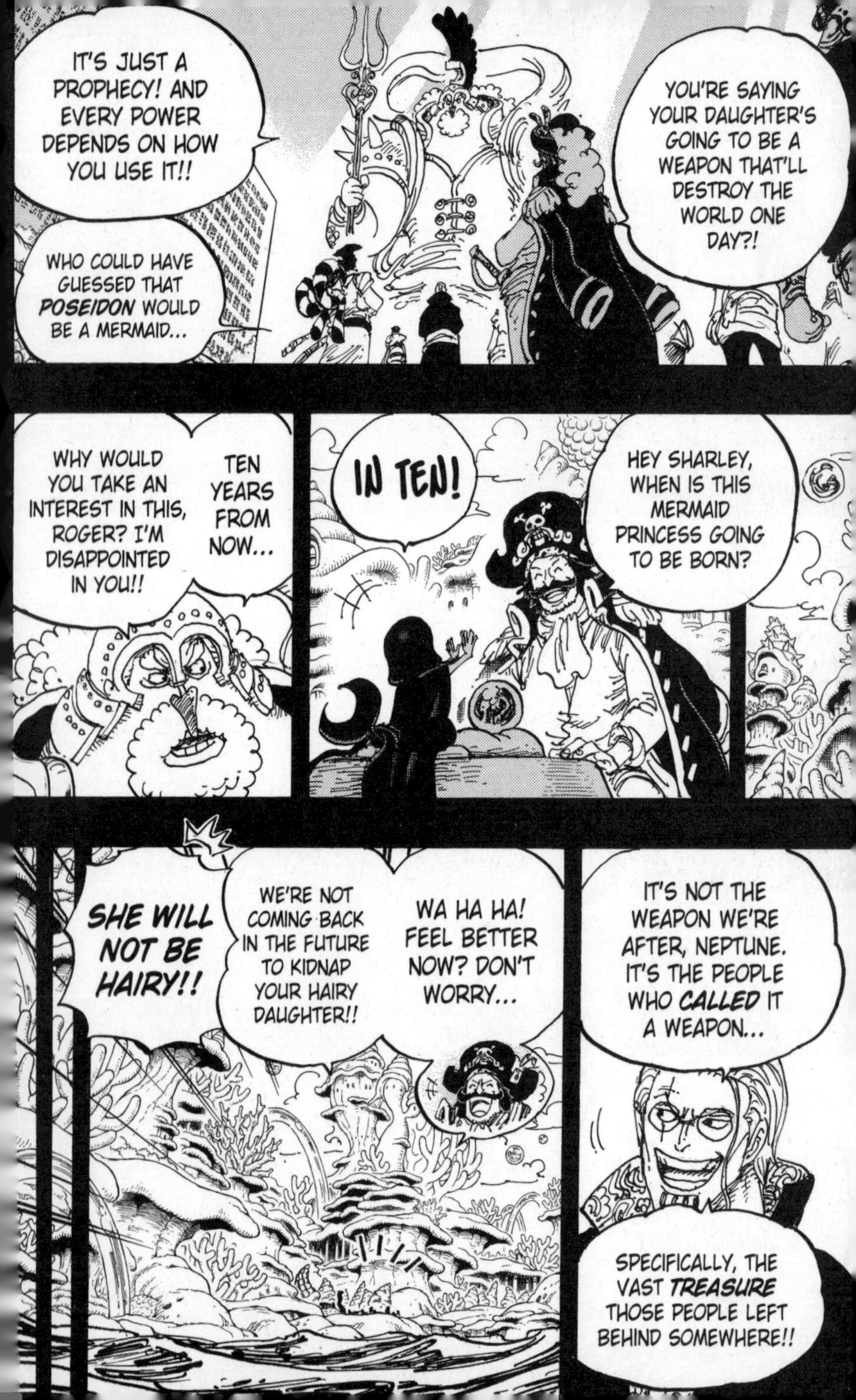

YOU'RE SAYING YOUR DAUGHTER'S GOING TO BE A WEAPON THAT'LL DESTROY THE WORLD ONE DAY?!
IT'S JUST A PROPHECY! AND EVERY POWER DEPENDS ON HOW YOU USE IT!!
WHO COULD HAVE GUESSED THAT POSEIDON WOULD BE A MERMAID...
HEY SHARLEY, WHEN IS THIS MERMAID PRINCESS GOING TO BE BORN?
IN TEN!
TEN YEARS FROM NOW...
WHY WOULD YOU TAKE AN INTEREST IN THIS, ROGER? I'M DISAPPOINTED IN YOU!!
IT'S NOT THE WEAPON WE'RE AFTER, NEPTUNE. IT'S THE PEOPLE WHO CALLED IT A WEAPON...
SPECIFICALLY, THE VAST TREASURE THOSE PEOPLE LEFT BEHIND SOMEWHERE!!
WA HA HA! FEEL BETTER NOW? DON'T WORRY...
WE'RE NOT COMING BACK IN THE FUTURE TO KIDNAP YOUR HAIRY DAUGHTER!!
SHE WILL NOT BE HAIRY!!

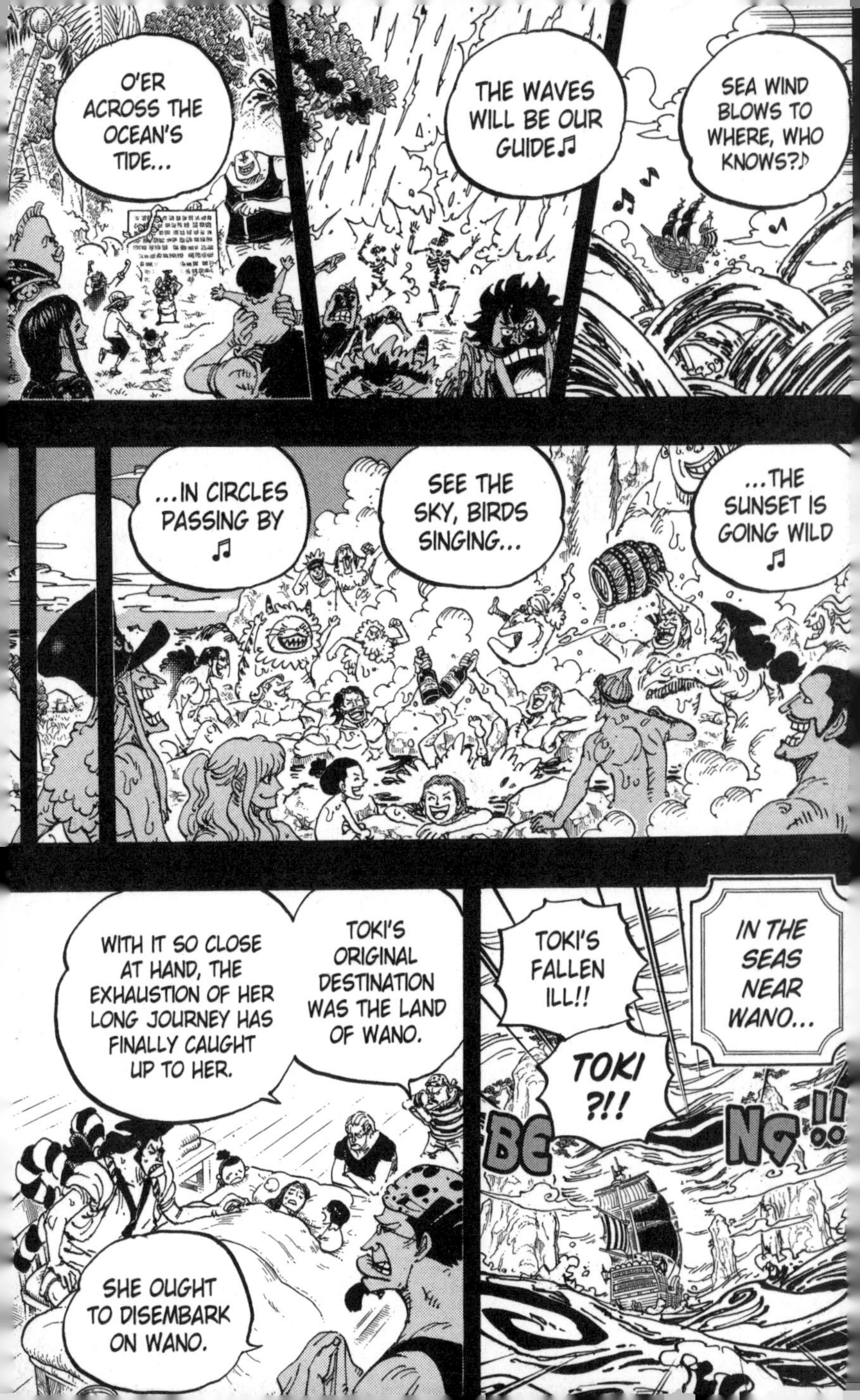
SEA WIND BLOWS TO WHERE, WHO KNOWS?♪
THE WAVES WILL BE OUR GUIDE♫
O'ER ACROSS THE OCEAN'S TIDE...
...THE SUNSET IS GOING WILD ♫
SEE THE SKY, BIRDS SINGING...
...IN CIRCLES PASSING BY ♫
IN THE SEAS NEAR WANO...
TOKI'S FALLEN ILL!!
TOKI ?!!
BENG!!
TOKI'S ORIGINAL DESTINATION WAS THE LAND OF WANO.
WITH IT SO CLOSE AT HAND, THE EXHAUSTION OF HER LONG JOURNEY HAS FINALLY CAUGHT UP TO HER.
SHE OUGHT TO DISEMBARK ON WANO.

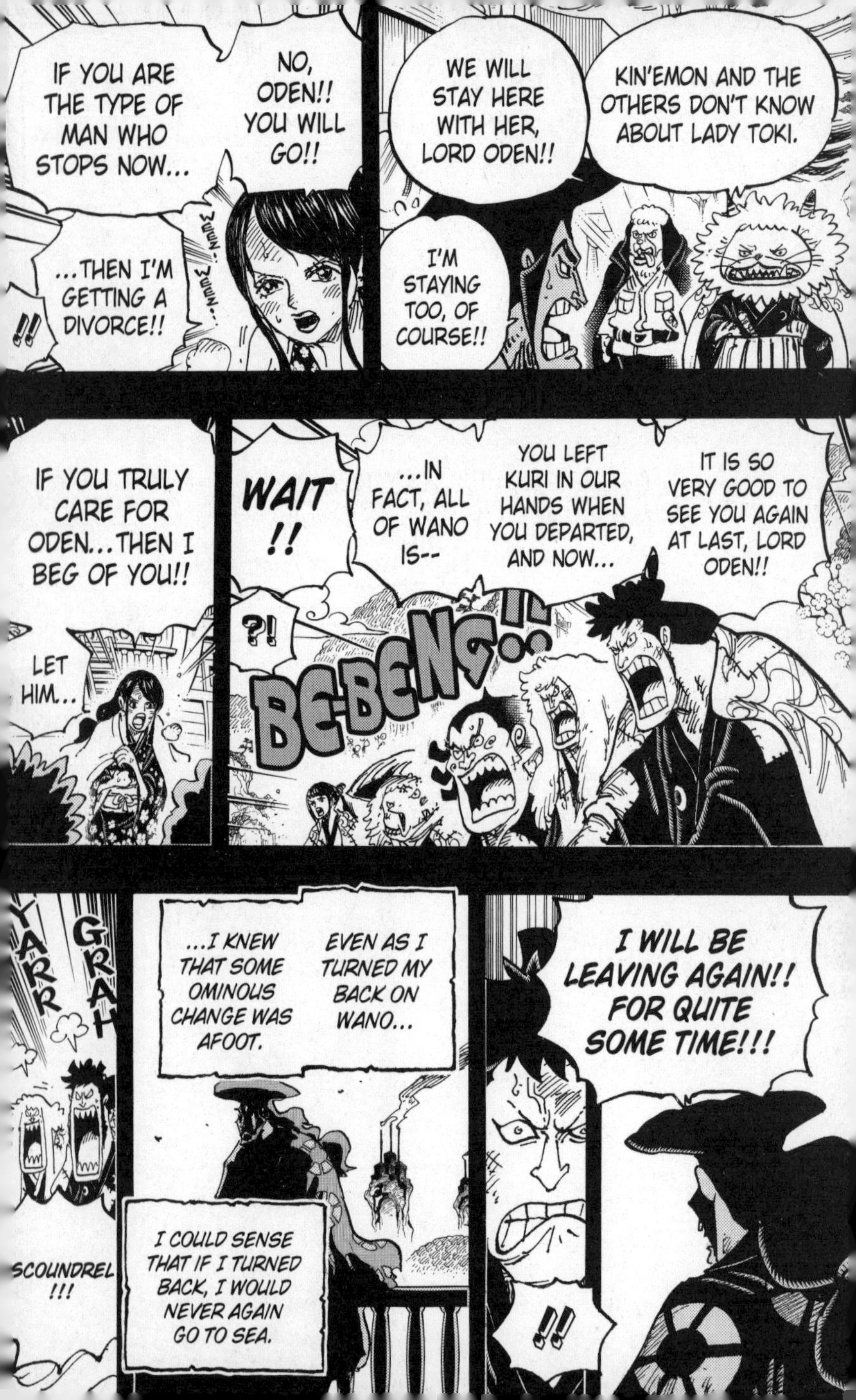
KIN'EMON AND THE OTHERS DON'T KNOW ABOUT LADY TOKI.
WE WILL STAY HERE WITH HER, LORD ODEN!!
I'M STAYING TOO, OF COURSE!!
NO, ODEN!! YOU WILL GO!!
IF YOU ARE THE TYPE OF MAN WHO STOPS NOW...
WEEN! WEEN...
...THEN I'M GETTING A DIVORCE!!
!!
IT IS SO VERY GOOD TO SEE YOU AGAIN AT LAST, LORD ODEN!!
YOU LEFT KURI IN OUR HANDS WHEN YOU DEPARTED, AND NOW...
...IN FACT, ALL OF WANO IS--
WAIT!!
BE-BENG!!
?!
IF YOU TRULY CARE FOR ODEN...THEN I BEG OF YOU!!
LET HIM...
I WILL BE LEAVING AGAIN!! FOR QUITE SOME TIME!!!
!!
EVEN AS I TURNED MY BACK ON WANO...
...I KNEW THAT SOME OMINOUS CHANGE WAS AFOOT.
I COULD SENSE THAT IF I TURNED BACK, I WOULD NEVER AGAIN GO TO SEA.
GRAH
YARR
SCOUNDREL!!!

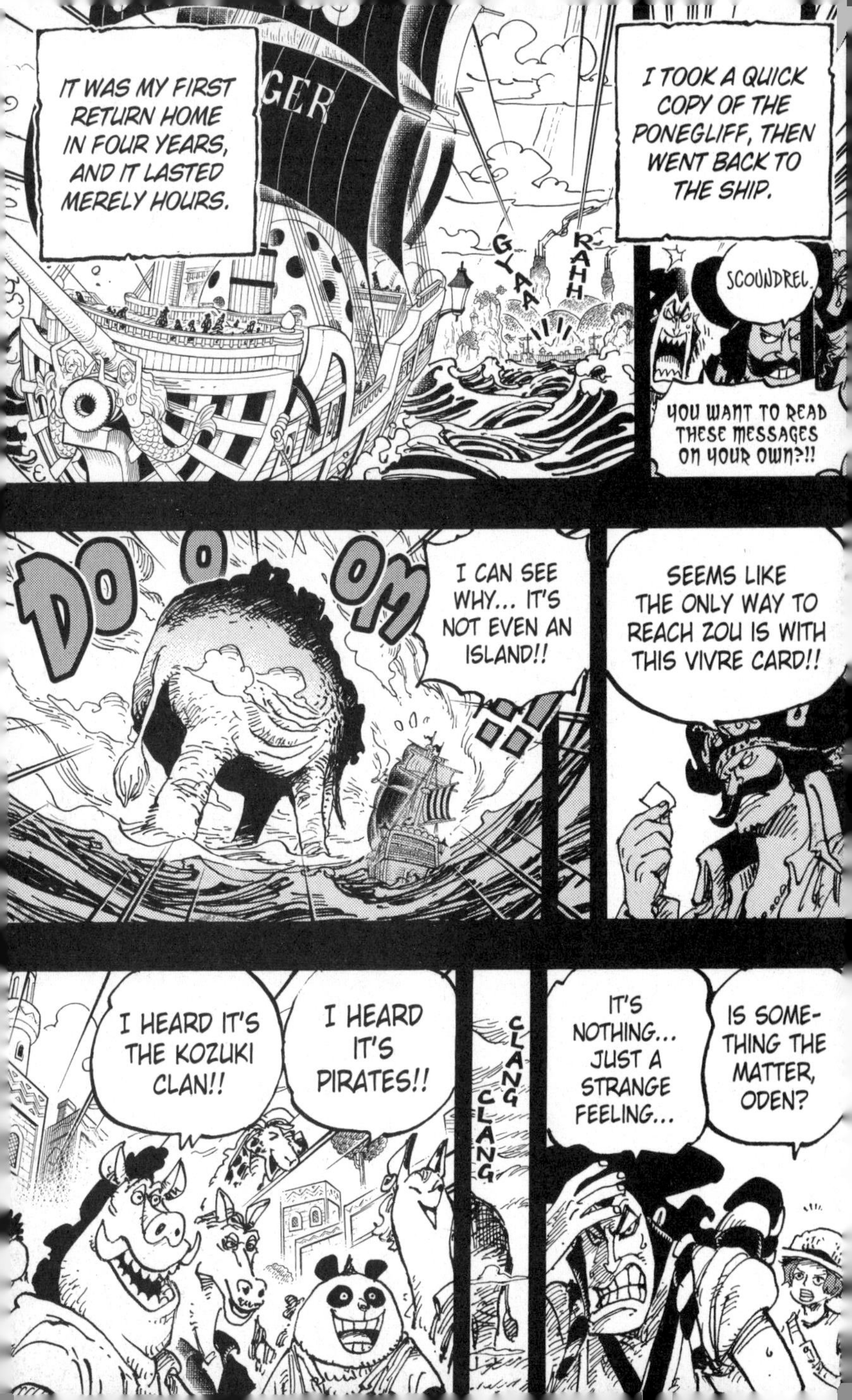
I TOOK A QUICK COPY OF THE PONEGLIFF, THEN WENT BACK TO THE SHIP.
SCOUNDREL.
YOU WANT TO READ THESE MESSAGES ON YOUR OWN?!!
RAHH
GYAAA
IT WAS MY FIRST RETURN HOME IN FOUR YEARS, AND IT LASTED MERELY HOURS.
SEEMS LIKE THE ONLY WAY TO REACH ZOU IS WITH THIS VIVRE CARD!!
I CAN SEE WHY... IT'S NOT EVEN AN ISLAND!!
DOOOOM
IS SOME-THING THE MATTER, ODEN?
IT'S NOTHING... JUST A STRANGE FEELING...
CLANG CLANG
I HEARD IT'S PIRATES!!
I HEARD IT'S THE KOZUKI CLAN!!

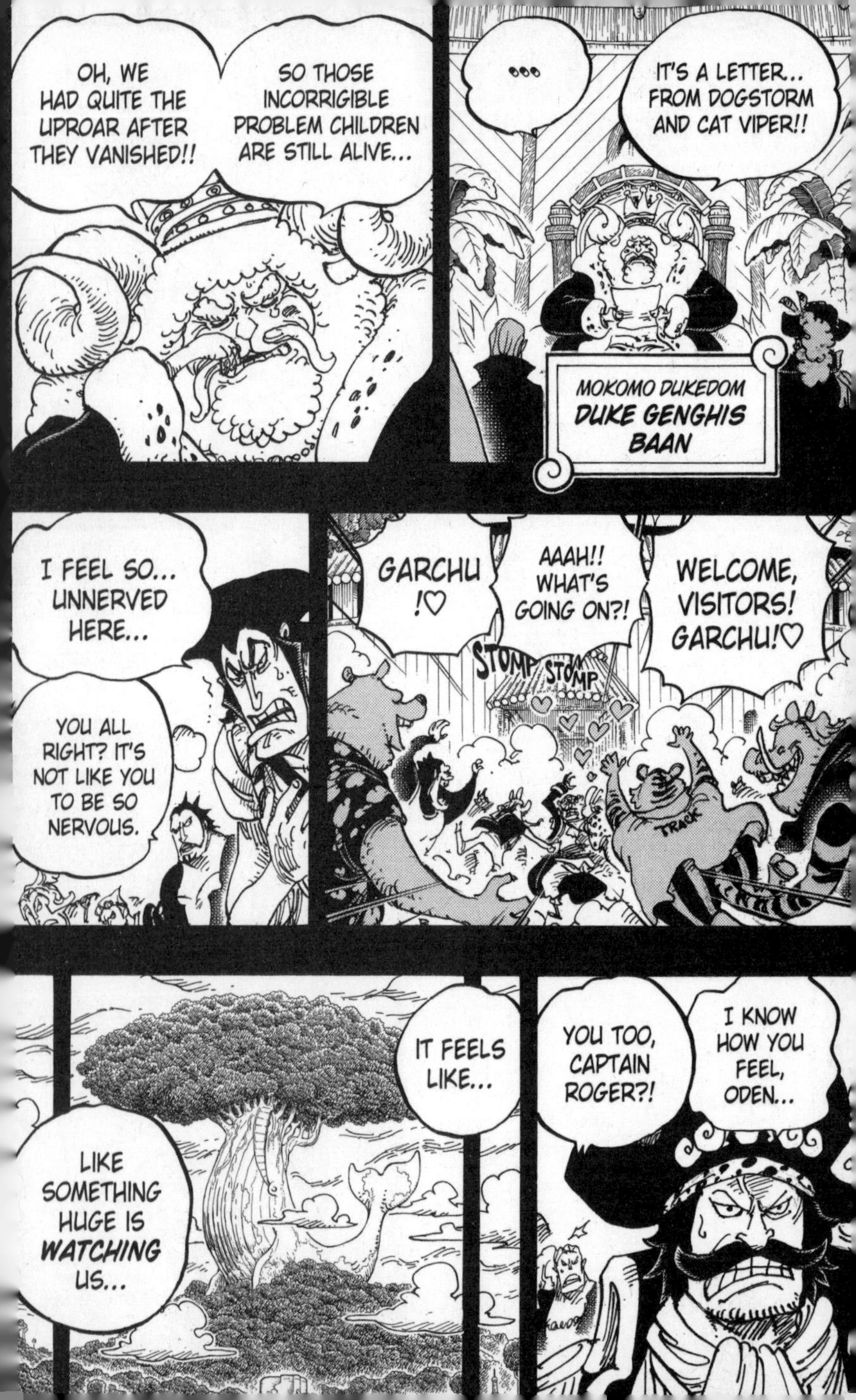
IT'S A LETTER... FROM DOGSTORM AND CAT VIPER!!
...
MOKOMO DUKEDOM
DUKE GENGHIS BAAN
SO THOSE INCORRIGIBLE PROBLEM CHILDREN ARE STILL ALIVE...
OH, WE HAD QUITE THE UPROAR AFTER THEY VANISHED!!
WELCOME, VISITORS! GARCHU!♡
AAAH!! WHAT'S GOING ON?!
GARCHU !♡
STOMP STOMP
TRACK
I FEEL SO... UNNERVED HERE...
YOU ALL RIGHT? IT'S NOT LIKE YOU TO BE SO NERVOUS.
I KNOW HOW YOU FEEL, ODEN...
YOU TOO, CAPTAIN ROGER?!
IT FEELS LIKE...
LIKE SOMETHING HUGE IS WATCHING US...

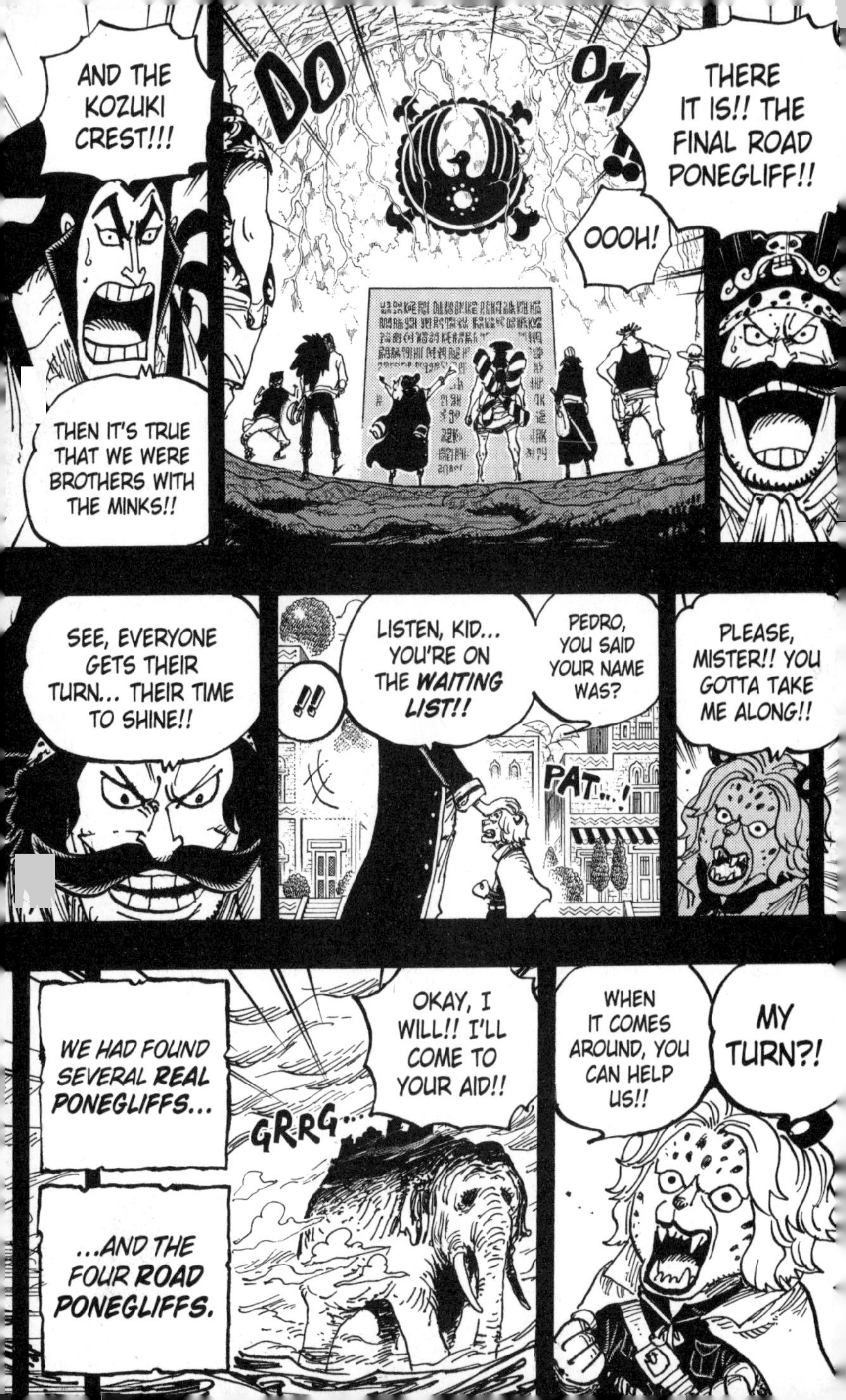
THERE IT IS!! THE FINAL ROAD PONEGLIFF!!
DO
OM
OOOH!
AND THE KOZUKI CREST!!!
THEN IT'S TRUE THAT WE WERE BROTHERS WITH THE MINKS!!
PLEASE, MISTER!! YOU GOTTA TAKE ME ALONG!!
PEDRO, YOU SAID YOUR NAME WAS?
LISTEN, KID... YOU'RE ON THE WAITING LIST!!
PAT...!
!!
SEE, EVERYONE GETS THEIR TURN... THEIR TIME TO SHINE!!
MY TURN?!
WHEN IT COMES AROUND, YOU CAN HELP US!!
OKAY, I WILL!! I'LL COME TO YOUR AID!!
GRRG...
WE HAD FOUND SEVERAL REAL PONEGLIFFS...
...AND THE FOUR ROAD PONEGLIFFS.

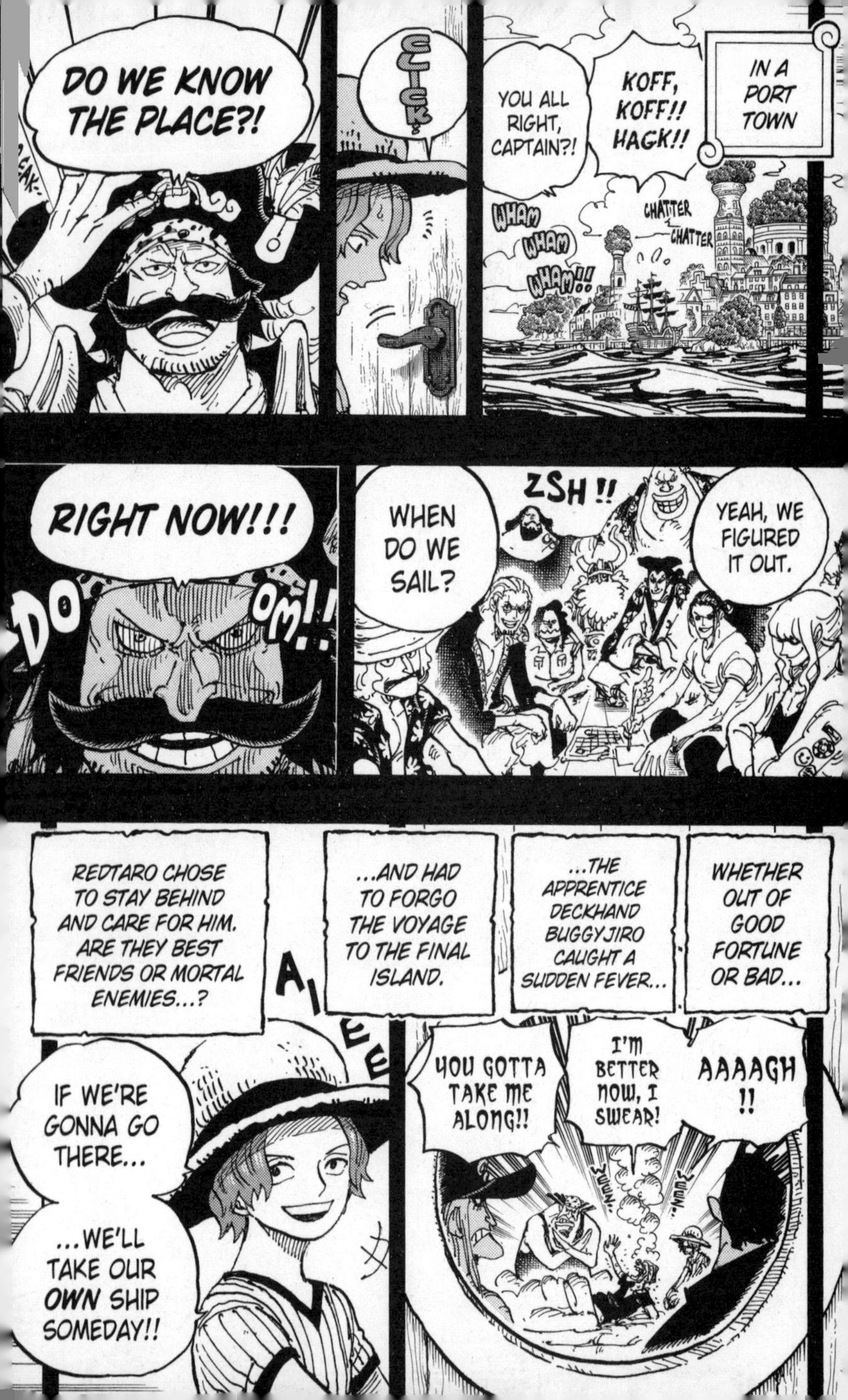
IN A PORT TOWN
KOFF, KOFF!! HAGK!!
YOU ALL RIGHT, CAPTAIN?!
WHAM WHAM WHAM!!
CHATTER CHATTER
CLICK
DO WE KNOW THE PLACE?!
YEAH, WE FIGURED IT OUT.
ZSH!!
WHEN DO WE SAIL?
RIGHT NOW!!!
DOOM!!
WHETHER OUT OF GOOD FORTUNE OR BAD...
...THE APPRENTICE DECKHAND BUGGYJIRO CAUGHT A SUDDEN FEVER...
...AND HAD TO FORGO THE VOYAGE TO THE FINAL ISLAND.
REDTARO CHOSE TO STAY BEHIND AND CARE FOR HIM. ARE THEY BEST FRIENDS OR MORTAL ENEMIES...?
AAAAGH!!
I'M BETTER NOW, I SWEAR!
YOU GOTTA TAKE ME ALONG!!
AIEE
IF WE'RE GONNA GO THERE...
...WE'LL TAKE OUR OWN SHIP SOMEDAY!!

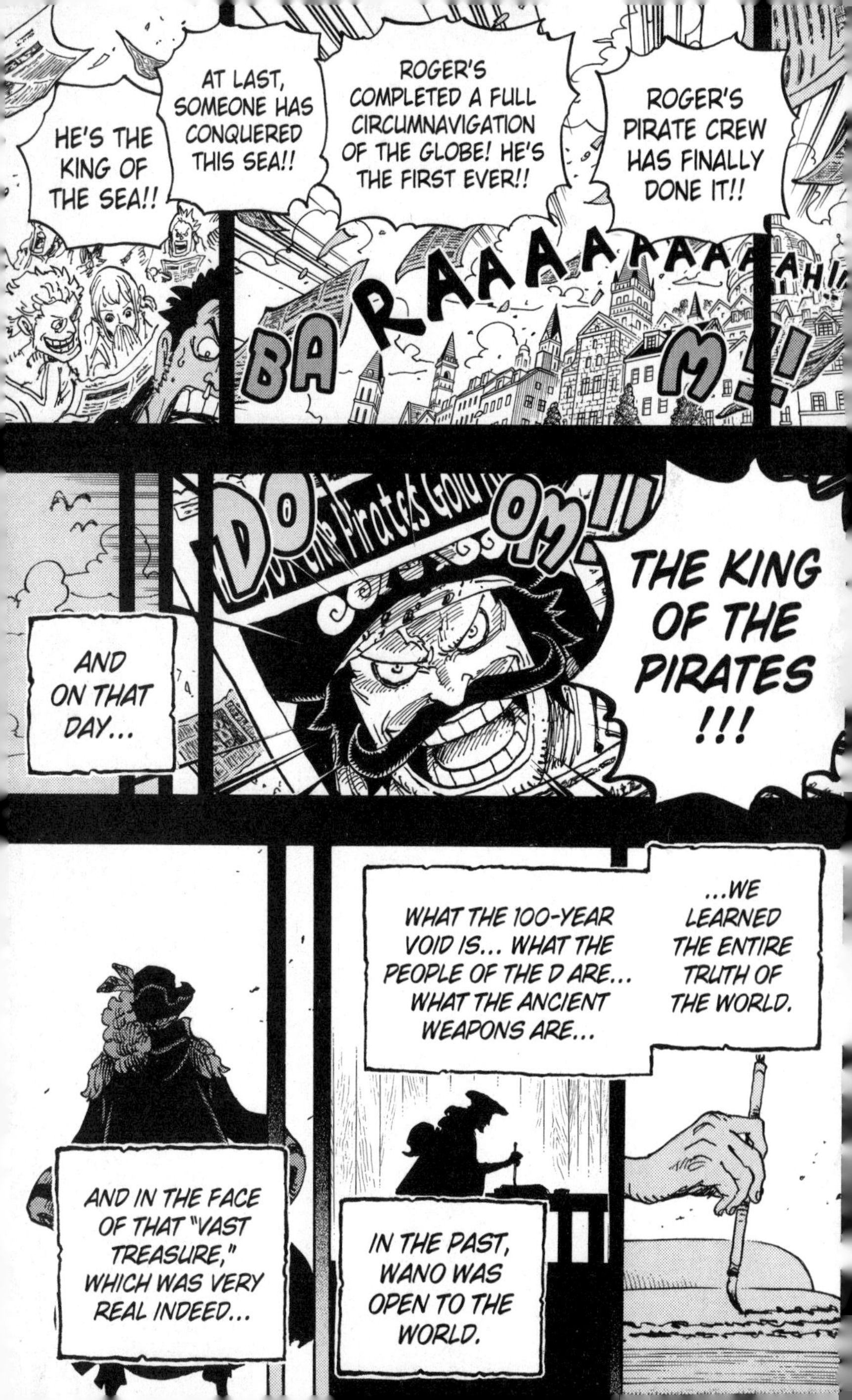
ROGER'S PIRATE CREW HAS FINALLY DONE IT!!
ROGER'S COMPLETED A FULL CIRCUMNAVIGATION OF THE GLOBE! HE'S THE FIRST EVER!!
AT LAST, SOMEONE HAS CONQUERED THIS SEA!!
HE'S THE KING OF THE SEA!!
BARAAAAAAAAAAH!!
M!!
THE KING OF THE PIRATES!!!
DOOM!!
AND ON THAT DAY...
...WE LEARNED THE ENTIRE TRUTH OF THE WORLD.
WHAT THE 100-YEAR VOID IS... WHAT THE PEOPLE OF THE D ARE... WHAT THE ANCIENT WEAPONS ARE...
IN THE PAST, WANO WAS OPEN TO THE WORLD.
AND IN THE FACE OF THAT "VAST TREASURE," WHICH WAS VERY REAL INDEED...

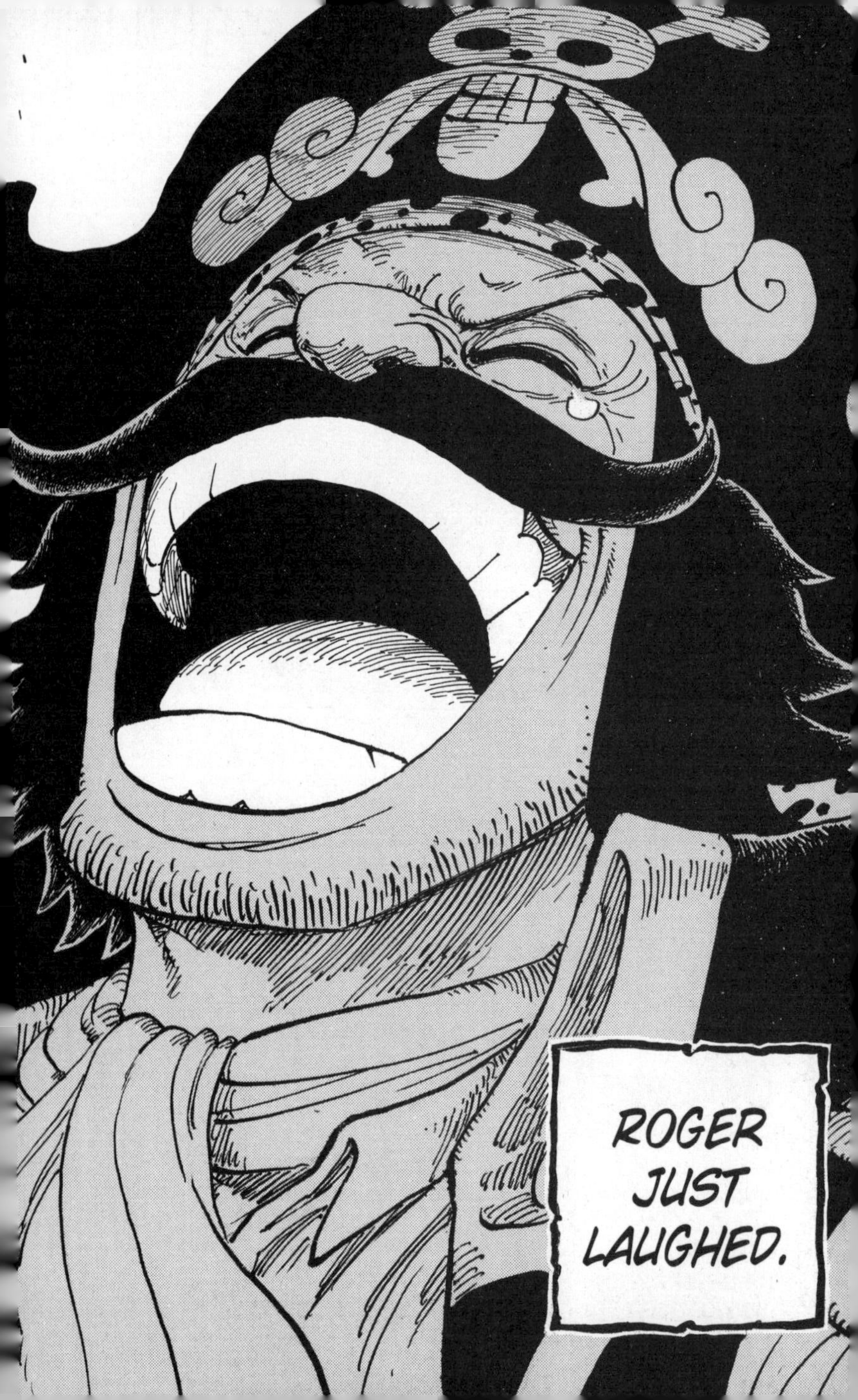
ROGER JUST LAUGHED.

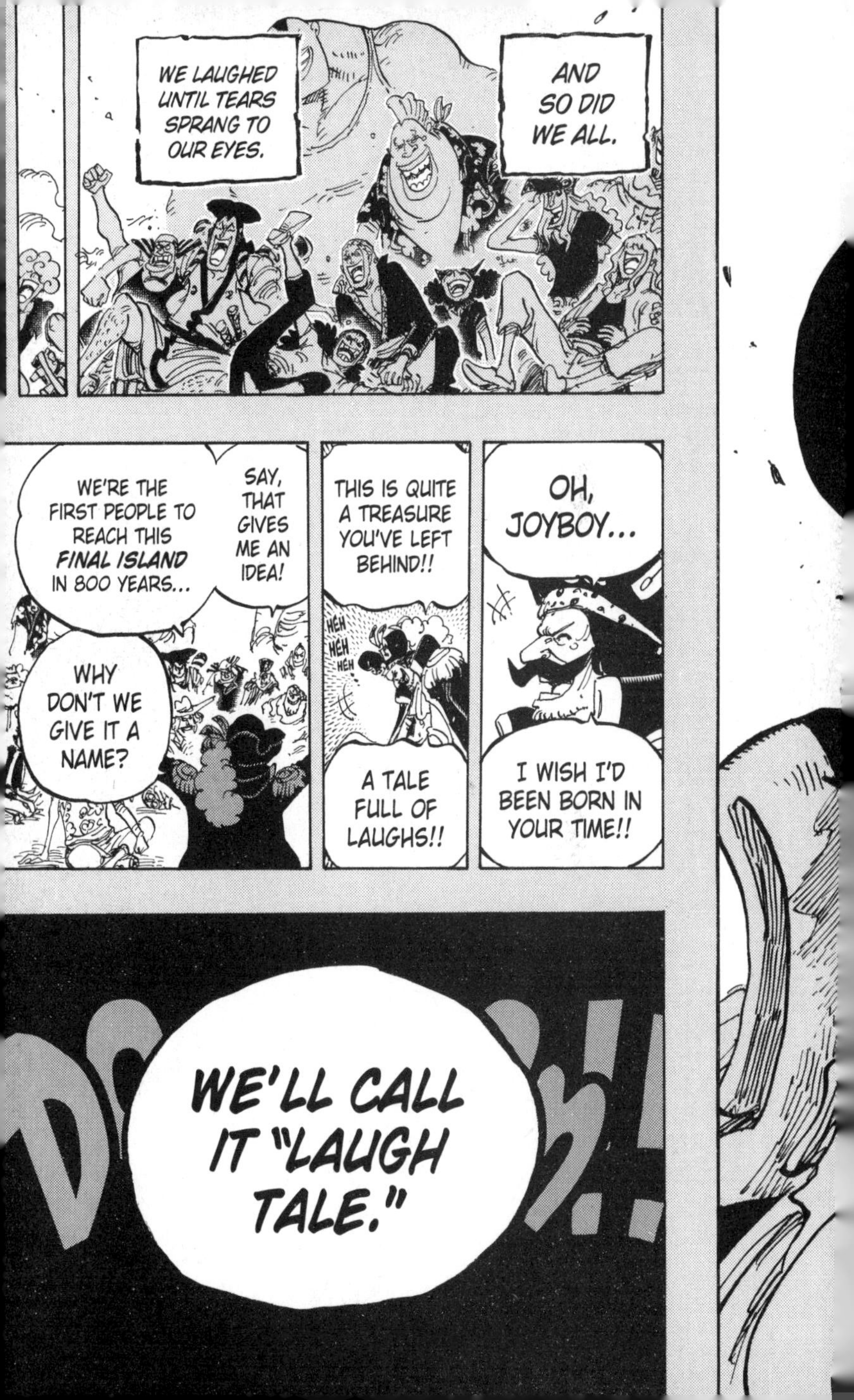
WE LAUGHED UNTIL TEARS SPRANG TO OUR EYES.
AND SO DID WE ALL.
OH, JOYBOY...
I WISH I'D BEEN BORN IN YOUR TIME!!
THIS IS QUITE A TREASURE YOU'VE LEFT BEHIND!!
HEH HEH HEH
A TALE FULL OF LAUGHS!!
SAY, THAT GIVES ME AN IDEA!
WE'RE THE FIRST PEOPLE TO REACH THIS ***FINAL ISLAND*** IN 800 YEARS...
WHY DON'T WE GIVE IT A NAME?
WE'LL CALL IT "LAUGH TALE."

SBS Question Corner

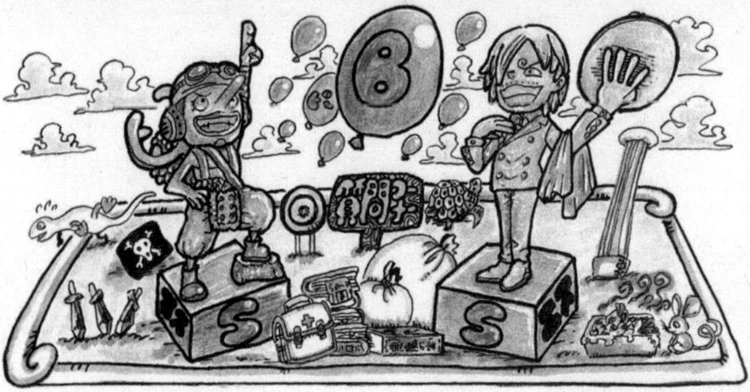

(420 Land, Hong Kong)

Q: So Nami likes all fruits, but especially tangerines. Does that mean she likes all other orange-like citrus fruits just as much as tangerines? I don't know, maybe she has a special attachment to tangerines... Please explain!

--Emerald Usa

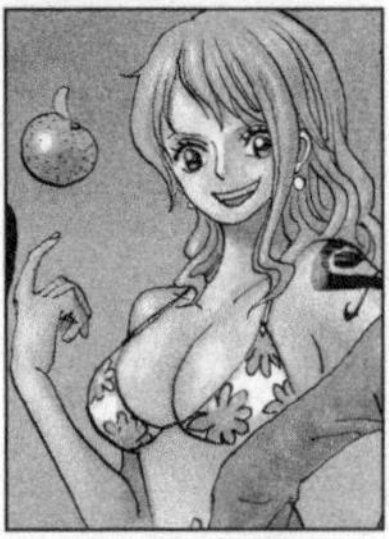

A: Hmm! Well, Nami's favorite fruit is tied closely to her upbringing. You see, this is actually revealed in the Arlong arc, from about the second half of volume 7 through the first half of volume 10. Nami grew up in a tangerine grove, and she has many memories of them associated with her late mother. That's why she loves them more than any other fruit. Thanks for your letter!

Q: Sanadacchi!! Give me all of your Nami figures.

--Captain Nobuo

A: Hey, hey, whoa!! Who do you think you're talking to?! Don't do that, especially if it's something dirty! I was just talking about some nice, heartfelt stuff! I'm not putting any of Sanada's gross stuff in this segment this time.

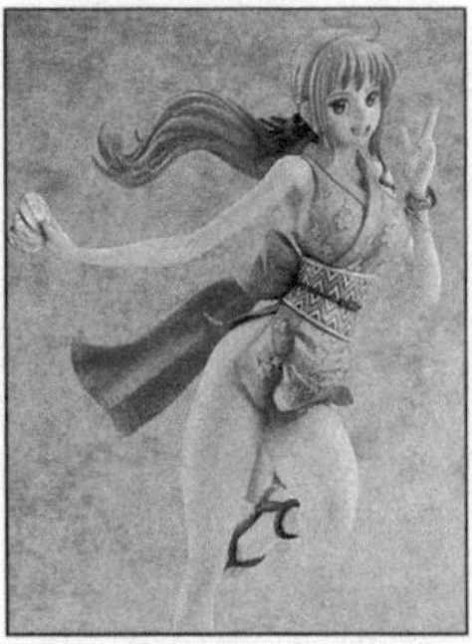

Q: Please give me the towel Onami used in the bathhouse!

--Sanadacchi

A: Nooo!! Get lost, Sanada!! Officer, he's over here!!

Q: This might be a weird question, but as the sole feminine member of the Akazaya Nine, does Okiku bathe separately from the others?

--Crybaby Kyoshiro

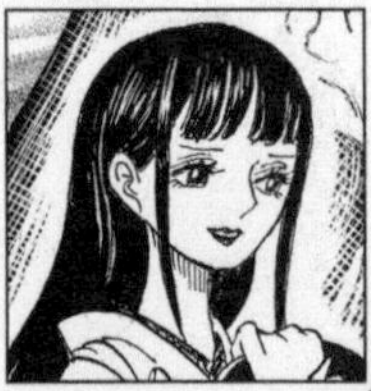

A: Not at all. She goes in with the group. She's known them since she was a little kid, after all.

Chapter 968:
ODEN'S RETURN

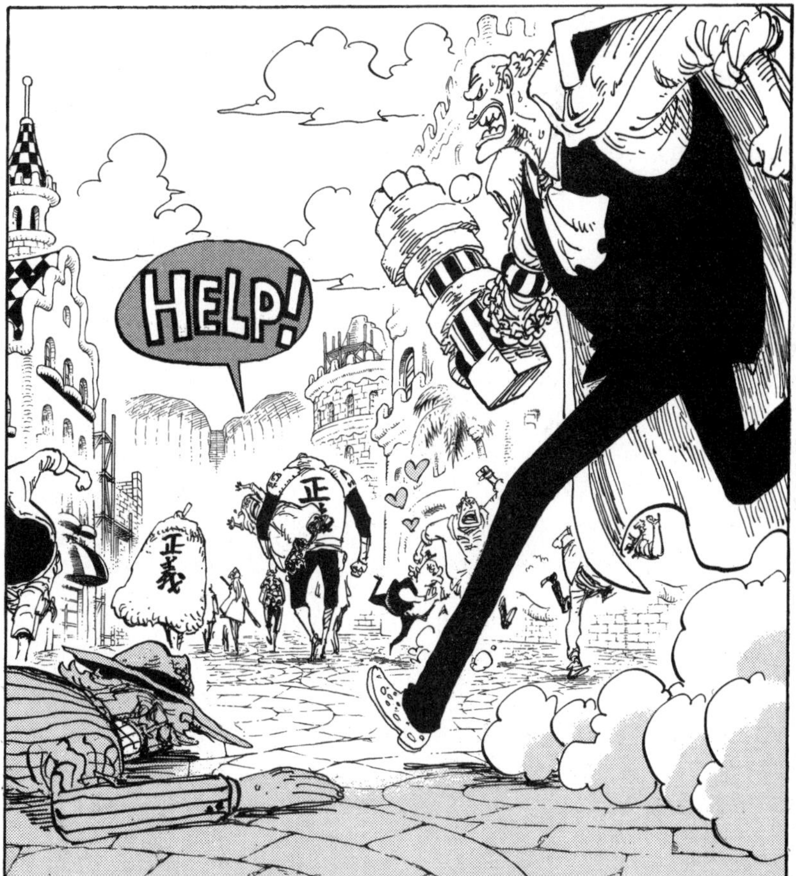
HELP!

GANG BEGE'S OH MY FAMILY
VOL. 17: "SAVE THE BOSS'S WIFE, GOTTI!!"

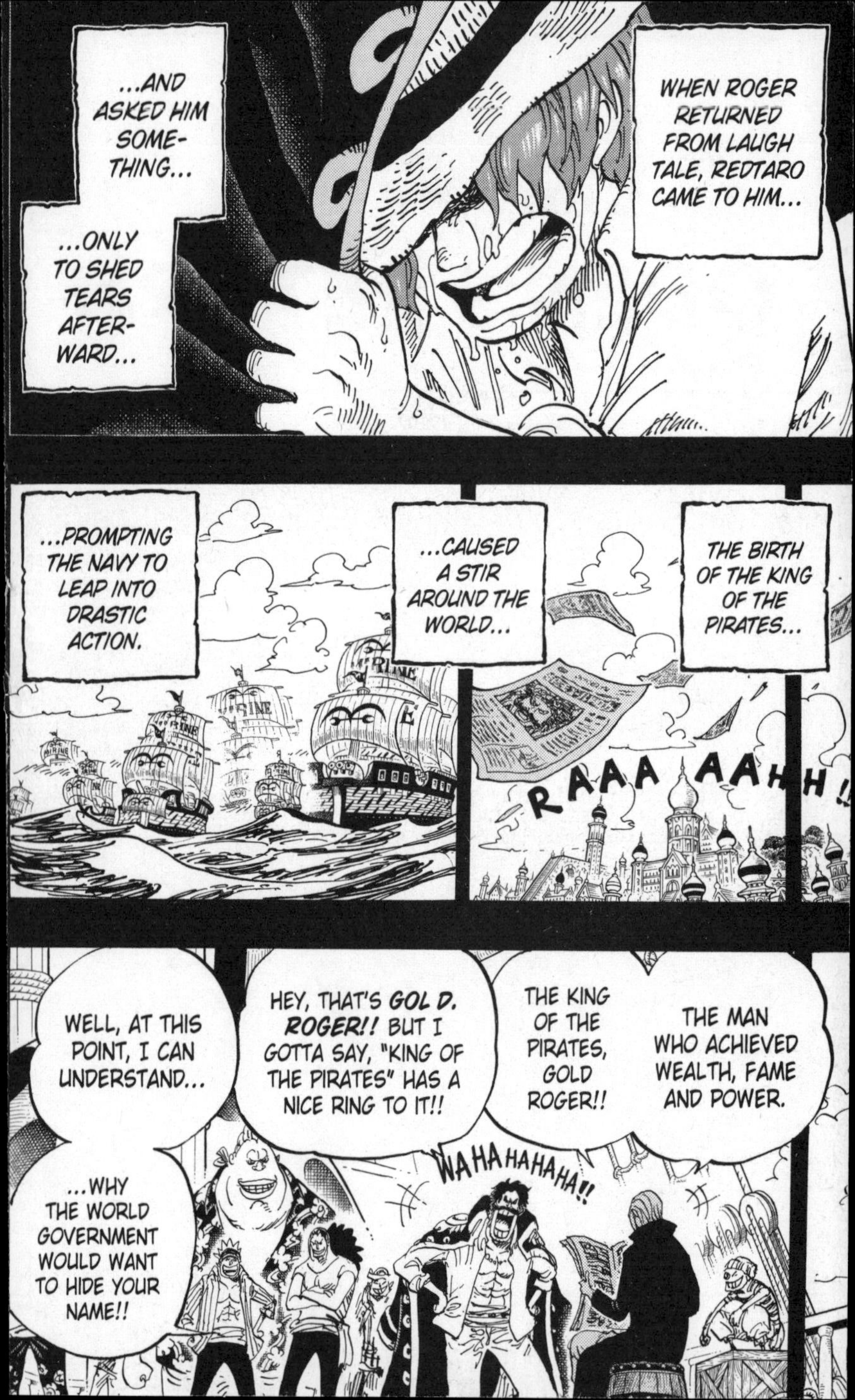
WHEN ROGER RETURNED FROM LAUGH TALE, REDTARO CAME TO HIM...
...AND ASKED HIM SOME-THING...
...ONLY TO SHED TEARS AFTER-WARD...
THE BIRTH OF THE KING OF THE PIRATES...
...CAUSED A STIR AROUND THE WORLD...
RAAAAAHH!!
...PROMPTING THE NAVY TO LEAP INTO DRASTIC ACTION.
THE MAN WHO ACHIEVED WEALTH, FAME AND POWER.
THE KING OF THE PIRATES, GOLD ROGER!!
HEY, THAT'S GOL D. ROGER!! BUT I GOTTA SAY, "KING OF THE PIRATES" HAS A NICE RING TO IT!!
WAHAHAHAHAHA!!
WELL, AT THIS POINT, I CAN UNDERSTAND...
...WHY THE WORLD GOVERNMENT WOULD WANT TO HIDE YOUR NAME!!

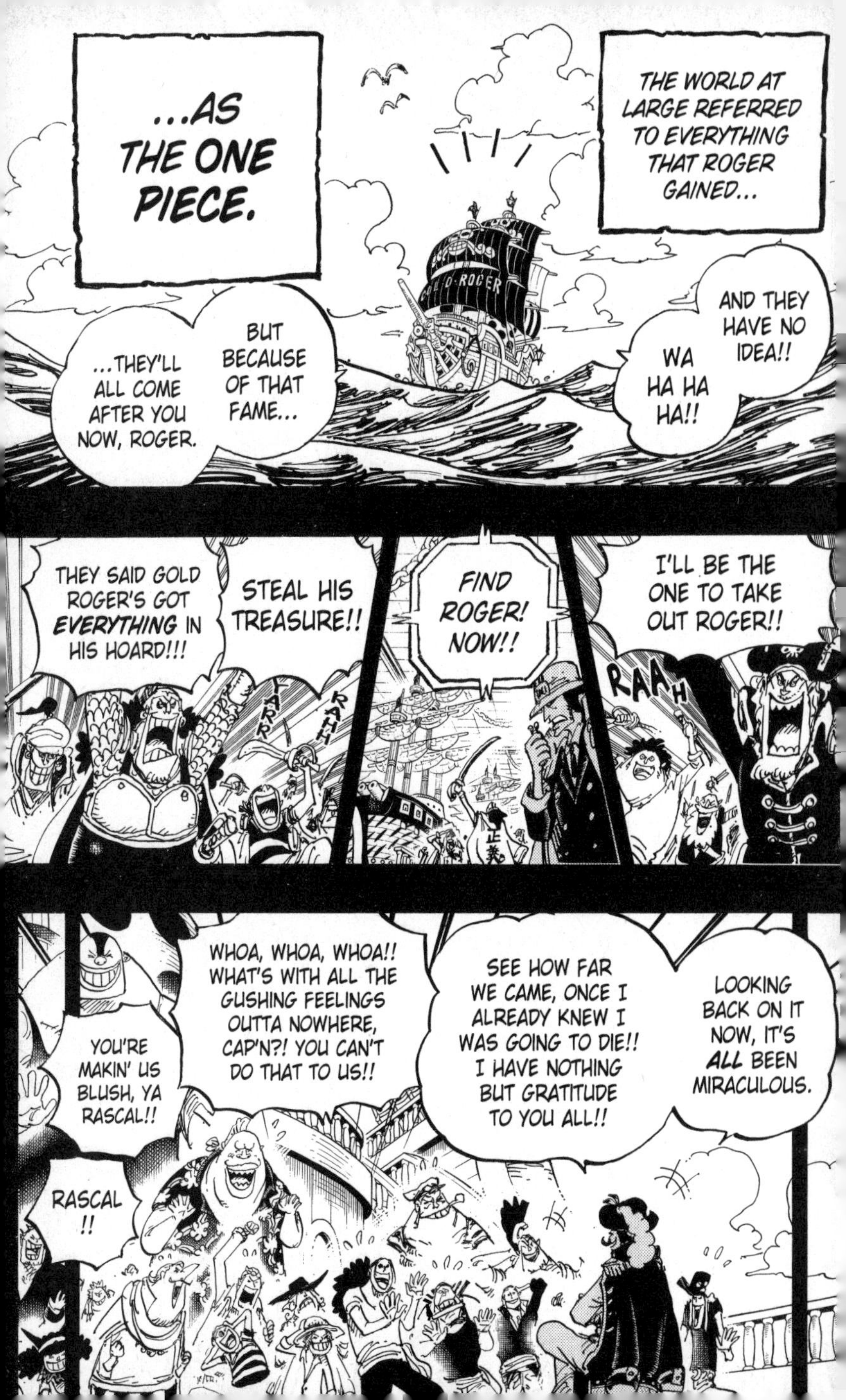
THE WORLD AT LARGE REFERRED TO EVERYTHING THAT ROGER GAINED...
...AS THE ONE PIECE.
AND THEY HAVE NO IDEA!!
WA HA HA HA!!
BUT BECAUSE OF THAT FAME...
...THEY'LL ALL COME AFTER YOU NOW, ROGER.
I'LL BE THE ONE TO TAKE OUT ROGER!!
RAAH
FIND ROGER! NOW!!
STEAL HIS TREASURE!!
RAHH
YARR
THEY SAID GOLD ROGER'S GOT EVERYTHING IN HIS HOARD!!!
LOOKING BACK ON IT NOW, IT'S ALL BEEN MIRACULOUS.
SEE HOW FAR WE CAME, ONCE I ALREADY KNEW I WAS GOING TO DIE!! I HAVE NOTHING BUT GRATITUDE TO YOU ALL!!
WHOA, WHOA, WHOA!! WHAT'S WITH ALL THE GUSHING FEELINGS OUTTA NOWHERE, CAP'N?! YOU CAN'T DO THAT TO US!!
YOU'RE MAKIN' US BLUSH, YA RASCAL!!
RASCAL !!

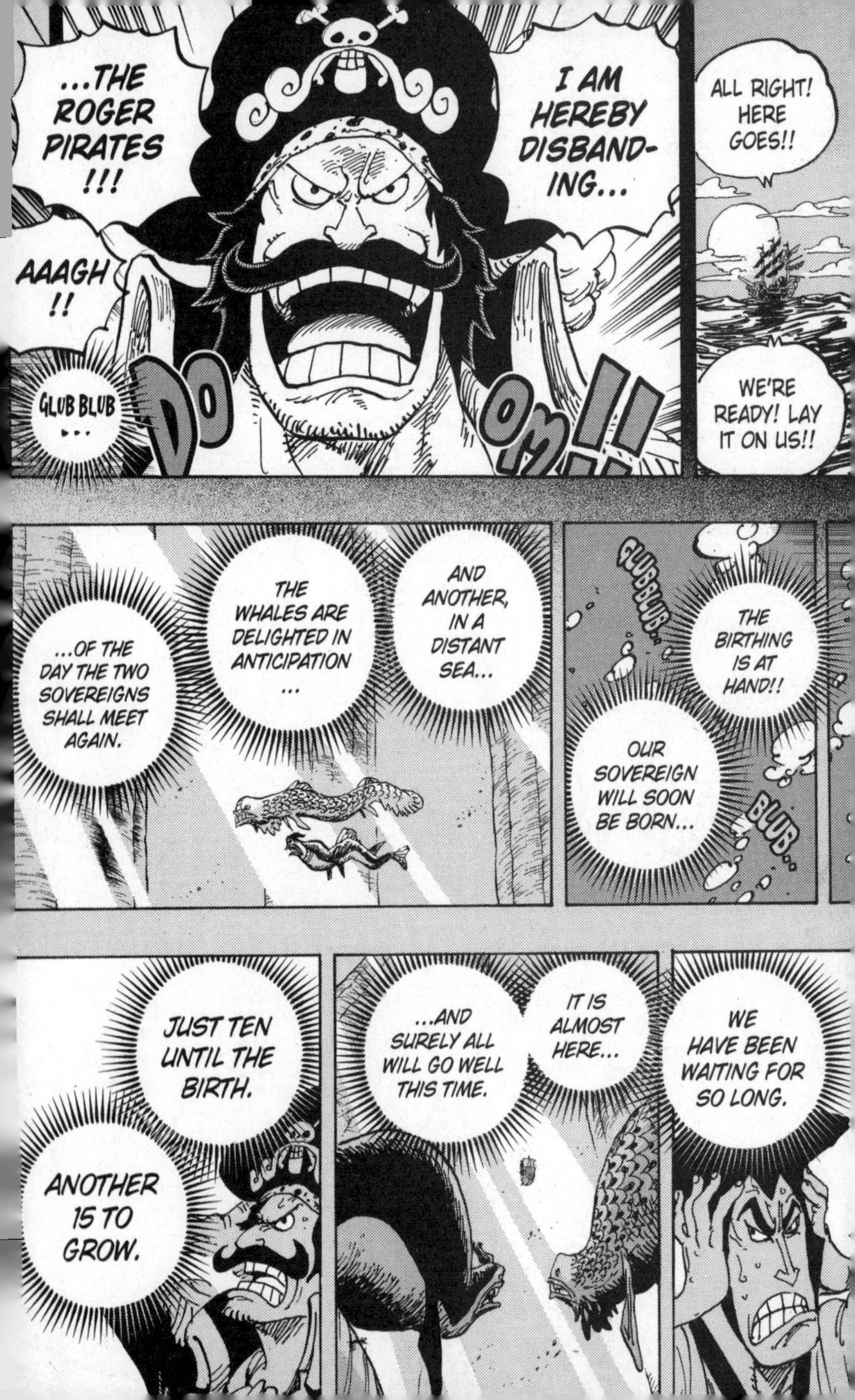
ALL RIGHT! HERE GOES!!
WE'RE READY! LAY IT ON US!!
I AM HEREBY DISBANDING...
...THE ROGER PIRATES!!!
AAAGH!!
DOOM!!
GLUB BLUB...
GLUBBLUB
THE BIRTHING IS AT HAND!!
OUR SOVEREIGN WILL SOON BE BORN...
BLUB...
AND ANOTHER, IN A DISTANT SEA...
THE WHALES ARE DELIGHTED IN ANTICIPATION...
...OF THE DAY THE TWO SOVEREIGNS SHALL MEET AGAIN.
WE HAVE BEEN WAITING FOR SO LONG.
IT IS ALMOST HERE...
...AND SURELY ALL WILL GO WELL THIS TIME.
JUST TEN UNTIL THE BIRTH.
ANOTHER 15 TO GROW.

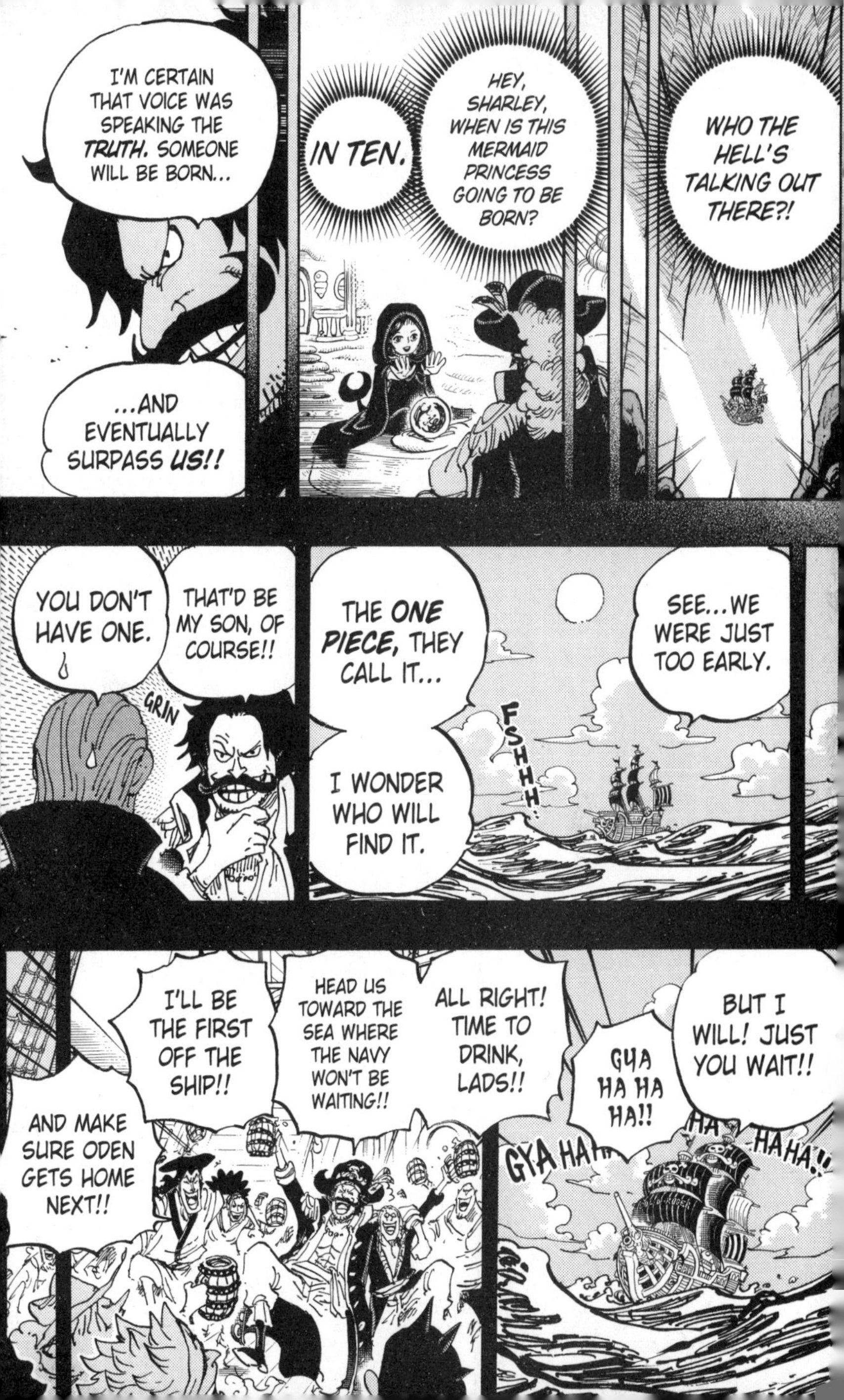
WHO THE HELL'S TALKING OUT THERE?!
HEY, SHARLEY, WHEN IS THIS MERMAID PRINCESS GOING TO BE BORN?
IN TEN.
I'M CERTAIN THAT VOICE WAS SPEAKING THE TRUTH. SOMEONE WILL BE BORN...
...AND EVENTUALLY SURPASS US!!
SEE...WE WERE JUST TOO EARLY.
THE ONE PIECE, THEY CALL IT...
FSHHH
I WONDER WHO WILL FIND IT.
THAT'D BE MY SON, OF COURSE!!
GRIN
YOU DON'T HAVE ONE.
BUT I WILL! JUST YOU WAIT!!
GYA HA HA HA!!
HA HA HA HA!!
GYA HA
ALL RIGHT! TIME TO DRINK, LADS!!
HEAD US TOWARD THE SEA WHERE THE NAVY WON'T BE WAITING!!
I'LL BE THE FIRST OFF THE SHIP!!
AND MAKE SURE ODEN GETS HOME NEXT!!

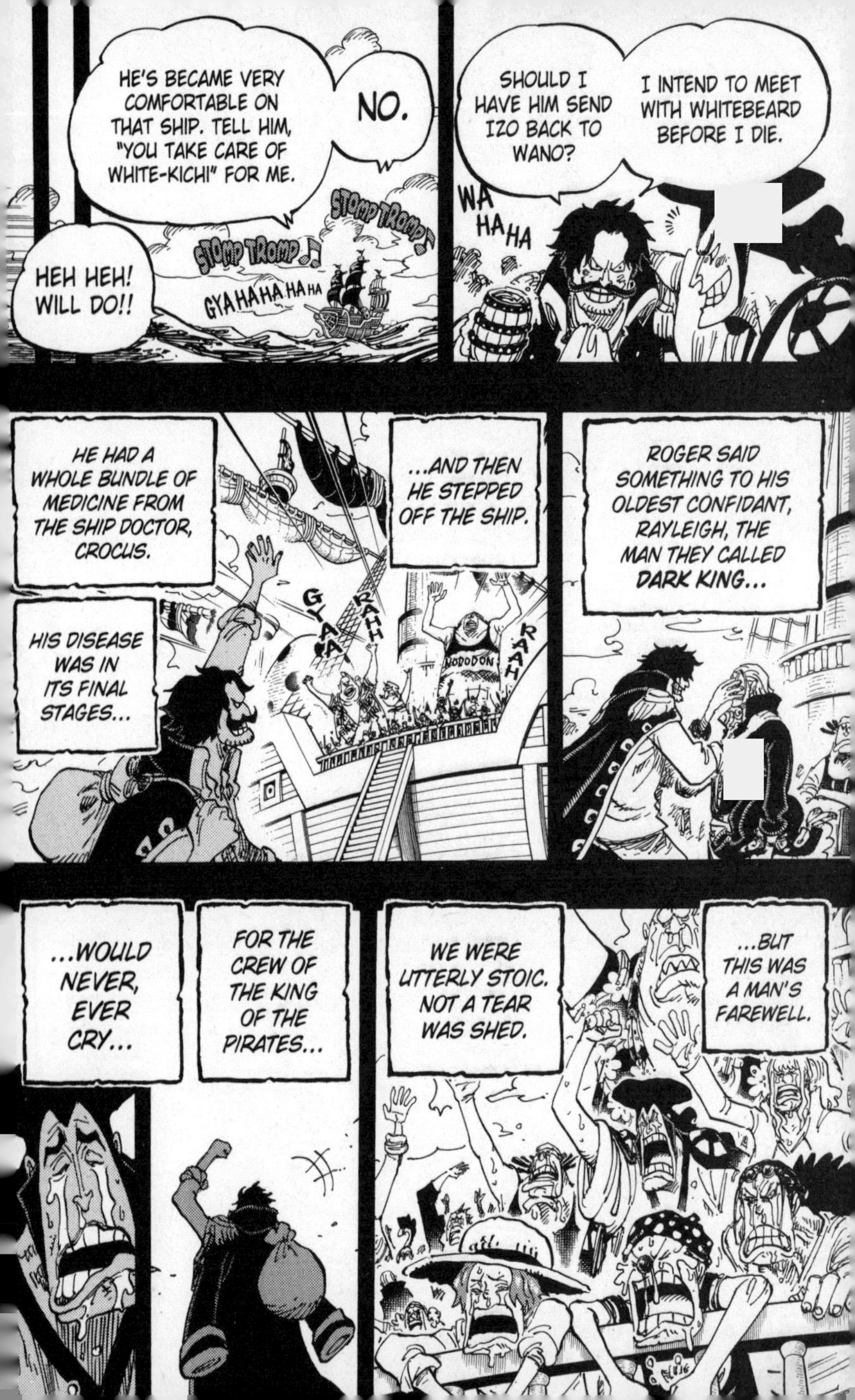
I INTEND TO MEET WITH WHITEBEARD BEFORE I DIE.
SHOULD I HAVE HIM SEND IZO BACK TO WANO?
WA HA HA
NO.
HE'S BECAME VERY COMFORTABLE ON THAT SHIP. TELL HIM, "YOU TAKE CARE OF WHITE-KICHI" FOR ME.
STOMP TROMP♪
STOMP TROMP♪
GYAHAHA HA HA HA
HEH HEH! WILL DO!!
ROGER SAID SOMETHING TO HIS OLDEST CONFIDANT, RAYLEIGH, THE MAN THEY CALLED DARK KING...
...AND THEN HE STEPPED OFF THE SHIP.
GYAA
RAHH
NODODON
RAAH
HE HAD A WHOLE BUNDLE OF MEDICINE FROM THE SHIP DOCTOR, CROCUS.
HIS DISEASE WAS IN ITS FINAL STAGES...
...BUT THIS WAS A MAN'S FAREWELL.
WE WERE UTTERLY STOIC. NOT A TEAR WAS SHED.
FOR THE CREW OF THE KING OF THE PIRATES...
...WOULD NEVER, EVER CRY...

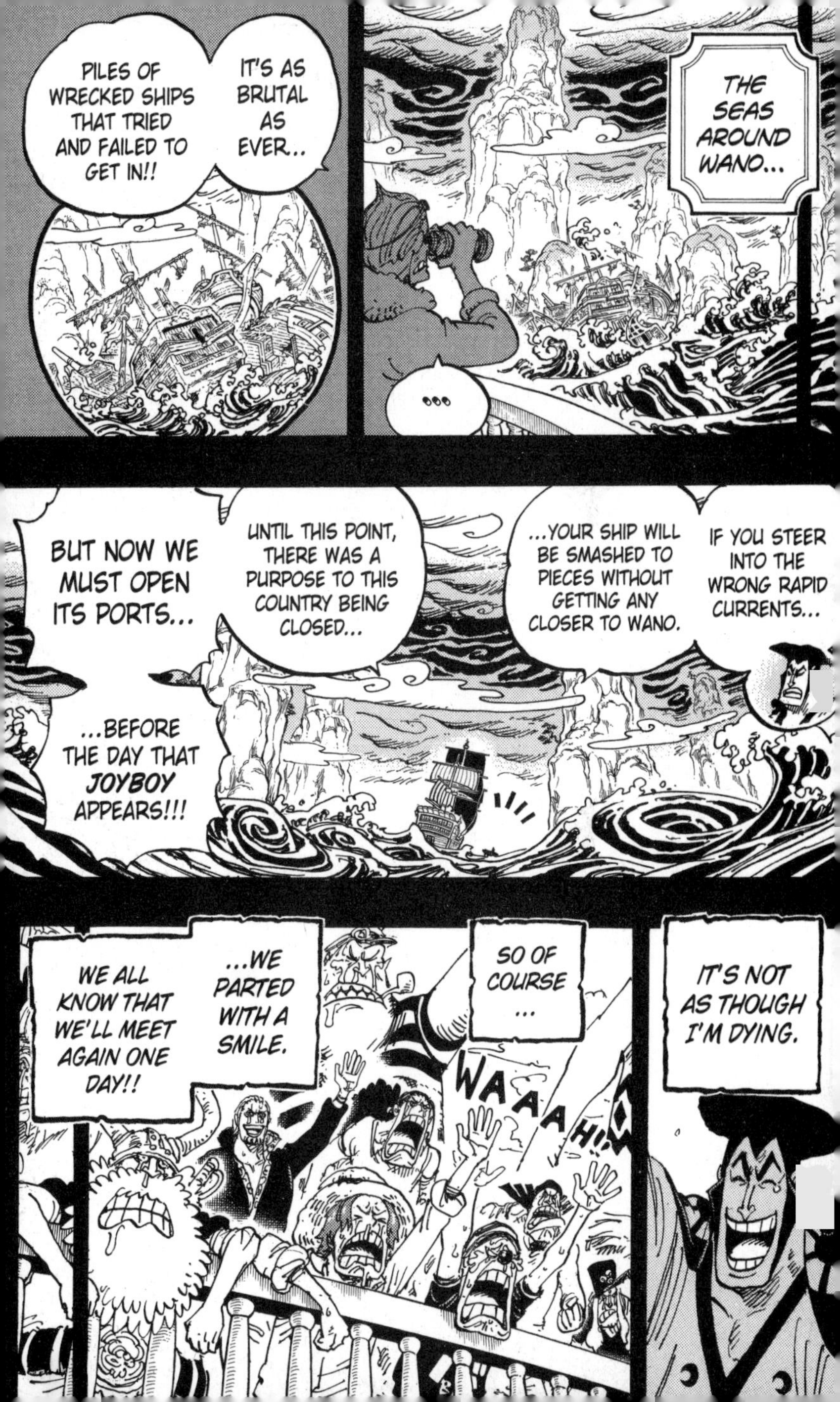
THE SEAS AROUND WANO...
...
IT'S AS BRUTAL AS EVER...
PILES OF WRECKED SHIPS THAT TRIED AND FAILED TO GET IN!!
IF YOU STEER INTO THE WRONG RAPID CURRENTS...
...YOUR SHIP WILL BE SMASHED TO PIECES WITHOUT GETTING ANY CLOSER TO WANO.
UNTIL THIS POINT, THERE WAS A PURPOSE TO THIS COUNTRY BEING CLOSED...
BUT NOW WE MUST OPEN ITS PORTS...
...BEFORE THE DAY THAT JOYBOY APPEARS!!!
IT'S NOT AS THOUGH I'M DYING.
SO OF COURSE ...
...WE PARTED WITH A SMILE.
WE ALL KNOW THAT WE'LL MEET AGAIN ONE DAY!!
WAAAAH!!

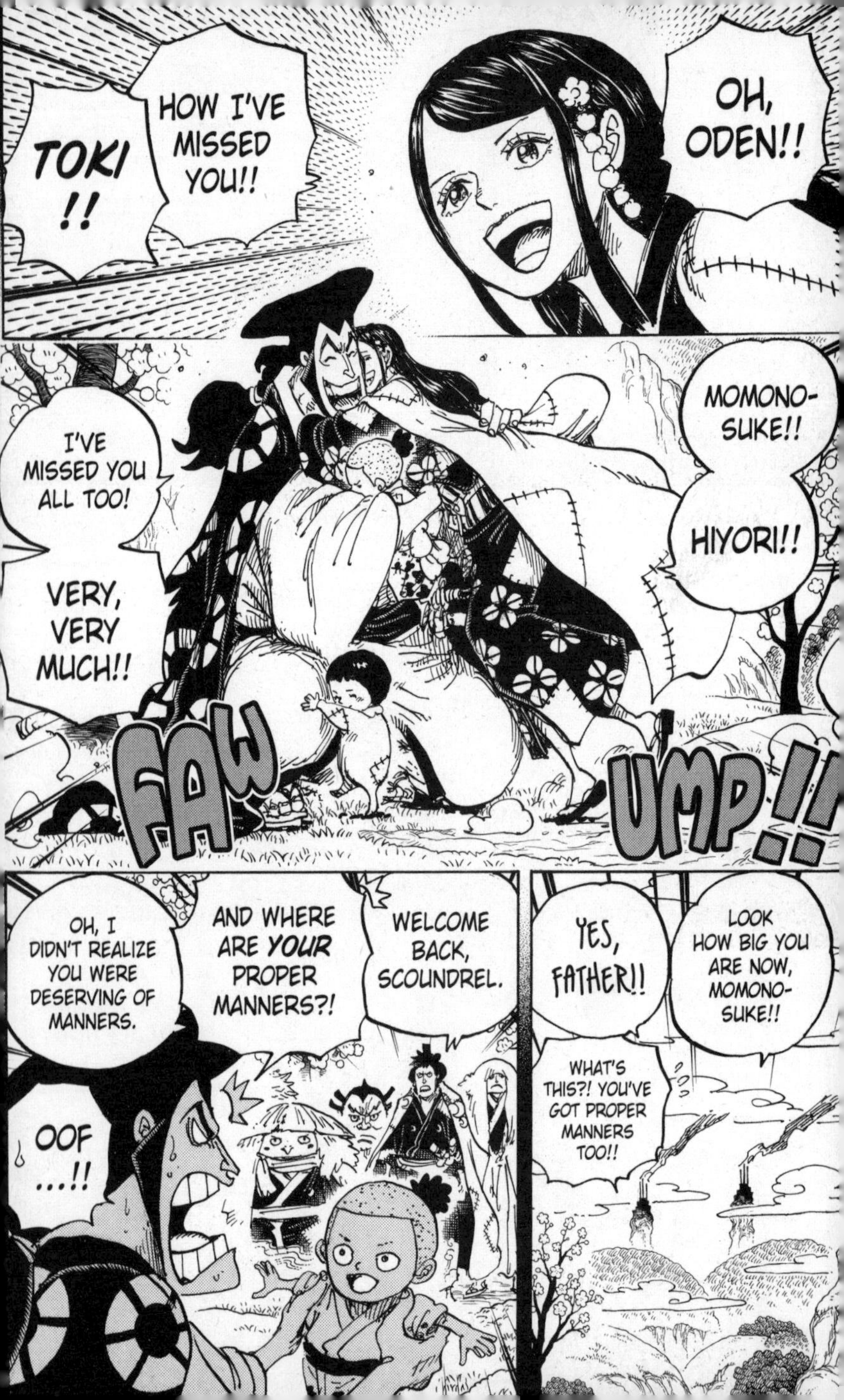
OH, ODEN!!
HOW I'VE MISSED YOU!!
TOKI!!
MOMONOSUKE!!
HIYORI!!
I'VE MISSED YOU ALL TOO!
VERY, VERY MUCH!!
FAWUMP!!
LOOK HOW BIG YOU ARE NOW, MOMONOSUKE!!
YES, FATHER!!
WHAT'S THIS?! YOU'VE GOT PROPER MANNERS TOO!!
WELCOME BACK, SCOUNDREL.
AND WHERE ARE *YOUR* PROPER MANNERS?!
OH, I DIDN'T REALIZE YOU WERE DESERVING OF MANNERS.
OOF ...!!

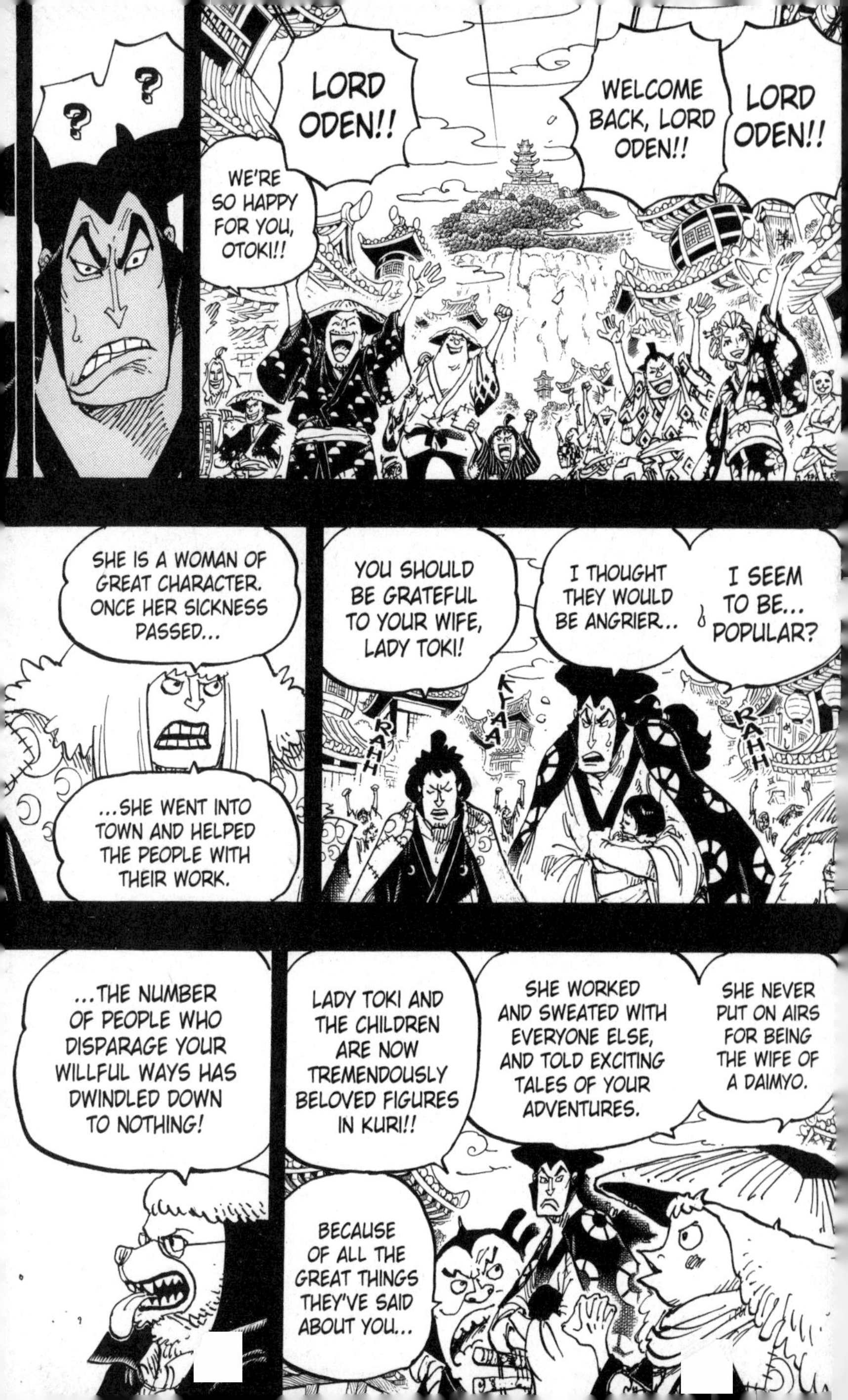
LORD ODEN!!
WELCOME BACK, LORD ODEN!!
LORD ODEN!!
WE'RE SO HAPPY FOR YOU, OTOKI!!
? ?
I SEEM TO BE... POPULAR?
I THOUGHT THEY WOULD BE ANGRIER...
RAHH
KYAA
RAHH
YOU SHOULD BE GRATEFUL TO YOUR WIFE, LADY TOKI!
SHE IS A WOMAN OF GREAT CHARACTER. ONCE HER SICKNESS PASSED...
...SHE WENT INTO TOWN AND HELPED THE PEOPLE WITH THEIR WORK.
SHE NEVER PUT ON AIRS FOR BEING THE WIFE OF A DAIMYO.
SHE WORKED AND SWEATED WITH EVERYONE ELSE, AND TOLD EXCITING TALES OF YOUR ADVENTURES.
LADY TOKI AND THE CHILDREN ARE NOW TREMENDOUSLY BELOVED FIGURES IN KURI!!
BECAUSE OF ALL THE GREAT THINGS THEY'VE SAID ABOUT YOU...
...THE NUMBER OF PEOPLE WHO DISPARAGE YOUR WILLFUL WAYS HAS DWINDLED DOWN TO NOTHING!

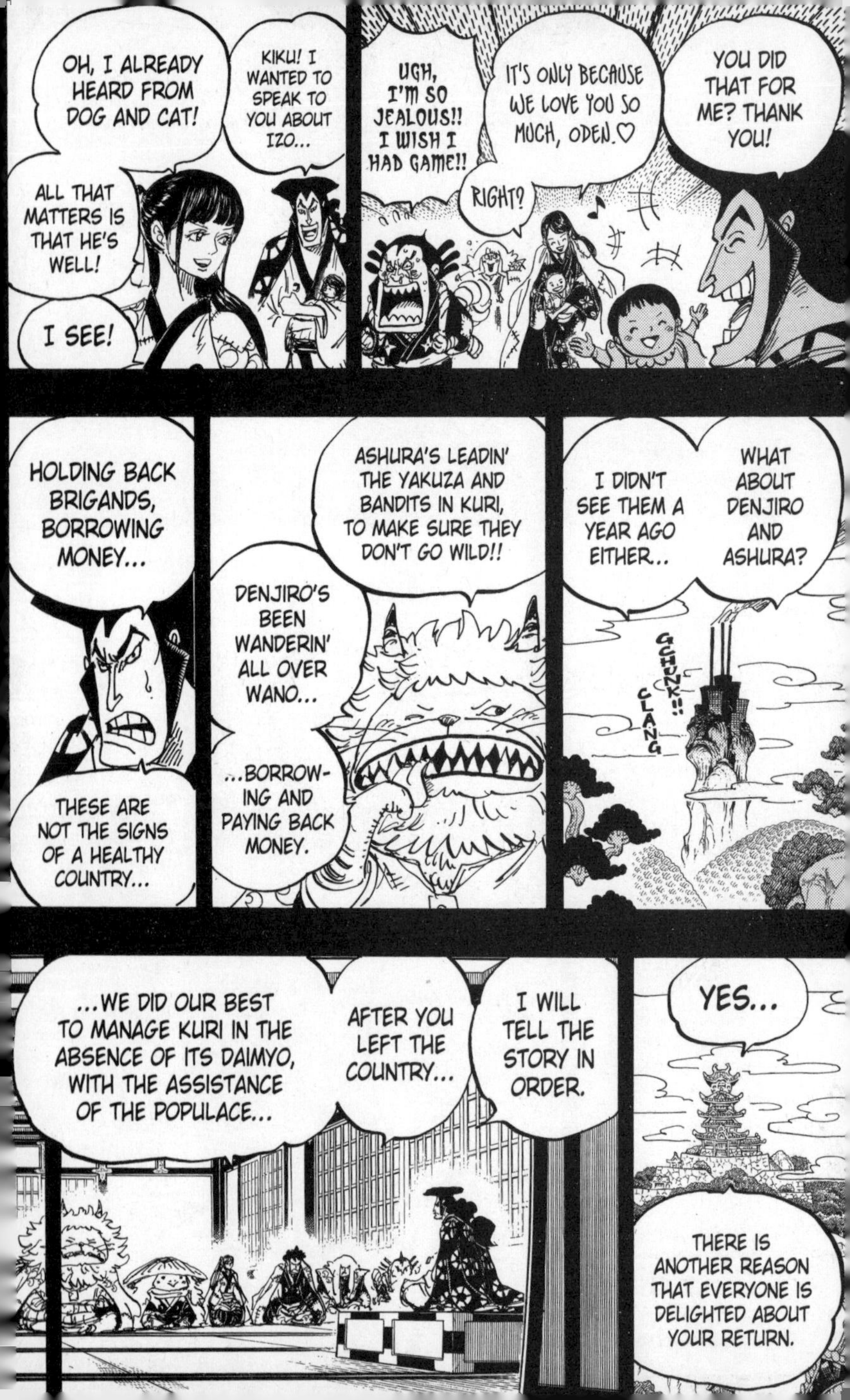
YOU DID THAT FOR ME? THANK YOU!
IT'S ONLY BECAUSE WE LOVE YOU SO MUCH, ODEN.♡
UGH, I'M SO JEALOUS!! I WISH I HAD GAME!!
RIGHT?
KIKU! I WANTED TO SPEAK TO YOU ABOUT IZO...
OH, I ALREADY HEARD FROM DOG AND CAT!
ALL THAT MATTERS IS THAT HE'S WELL!
I SEE!
WHAT ABOUT DENJIRO AND ASHURA?
I DIDN'T SEE THEM A YEAR AGO EITHER...
GCHUNK!!
CLANG
ASHURA'S LEADIN' THE YAKUZA AND BANDITS IN KURI, TO MAKE SURE THEY DON'T GO WILD!!
DENJIRO'S BEEN WANDERIN' ALL OVER WANO...
...BORROWING AND PAYING BACK MONEY.
HOLDING BACK BRIGANDS, BORROWING MONEY...
THESE ARE NOT THE SIGNS OF A HEALTHY COUNTRY...
YES...
THERE IS ANOTHER REASON THAT EVERYONE IS DELIGHTED ABOUT YOUR RETURN.
I WILL TELL THE STORY IN ORDER.
AFTER YOU LEFT THE COUNTRY...
...WE DID OUR BEST TO MANAGE KURI IN THE ABSENCE OF ITS DAIMYO, WITH THE ASSISTANCE OF THE POPULACE...

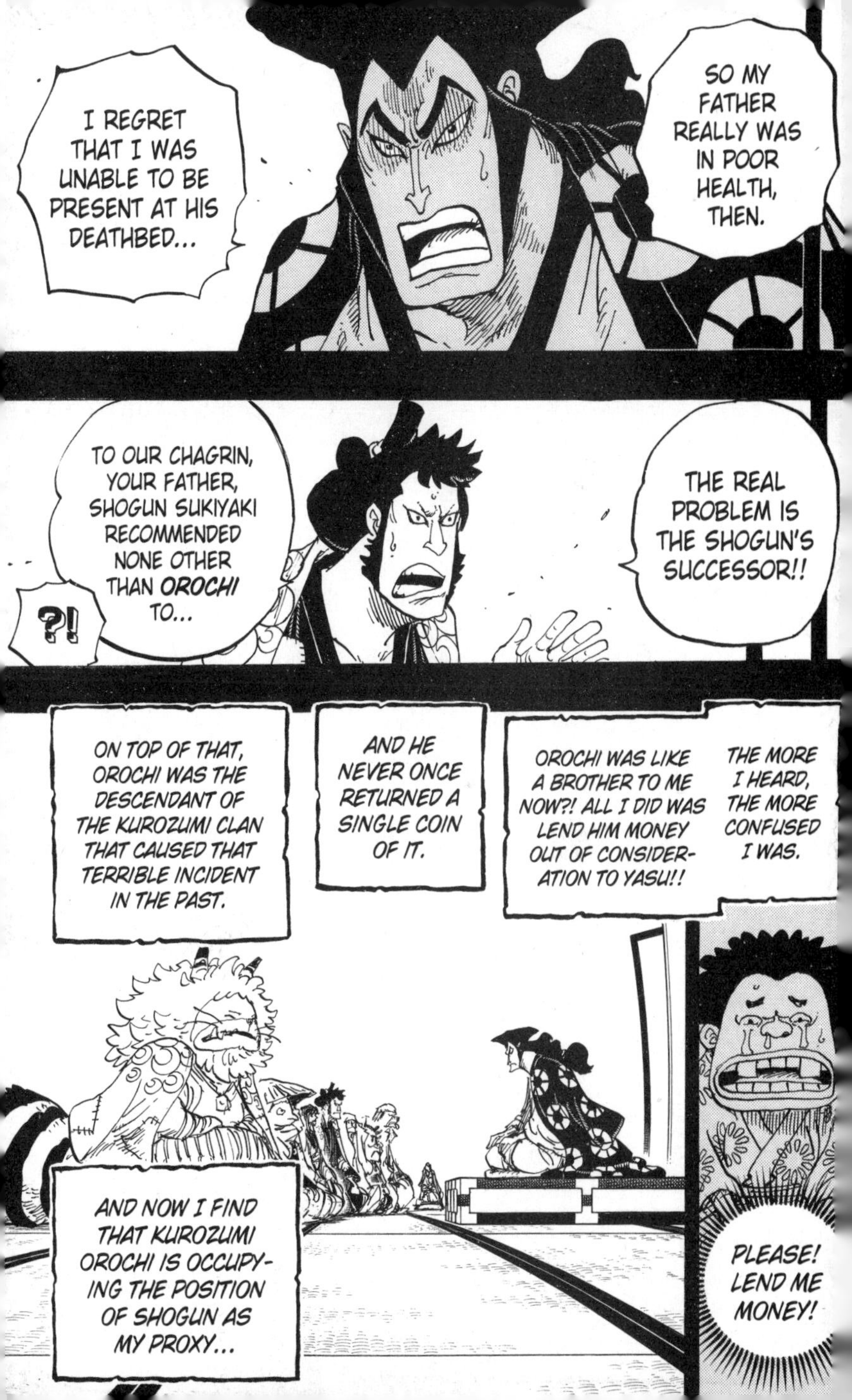
SO MY FATHER REALLY WAS IN POOR HEALTH, THEN.
I REGRET THAT I WAS UNABLE TO BE PRESENT AT HIS DEATHBED...
THE REAL PROBLEM IS THE SHOGUN'S SUCCESSOR!!
TO OUR CHAGRIN, YOUR FATHER, SHOGUN SUKIYAKI RECOMMENDED NONE OTHER THAN **OROCHI** TO...
?!
THE MORE I HEARD, THE MORE CONFUSED I WAS.
OROCHI WAS LIKE A BROTHER TO ME NOW?! ALL I DID WAS LEND HIM MONEY OUT OF CONSIDERATION TO YASU!!
AND HE NEVER ONCE RETURNED A SINGLE COIN OF IT.
ON TOP OF THAT, OROCHI WAS THE DESCENDANT OF THE KUROZUMI CLAN THAT CAUSED THAT TERRIBLE INCIDENT IN THE PAST.
PLEASE! LEND ME MONEY!
AND NOW I FIND THAT KUROZUMI OROCHI IS OCCUPYING THE POSITION OF SHOGUN AS MY PROXY...

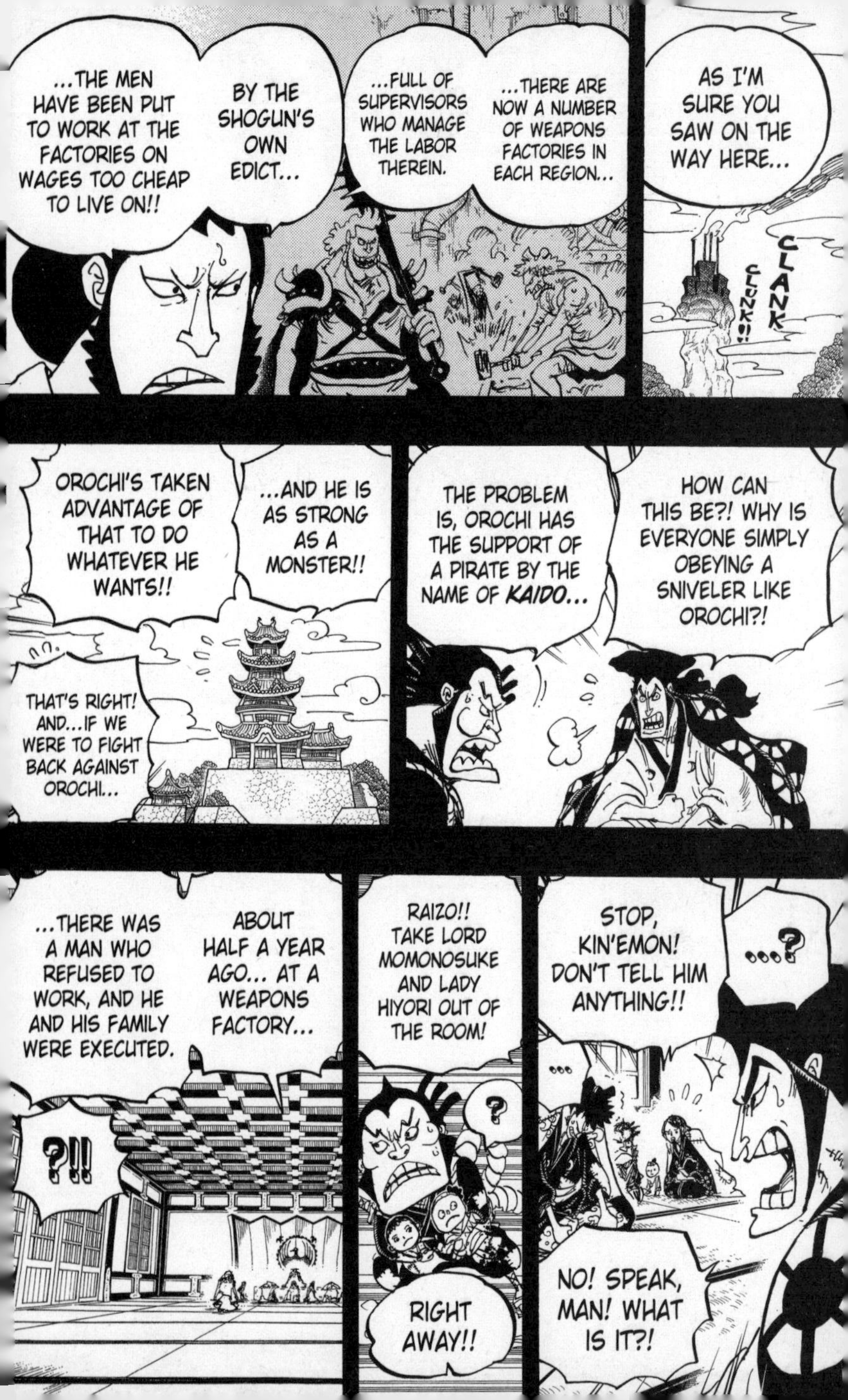
AS I'M SURE YOU SAW ON THE WAY HERE...
CLANK
CLUNK!!
...THERE ARE NOW A NUMBER OF WEAPONS FACTORIES IN EACH REGION...
...FULL OF SUPERVISORS WHO MANAGE THE LABOR THEREIN.
BY THE SHOGUN'S OWN EDICT...
...THE MEN HAVE BEEN PUT TO WORK AT THE FACTORIES ON WAGES TOO CHEAP TO LIVE ON!!
HOW CAN THIS BE?! WHY IS EVERYONE SIMPLY OBEYING A SNIVELER LIKE OROCHI?!
THE PROBLEM IS, OROCHI HAS THE SUPPORT OF A PIRATE BY THE NAME OF *KAIDO*...
...AND HE IS AS STRONG AS A MONSTER!!
OROCHI'S TAKEN ADVANTAGE OF THAT TO DO WHATEVER HE WANTS!!
THAT'S RIGHT! AND...IF WE WERE TO FIGHT BACK AGAINST OROCHI...
...?
STOP, KIN'EMON! DON'T TELL HIM ANYTHING!!
...
NO! SPEAK, MAN! WHAT IS IT?!
RAIZO!! TAKE LORD MOMONOSUKE AND LADY HIYORI OUT OF THE ROOM!
?
RIGHT AWAY!!
ABOUT HALF A YEAR AGO... AT A WEAPONS FACTORY...
...THERE WAS A MAN WHO REFUSED TO WORK, AND HE AND HIS FAMILY WERE EXECUTED.
?!!

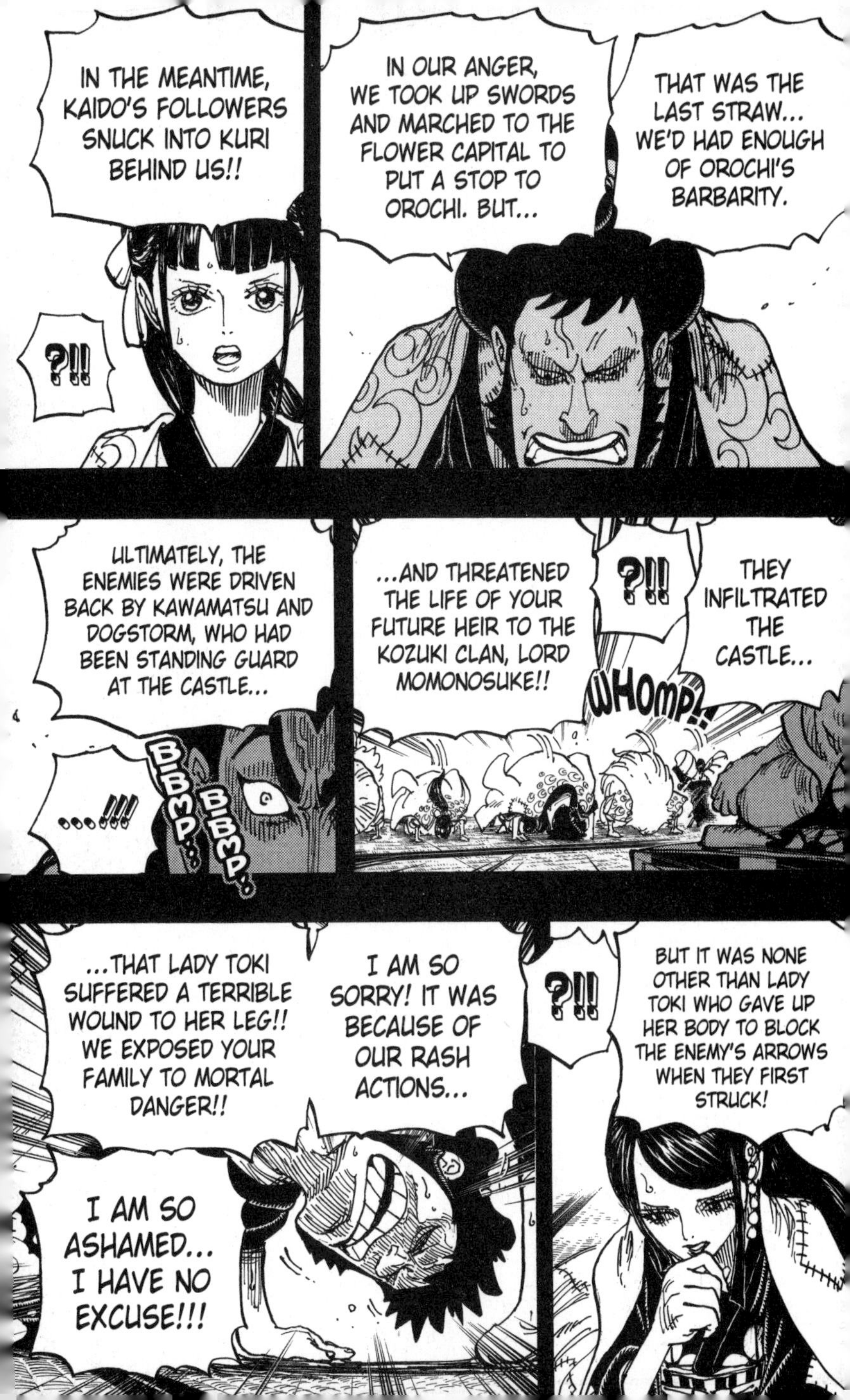
THAT WAS THE LAST STRAW... WE'D HAD ENOUGH OF OROCHI'S BARBARITY.
IN OUR ANGER, WE TOOK UP SWORDS AND MARCHED TO THE FLOWER CAPITAL TO PUT A STOP TO OROCHI. BUT...
IN THE MEANTIME, KAIDO'S FOLLOWERS SNUCK INTO KURI BEHIND US!!
?!!
THEY INFILTRATED THE CASTLE...
?!!
...AND THREATENED THE LIFE OF YOUR FUTURE HEIR TO THE KOZUKI CLAN, LORD MOMONOSUKE!!
WHOMP!!
ULTIMATELY, THE ENEMIES WERE DRIVEN BACK BY KAWAMATSU AND DOGSTORM, WHO HAD BEEN STANDING GUARD AT THE CASTLE...
...!!!
B-BMP
B-BMP
BUT IT WAS NONE OTHER THAN LADY TOKI WHO GAVE UP HER BODY TO BLOCK THE ENEMY'S ARROWS WHEN THEY FIRST STRUCK!
?!!
I AM SO SORRY! IT WAS BECAUSE OF OUR RASH ACTIONS...
...THAT LADY TOKI SUFFERED A TERRIBLE WOUND TO HER LEG!! WE EXPOSED YOUR FAMILY TO MORTAL DANGER!!
I AM SO ASHAMED... I HAVE NO EXCUSE!!!

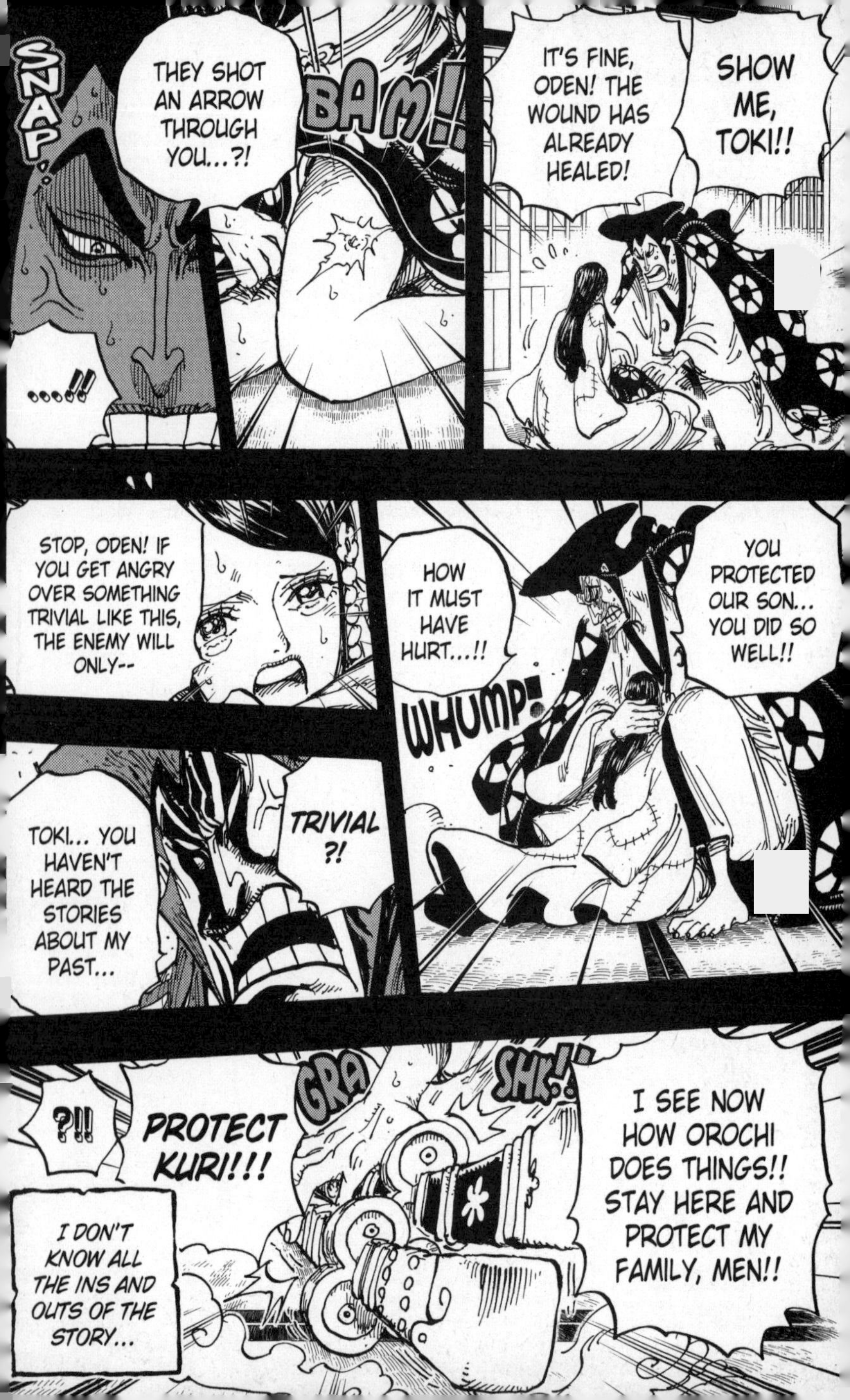
SHOW ME, TOKI!!
IT'S FINE, ODEN! THE WOUND HAS ALREADY HEALED!
BAM!!
THEY SHOT AN ARROW THROUGH YOU...?!
SNAP!
......!!
YOU PROTECTED OUR SON... YOU DID SO WELL!!
HOW IT MUST HAVE HURT...!!
WHUMP!
STOP, ODEN! IF YOU GET ANGRY OVER SOMETHING TRIVIAL LIKE THIS, THE ENEMY WILL ONLY--
TRIVIAL?!
TOKI... YOU HAVEN'T HEARD THE STORIES ABOUT MY PAST...
I SEE NOW HOW OROCHI DOES THINGS!! STAY HERE AND PROTECT MY FAMILY, MEN!!
GRA
SHK!!
PROTECT KURI!!!
?!!
I DON'T KNOW ALL THE INS AND OUTS OF THE STORY...

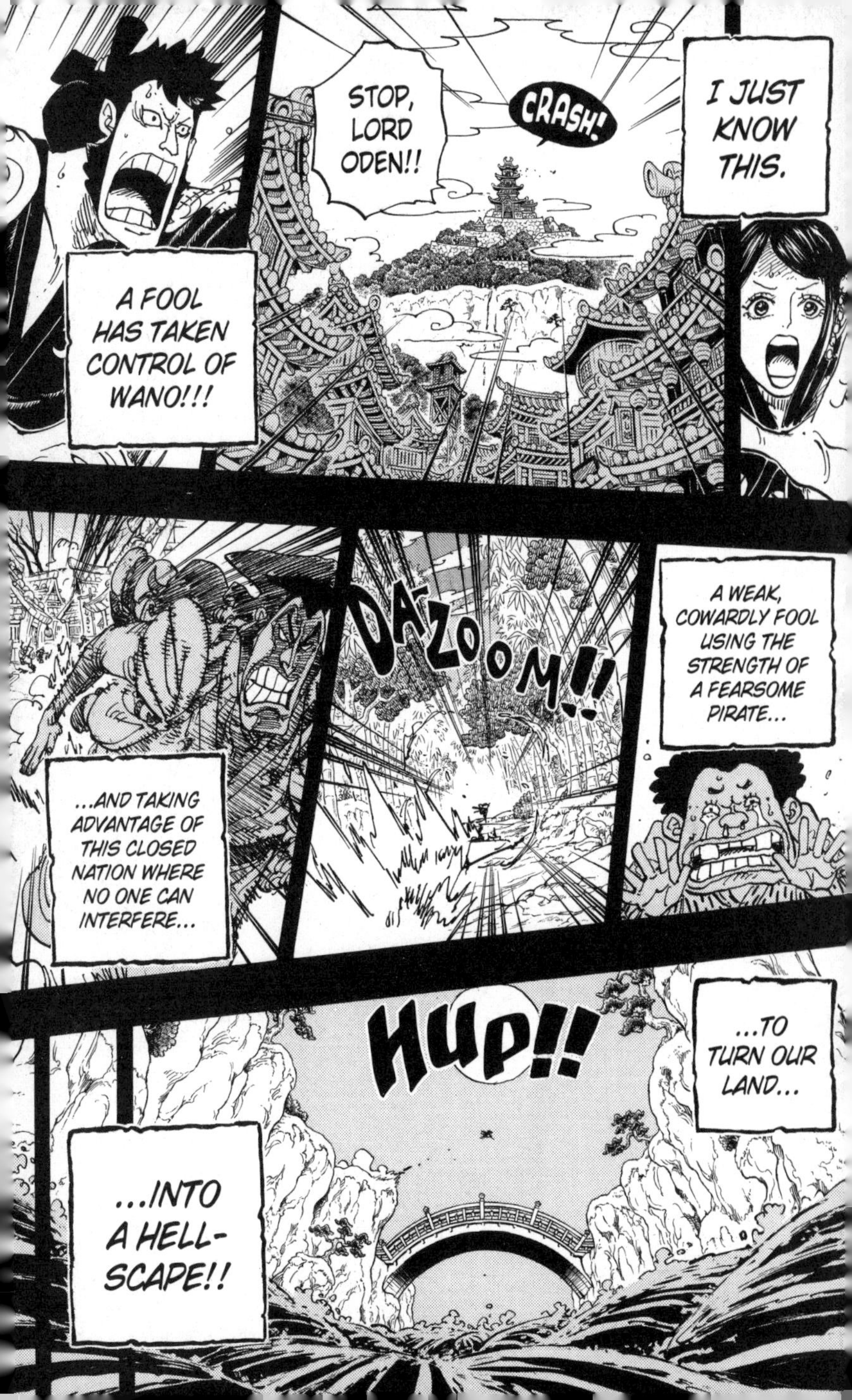
I JUST KNOW THIS.
CRASH!
STOP, LORD ODEN!!
A FOOL HAS TAKEN CONTROL OF WANO!!!
A WEAK, COWARDLY FOOL USING THE STRENGTH OF A FEARSOME PIRATE...
DAZOOM!!
...AND TAKING ADVANTAGE OF THIS CLOSED NATION WHERE NO ONE CAN INTERFERE...
...TO TURN OUR LAND...
HUP!!
...INTO A HELL-SCAPE!!

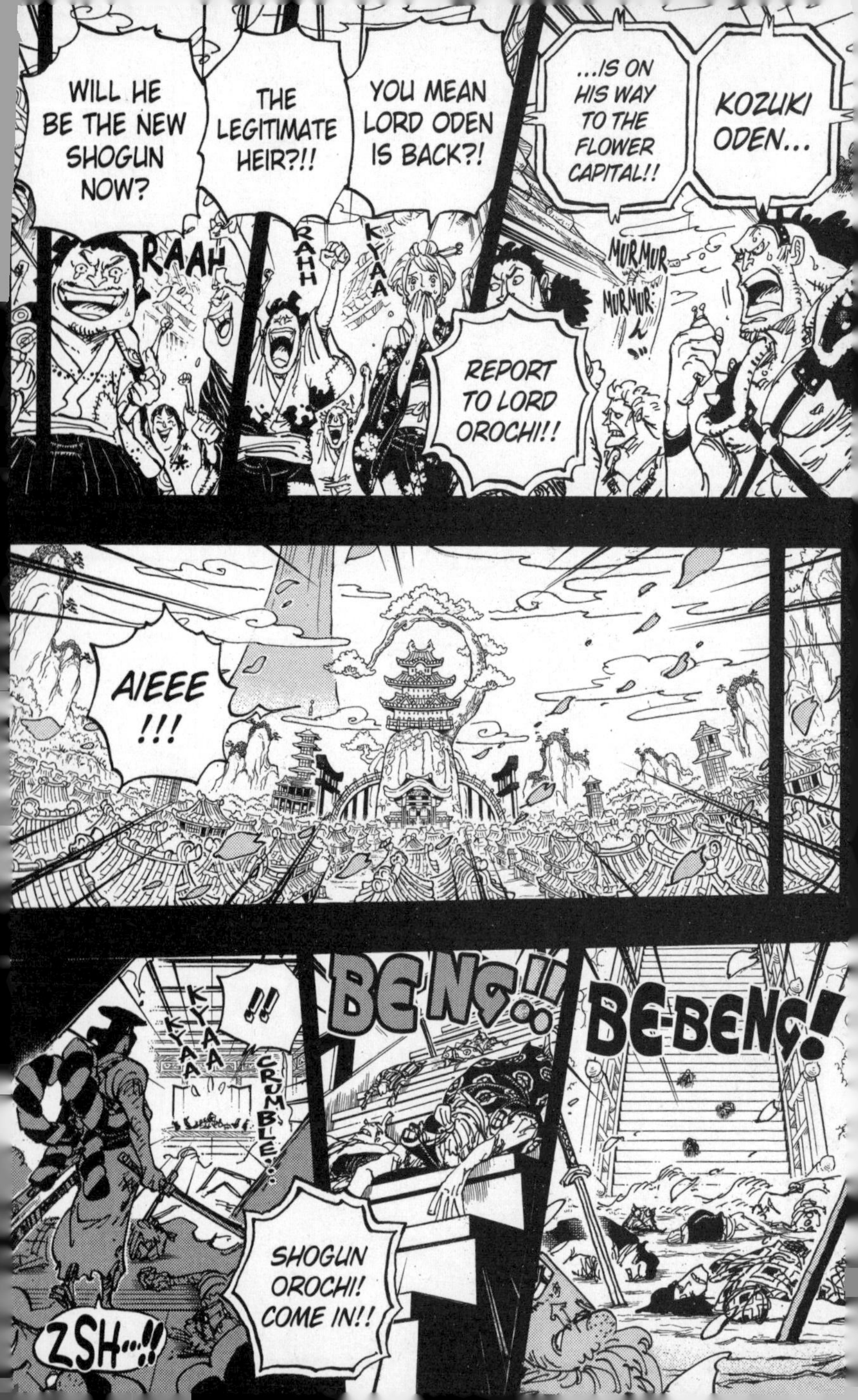
KOZUKI ODEN...
...IS ON HIS WAY TO THE FLOWER CAPITAL!!
MURMUR
MURMUR
REPORT TO LORD OROCHI!!
YOU MEAN LORD ODEN IS BACK?!
KYAA
RAHH
THE LEGITIMATE HEIR?!!
WILL HE BE THE NEW SHOGUN NOW?
RAAH
AIEEE!!!
BE-BENG!
BENG..!!
SHOGUN OROCHI! COME IN!!
!!
KYAA
KYAA
CRUMBLE
ZSH...!!

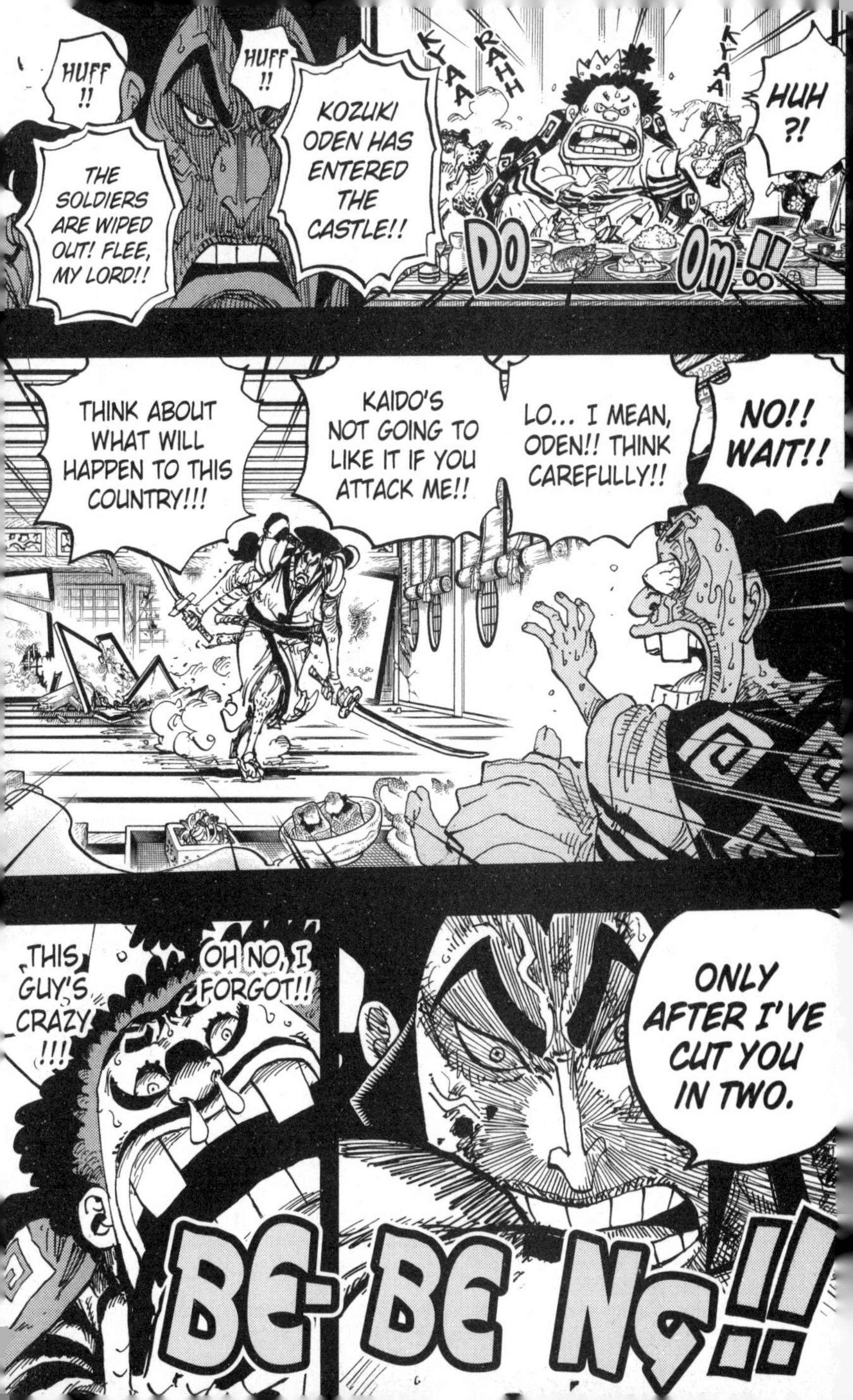
HUH ?!
KYAA
RAHH
KYAA
DO Om!!
HUFF !!
HUFF !!
KOZUKI ODEN HAS ENTERED THE CASTLE!!
THE SOLDIERS ARE WIPED OUT! FLEE, MY LORD!!
NO!! WAIT!!
LO... I MEAN, ODEN!! THINK CAREFULLY!!
KAIDO'S NOT GOING TO LIKE IT IF YOU ATTACK ME!!
THINK ABOUT WHAT WILL HAPPEN TO THIS COUNTRY!!!
ONLY AFTER I'VE CUT YOU IN TWO.
BE-BE NG!!
OH NO, I FORGOT!!
THIS GUY'S CRAZY!!!

エス
ビー
エス
くすくす
カッパー
ドジョー

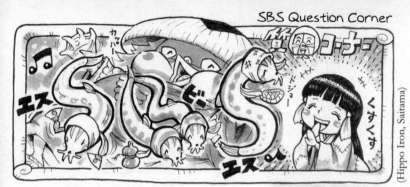

(Hippo Iron, Saitama)

Shimotsuki Yasuie
Shimotsuki Ryuma
Shimotsuki Ushimaru

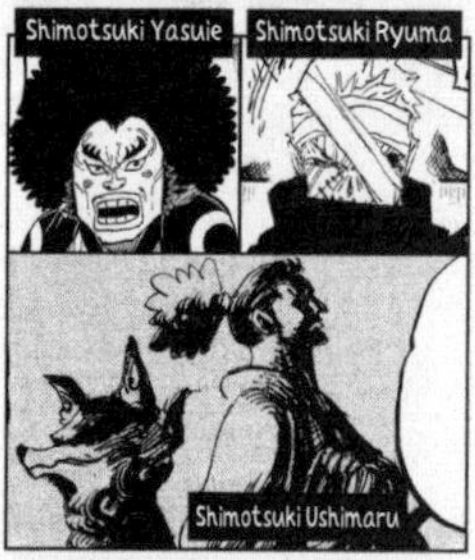

Q: Odacchi!! Here's a question!! We have Shimotsuki Yasuie, Shimotsuki Ryuma, Shimotsuki Kozaburo, Shimotsuki Onimaru--all of these people with the name of Shimotsuki. Is there a connection to the Frost Moon *(shimotsuki)* village that Zolo grew up in, and his teacher, Koshiro? Zolo said he learned about the word "sunacchi" from the old guy in his village. Plus you said in the SBS of volume 92 that they came to the East Blue from Wano!

--Yuu

ZOLOJURO, I WAS TOLD NOT TO SAY "SUNACCHI."
IT'S JUST SOMETHING THE OLD GUY IN MY VILLAGE TOLD ME. I'VE NEVER SAID IT MYSELF BEFORE.
WHAT ?!

Vol. 95, p.31

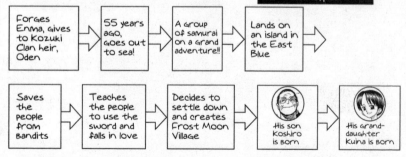

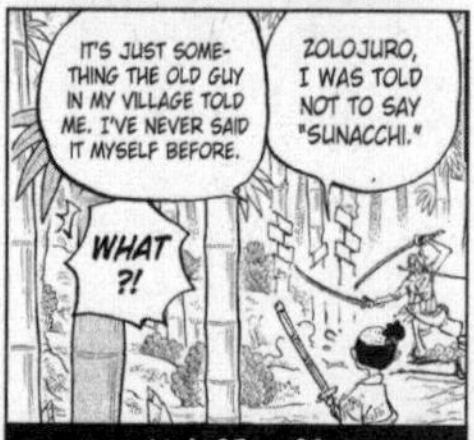

A: Okay. I think you can envision how this all fits together based on a close reading of the manga, but just to make it clear, allow me to explain! Here's the life of Shimotsuki Kozaburo, the blacksmith and swordsman.

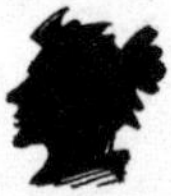

Forges Enma, gives to Kozuki Clan heir, Oden → 55 years ago, goes out to sea! → A group of samurai on a grand adventure!! → Lands on an island in the East Blue →

Saves the people from bandits → Teaches the people to use the sword and falls in love → Decides to settle down and creates Frost Moon Village → His son Koshiro is born → His granddaughter Kuina is born

So as you can see here, the "old guy in the village" Zolo knew was none other than old Shimotsuki Kozaburo, who originally sailed out of Wano. Huh? Wait, what does that mean for Zolo's bloodline...?
That's all for the story of Shimotsuki Kozaburo, the founder of Frost Moon Village, for today!! Be-beng!!

Chapter 969:
FOOL OF A LORD

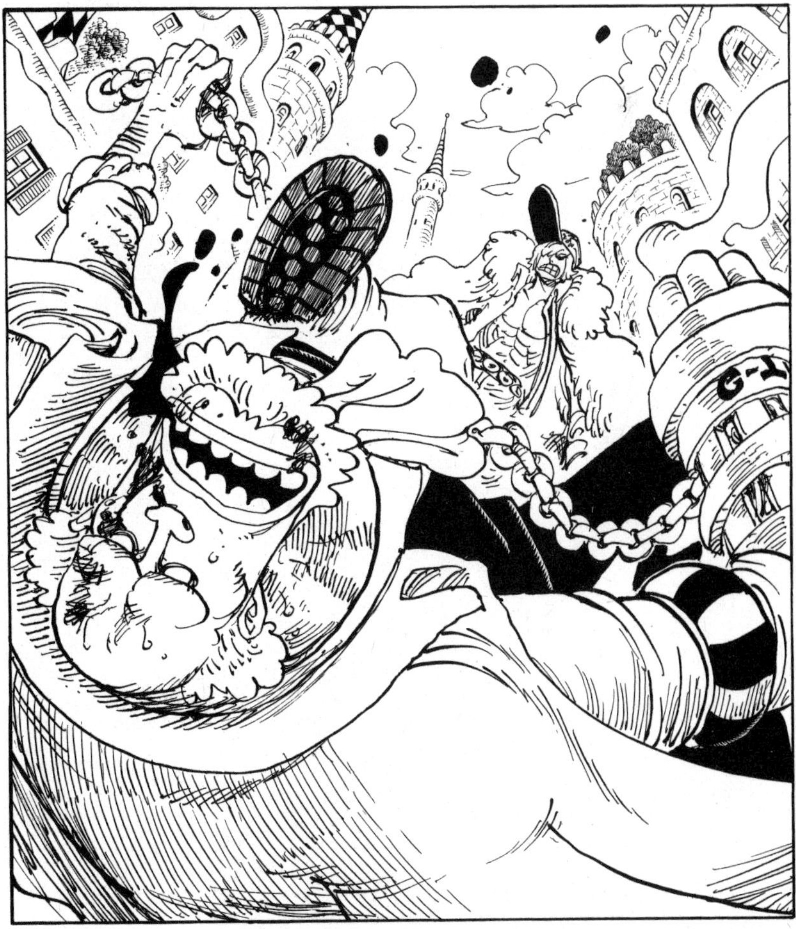

GANG BEGE'S OH MY FAMILY
VOL. 18: "GOTTI VS. NAVY"

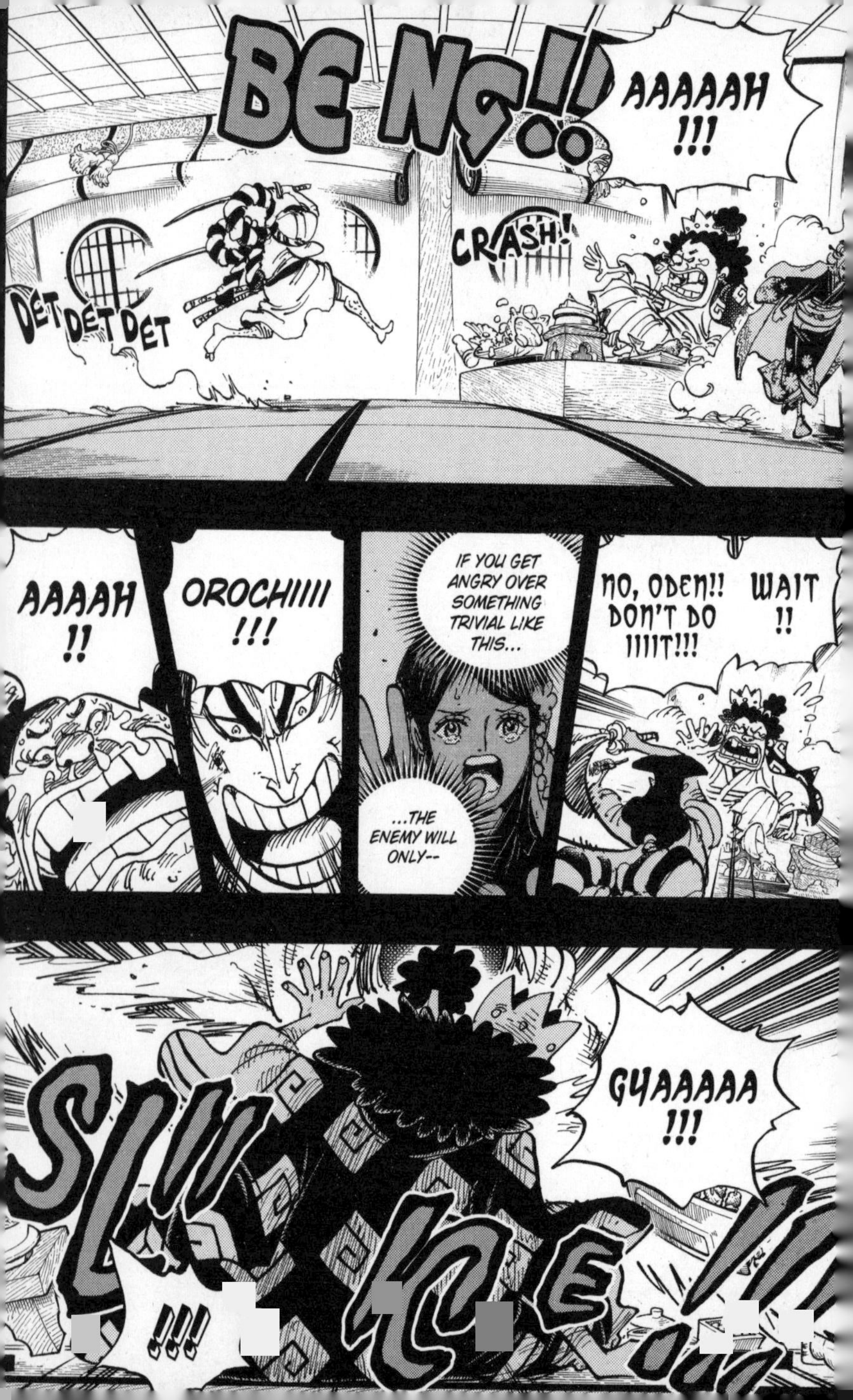
AAAAAH !!!
CRASH!
BE NG!!
DET DET DET
WAIT !!
NO, ODEN!! DON'T DO IIIIT!!!
IF YOU GET ANGRY OVER SOMETHING TRIVIAL LIKE THIS...
...THE ENEMY WILL ONLY--
OROCHIIIII !!!
AAAAH !!
GUAAAAA !!!
SL !!! NE

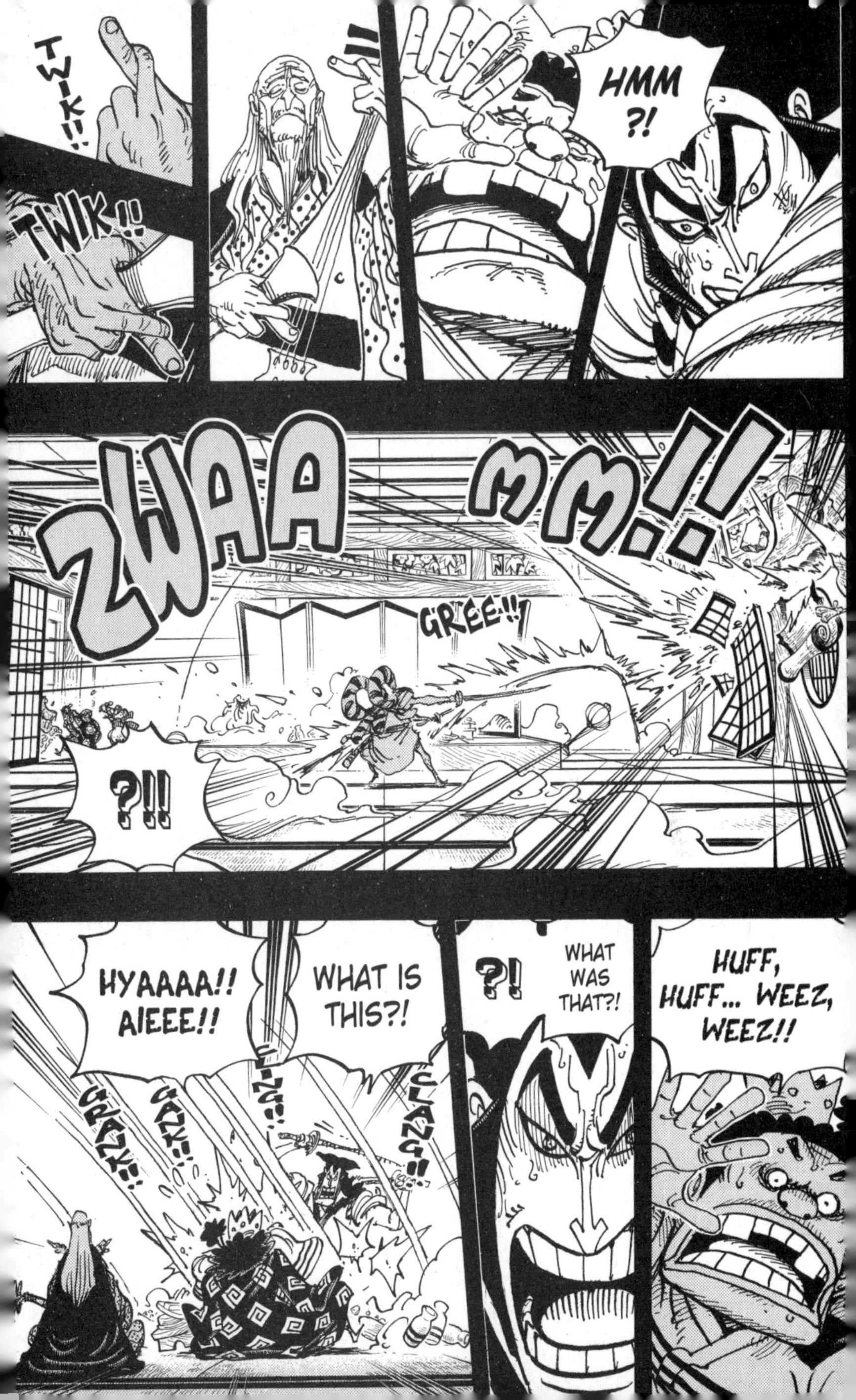
HMM ?!
TWIK!!
TWIK!!
ZWAAMM!!
GREE!!
?!!
HUFF, HUFF... WEEZ, WEEZ!!
WHAT WAS THAT?!
?!
WHAT IS THIS?!
HYAAAA!! AIEEE!!
CLANG!!
SING!!
GANK!!
GRANK!!

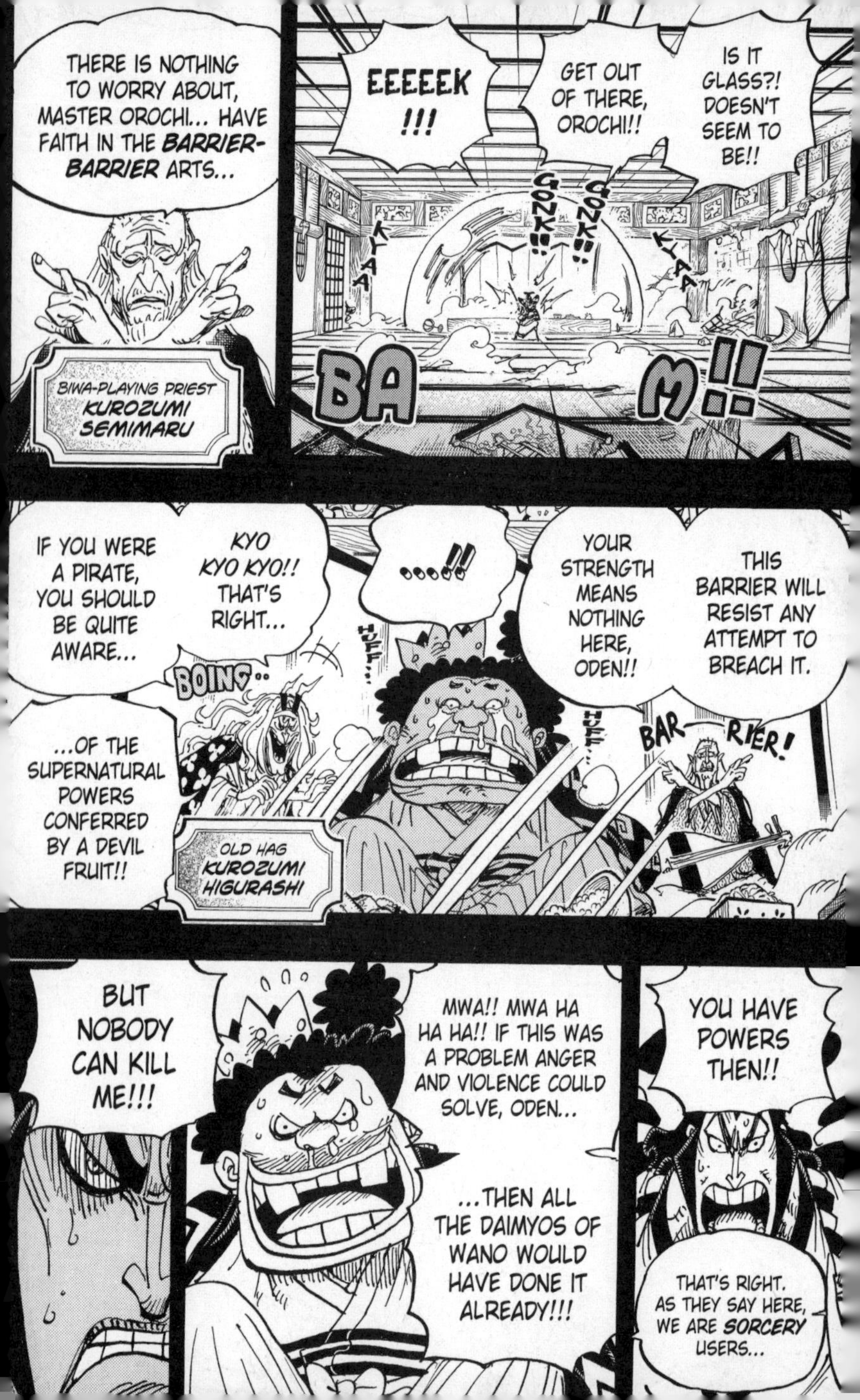
IS IT GLASS?! DOESN'T SEEM TO BE!!
GET OUT OF THERE, OROCHI!!
EEEEEK !!!
GONK!!
GONK!!
KYAA
KYAA
BAM!!
THERE IS NOTHING TO WORRY ABOUT, MASTER OROCHI... HAVE FAITH IN THE BARRIER-BARRIER ARTS...
BIWA-PLAYING PRIEST KUROZUMI SEMIMARU
THIS BARRIER WILL RESIST ANY ATTEMPT TO BREACH IT.
YOUR STRENGTH MEANS NOTHING HERE, ODEN!!
....!!
KYO KYO KYO!! THAT'S RIGHT...
IF YOU WERE A PIRATE, YOU SHOULD BE QUITE AWARE...
BAR-RIER!
HUFF...
HUFF...
BOING..
...OF THE SUPERNATURAL POWERS CONFERRED BY A DEVIL FRUIT!!
OLD HAG KUROZUMI HIGURASHI
YOU HAVE POWERS THEN!!
THAT'S RIGHT. AS THEY SAY HERE, WE ARE SORCERY USERS...
MWA!! MWA HA HA HA!! IF THIS WAS A PROBLEM ANGER AND VIOLENCE COULD SOLVE, ODEN...
...THEN ALL THE DAIMYOS OF WANO WOULD HAVE DONE IT ALREADY!!!
BUT NOBODY CAN KILL ME!!!

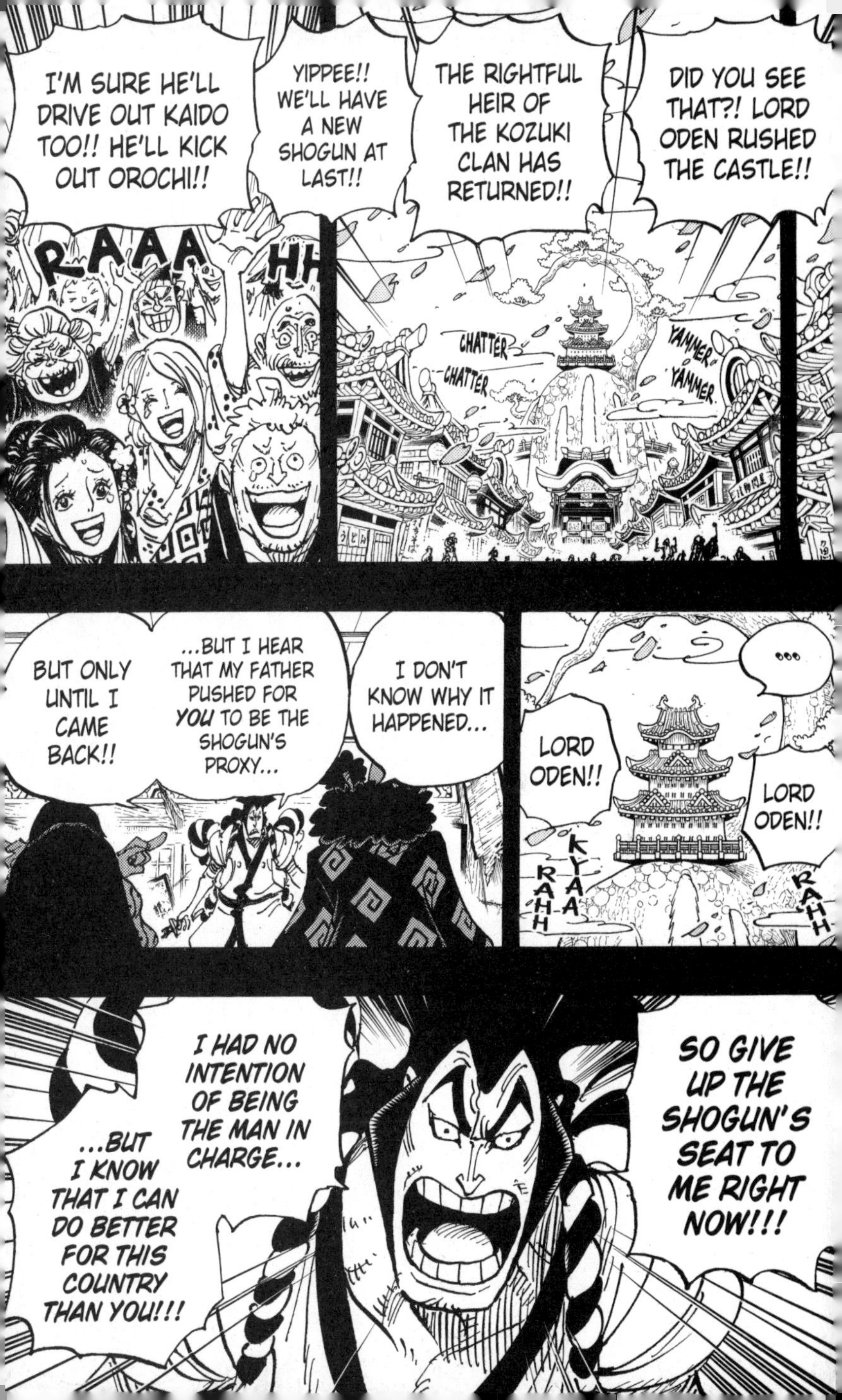
DID YOU SEE THAT?! LORD ODEN RUSHED THE CASTLE!!
THE RIGHTFUL HEIR OF THE KOZUKI CLAN HAS RETURNED!!
YAMMER YAMMER
CHATTER CHATTER
YIPPEE!! WE'LL HAVE A NEW SHOGUN AT LAST!!
I'M SURE HE'LL DRIVE OUT KAIDO TOO!! HE'LL KICK OUT OROCHI!!
RAAAHH
...
LORD ODEN!!
LORD ODEN!!
RAHH
KYAAA
RAHH
I DON'T KNOW WHY IT HAPPENED...
...BUT I HEAR THAT MY FATHER PUSHED FOR *YOU* TO BE THE SHOGUN'S PROXY...
BUT ONLY UNTIL I CAME BACK!!
SO GIVE UP THE SHOGUN'S SEAT TO ME RIGHT NOW!!!
I HAD NO INTENTION OF BEING THE MAN IN CHARGE...
...BUT I KNOW THAT I CAN DO BETTER FOR THIS COUNTRY THAN YOU!!!

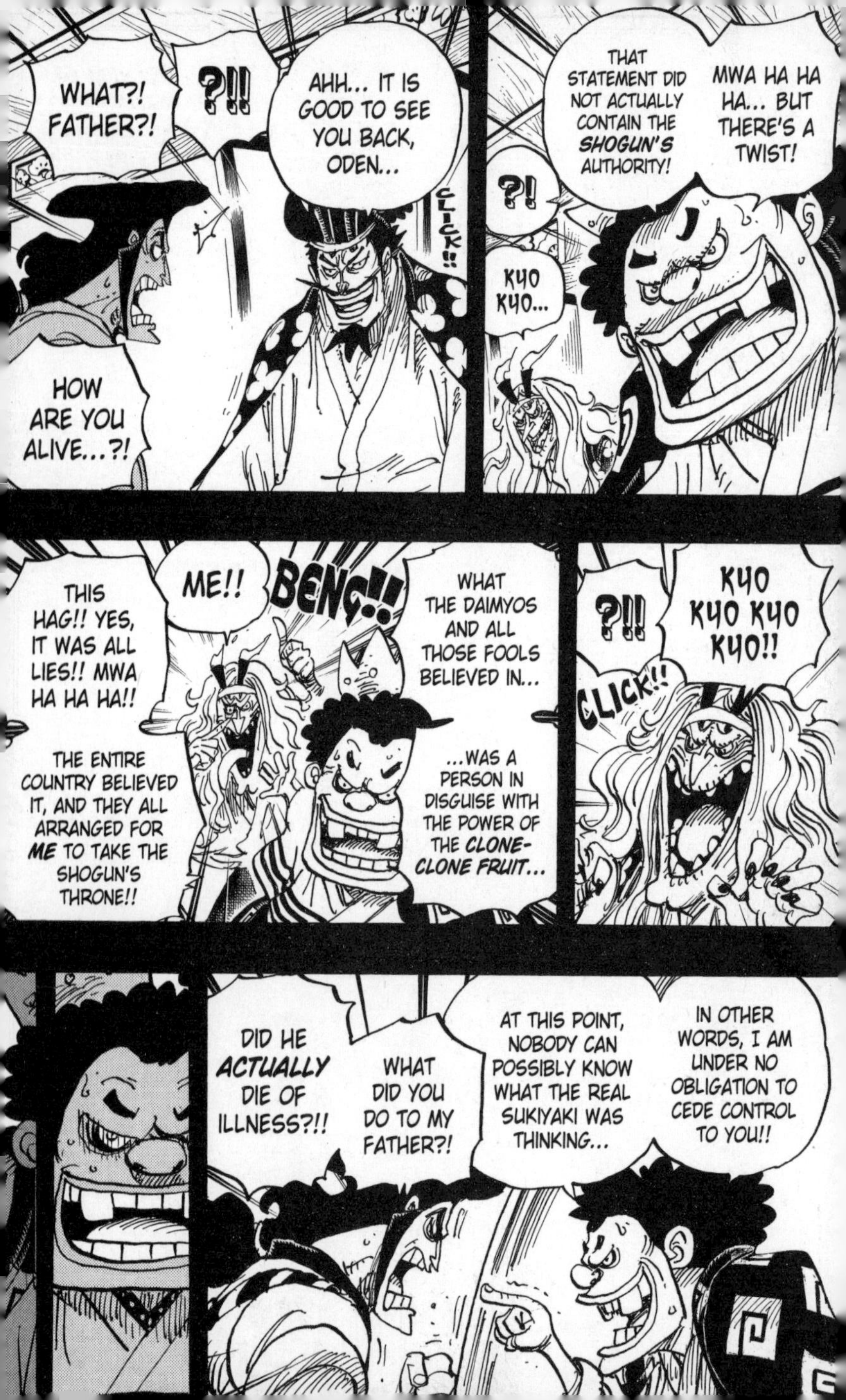
MWA HA HA HA... BUT THERE'S A TWIST!
THAT STATEMENT DID NOT ACTUALLY CONTAIN THE SHOGUN'S AUTHORITY!
?!
KYO KYO...
AHH... IT IS GOOD TO SEE YOU BACK, ODEN...
CLICK!!
?!!
WHAT?! FATHER?!
HOW ARE YOU ALIVE...?!
KYO KYO KYO KYO!!
?!!
CLICK!!
WHAT THE DAIMYOS AND ALL THOSE FOOLS BELIEVED IN...
...WAS A PERSON IN DISGUISE WITH THE POWER OF THE CLONE-CLONE FRUIT...
BENG!!
ME!!
THIS HAG!! YES, IT WAS ALL LIES!! MWA HA HA HA!!
THE ENTIRE COUNTRY BELIEVED IT, AND THEY ALL ARRANGED FOR ME TO TAKE THE SHOGUN'S THRONE!!
IN OTHER WORDS, I AM UNDER NO OBLIGATION TO CEDE CONTROL TO YOU!!
AT THIS POINT, NOBODY CAN POSSIBLY KNOW WHAT THE REAL SUKIYAKI WAS THINKING...
WHAT DID YOU DO TO MY FATHER?!
DID HE ACTUALLY DIE OF ILLNESS?!!

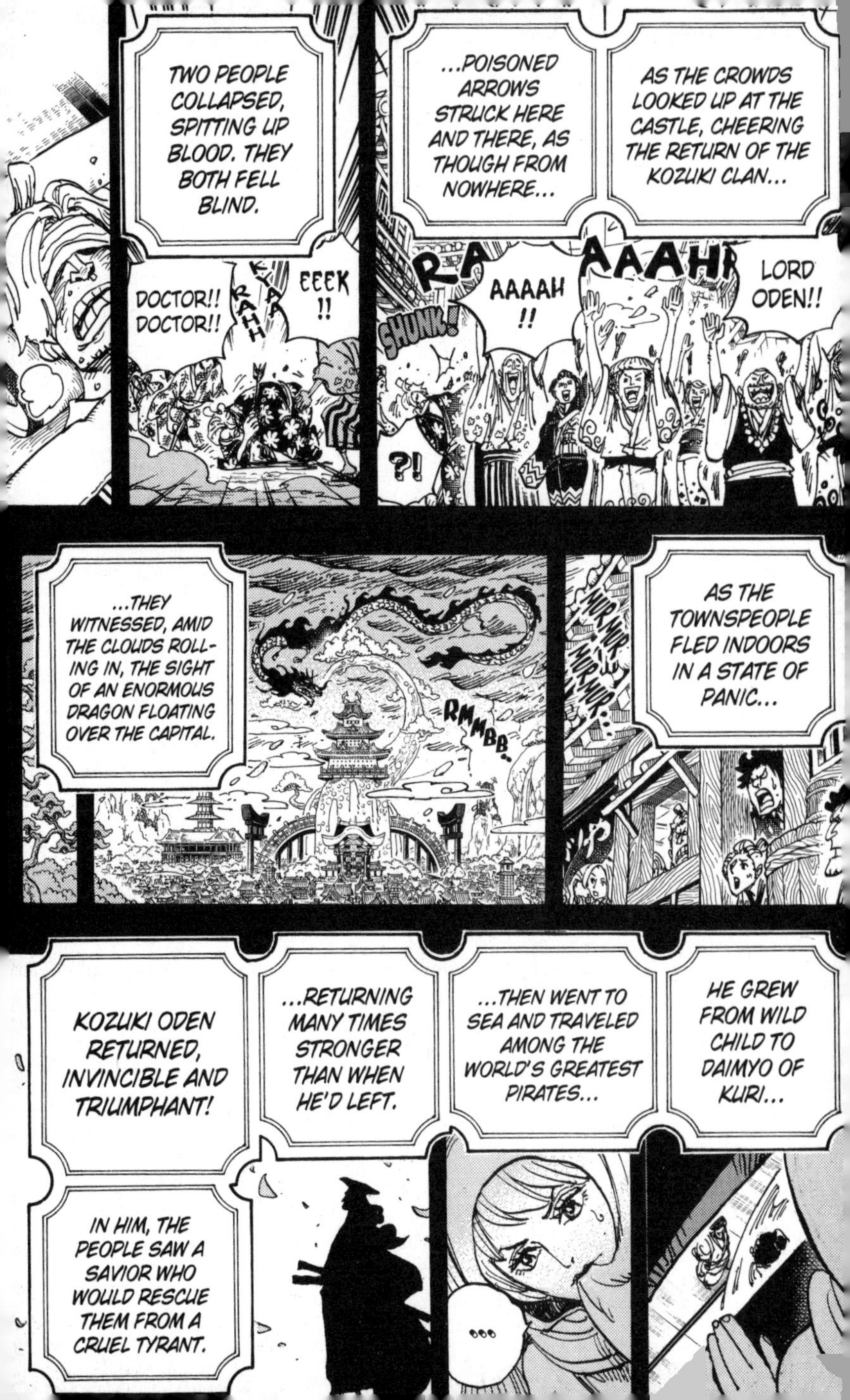
AS THE CROWDS LOOKED UP AT THE CASTLE, CHEERING THE RETURN OF THE KOZUKI CLAN...
...POISONED ARROWS STRUCK HERE AND THERE, AS THOUGH FROM NOWHERE...
LORD ODEN!!
AAAHH
AAAAH !!
RA
SHUNK!
?!
TWO PEOPLE COLLAPSED, SPITTING UP BLOOD. THEY BOTH FELL BLIND.
EEEK !!
KYAA
RAHH
DOCTOR!! DOCTOR!!
AS THE TOWNSPEOPLE FLED INDOORS IN A STATE OF PANIC...
MURMUR... MURMUR...
...THEY WITNESSED, AMID THE CLOUDS ROLLING IN, THE SIGHT OF AN ENORMOUS DRAGON FLOATING OVER THE CAPITAL.
RMMBB..
HE GREW FROM WILD CHILD TO DAIMYO OF KURI...
...THEN WENT TO SEA AND TRAVELED AMONG THE WORLD'S GREATEST PIRATES...
...RETURNING MANY TIMES STRONGER THAN WHEN HE'D LEFT.
KOZUKI ODEN RETURNED, INVINCIBLE AND TRIUMPHANT!
IN HIM, THE PEOPLE SAW A SAVIOR WHO WOULD RESCUE THEM FROM A CRUEL TYRANT.
...

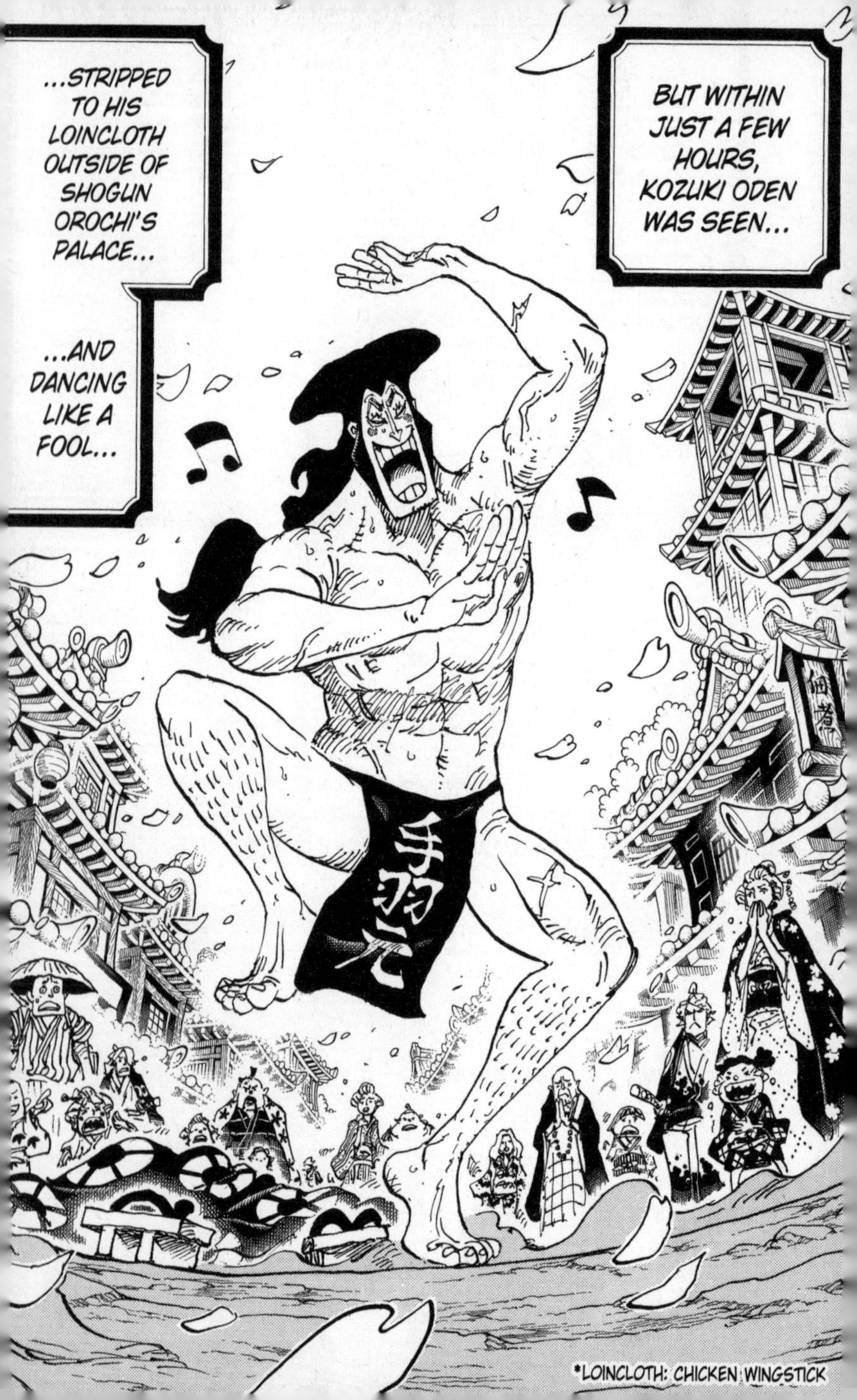
BUT WITHIN JUST A FEW HOURS, KOZUKI ODEN WAS SEEN...
...STRIPPED TO HIS LOINCLOTH OUTSIDE OF SHOGUN OROCHI'S PALACE...
...AND DANCING LIKE A FOOL...
手羽元
*LOINCLOTH: CHICKEN WINGSTICK

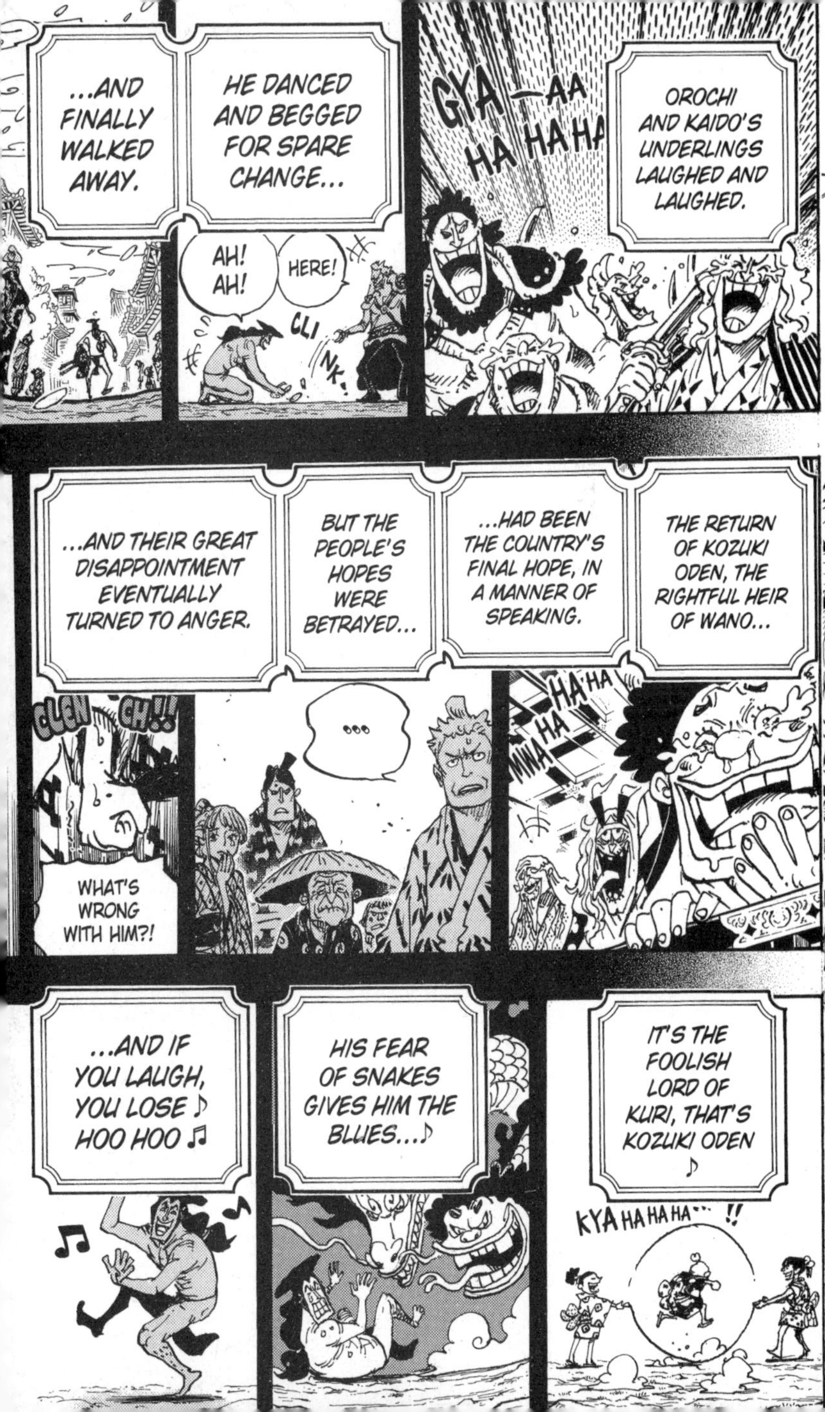
OROCHI AND KAIDO'S UNDERLINGS LAUGHED AND LAUGHED.
GYA—AA HA HA HA
HE DANCED AND BEGGED FOR SPARE CHANGE...
HERE!
AH! AH!
CLINK!
...AND FINALLY WALKED AWAY.
THE RETURN OF KOZUKI ODEN, THE RIGHTFUL HEIR OF WANO...
...HAD BEEN THE COUNTRY'S FINAL HOPE, IN A MANNER OF SPEAKING.
BUT THE PEOPLE'S HOPES WERE BETRAYED...
...AND THEIR GREAT DISAPPOINTMENT EVENTUALLY TURNED TO ANGER.
MMHA HA HA HA
...
CLENCH!!
WHAT'S WRONG WITH HIM?!
IT'S THE FOOLISH LORD OF KURI, THAT'S KOZUKI ODEN ♪
KYA HA HA HA...!!
HIS FEAR OF SNAKES GIVES HIM THE BLUES...♪
...AND IF YOU LAUGH, YOU LOSE ♪ HOO HOO ♫

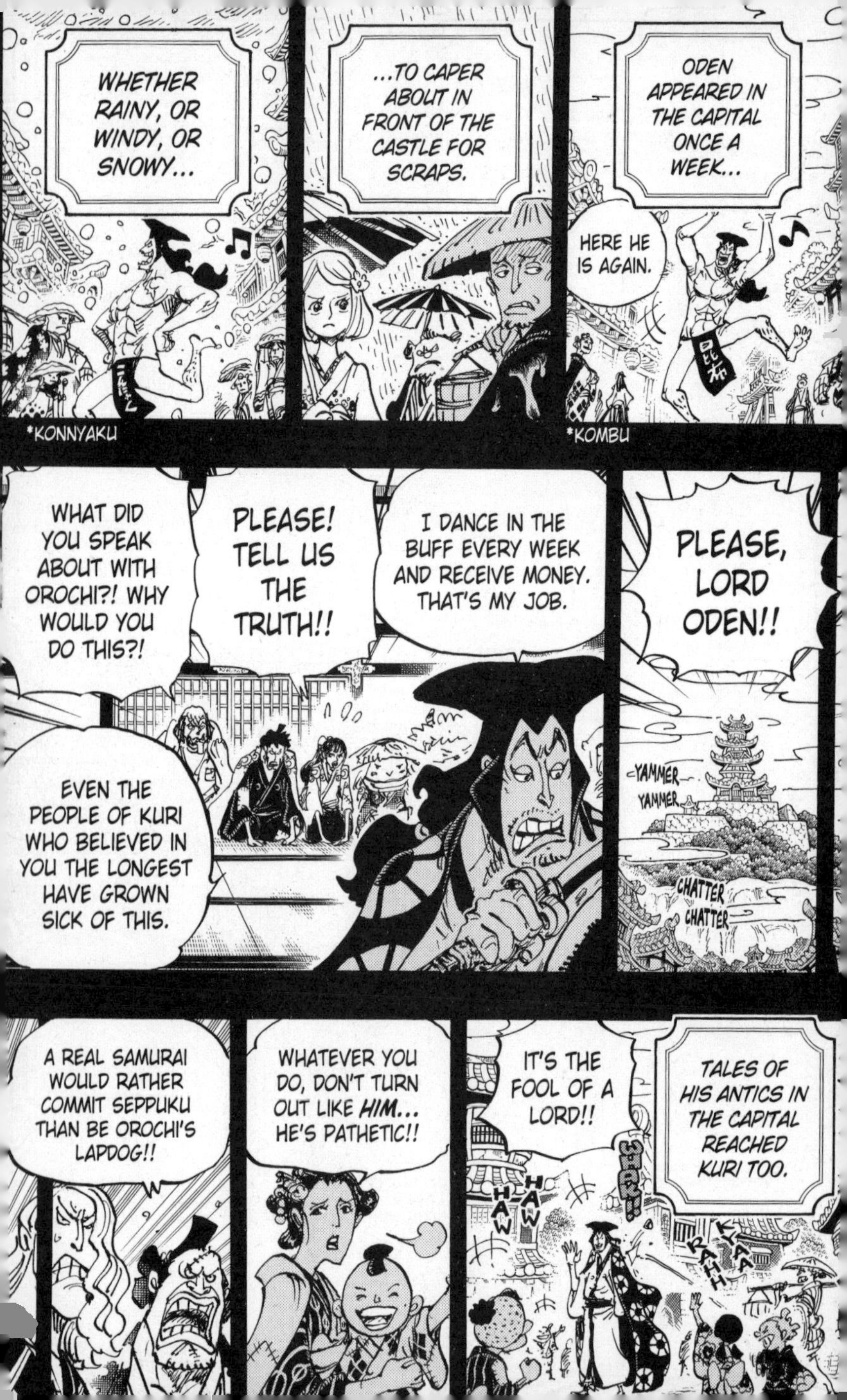
ODEN APPEARED IN THE CAPITAL ONCE A WEEK...
HERE HE IS AGAIN.
*KOMBU
...TO CAPER ABOUT IN FRONT OF THE CASTLE FOR SCRAPS.
WHETHER RAINY, OR WINDY, OR SNOWY...
*KONNYAKU
PLEASE, LORD ODEN!!
YAMMER YAMMER
CHATTER CHATTER
I DANCE IN THE BUFF EVERY WEEK AND RECEIVE MONEY. THAT'S MY JOB.
PLEASE! TELL US THE TRUTH!!
WHAT DID YOU SPEAK ABOUT WITH OROCHI?! WHY WOULD YOU DO THIS?!
EVEN THE PEOPLE OF KURI WHO BELIEVED IN YOU THE LONGEST HAVE GROWN SICK OF THIS.
TALES OF HIS ANTICS IN THE CAPITAL REACHED KURI TOO.
IT'S THE FOOL OF A LORD!!
KYAA
RAHH
HAW HAW
HAW HAW
WHATEVER YOU DO, DON'T TURN OUT LIKE HIM... HE'S PATHETIC!!
A REAL SAMURAI WOULD RATHER COMMIT SEPPUKU THAN BE OROCHI'S LAPDOG!!

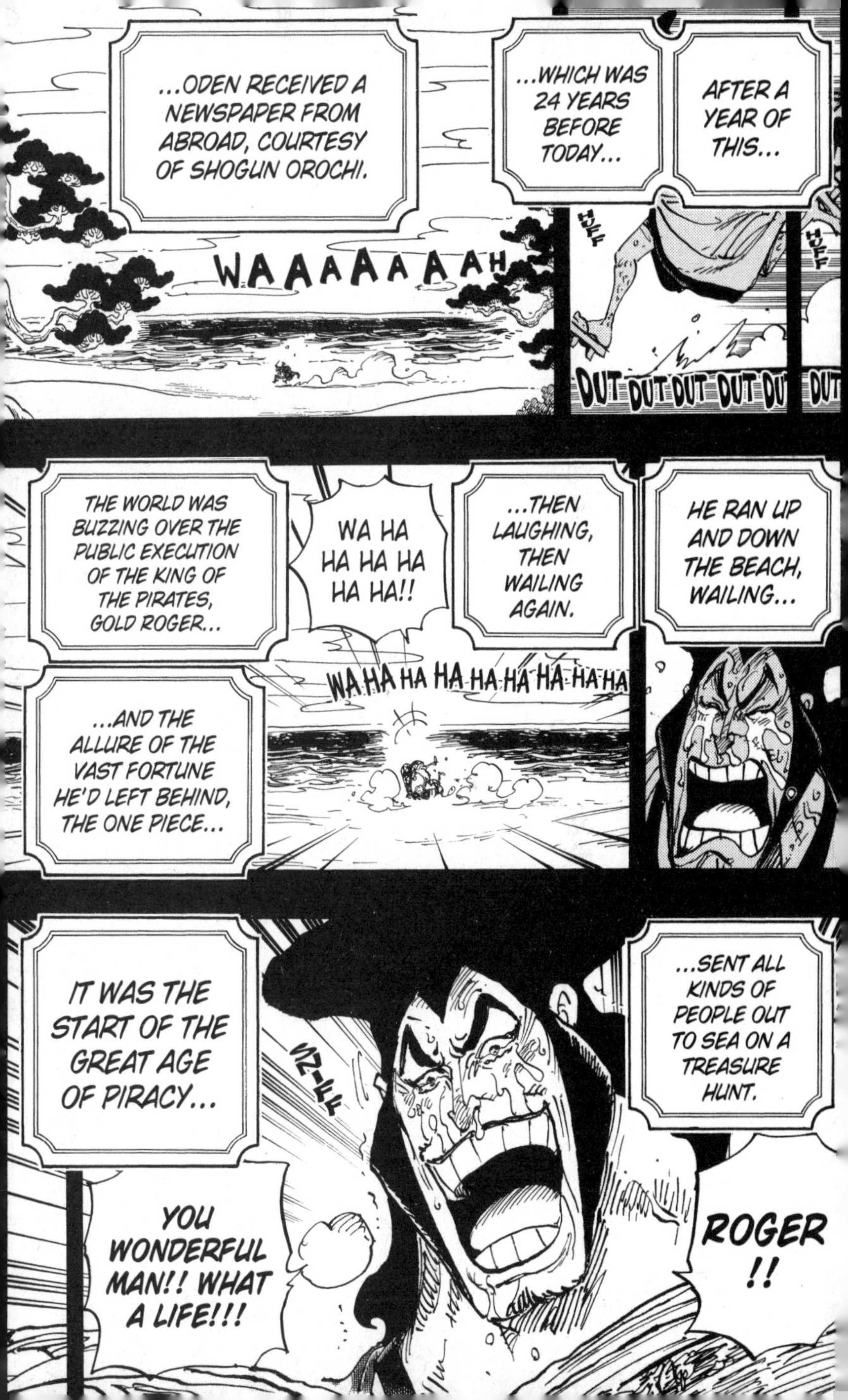
AFTER A YEAR OF THIS...
...WHICH WAS 24 YEARS BEFORE TODAY...
HUFF
HUFF
DUT DUT DUT DUT DU DUT
...ODEN RECEIVED A NEWSPAPER FROM ABROAD, COURTESY OF SHOGUN OROCHI.
WAAAAAAAH
HE RAN UP AND DOWN THE BEACH, WAILING...
...THEN LAUGHING, THEN WAILING AGAIN.
WA HA HA HA HA HA HA!!
THE WORLD WAS BUZZING OVER THE PUBLIC EXECUTION OF THE KING OF THE PIRATES, GOLD ROGER...
WA HA HA HA HA HA HA HA HA
...AND THE ALLURE OF THE VAST FORTUNE HE'D LEFT BEHIND, THE ONE PIECE...
...SENT ALL KINDS OF PEOPLE OUT TO SEA ON A TREASURE HUNT.
IT WAS THE START OF THE GREAT AGE OF PIRACY...
SNIFF
ROGER !!
YOU WONDERFUL MAN!! WHAT A LIFE!!!

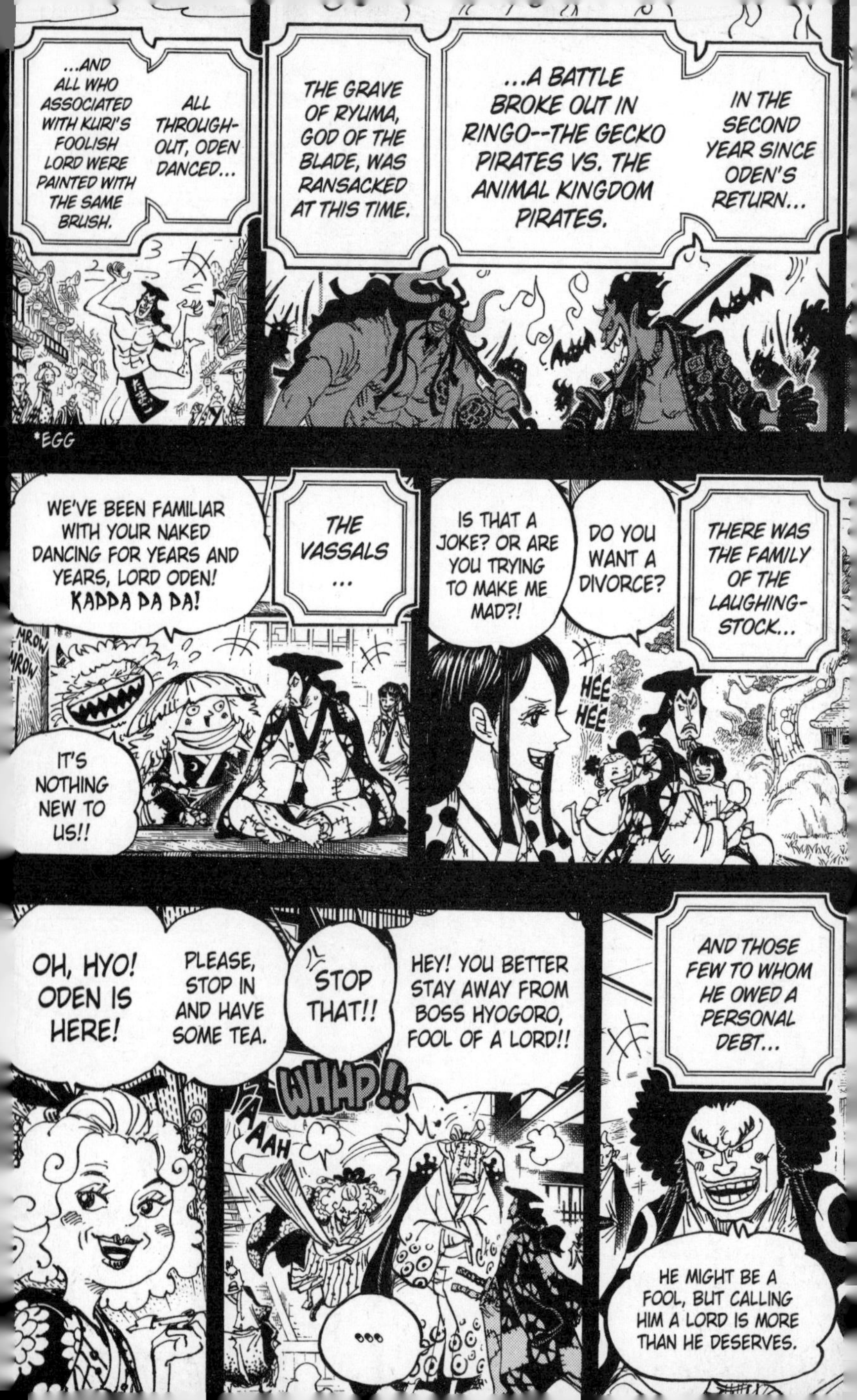
IN THE SECOND YEAR SINCE ODEN'S RETURN...
...A BATTLE BROKE OUT IN RINGO--THE GECKO PIRATES VS. THE ANIMAL KINGDOM PIRATES.
THE GRAVE OF RYUMA, GOD OF THE BLADE, WAS RANSACKED AT THIS TIME.
ALL THROUGHOUT, ODEN DANCED...
...AND ALL WHO ASSOCIATED WITH KURI'S FOOLISH LORD WERE PAINTED WITH THE SAME BRUSH.
*EGG
THERE WAS THE FAMILY OF THE LAUGHING-STOCK...
DO YOU WANT A DIVORCE?
IS THAT A JOKE? OR ARE YOU TRYING TO MAKE ME MAD?!
HEE HEE
THE VASSALS ...
WE'VE BEEN FAMILIAR WITH YOUR NAKED DANCING FOR YEARS AND YEARS, LORD ODEN! KAPPA PA PA!
MROW MROW
IT'S NOTHING NEW TO US!!
AND THOSE FEW TO WHOM HE OWED A PERSONAL DEBT...
HE MIGHT BE A FOOL, BUT CALLING HIM A LORD IS MORE THAN HE DESERVES.
HEY! YOU BETTER STAY AWAY FROM BOSS HYOGORO, FOOL OF A LORD!!
STOP THAT!!
WHHP!!
AAAAH
...
OH, HYO! ODEN IS HERE!
PLEASE, STOP IN AND HAVE SOME TEA.

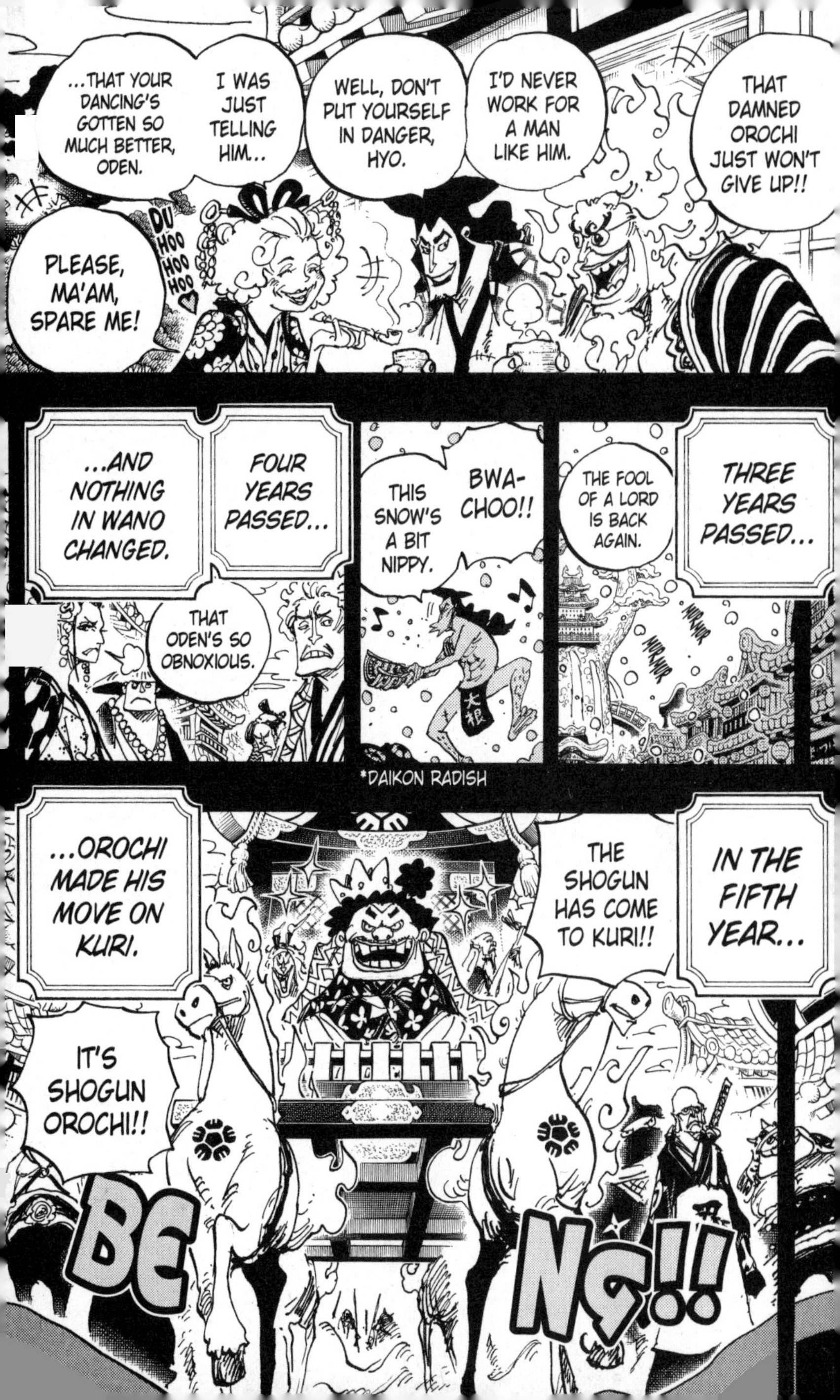

THAT DAMNED OROCHI JUST WON'T GIVE UP!!
I'D NEVER WORK FOR A MAN LIKE HIM.
WELL, DON'T PUT YOURSELF IN DANGER, HYO.
I WAS JUST TELLING HIM...
...THAT YOUR DANCING'S GOTTEN SO MUCH BETTER, ODEN.
DU HOO HOO HOO
PLEASE, MA'AM, SPARE ME!
THREE YEARS PASSED...
THE FOOL OF A LORD IS BACK AGAIN.
BWA-CHOO!!
THIS SNOW'S A BIT NIPPY.
大根
FOUR YEARS PASSED...
...AND NOTHING IN WANO CHANGED.
THAT ODEN'S SO OBNOXIOUS.
*DAIKON RADISH
IN THE FIFTH YEAR...
THE SHOGUN HAS COME TO KURI!!
...OROCHI MADE HIS MOVE ON KURI.
IT'S SHOGUN OROCHI!!
BENG!!

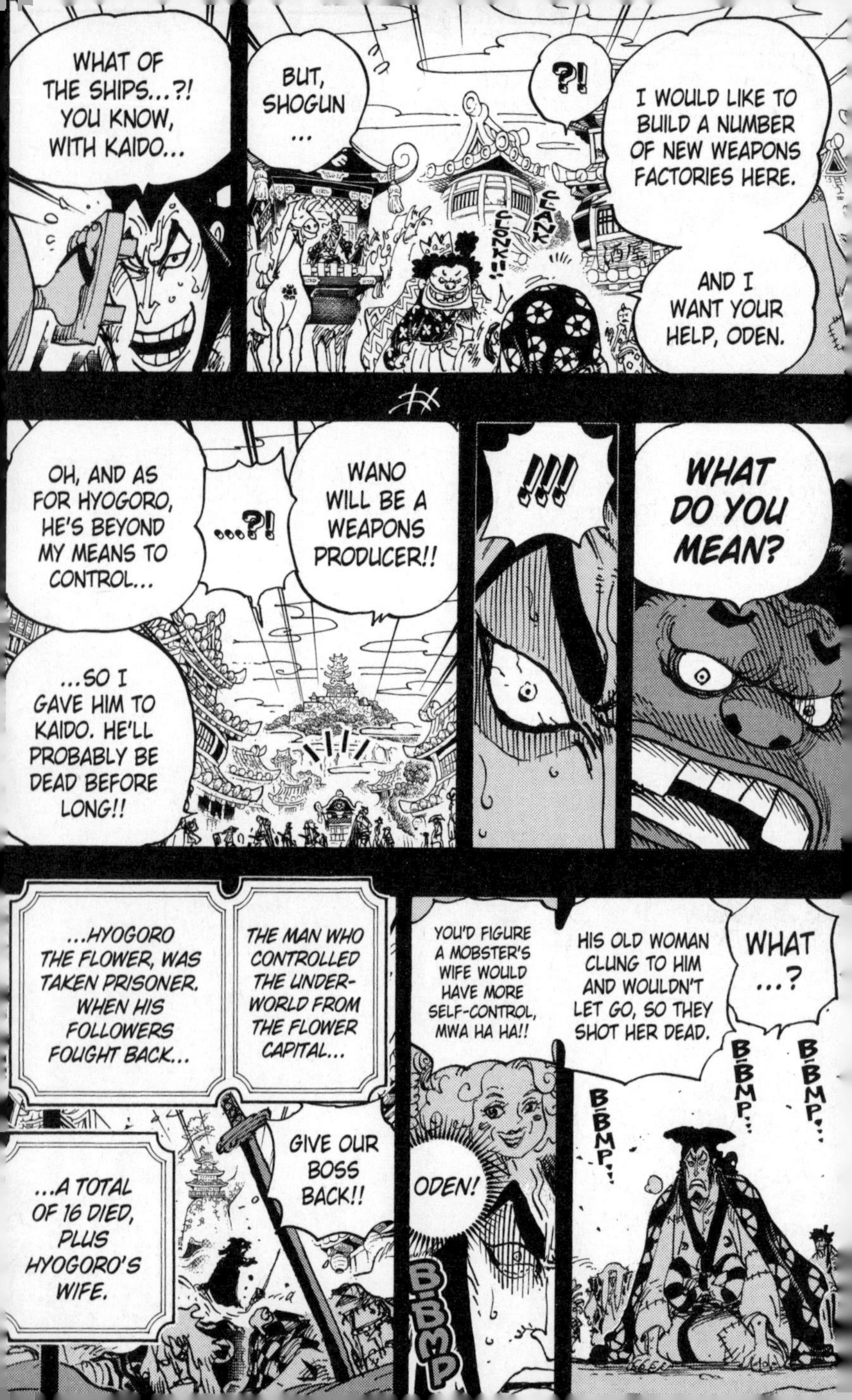

I WOULD LIKE TO BUILD A NUMBER OF NEW WEAPONS FACTORIES HERE.
?!
AND I WANT YOUR HELP, ODEN.
CLANK
CLONK!!
BUT, SHOGUN ...
WHAT OF THE SHIPS...?! YOU KNOW, WITH KAIDO...
WHAT DO YOU MEAN?
!!!
WANO WILL BE A WEAPONS PRODUCER!!
...?!
OH, AND AS FOR HYOGORO, HE'S BEYOND MY MEANS TO CONTROL...
...SO I GAVE HIM TO KAIDO. HE'LL PROBABLY BE DEAD BEFORE LONG!!
WHAT ...?
B-BMP...
HIS OLD WOMAN CLUNG TO HIM AND WOULDN'T LET GO, SO THEY SHOT HER DEAD.
B-BMP...
YOU'D FIGURE A MOBSTER'S WIFE WOULD HAVE MORE SELF-CONTROL, MWA HA HA!!
B-BMP...
ODEN!
B-BMP
THE MAN WHO CONTROLLED THE UNDER-WORLD FROM THE FLOWER CAPITAL...
...HYOGORO THE FLOWER, WAS TAKEN PRISONER. WHEN HIS FOLLOWERS FOUGHT BACK...
GIVE OUR BOSS BACK!!
...A TOTAL OF 16 DIED, PLUS HYOGORO'S WIFE.

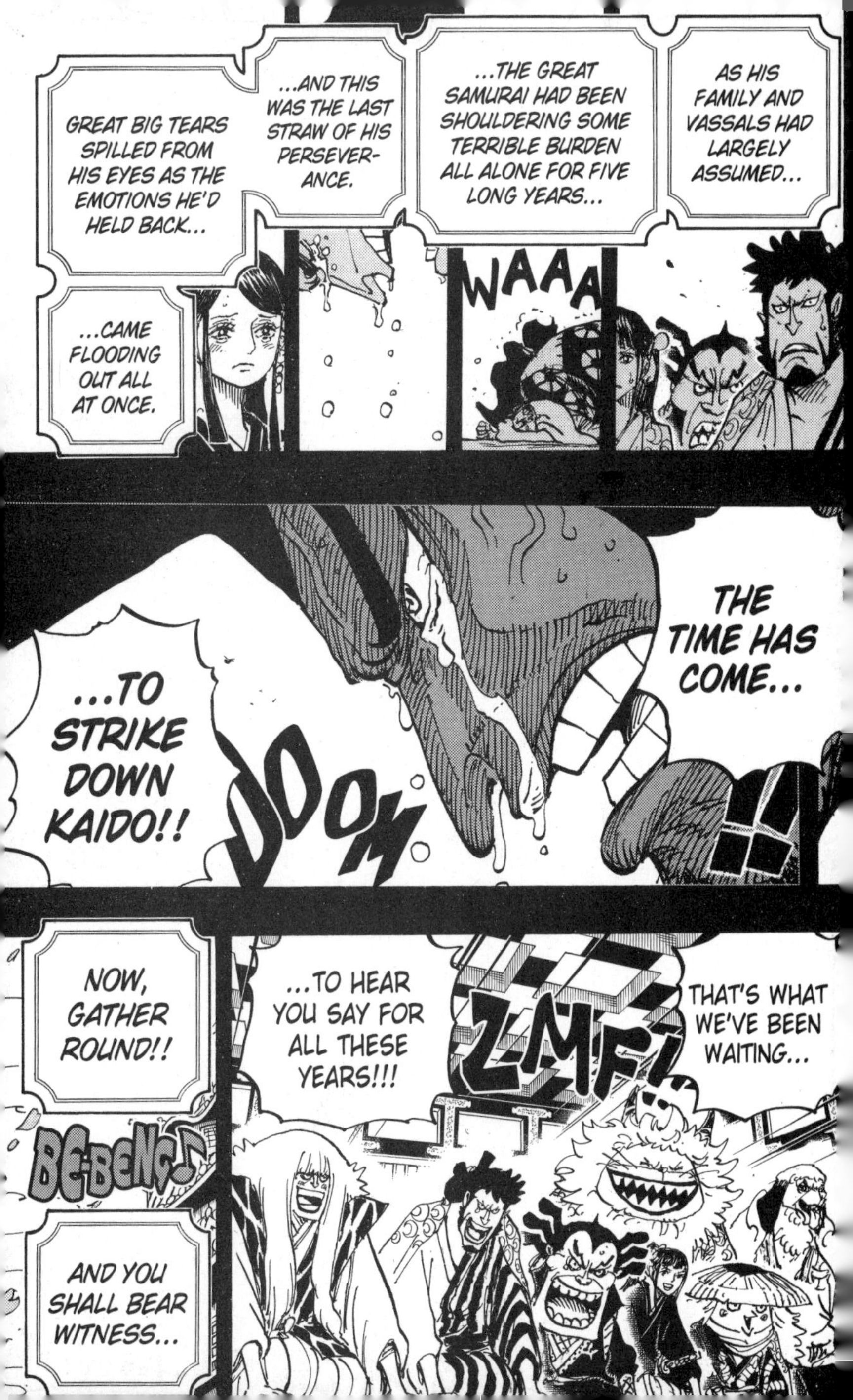
AS HIS FAMILY AND VASSALS HAD LARGELY ASSUMED...
...THE GREAT SAMURAI HAD BEEN SHOULDERING SOME TERRIBLE BURDEN ALL ALONE FOR FIVE LONG YEARS...
WAAA
...AND THIS WAS THE LAST STRAW OF HIS PERSEVER-ANCE.
GREAT BIG TEARS SPILLED FROM HIS EYES AS THE EMOTIONS HE'D HELD BACK...
...CAME FLOODING OUT ALL AT ONCE.
THE TIME HAS COME...
DOOM
...TO STRIKE DOWN KAIDO!!
THAT'S WHAT WE'VE BEEN WAITING...
ZMF
...TO HEAR YOU SAY FOR ALL THESE YEARS!!!
NOW, GATHER ROUND!!
BE-BENG♪
AND YOU SHALL BEAR WITNESS...

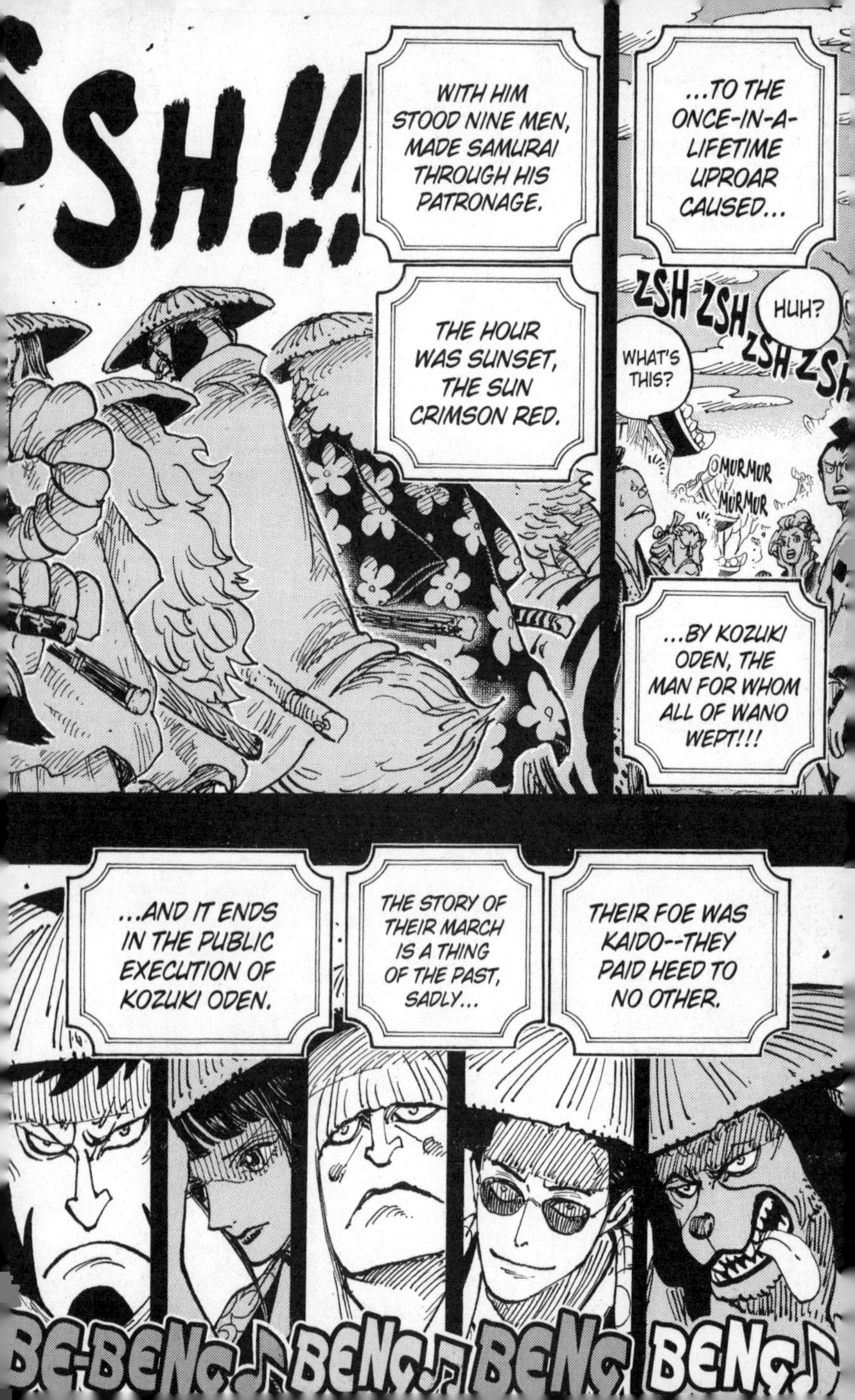
...TO THE ONCE-IN-A-LIFETIME UPROAR CAUSED...
ZSH ZSH ZSH ZSH
HUH?
WHAT'S THIS?
MURMUR
MURMUR
...BY KOZUKI ODEN, THE MAN FOR WHOM ALL OF WANO WEPT!!!
WITH HIM STOOD NINE MEN, MADE SAMURAI THROUGH HIS PATRONAGE.
SH!!
THE HOUR WAS SUNSET, THE SUN CRIMSON RED.
THEIR FOE WAS KAIDO--THEY PAID HEED TO NO OTHER.
THE STORY OF THEIR MARCH IS A THING OF THE PAST, SADLY...
...AND IT ENDS IN THE PUBLIC EXECUTION OF KOZUKI ODEN.
BENG♪
BENG
BENG♪
BE-BENG♪

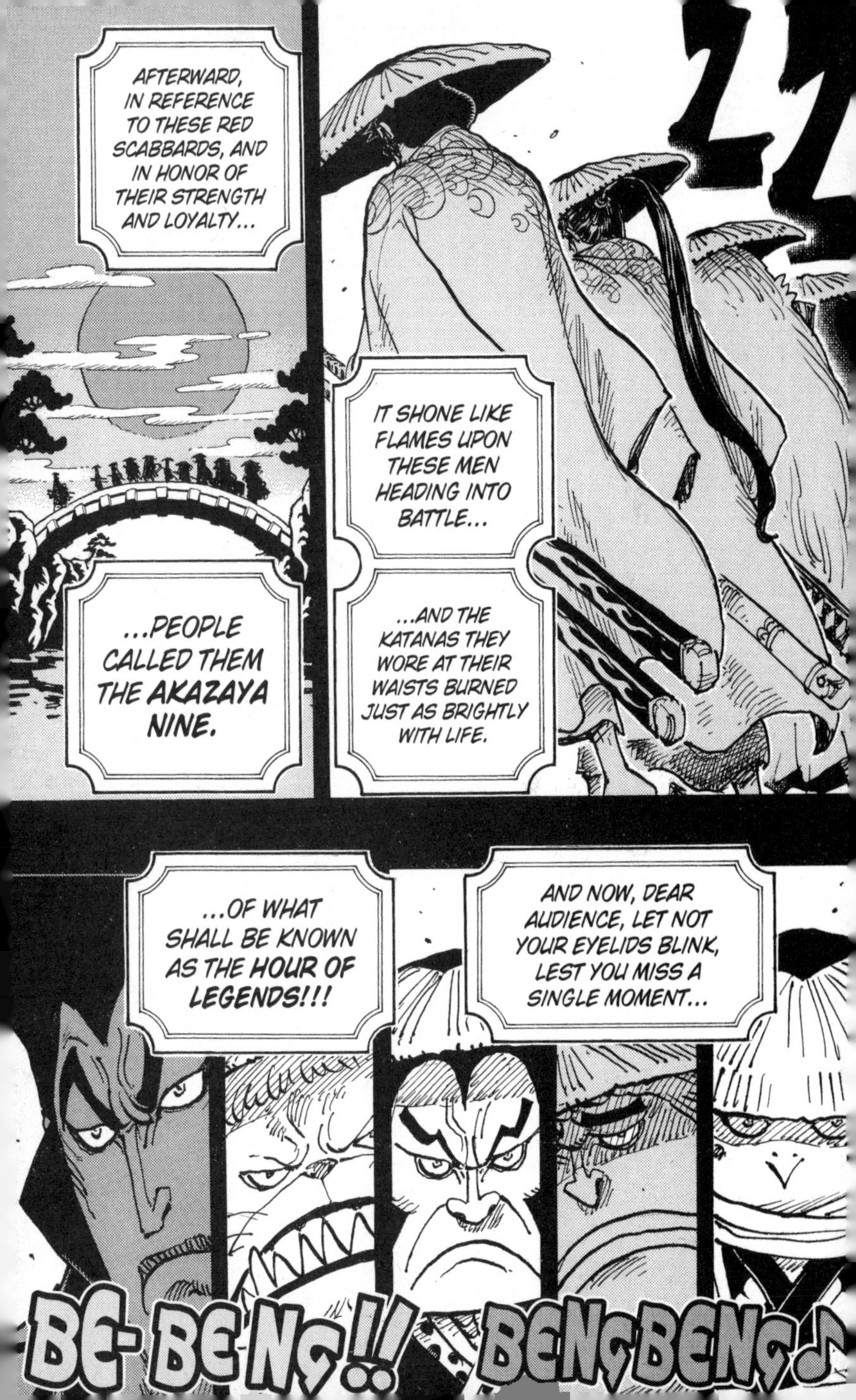

ZZ
IT SHONE LIKE FLAMES UPON THESE MEN HEADING INTO BATTLE...
...AND THE KATANAS THEY WORE AT THEIR WAISTS BURNED JUST AS BRIGHTLY WITH LIFE.
AFTERWARD, IN REFERENCE TO THESE RED SCABBARDS, AND IN HONOR OF THEIR STRENGTH AND LOYALTY...
...PEOPLE CALLED THEM THE **AKAZAYA NINE.**
AND NOW, DEAR AUDIENCE, LET NOT YOUR EYELIDS BLINK, LEST YOU MISS A SINGLE MOMENT...
...OF WHAT SHALL BE KNOWN AS THE **HOUR OF LEGENDS!!!**
BENGBENG♪
BE-BENG!!

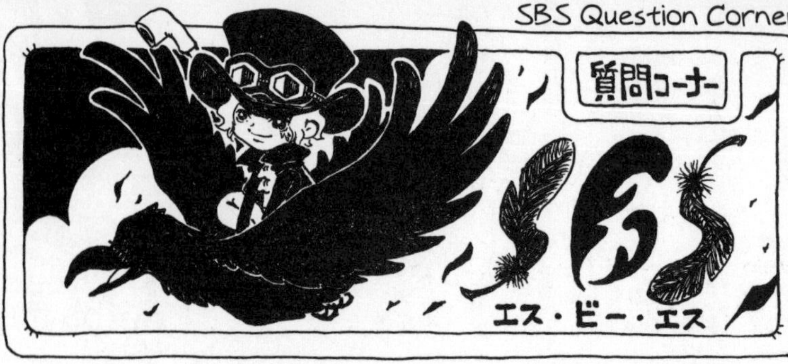
質問コーナー
SBS
エス・ビー・エス

(I ♡ OP, Ishikawa)

Q: Odacchi!! Is Shinobu modeled after Jane?!

--World Economic Part-Timer

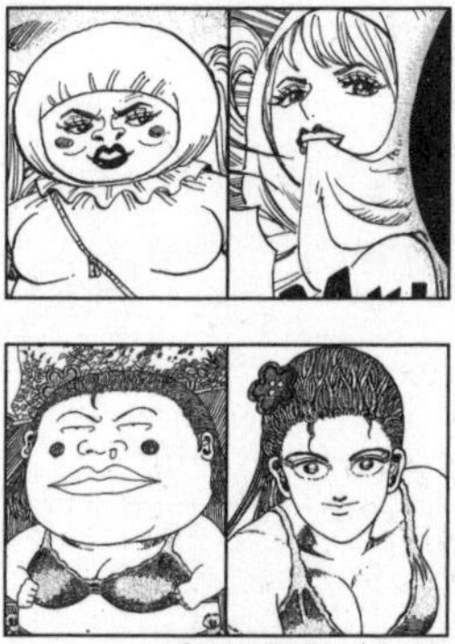

©Masaya Tokuhiro / Shueisha

A: Oh! You think so?! Yeah, I kinda figured it out along the way, myself. Initially I was thinking about how the comedian and actress Naomi Watanabe has such an incredible and vibrant presence, so I based Shinobu on her, but eventually I started thinking, You know, she reminds me of someone... Then I figured out that it was none other than the legendary character Jane from my manga mentor Masaya Tokuhiro's classic series, *King of the Jungle Tar-chan.* Plus, Jane was beautiful when she was younger too, so it's really impossible to deny!

Q: We now know that Kawamatsu isn't a real kappa, but a fish-man. What kind of fish-man is he?

--Gum-Flame Fruit

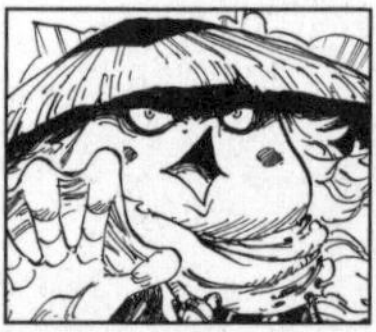

A: He's a tiger pufferfish. But he claims that he's a kappa, so let's just say he's a kappa!

Q: Odacchi! I want to see the human form of Brook's weapon, Soul Solid. I think it should be female, like Mihawk's swords. I think Brook would be very happy with that.

--Odamania's Big Brother

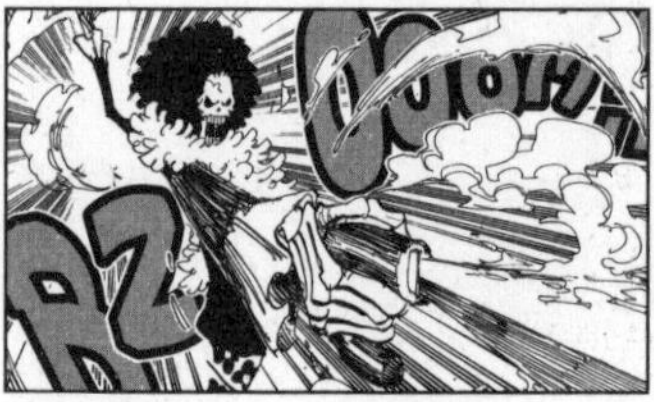

A: A woman. Got it!

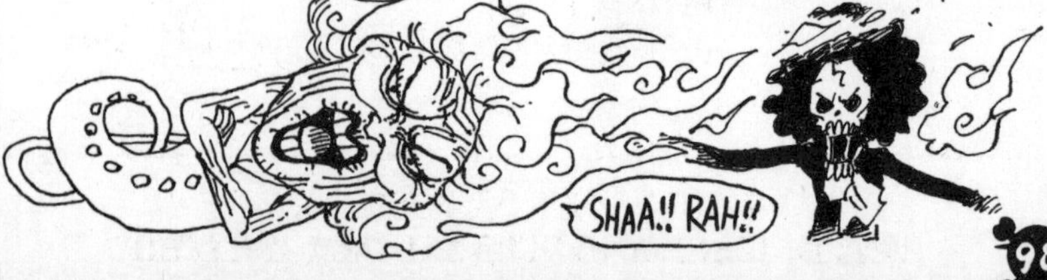
SHAA!! RAH!!

Chapter 970:
ODEN VS. KAIDO

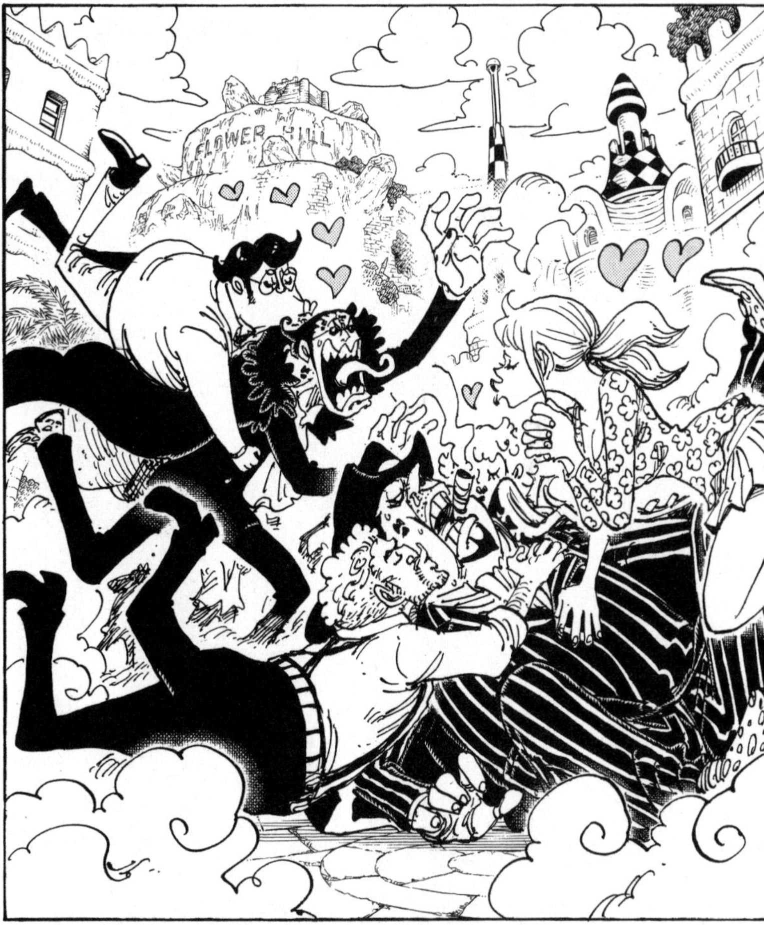
FLOWER HILL

GANG BEGE'S OH MY FAMILY
VOL. 19: "BEGE AND VITO ARE IMMOBILIZED"

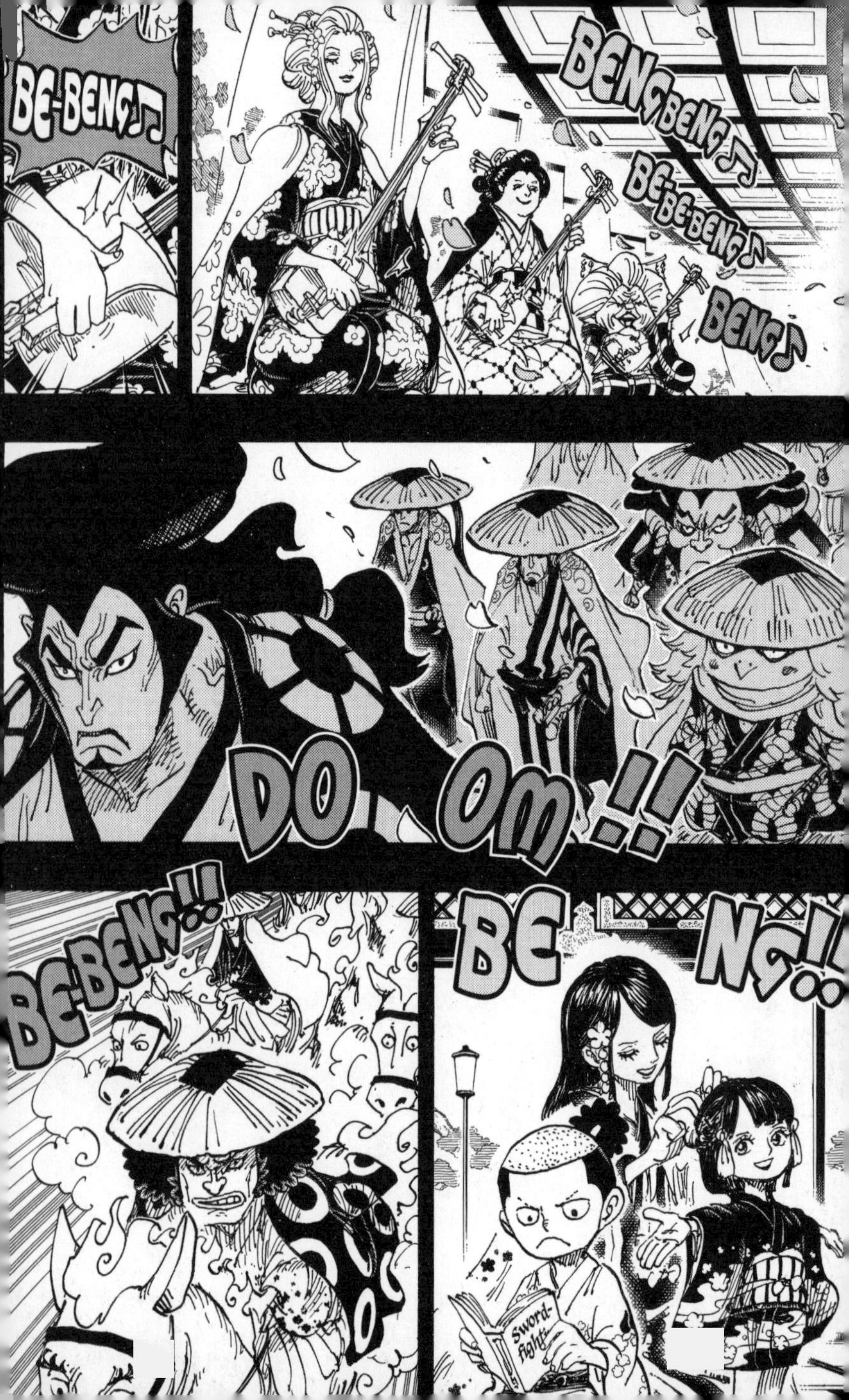
BENG BENG♪
BE-BE-BENG♪
BENG♪
BE-BENG♪
DO OM!!
BE NG!!
Sword-fight
BE-BENG!!

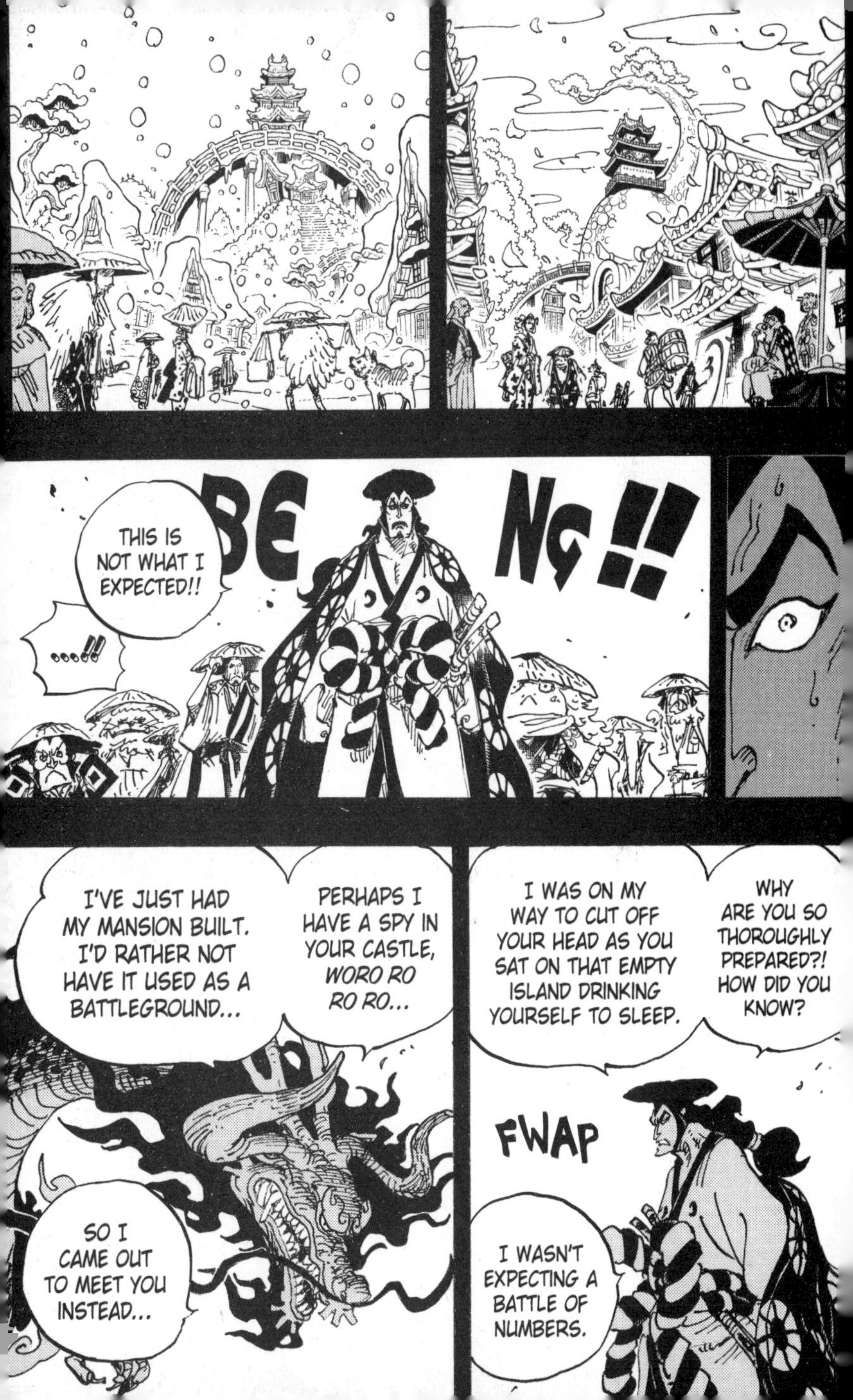

BE NG!!
THIS IS NOT WHAT I EXPECTED!!
....!!
WHY ARE YOU SO THOROUGHLY PREPARED?! HOW DID YOU KNOW?
I WAS ON MY WAY TO CUT OFF YOUR HEAD AS YOU SAT ON THAT EMPTY ISLAND DRINKING YOURSELF TO SLEEP.
FWAP
I WASN'T EXPECTING A BATTLE OF NUMBERS.
PERHAPS I HAVE A SPY IN YOUR CASTLE, *WORO RO RO RO...*
I'VE JUST HAD MY MANSION BUILT. I'D RATHER NOT HAVE IT USED AS A BATTLEGROUND...
SO I CAME OUT TO MEET YOU INSTEAD...

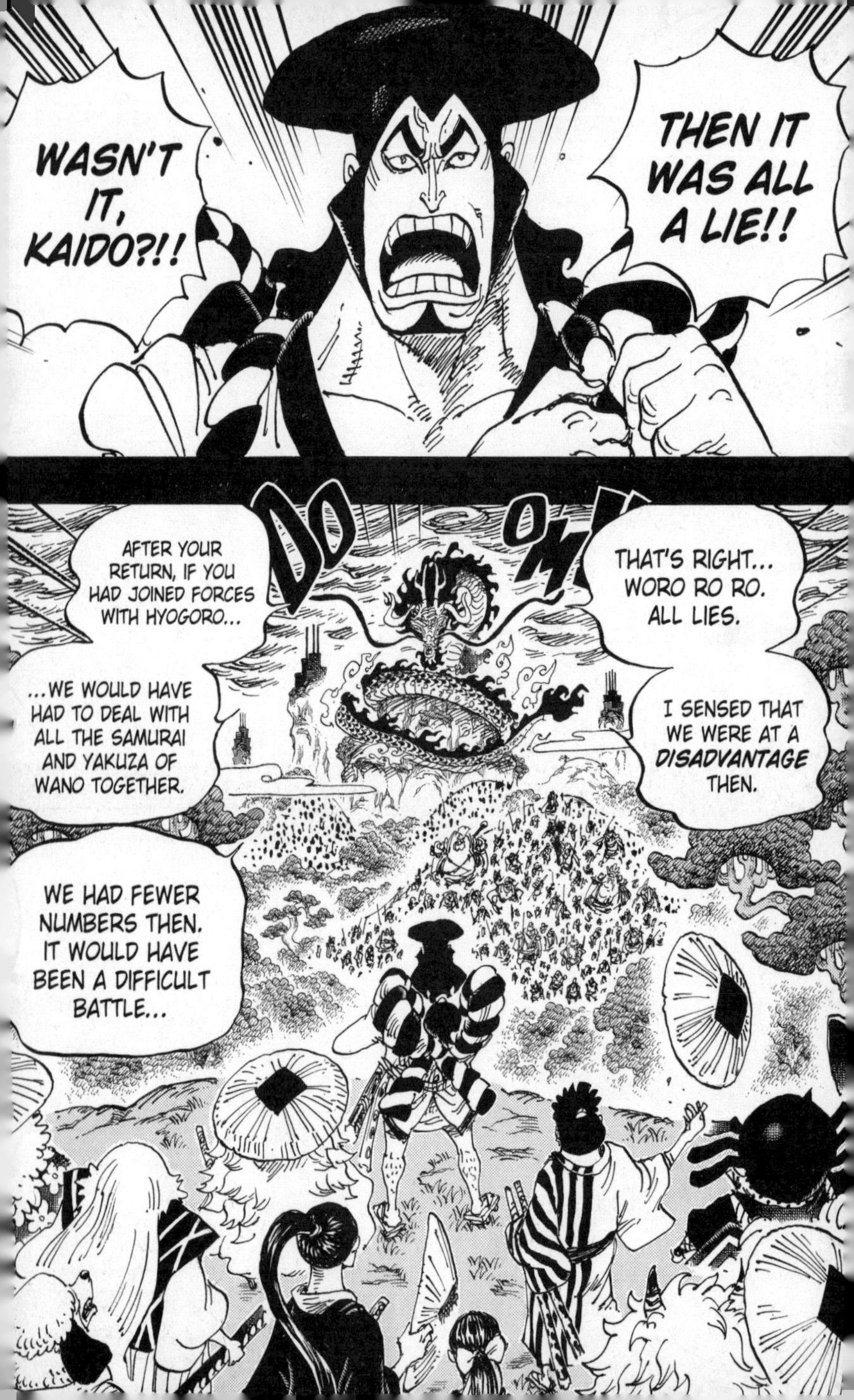
THEN IT WAS ALL A LIE!!
WASN'T IT, KAIDO?!!
DOOM
THAT'S RIGHT... WORO RO RO. ALL LIES.
I SENSED THAT WE WERE AT A *DISADVANTAGE* THEN.
AFTER YOUR RETURN, IF YOU HAD JOINED FORCES WITH HYOGORO...
...WE WOULD HAVE HAD TO DEAL WITH ALL THE SAMURAI AND YAKUZA OF WANO TOGETHER.
WE HAD FEWER NUMBERS THEN. IT WOULD HAVE BEEN A DIFFICULT BATTLE...

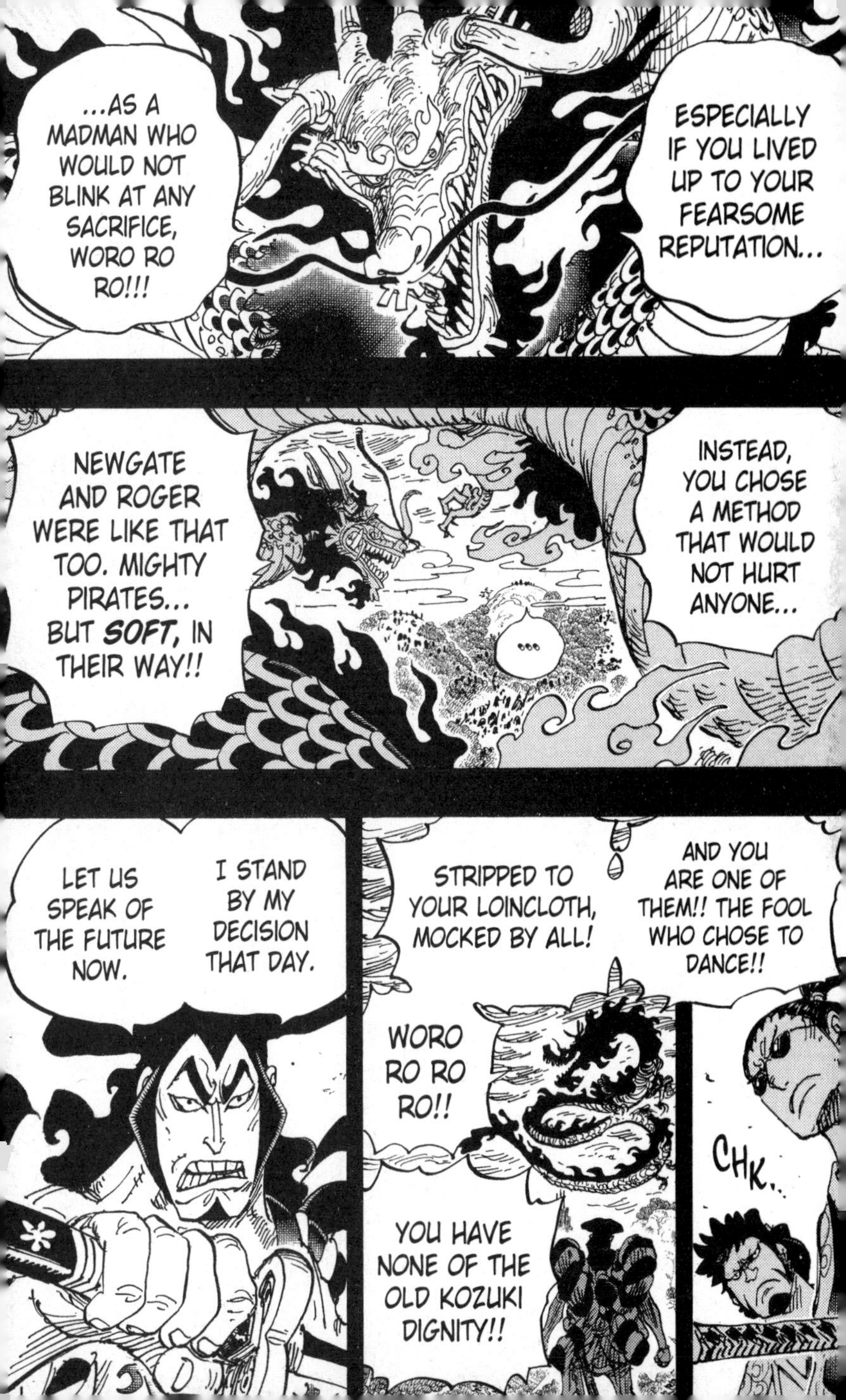
ESPECIALLY IF YOU LIVED UP TO YOUR FEARSOME REPUTATION...
...AS A MADMAN WHO WOULD NOT BLINK AT ANY SACRIFICE, WORO RO RO!!!
INSTEAD, YOU CHOSE A METHOD THAT WOULD NOT HURT ANYONE...
...
NEWGATE AND ROGER WERE LIKE THAT TOO. MIGHTY PIRATES... BUT **SOFT,** IN THEIR WAY!!
AND YOU ARE ONE OF THEM!! THE FOOL WHO CHOSE TO DANCE!!
STRIPPED TO YOUR LOINCLOTH, MOCKED BY ALL!
WORO RO RO RO!!
YOU HAVE NONE OF THE OLD KOZUKI DIGNITY!!
CHK...
I STAND BY MY DECISION THAT DAY.
LET US SPEAK OF THE FUTURE NOW.

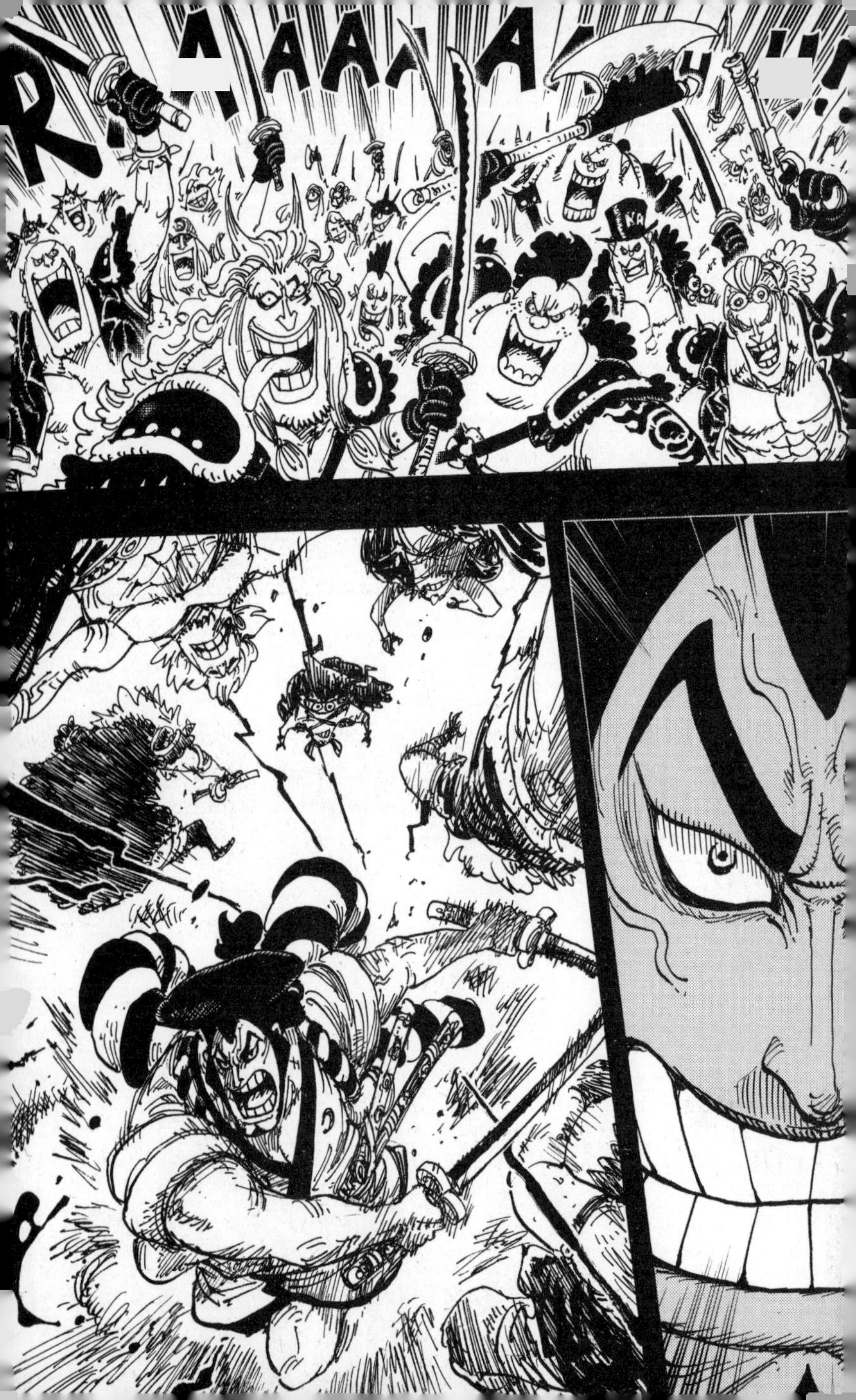

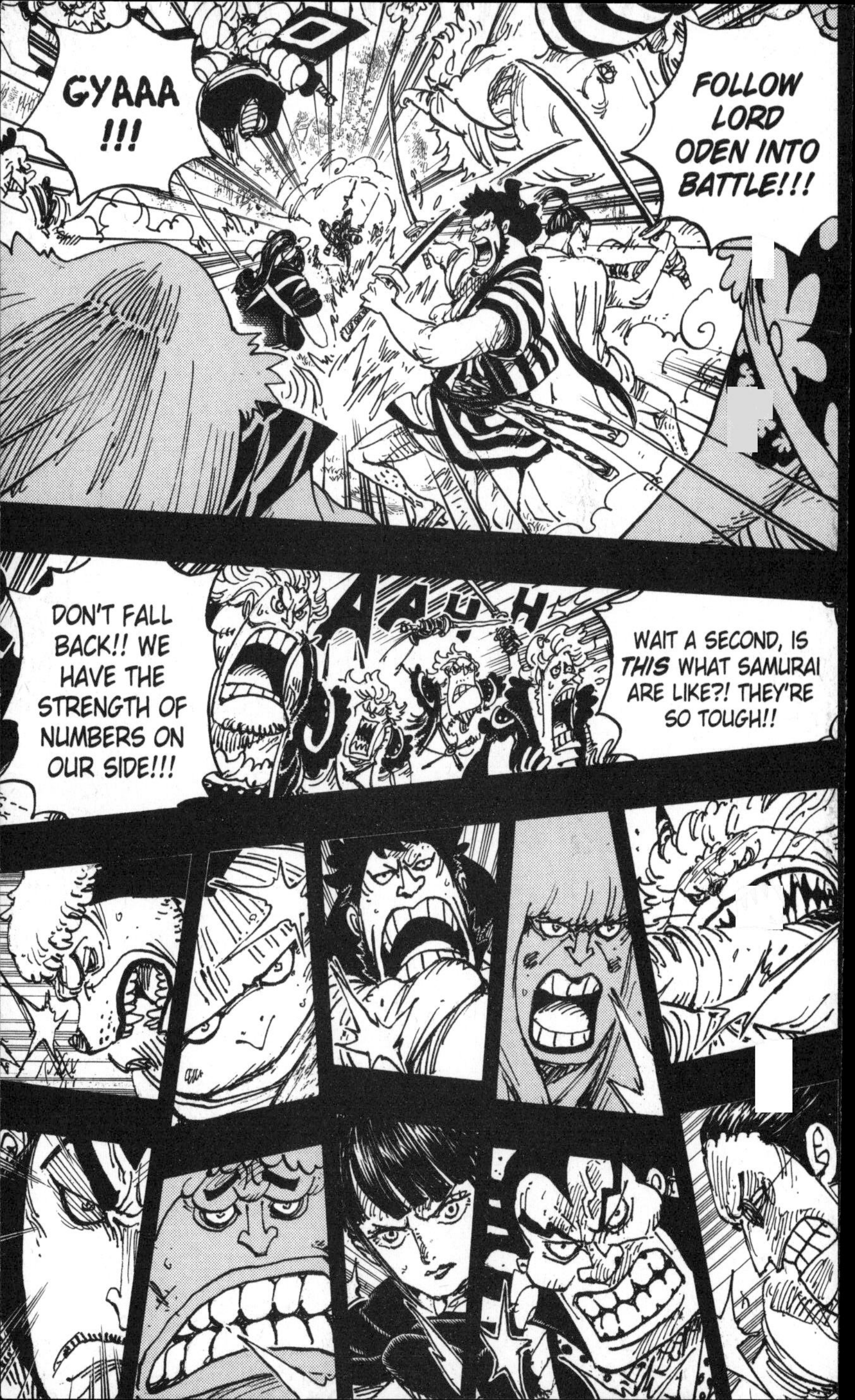
FOLLOW LORD ODEN INTO BATTLE!!!
GYAAA !!!
WAIT A SECOND, IS THIS WHAT SAMURAI ARE LIKE?! THEY'RE SO TOUGH!!
AAUGH
DON'T FALL BACK!! WE HAVE THE STRENGTH OF NUMBERS ON OUR SIDE!!!

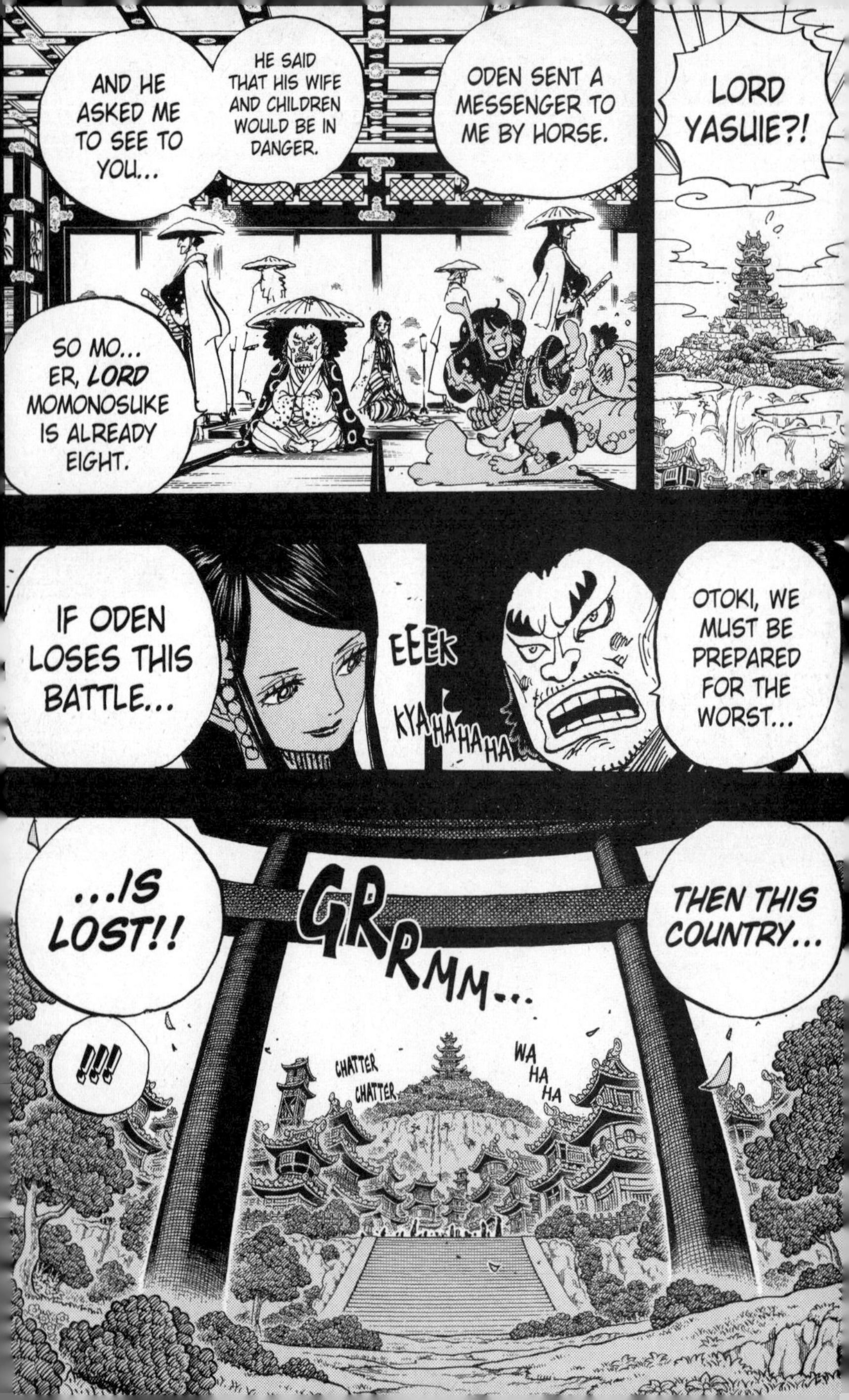
LORD YASUIE?!
ODEN SENT A MESSENGER TO ME BY HORSE.
HE SAID THAT HIS WIFE AND CHILDREN WOULD BE IN DANGER.
AND HE ASKED ME TO SEE TO YOU...
SO MO... ER, *LORD* MOMONOSUKE IS ALREADY EIGHT.
OTOKI, WE MUST BE PREPARED FOR THE WORST...
EEEK
KYAHAHAHAHA
IF ODEN LOSES THIS BATTLE...
THEN THIS COUNTRY...
GRRMM...
...IS LOST!!
WA HA HA
CHATTER CHATTER
!!!

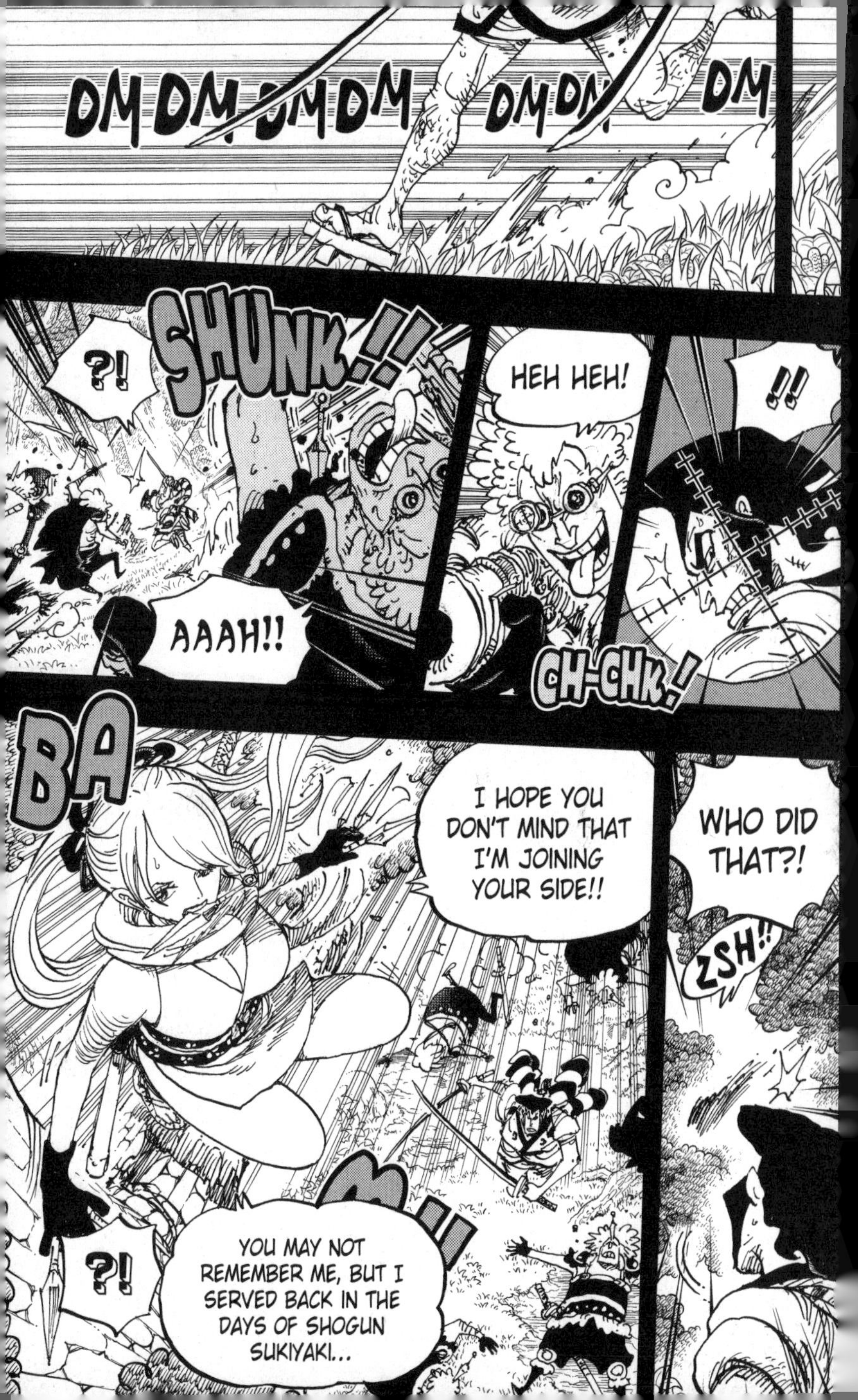
DM DM DM DM DM DM DM
!!
CH-CHK!
HEH HEH!
SHUNK!!!
?!
AAAH!!
WHO DID THAT?!
ZSH!!
I HOPE YOU DON'T MIND THAT I'M JOINING YOUR SIDE!!
BA
?!
YOU MAY NOT REMEMBER ME, BUT I SERVED BACK IN THE DAYS OF SHOGUN SUKIYAKI...

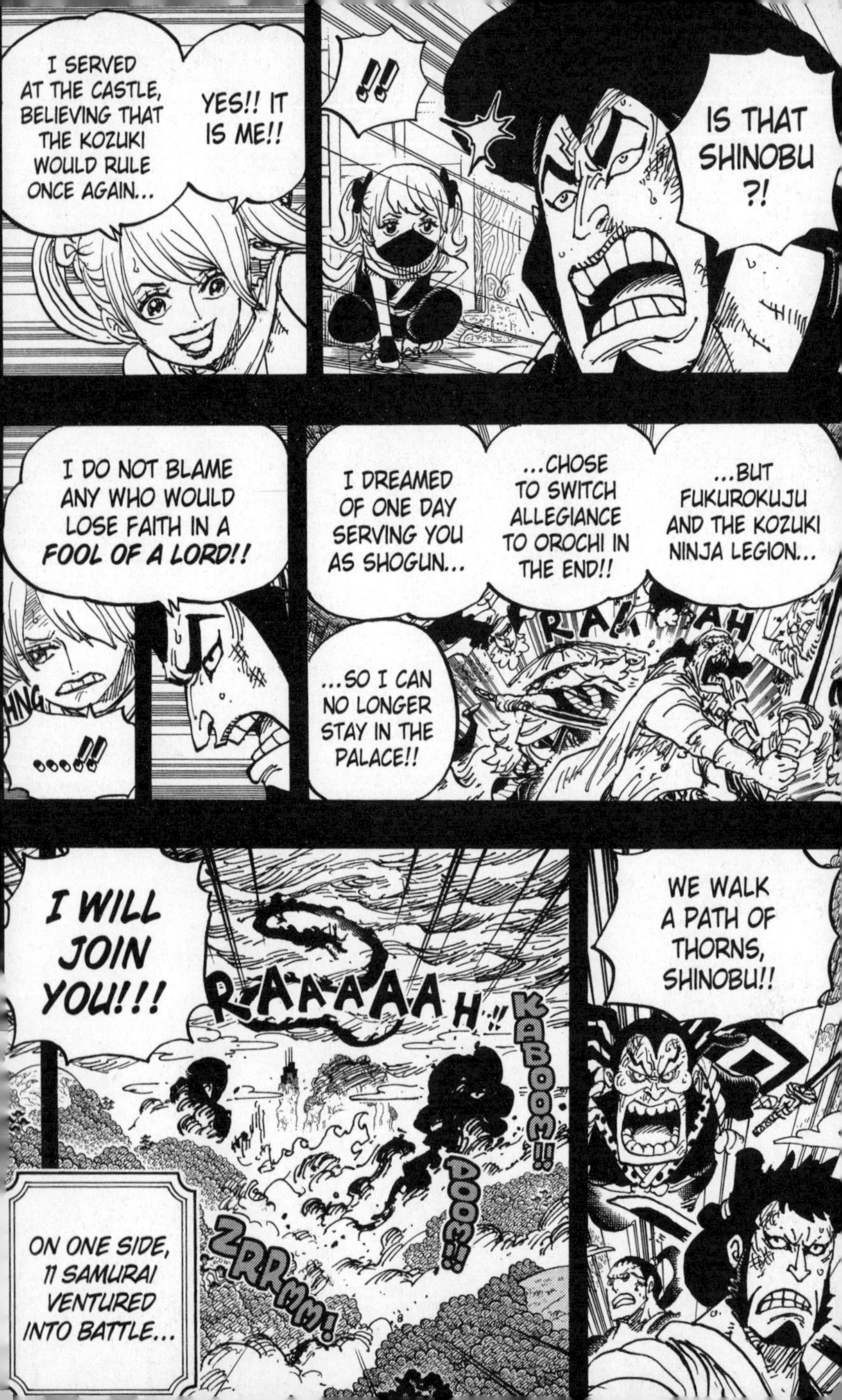
IS THAT SHINOBU ?!
!!
YES!! IT IS ME!!
I SERVED AT THE CASTLE, BELIEVING THAT THE KOZUKI WOULD RULE ONCE AGAIN...
...BUT FUKUROKUJU AND THE KOZUKI NINJA LEGION...
...CHOSE TO SWITCH ALLEGIANCE TO OROCHI IN THE END!!
I DREAMED OF ONE DAY SERVING YOU AS SHOGUN...
...SO I CAN NO LONGER STAY IN THE PALACE!!
I DO NOT BLAME ANY WHO WOULD LOSE FAITH IN A *FOOL OF A LORD!!*
HNG
....!!
WE WALK A PATH OF THORNS, SHINOBU!!
I WILL JOIN YOU!!!
RAAAAAH!!
KABOOM!!
DOOM!!
ZRRMM!
ON ONE SIDE, 11 SAMURAI VENTURED INTO BATTLE...

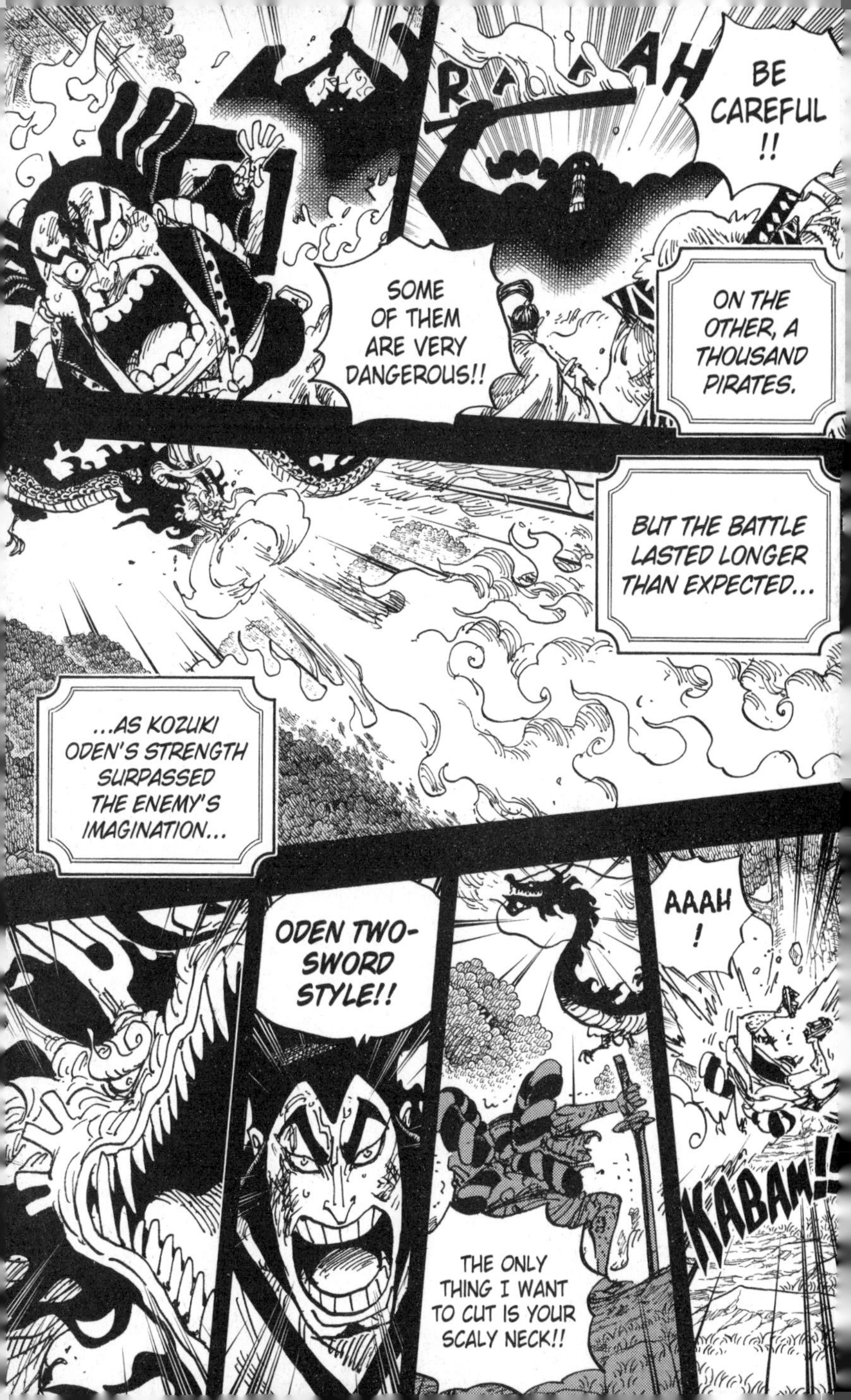
BE CAREFUL!!
ON THE OTHER, A THOUSAND PIRATES.
SOME OF THEM ARE VERY DANGEROUS!!
BUT THE BATTLE LASTED LONGER THAN EXPECTED...
...AS KOZUKI ODEN'S STRENGTH SURPASSED THE ENEMY'S IMAGINATION...
AAAH!
KABAM!!
THE ONLY THING I WANT TO CUT IS YOUR SCALY NECK!!
ODEN TWO-SWORD STYLE!!

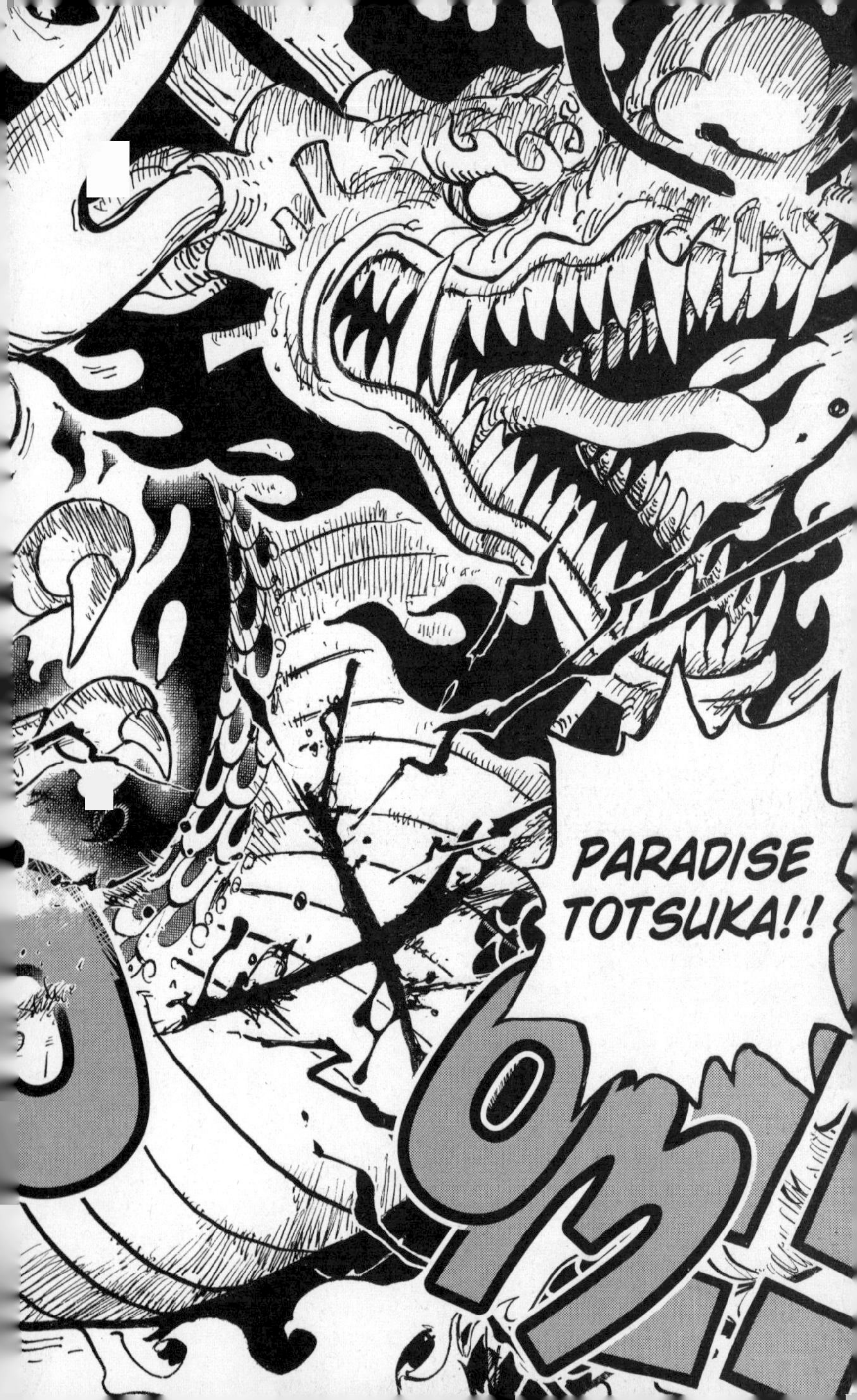
PARADISE TOTSUKA!!

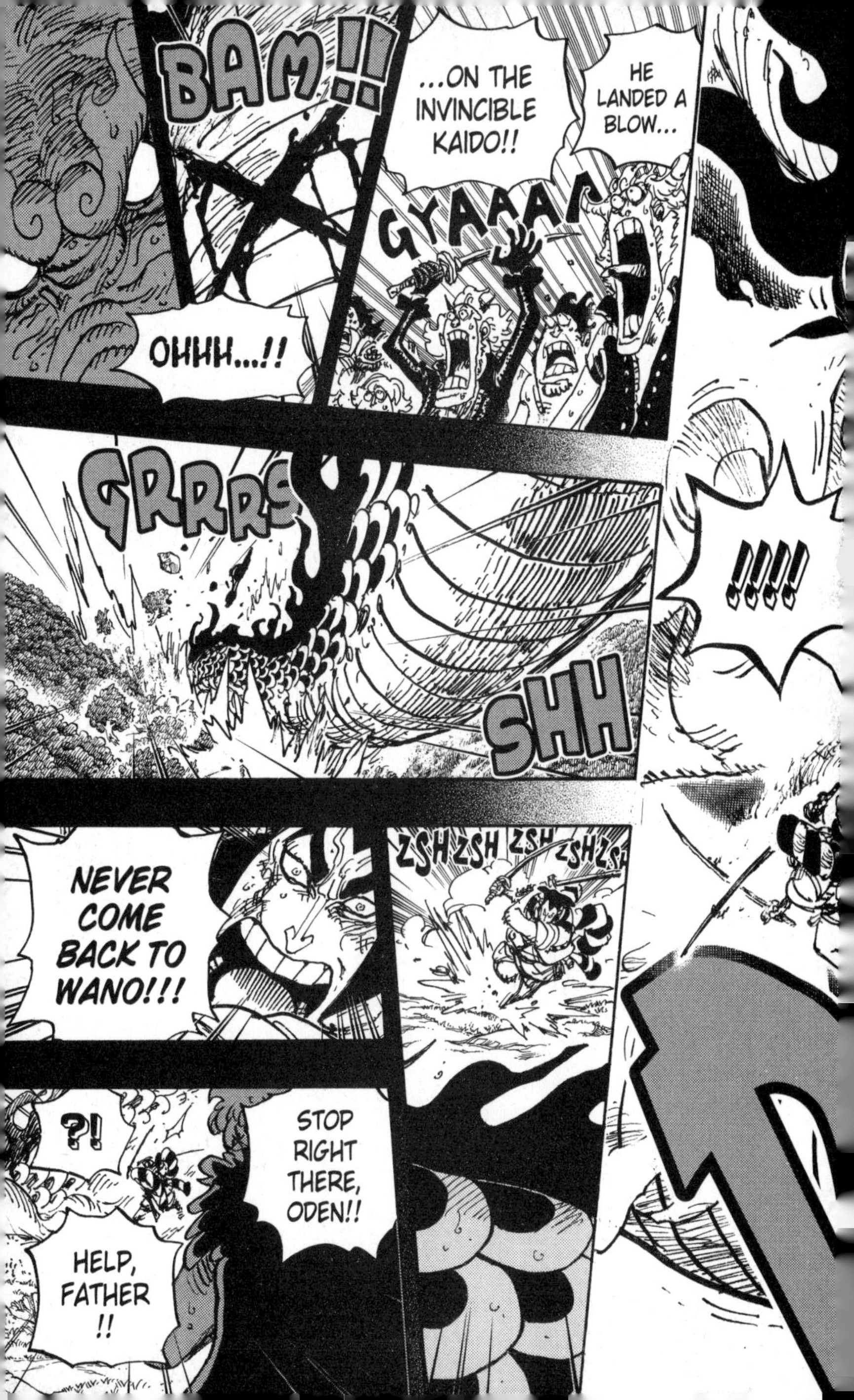
!!!!
HE LANDED A BLOW...
...ON THE INVINCIBLE KAIDO!!
GYAAAA
BAM!!
OHHH...!!
GRRRS
SHH
ZSH ZSH ZSH ZSH ZSH
NEVER COME BACK TO WANO!!!
STOP RIGHT THERE, ODEN!!
?!
HELP, FATHER!!

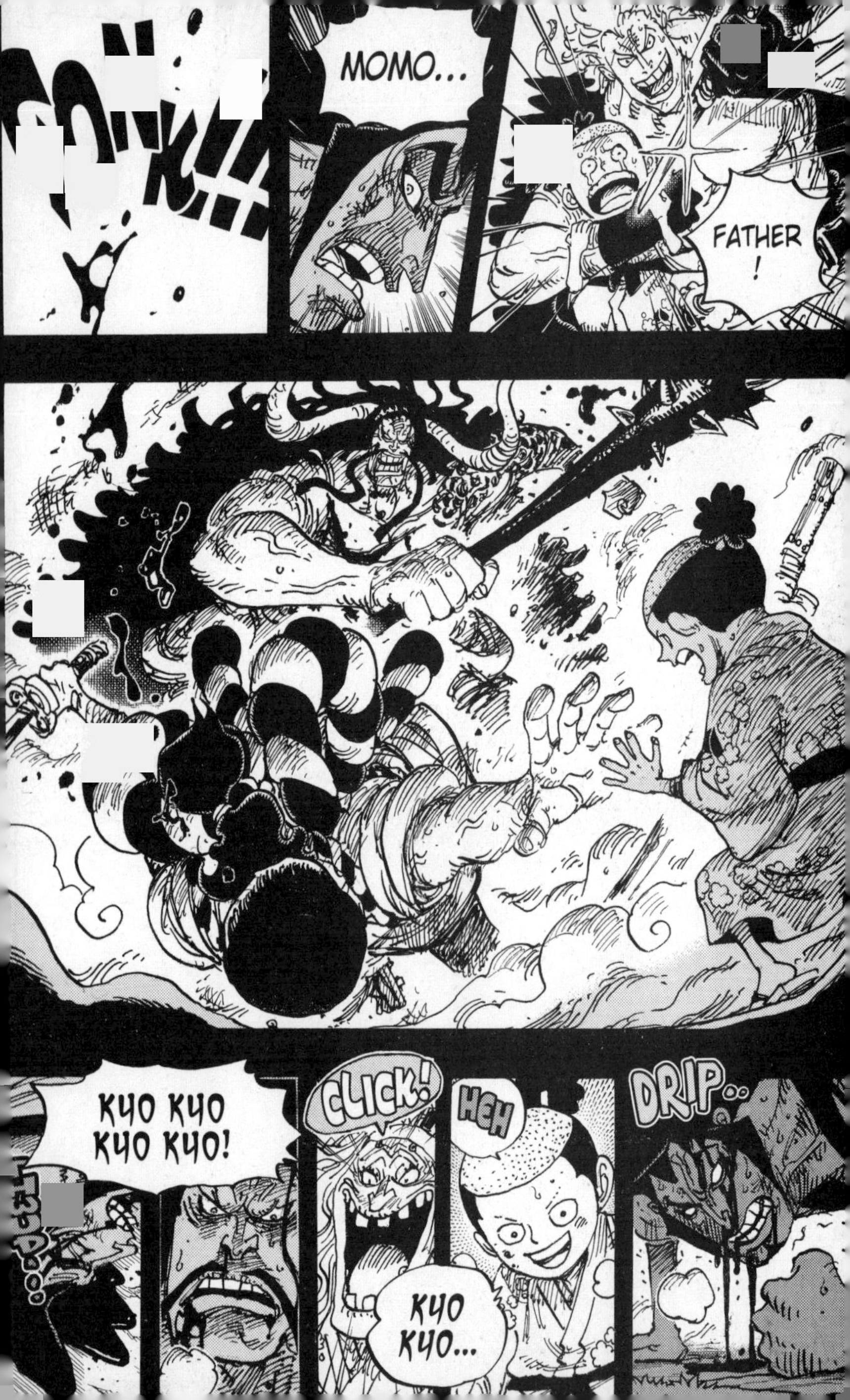
FATHER !
MOMO...
DRIP..
HEH
KYO KYO...
CLICK!
KYO KYO
KYO KYO!

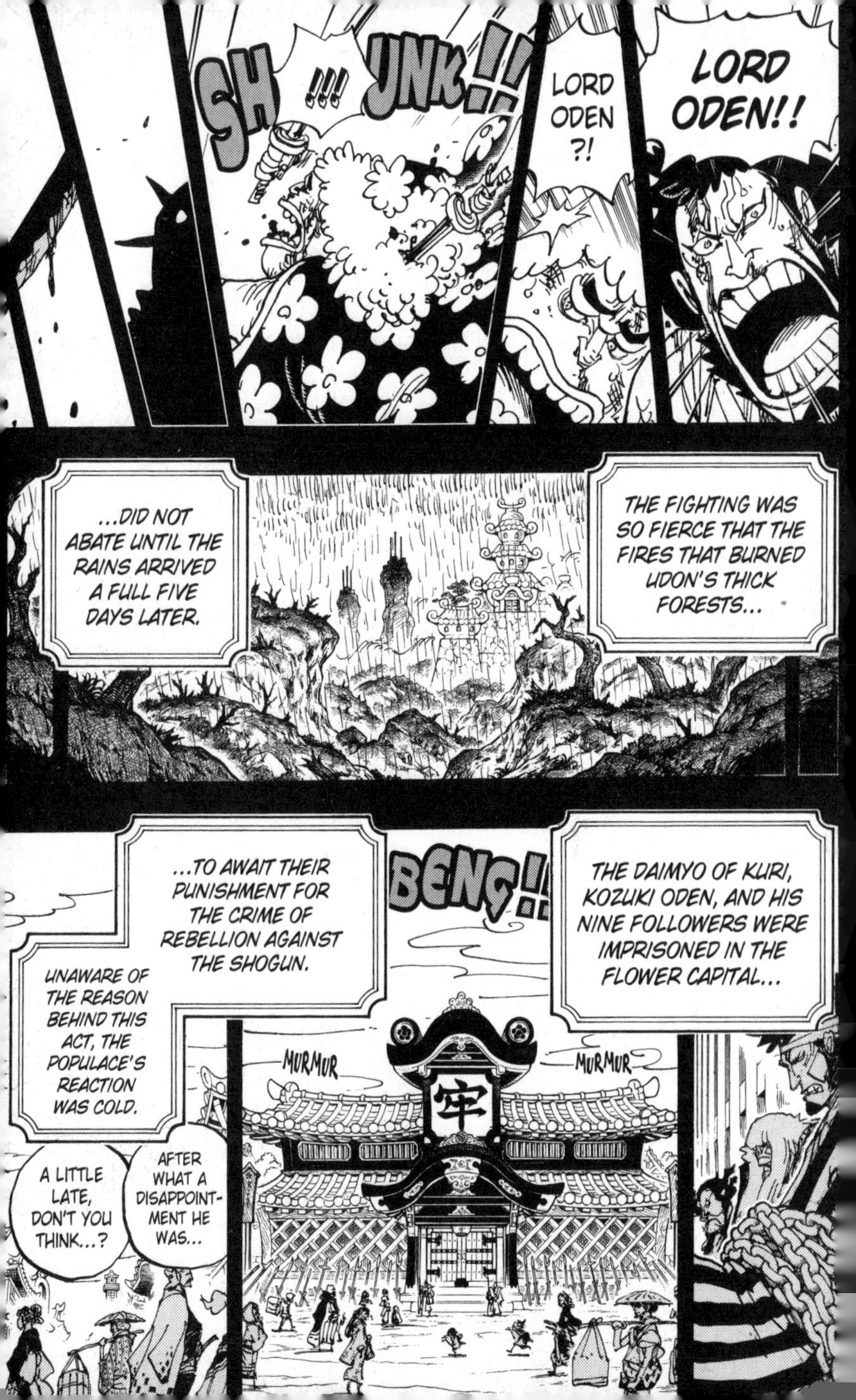
LORD ODEN!!
LORD ODEN ?!
SH!!! UNK!!!
THE FIGHTING WAS SO FIERCE THAT THE FIRES THAT BURNED UDON'S THICK FORESTS...
...DID NOT ABATE UNTIL THE RAINS ARRIVED A FULL FIVE DAYS LATER.
THE DAIMYO OF KURI, KOZUKI ODEN, AND HIS NINE FOLLOWERS WERE IMPRISONED IN THE FLOWER CAPITAL...
BENG!!
...TO AWAIT THEIR PUNISHMENT FOR THE CRIME OF REBELLION AGAINST THE SHOGUN.
UNAWARE OF THE REASON BEHIND THIS ACT, THE POPULACE'S REACTION WAS COLD.
MURMUR
MURMUR
牢
AFTER WHAT A DISAPPOINTMENT HE WAS...
A LITTLE LATE, DON'T YOU THINK...?

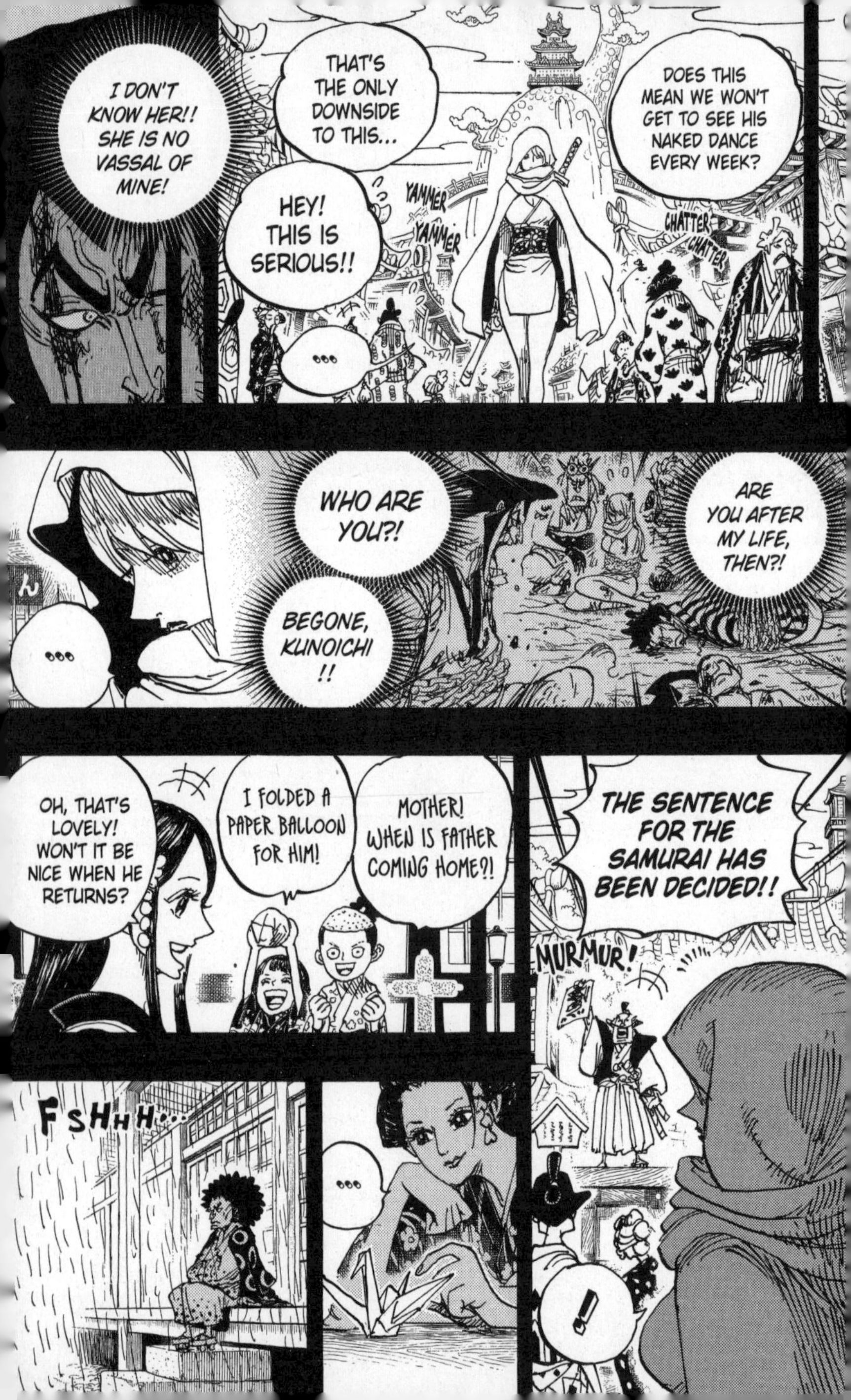
DOES THIS MEAN WE WON'T GET TO SEE HIS NAKED DANCE EVERY WEEK?
CHATTER CHATTER
THAT'S THE ONLY DOWNSIDE TO THIS...
YAMMER YAMMER
HEY! THIS IS SERIOUS!!
...
I DON'T KNOW HER!! SHE IS NO VASSAL OF MINE!
ARE YOU AFTER MY LIFE, THEN?!
WHO ARE YOU?!
BEGONE, KUNOICHI!!
...
THE SENTENCE FOR THE SAMURAI HAS BEEN DECIDED!!
MURMUR!
!
MOTHER! WHEN IS FATHER COMING HOME?!
I FOLDED A PAPER BALLOON FOR HIM!
OH, THAT'S LOVELY! WON'T IT BE NICE WHEN HE RETURNS?
...
FSHHH...

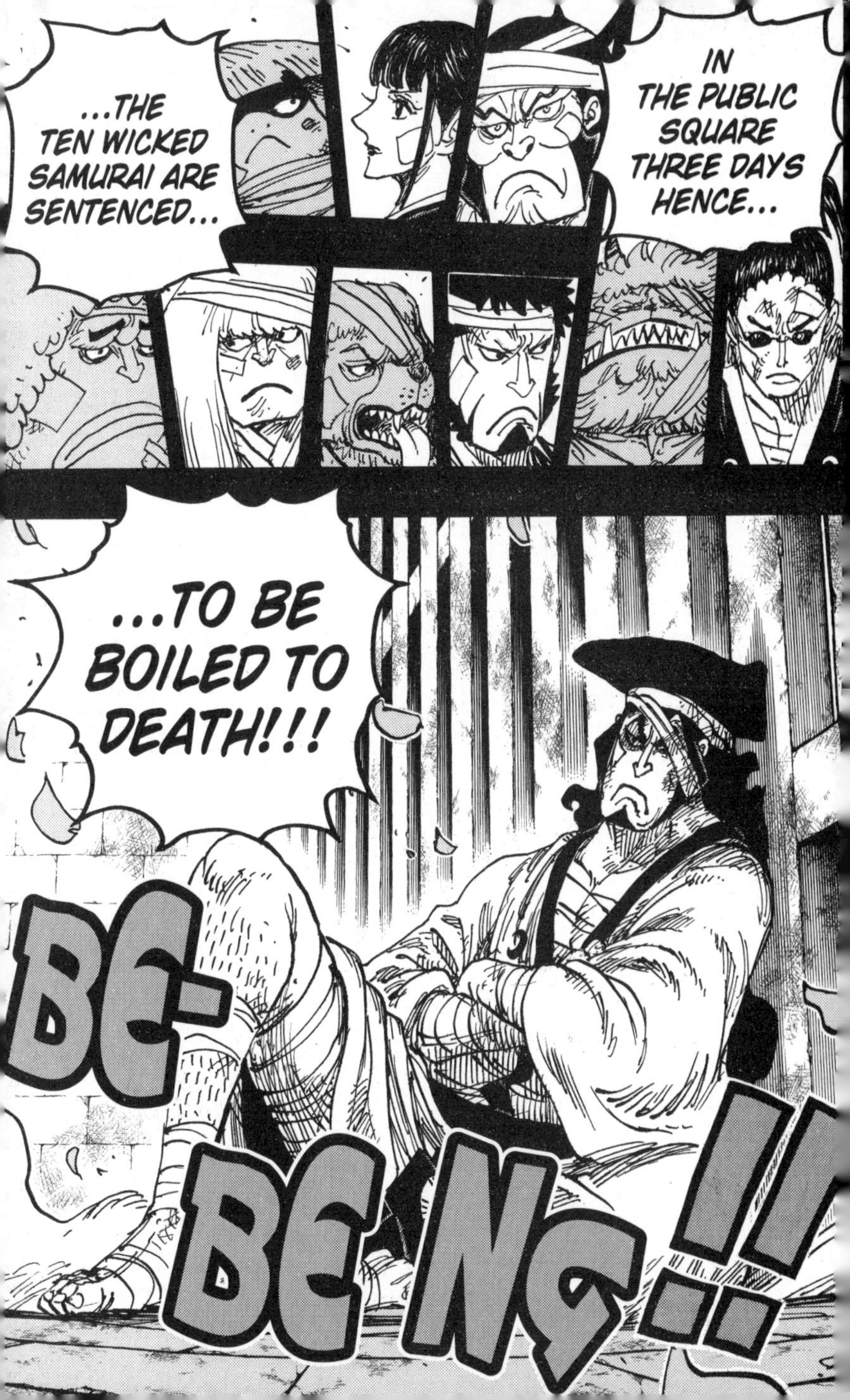
...THE TEN WICKED SAMURAI ARE SENTENCED...
IN THE PUBLIC SQUARE THREE DAYS HENCE...
...TO BE BOILED TO DEATH!!!
BO-BONG..!!

SBS Question Corner

(Buchonosuke, Tochigi)

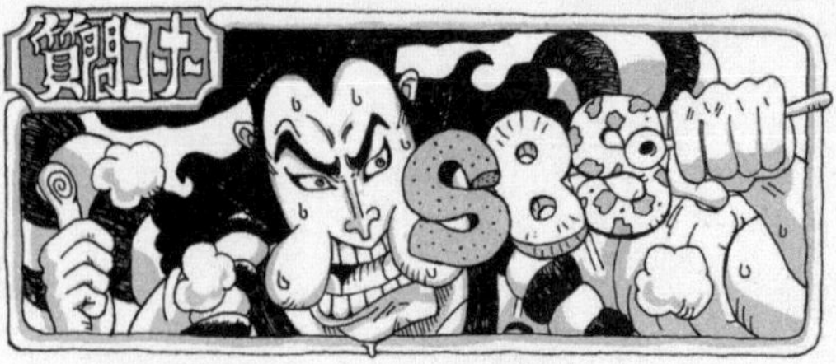

Q: Odacchi!!!♡♡♡ Who is he?! Tell me his name!!

--420 Land

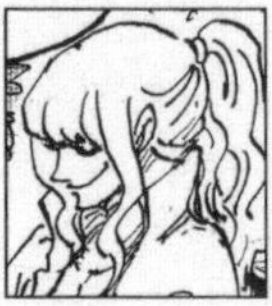

A: You're talking about one of the Roger Pirates. I had lots of questions about Roger's crew, so I'll just put up my rough design sketches of the main members of the group. It'll continue later on page 154, so check them out!! Don't worry, you don't need to know their names!!

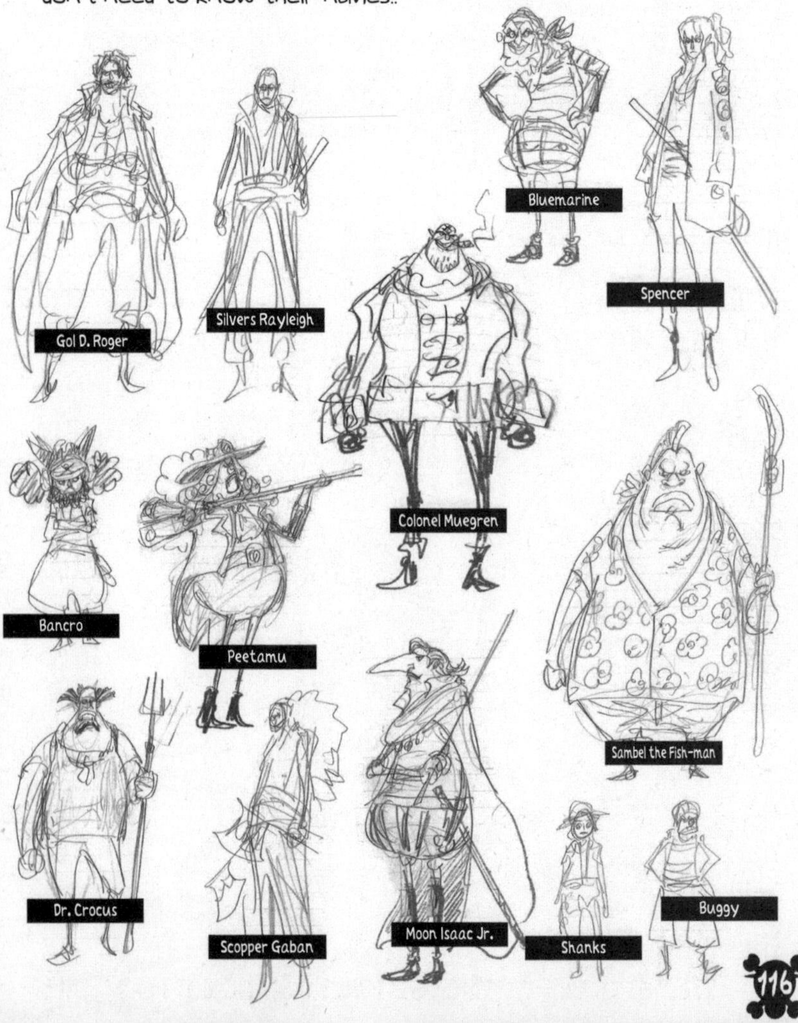

Gol D. Roger
Silvers Rayleigh
Bluemarine
Spencer
Colonel Muegren
Bancro
Peetamu
Sambel the Fish-man
Dr. Crocus
Scopper Gaban
Moon Isaac Jr.
Shanks
Buggy

Chapter 971:
SENTENCED TO BOIL

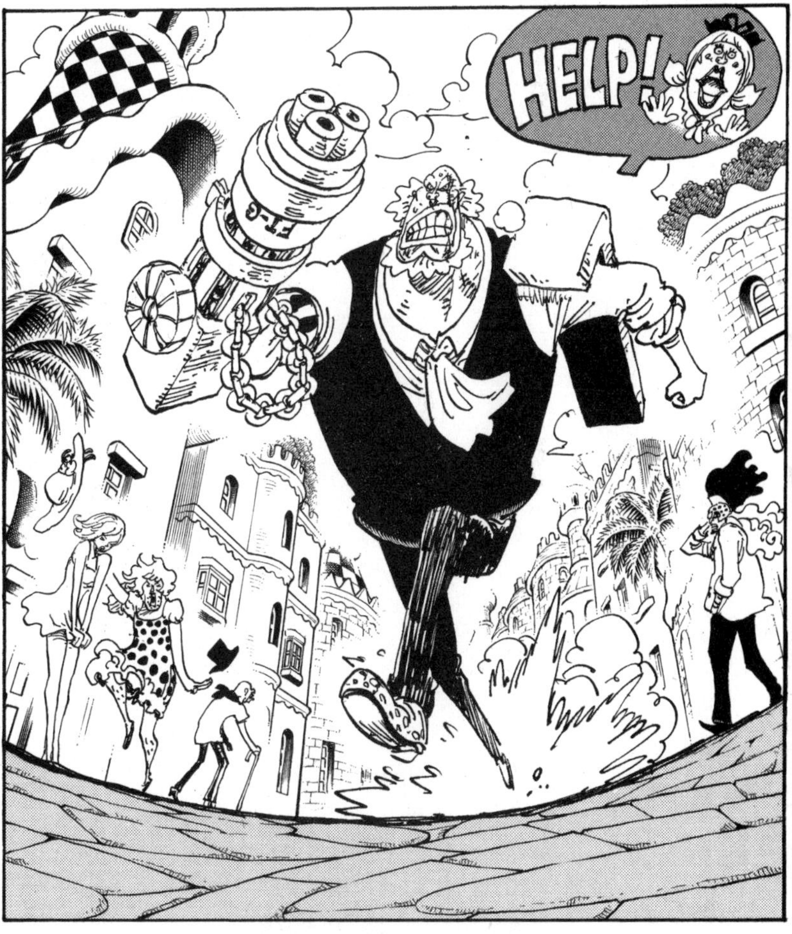
HELP!
FT-G

GANG BEGE'S OH MY FAMILY
VOL. 20: "KEEP GOING, GOTTI! IT'S ALL UP TO YOU!!"

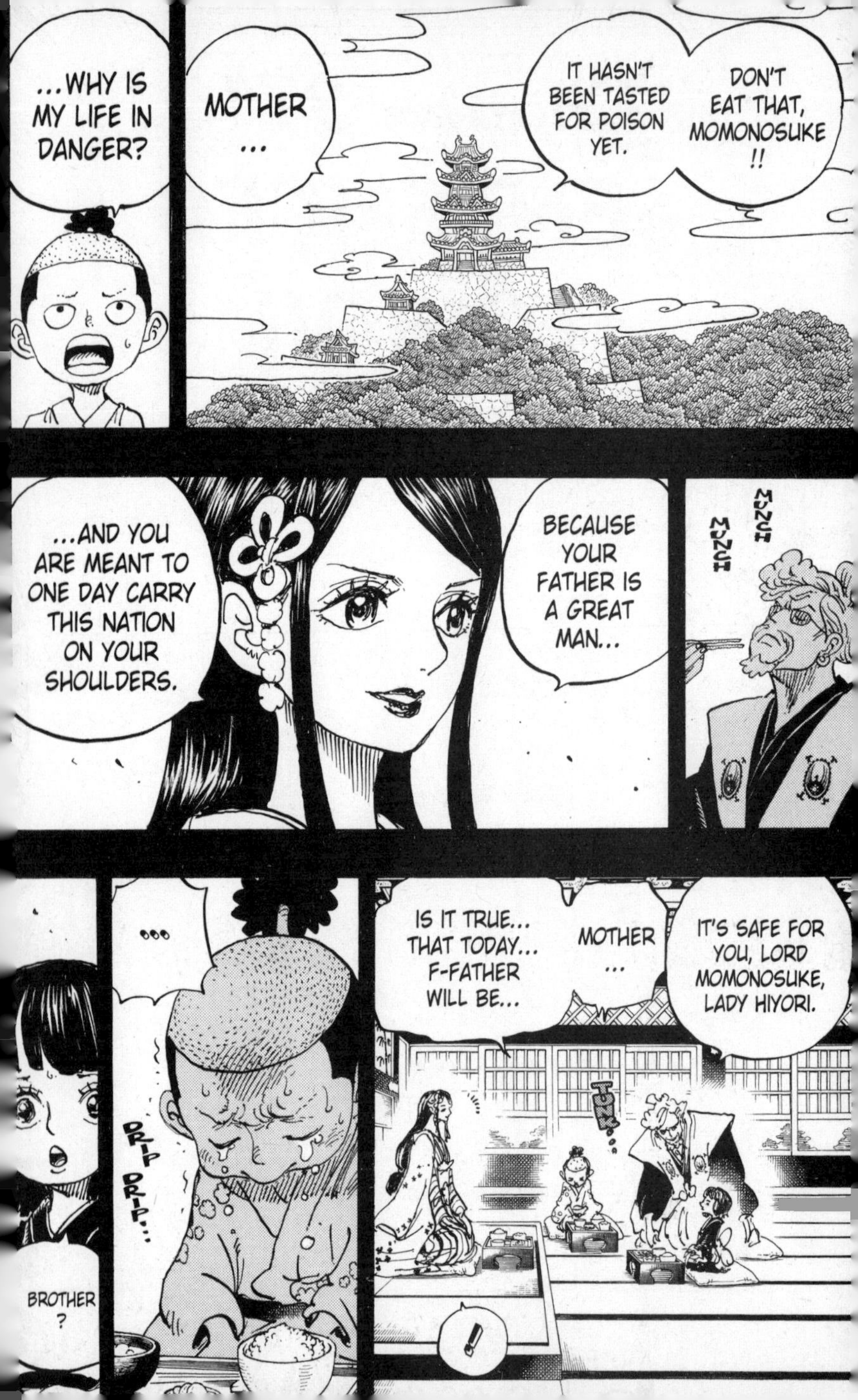
DON'T EAT THAT, MOMONOSUKE!!
IT HASN'T BEEN TASTED FOR POISON YET.
MOTHER...
...WHY IS MY LIFE IN DANGER?
MUNCH
MUNCH
BECAUSE YOUR FATHER IS A GREAT MAN...
...AND YOU ARE MEANT TO ONE DAY CARRY THIS NATION ON YOUR SHOULDERS.
IT'S SAFE FOR YOU, LORD MOMONOSUKE, LADY HIYORI.
MOTHER...
IS IT TRUE... THAT TODAY... F-FATHER WILL BE...
TUNK...
!
...
DRIP DRIP...
BROTHER?

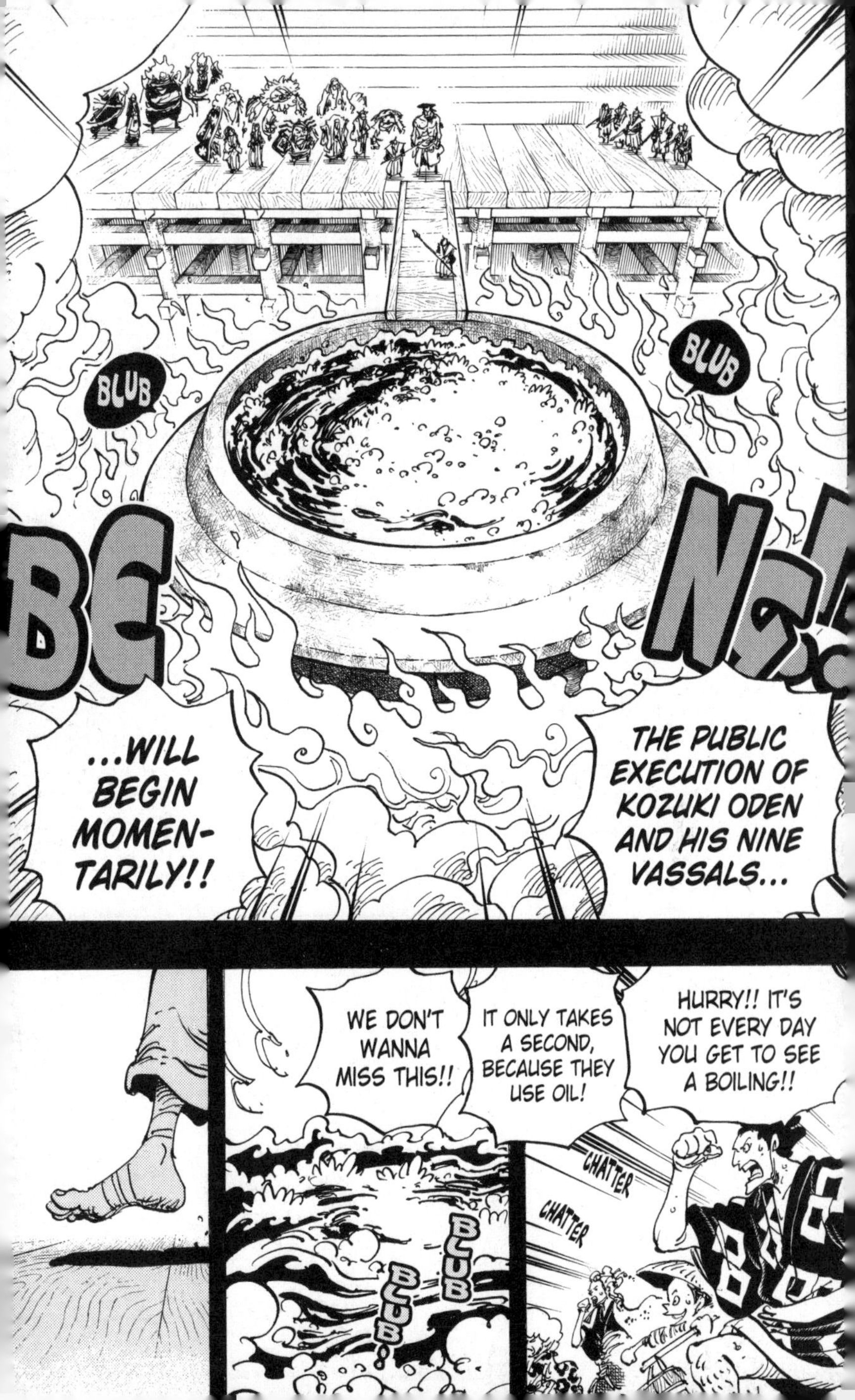
BLUB
BLUB
THE PUBLIC EXECUTION OF KOZUKI ODEN AND HIS NINE VASSALS...
...WILL BEGIN MOMENTARILY!!
HURRY!! IT'S NOT EVERY DAY YOU GET TO SEE A BOILING!!
IT ONLY TAKES A SECOND, BECAUSE THEY USE OIL!
WE DON'T WANNA MISS THIS!!
CHATTER
CHATTER
BLUB
BLUB

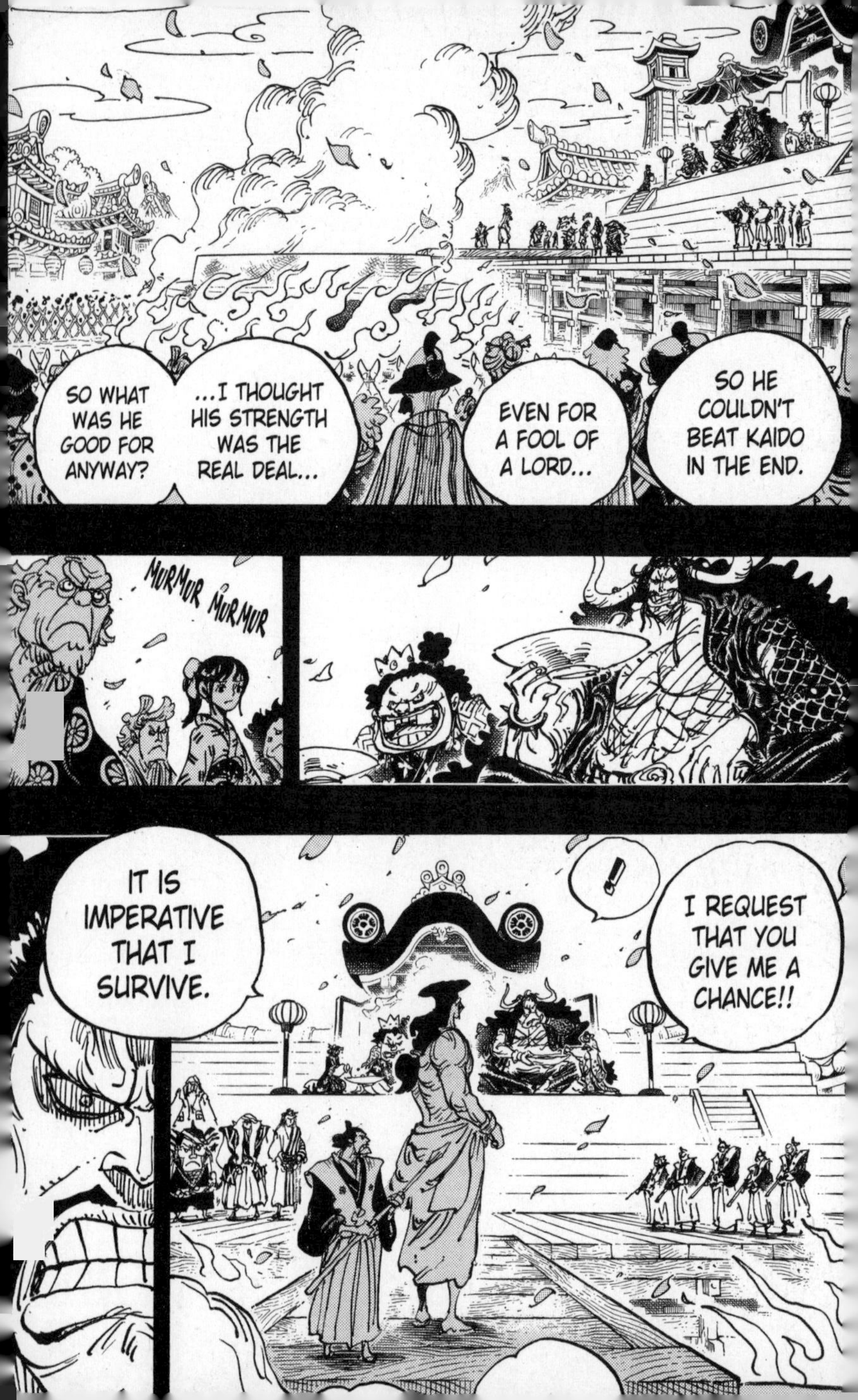
SO HE COULDN'T BEAT KAIDO IN THE END.
EVEN FOR A FOOL OF A LORD...
...I THOUGHT HIS STRENGTH WAS THE REAL DEAL...
SO WHAT WAS HE GOOD FOR ANYWAY?
MURMUR MURMUR
I REQUEST THAT YOU GIVE ME A CHANCE!!
!
IT IS IMPERATIVE THAT I SURVIVE.

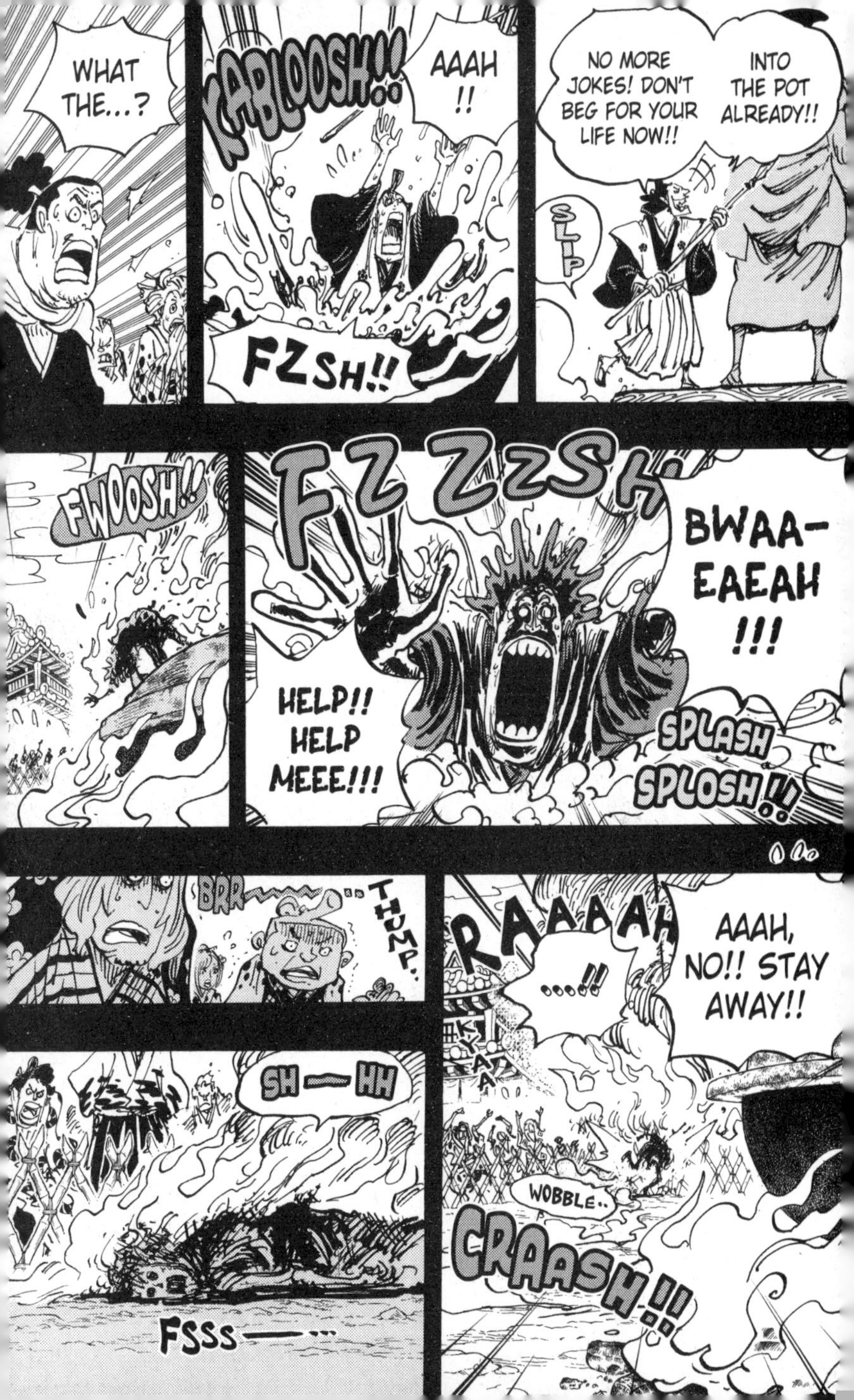
INTO THE POT ALREADY!!
NO MORE JOKES! DON'T BEG FOR YOUR LIFE NOW!!
SLIP
AAAH !!
KABLOOSH!!
FZSH!!
WHAT THE...?
FZZZSH
BWAA-EAEAH!!!
HELP!! HELP MEEE!!!
SPLASH SPLOSH!!
FWOOSH!!
AAAH, NO!! STAY AWAY!!
RAAAAH
....!!
KYAA
WOBBLE..
CRAASH!!
BRR..
THUMP..
SH—HH
FSSS—...

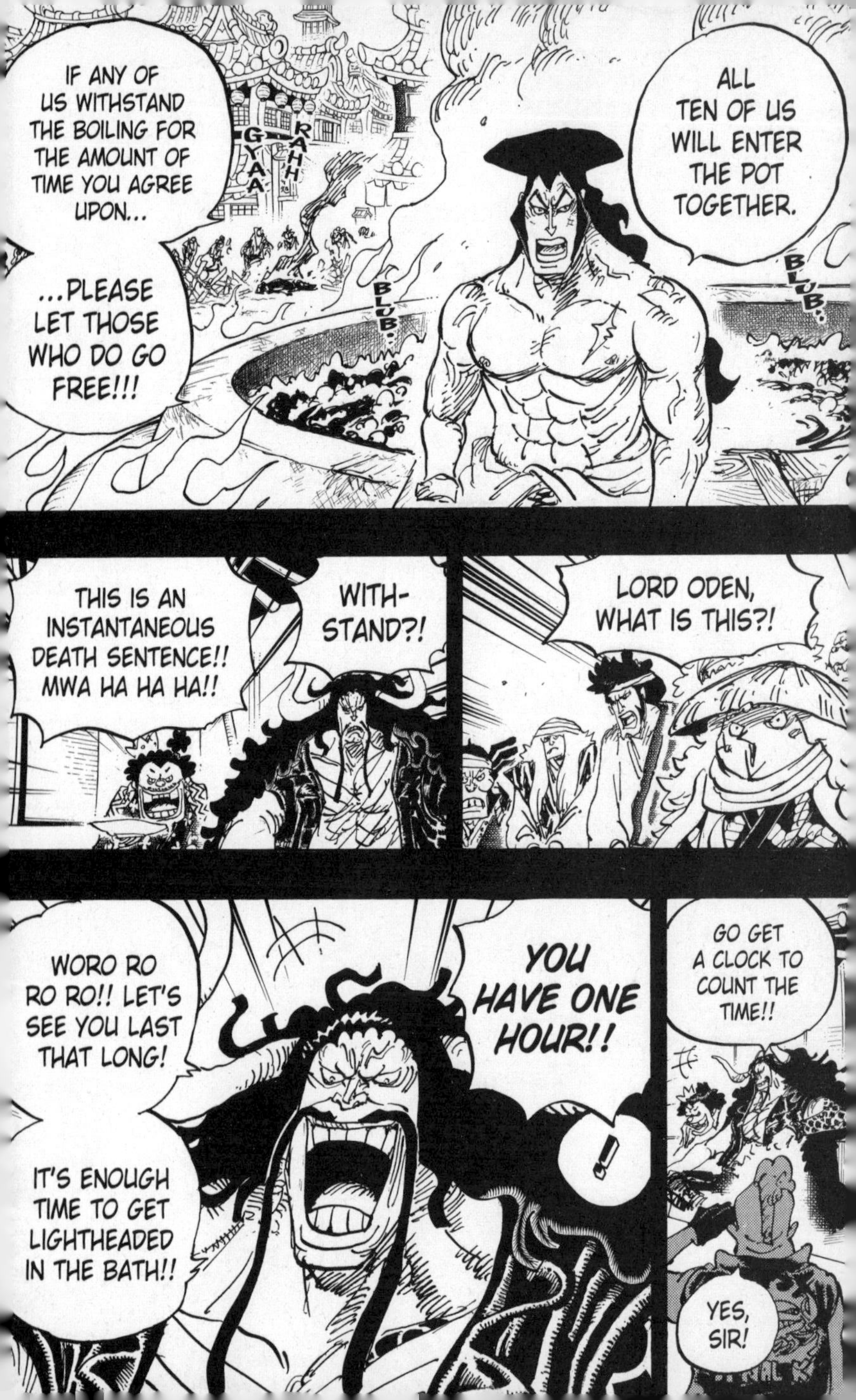
ALL TEN OF US WILL ENTER THE POT TOGETHER.
BLUB
BLUB
GYAA
RAHH
IF ANY OF US WITHSTAND THE BOILING FOR THE AMOUNT OF TIME YOU AGREE UPON...
...PLEASE LET THOSE WHO DO GO FREE!!!
LORD ODEN, WHAT IS THIS?!
WITH-STAND?!
THIS IS AN INSTANTANEOUS DEATH SENTENCE!! MWA HA HA HA!!
GO GET A CLOCK TO COUNT THE TIME!!
YES, SIR!
YOU HAVE ONE HOUR!!
WORO RO RO RO!! LET'S SEE YOU LAST THAT LONG!
!
IT'S ENOUGH TIME TO GET LIGHTHEADED IN THE BATH!!

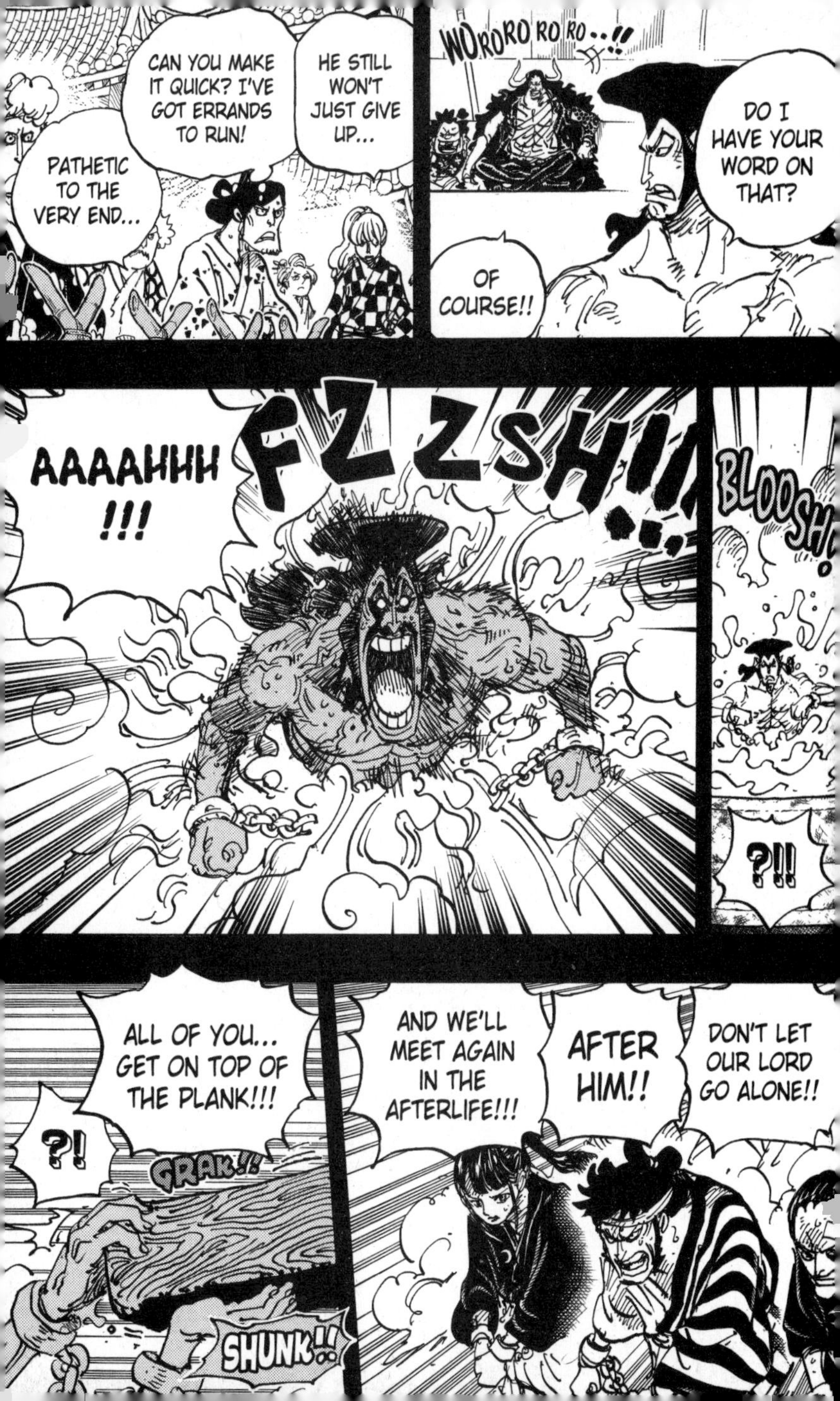
WORORO RO RO..!!
DO I HAVE YOUR WORD ON THAT?
OF COURSE!!
HE STILL WON'T JUST GIVE UP...
CAN YOU MAKE IT QUICK? I'VE GOT ERRANDS TO RUN!
PATHETIC TO THE VERY END...
BLOOSH!
?!!
FZZSH!!
AAAAHHH!!!
DON'T LET OUR LORD GO ALONE!!
AFTER HIM!!
AND WE'LL MEET AGAIN IN THE AFTERLIFE!!!
ALL OF YOU... GET ON TOP OF THE PLANK!!!
?!
GRAK!!
SHUNK!!

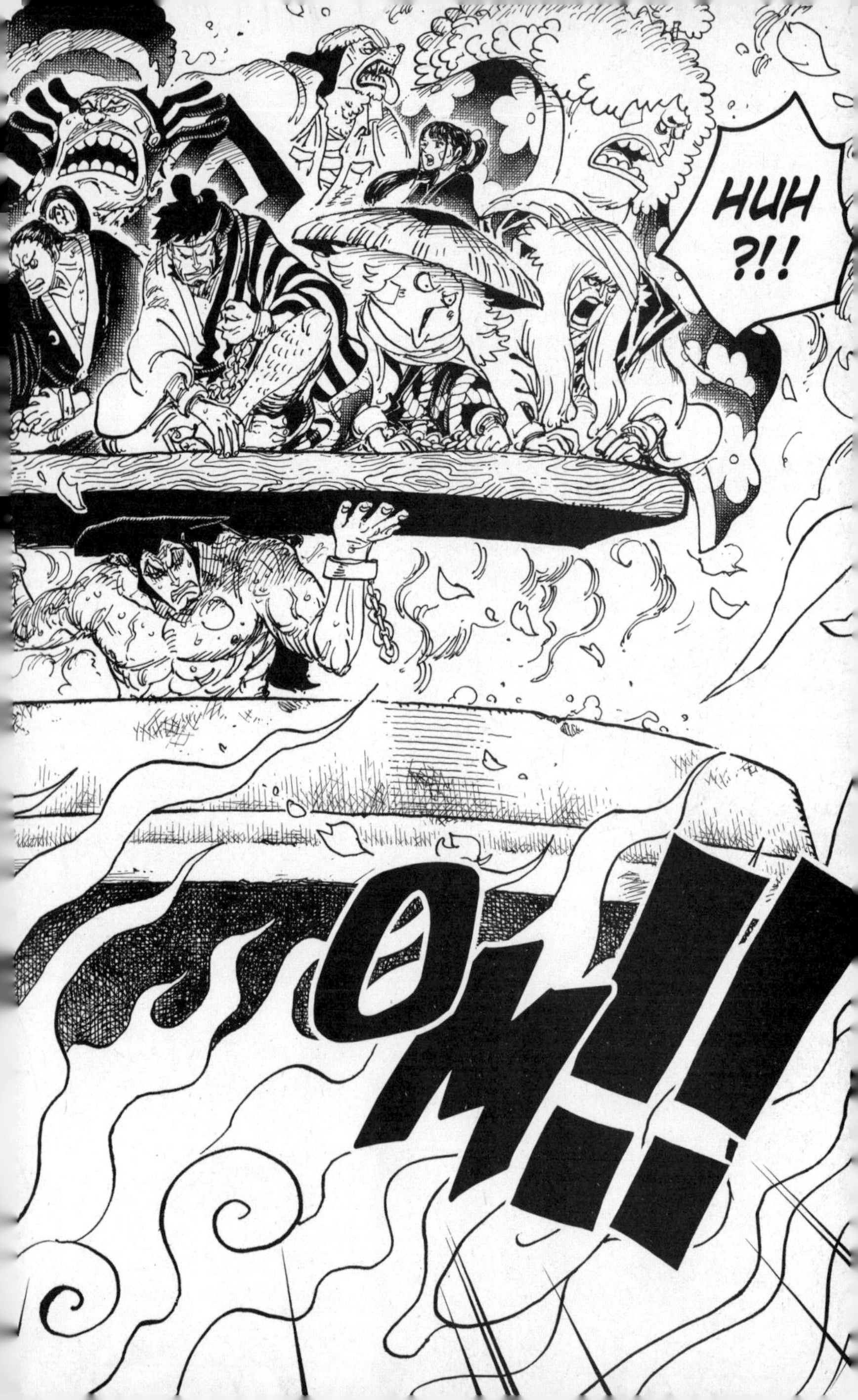
HUH ?!!
OH!!

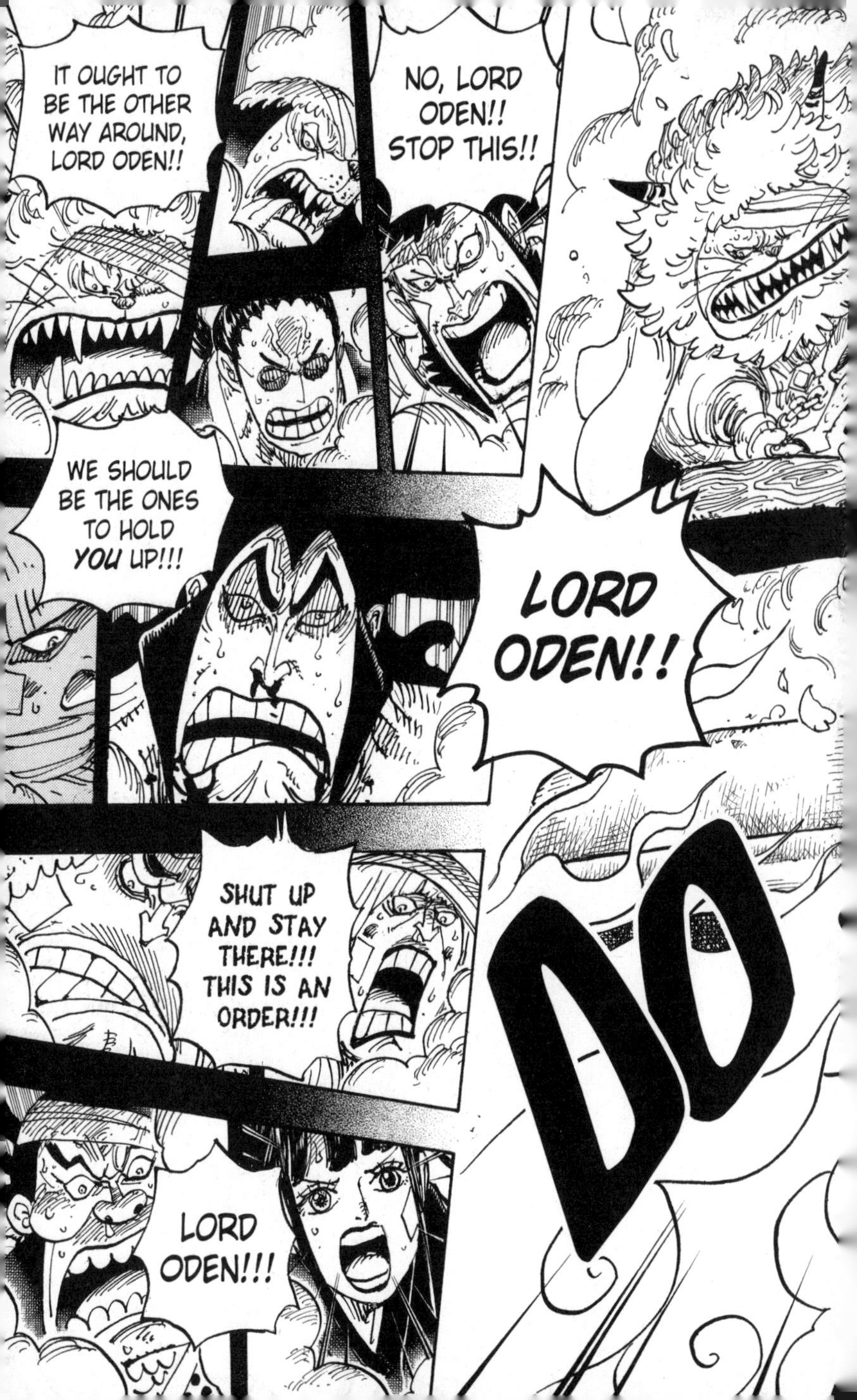

NO, LORD ODEN!! STOP THIS!!
IT OUGHT TO BE THE OTHER WAY AROUND, LORD ODEN!!
WE SHOULD BE THE ONES TO HOLD *YOU* UP!!!
LORD ODEN!!
SHUT UP AND STAY THERE!!! THIS IS AN ORDER!!!
LORD ODEN!!!
DO

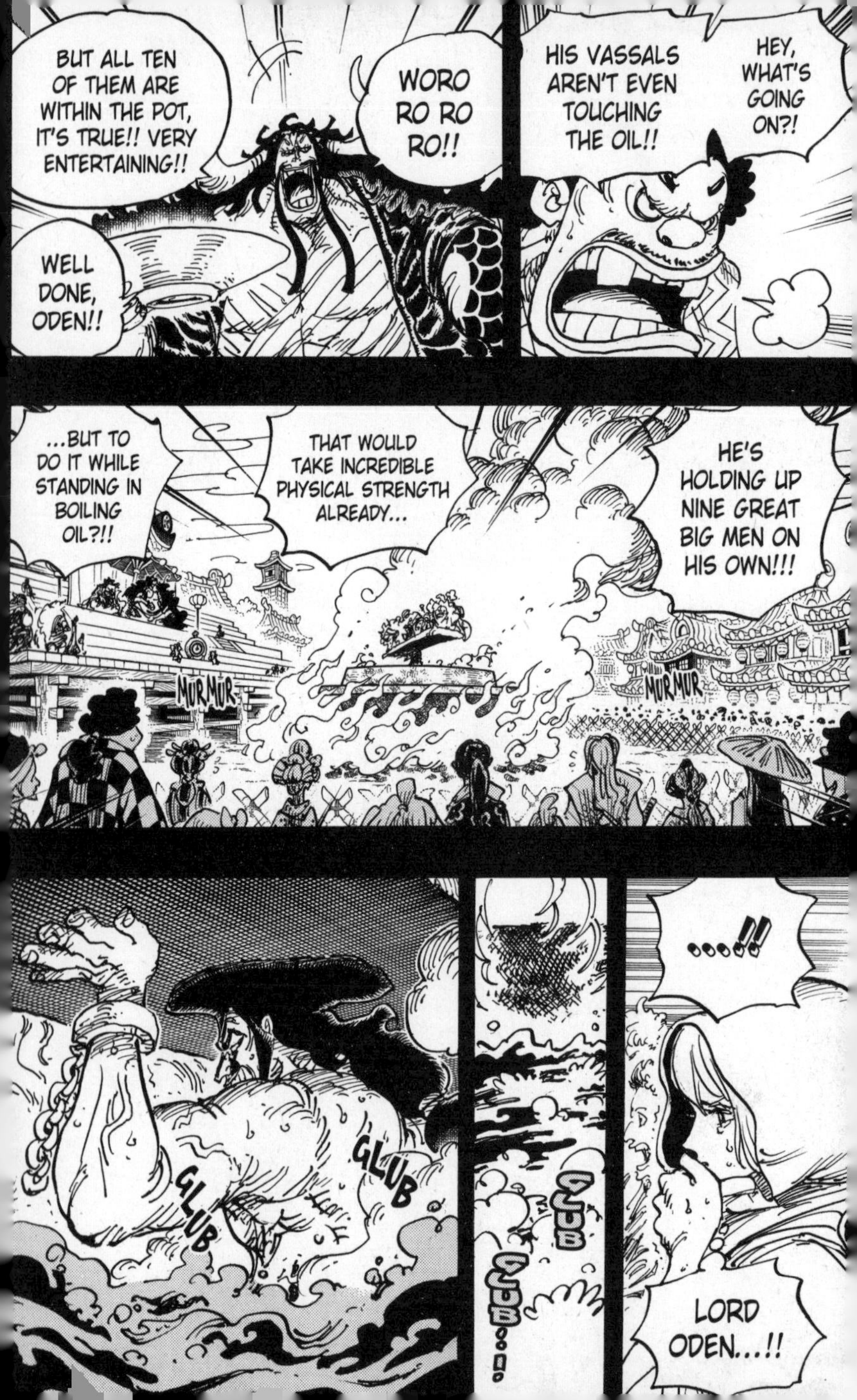
HEY, WHAT'S GOING ON?!
HIS VASSALS AREN'T EVEN TOUCHING THE OIL!!
WORO RO RO!!
BUT ALL TEN OF THEM ARE WITHIN THE POT, IT'S TRUE!! VERY ENTERTAINING!!
WELL DONE, ODEN!!
HE'S HOLDING UP NINE GREAT BIG MEN ON HIS OWN!!!
THAT WOULD TAKE INCREDIBLE PHYSICAL STRENGTH ALREADY...
...BUT TO DO IT WHILE STANDING IN BOILING OIL?!!
MURMUR
MURMUR
...!!
LORD ODEN...!!
GLUB
GLUB...
GLUB
GLUB

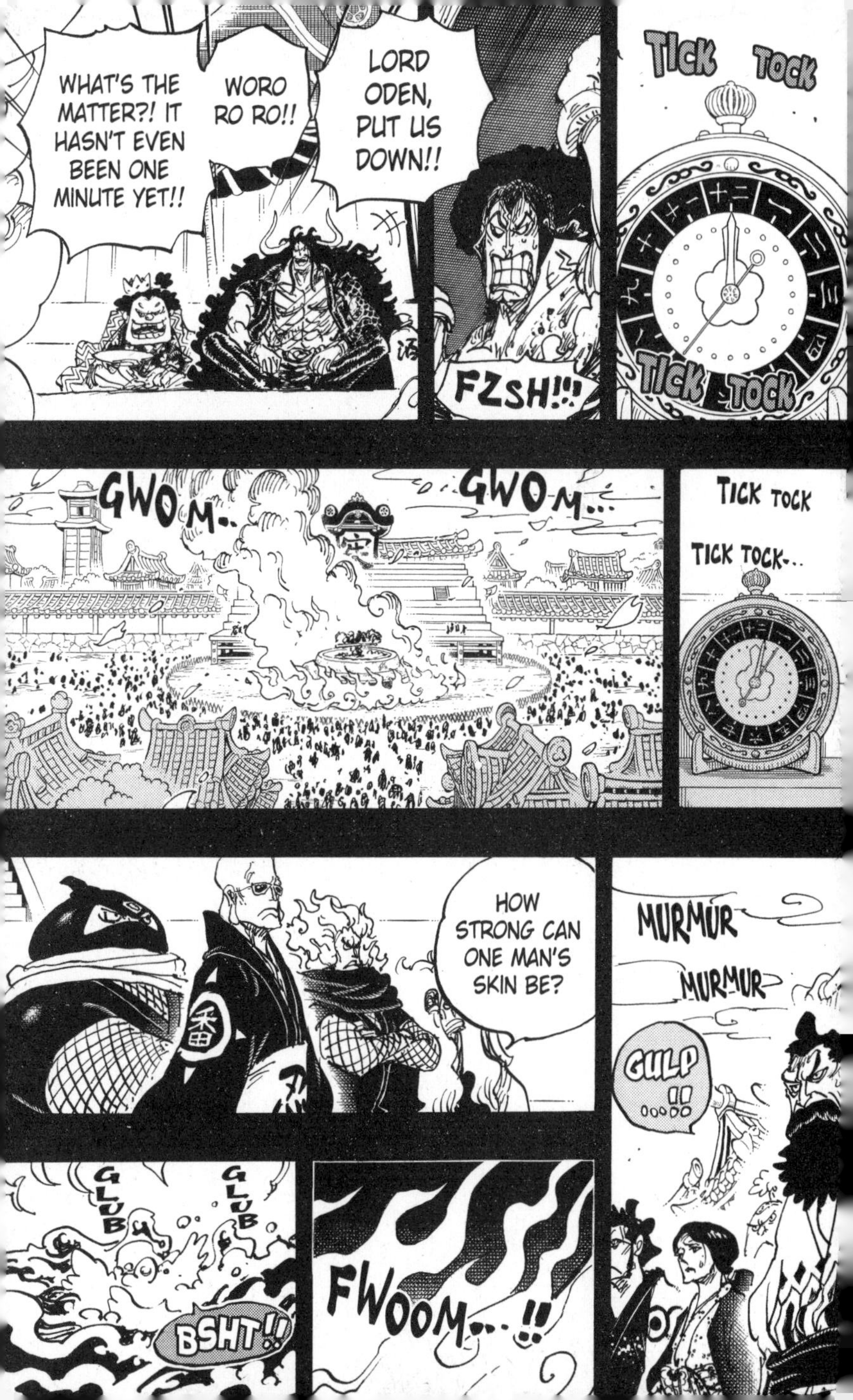
TICK TOCK
TICK TOCK
FZSH!!
LORD ODEN, PUT US DOWN!!
WORO RO RO!!
WHAT'S THE MATTER?! IT HASN'T EVEN BEEN ONE MINUTE YET!!
TICK TOCK
TICK TOCK...
GWOM...
GWOM...
MURMUR
MURMUR
GULP!!
HOW STRONG CAN ONE MAN'S SKIN BE?
FWOOM...!!
GLUB
GLUB
BSHT!!

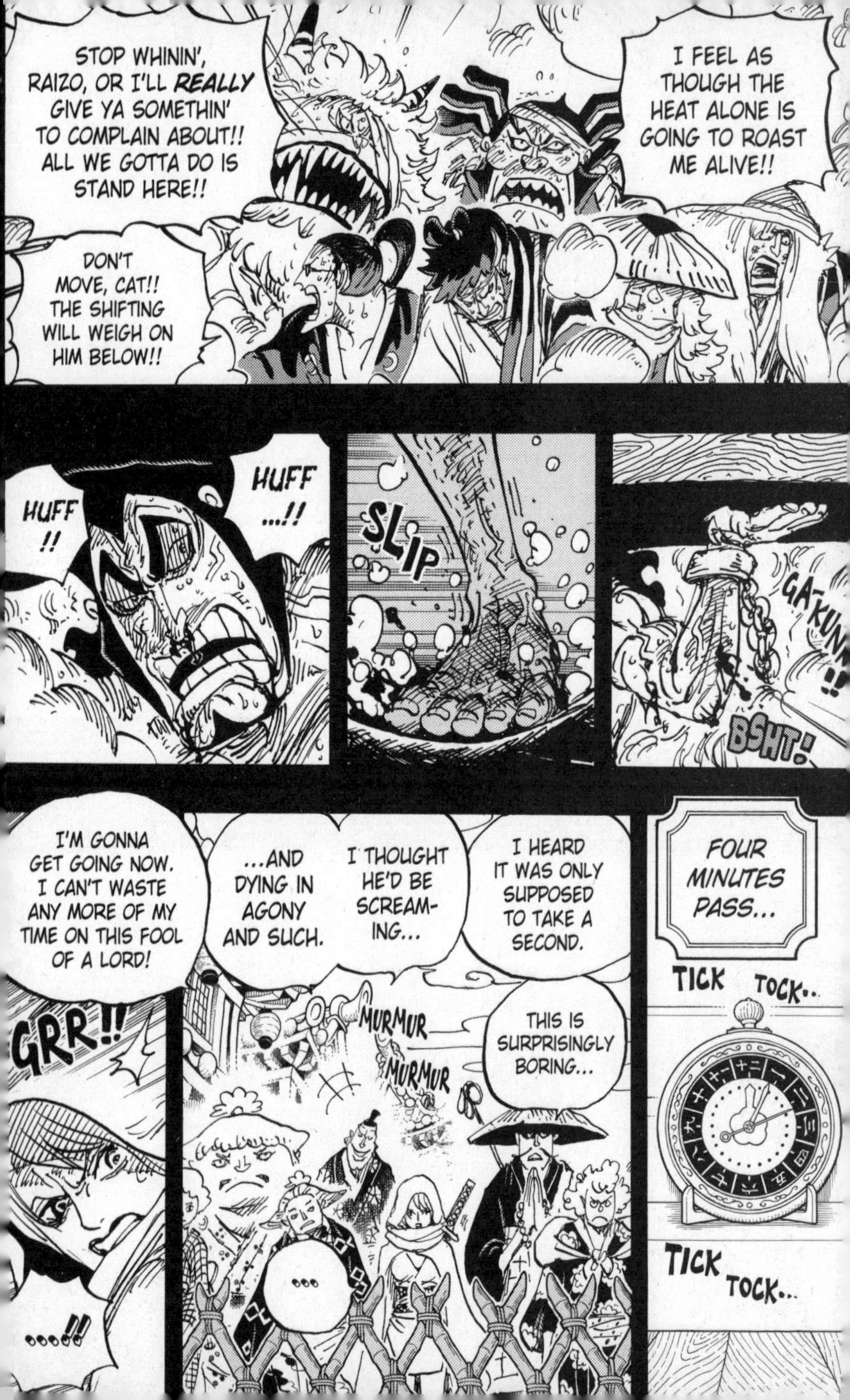
I FEEL AS THOUGH THE HEAT ALONE IS GOING TO ROAST ME ALIVE!!
STOP WHININ', RAIZO, OR I'LL **REALLY** GIVE YA SOMETHIN' TO COMPLAIN ABOUT!! ALL WE GOTTA DO IS STAND HERE!!
DON'T MOVE, CAT!! THE SHIFTING WILL WEIGH ON HIM BELOW!!
GA-KUNN!!
BSHT!
SLIP
HUFF ...!!
HUFF !!
FOUR MINUTES PASS...
TICK TOCK...
TICK TOCK...
I HEARD IT WAS ONLY SUPPOSED TO TAKE A SECOND.
I THOUGHT HE'D BE SCREAM-ING...
...AND DYING IN AGONY AND SUCH.
MURMUR
MURMUR
THIS IS SURPRISINGLY BORING...
...
I'M GONNA GET GOING NOW. I CAN'T WASTE ANY MORE OF MY TIME ON THIS FOOL OF A LORD!
GRR!!
.....!!

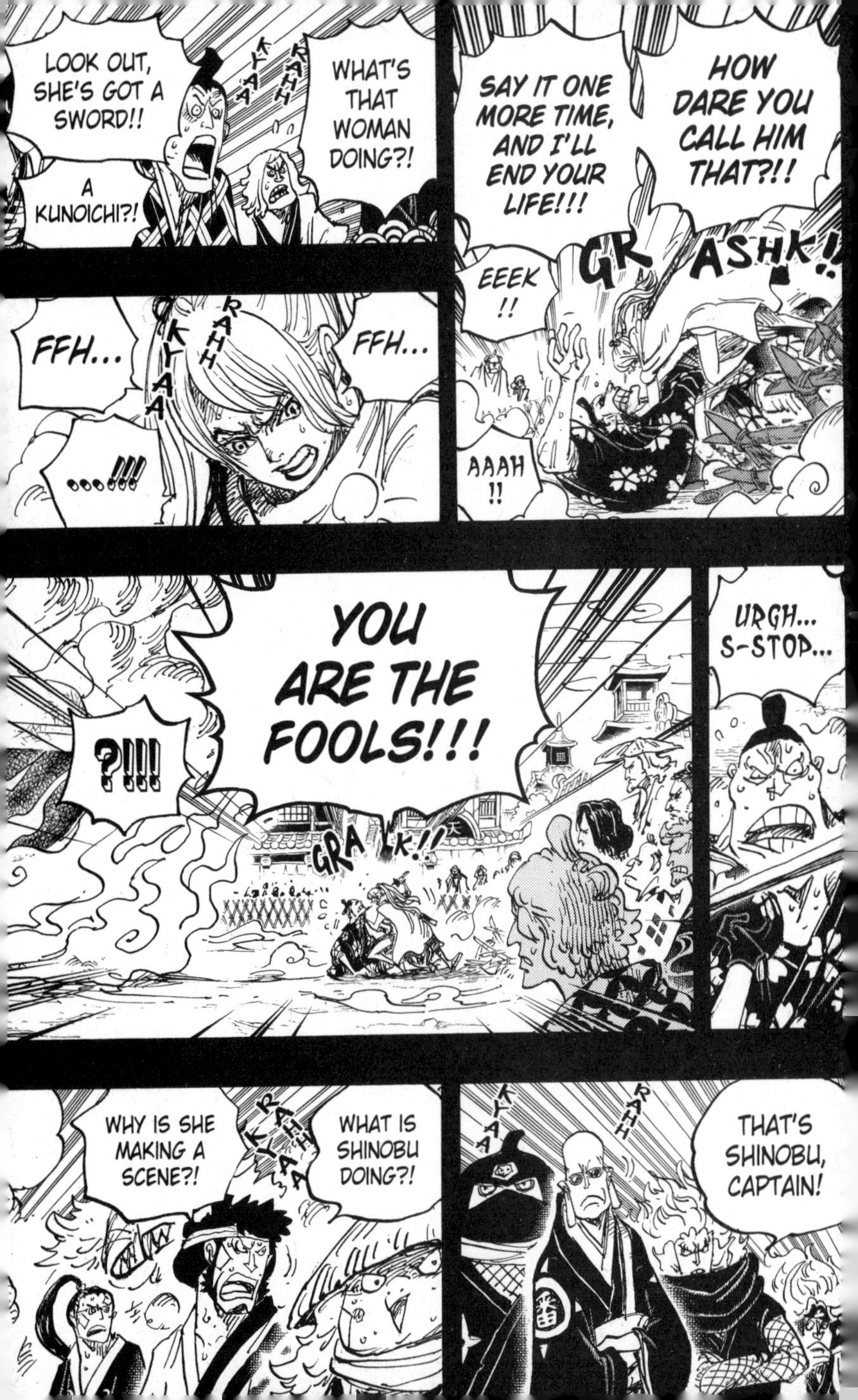
HOW DARE YOU CALL HIM THAT?!!
SAY IT ONE MORE TIME, AND I'LL END YOUR LIFE!!!
GRASHK!!
EEEK !!
AAAH !!
WHAT'S THAT WOMAN DOING?!
RAHH
KYAAA
LOOK OUT, SHE'S GOT A SWORD!!
A KUNOICHI?!
FFH...
RAHH
KYAAA
FFH...
...!!!
URGH... S-STOP...
YOU ARE THE FOOLS!!!
?!!!
GRALK!!
THAT'S SHINOBU, CAPTAIN!
RAHH
KYAA
WHAT IS SHINOBU DOING?!
RAHH
KYAAA
WHY IS SHE MAKING A SCENE?!

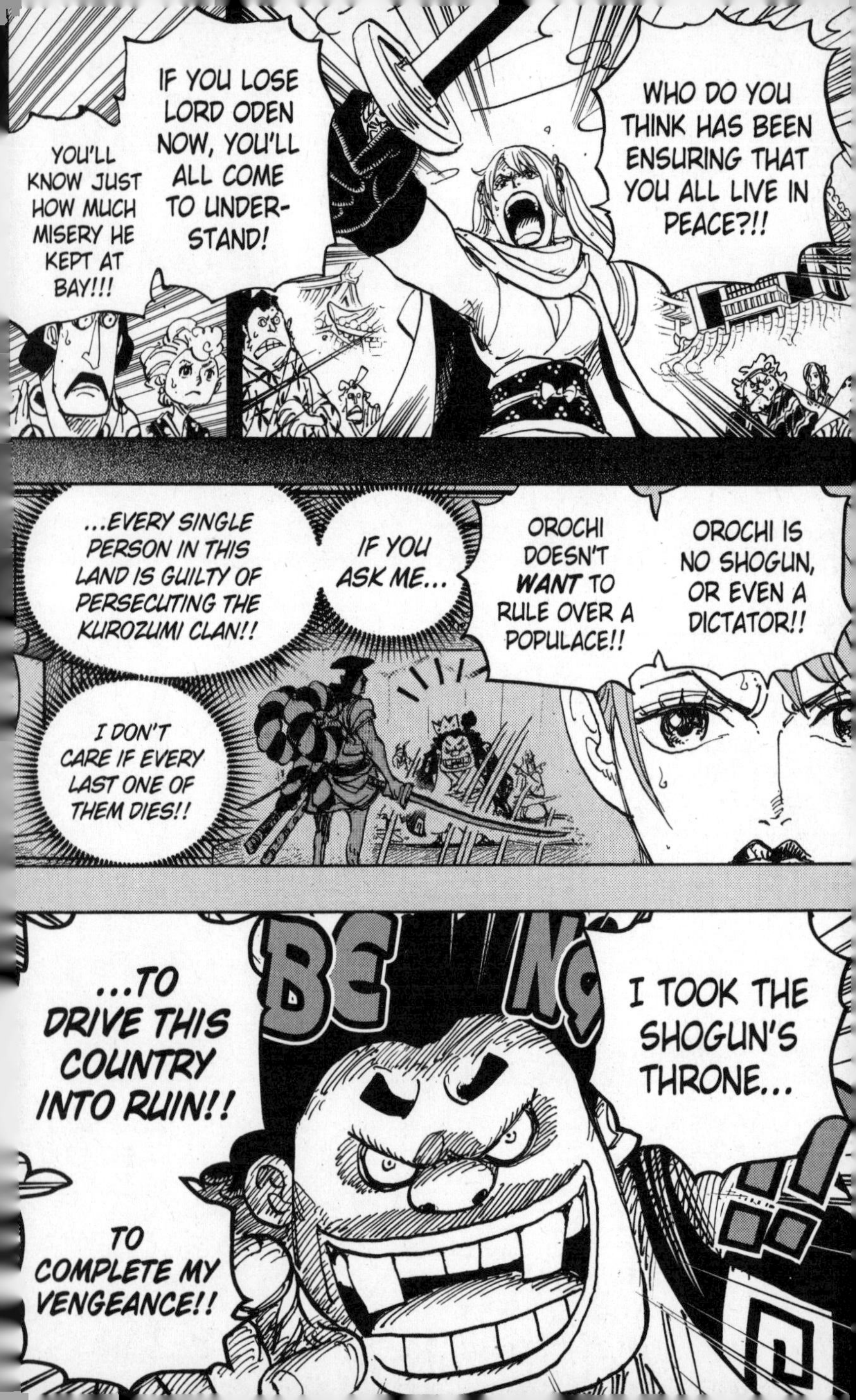
WHO DO YOU THINK HAS BEEN ENSURING THAT YOU ALL LIVE IN PEACE?!!
IF YOU LOSE LORD ODEN NOW, YOU'LL ALL COME TO UNDER-STAND!
YOU'LL KNOW JUST HOW MUCH MISERY HE KEPT AT BAY!!!
OROCHI IS NO SHOGUN, OR EVEN A DICTATOR!!
OROCHI DOESN'T WANT TO RULE OVER A POPULACE!!
IF YOU ASK ME...
...EVERY SINGLE PERSON IN THIS LAND IS GUILTY OF PERSECUTING THE KUROZUMI CLAN!!
I DON'T CARE IF EVERY LAST ONE OF THEM DIES!!
I TOOK THE SHOGUN'S THRONE...
...TO DRIVE THIS COUNTRY INTO RUIN!!
TO COMPLETE MY VENGEANCE!!

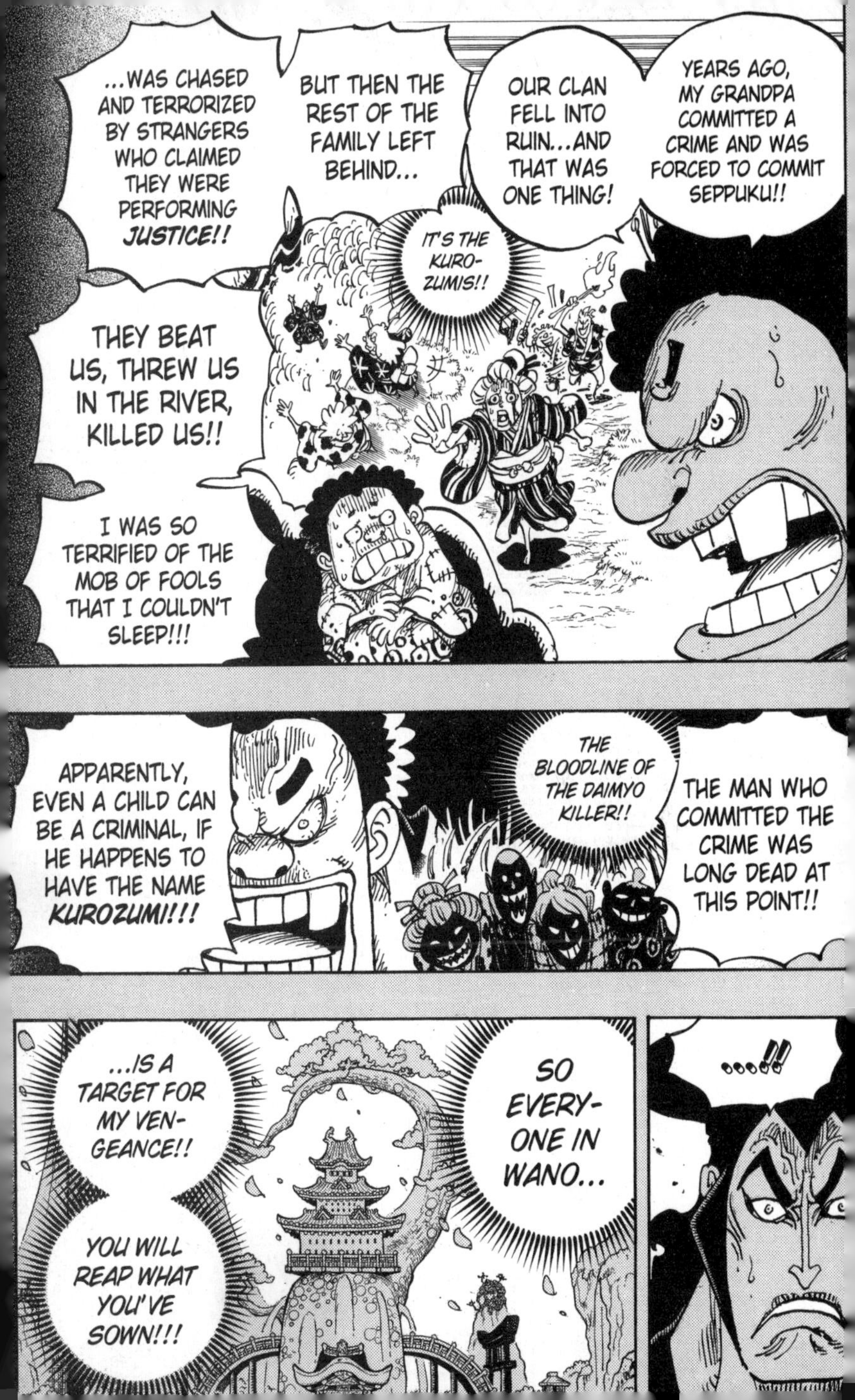
YEARS AGO, MY GRANDPA COMMITTED A CRIME AND WAS FORCED TO COMMIT SEPPUKU!!
OUR CLAN FELL INTO RUIN...AND THAT WAS ONE THING!
BUT THEN THE REST OF THE FAMILY LEFT BEHIND...
...WAS CHASED AND TERRORIZED BY STRANGERS WHO CLAIMED THEY WERE PERFORMING ***JUSTICE!!***
IT'S THE KURO-ZUMIS!!
THEY BEAT US, THREW US IN THE RIVER, KILLED US!!
I WAS SO TERRIFIED OF THE MOB OF FOOLS THAT I COULDN'T SLEEP!!!
THE MAN WHO COMMITTED THE CRIME WAS LONG DEAD AT THIS POINT!!
THE BLOODLINE OF THE DAIMYO KILLER!!
APPARENTLY, EVEN A CHILD CAN BE A CRIMINAL, IF HE HAPPENS TO HAVE THE NAME ***KUROZUMI!!!***
...!!
SO EVERY-ONE IN WANO...
...IS A TARGET FOR MY VEN-GEANCE!!
YOU WILL REAP WHAT YOU'VE SOWN!!!

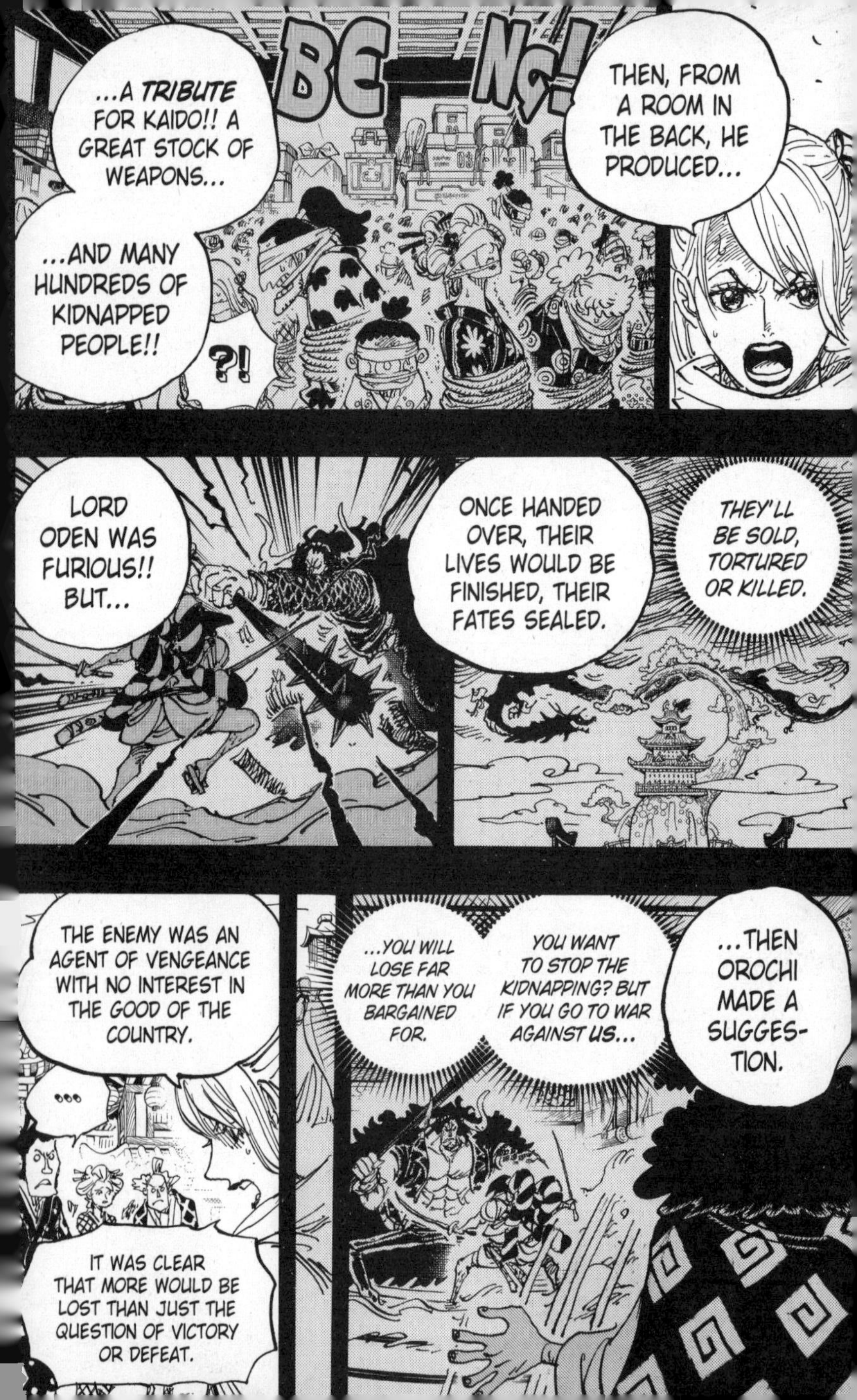
THEN, FROM A ROOM IN THE BACK, HE PRODUCED...
BE—NG!
...A *TRIBUTE* FOR KAIDO!! A GREAT STOCK OF WEAPONS...
...AND MANY HUNDREDS OF KIDNAPPED PEOPLE!!
?!
ONCE HANDED OVER, THEIR LIVES WOULD BE FINISHED, THEIR FATES SEALED.
THEY'LL BE SOLD, TORTURED OR KILLED.
LORD ODEN WAS FURIOUS!! BUT...
...THEN OROCHI MADE A SUGGES-TION.
YOU WANT TO STOP THE KIDNAPPING? BUT IF YOU GO TO WAR AGAINST ***US...***
...YOU WILL LOSE FAR MORE THAN YOU BARGAINED FOR.
THE ENEMY WAS AN AGENT OF VENGEANCE WITH NO INTEREST IN THE GOOD OF THE COUNTRY.
...
IT WAS CLEAR THAT MORE WOULD BE LOST THAN JUST THE QUESTION OF VICTORY OR DEFEAT.

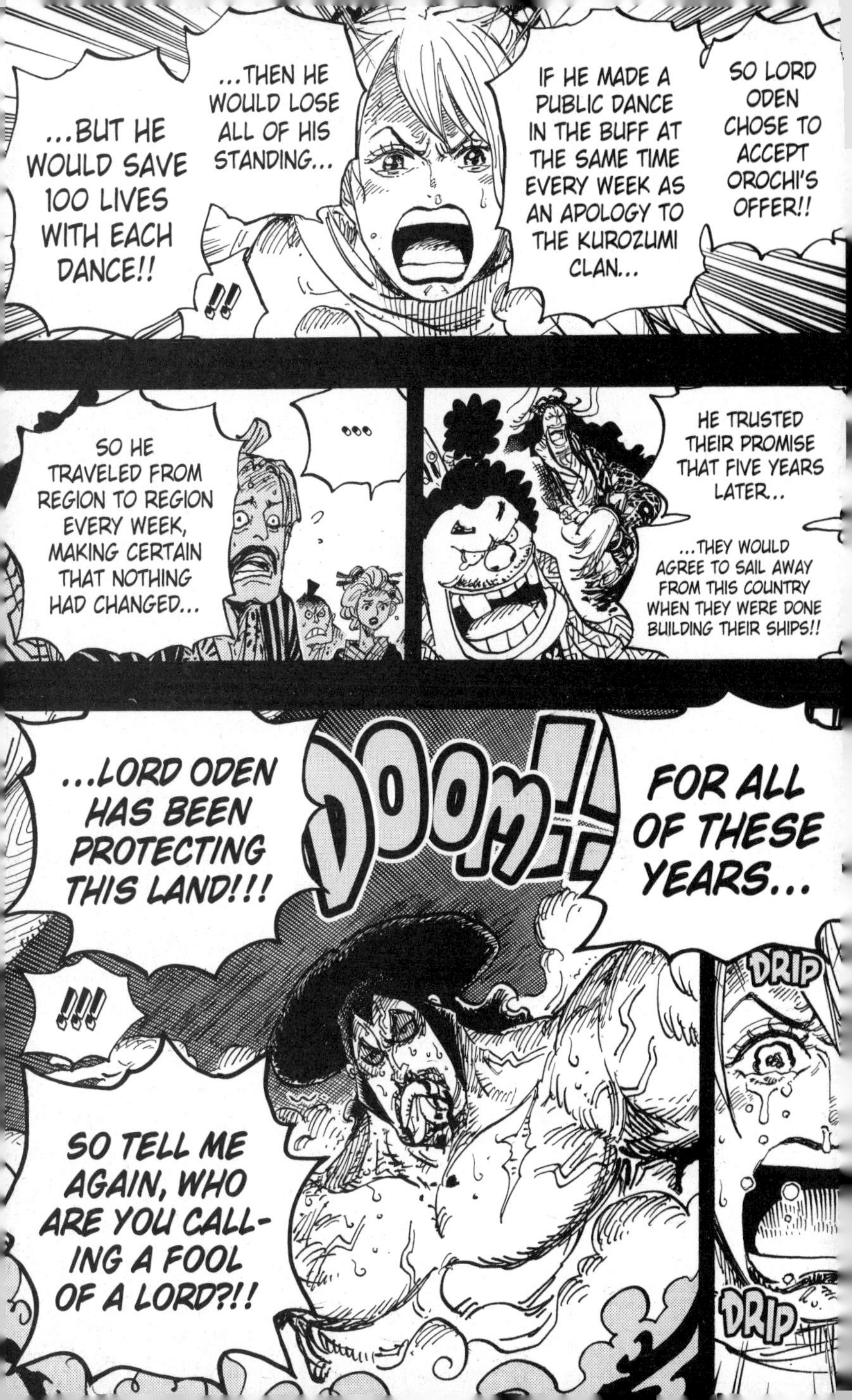
SO LORD ODEN CHOSE TO ACCEPT OROCHI'S OFFER!!
IF HE MADE A PUBLIC DANCE IN THE BUFF AT THE SAME TIME EVERY WEEK AS AN APOLOGY TO THE KUROZUMI CLAN...
...THEN HE WOULD LOSE ALL OF HIS STANDING...
...BUT HE WOULD SAVE 100 LIVES WITH EACH DANCE!!
!!
HE TRUSTED THEIR PROMISE THAT FIVE YEARS LATER...
...THEY WOULD AGREE TO SAIL AWAY FROM THIS COUNTRY WHEN THEY WERE DONE BUILDING THEIR SHIPS!!
...
SO HE TRAVELED FROM REGION TO REGION EVERY WEEK, MAKING CERTAIN THAT NOTHING HAD CHANGED...
FOR ALL OF THESE YEARS...
DOOM!!
...LORD ODEN HAS BEEN PROTECTING THIS LAND!!!
DRIP
DRIP
!!!
SO TELL ME AGAIN, WHO ARE YOU CALLING A FOOL OF A LORD?!!

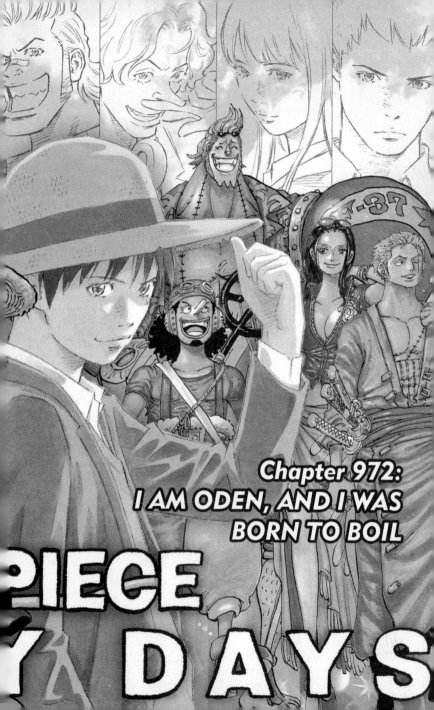

Chapter 972:
I AM ODEN, AND I WAS
BORN TO BOIL

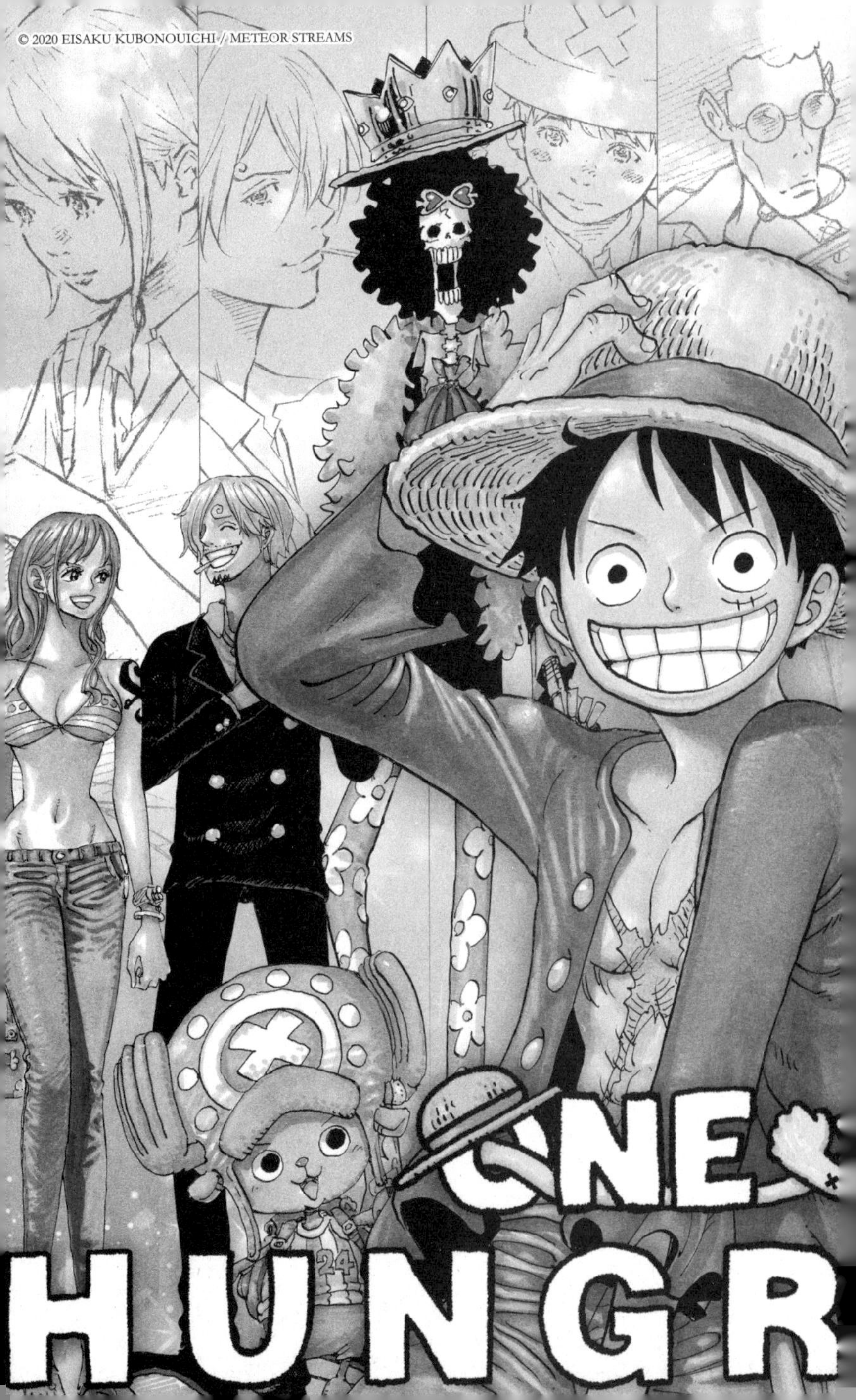
© 2020 EISAKU KUBONOUICHI / METEOR STREAMS
ONE
HUNGR

vol.96
ONE PIECE

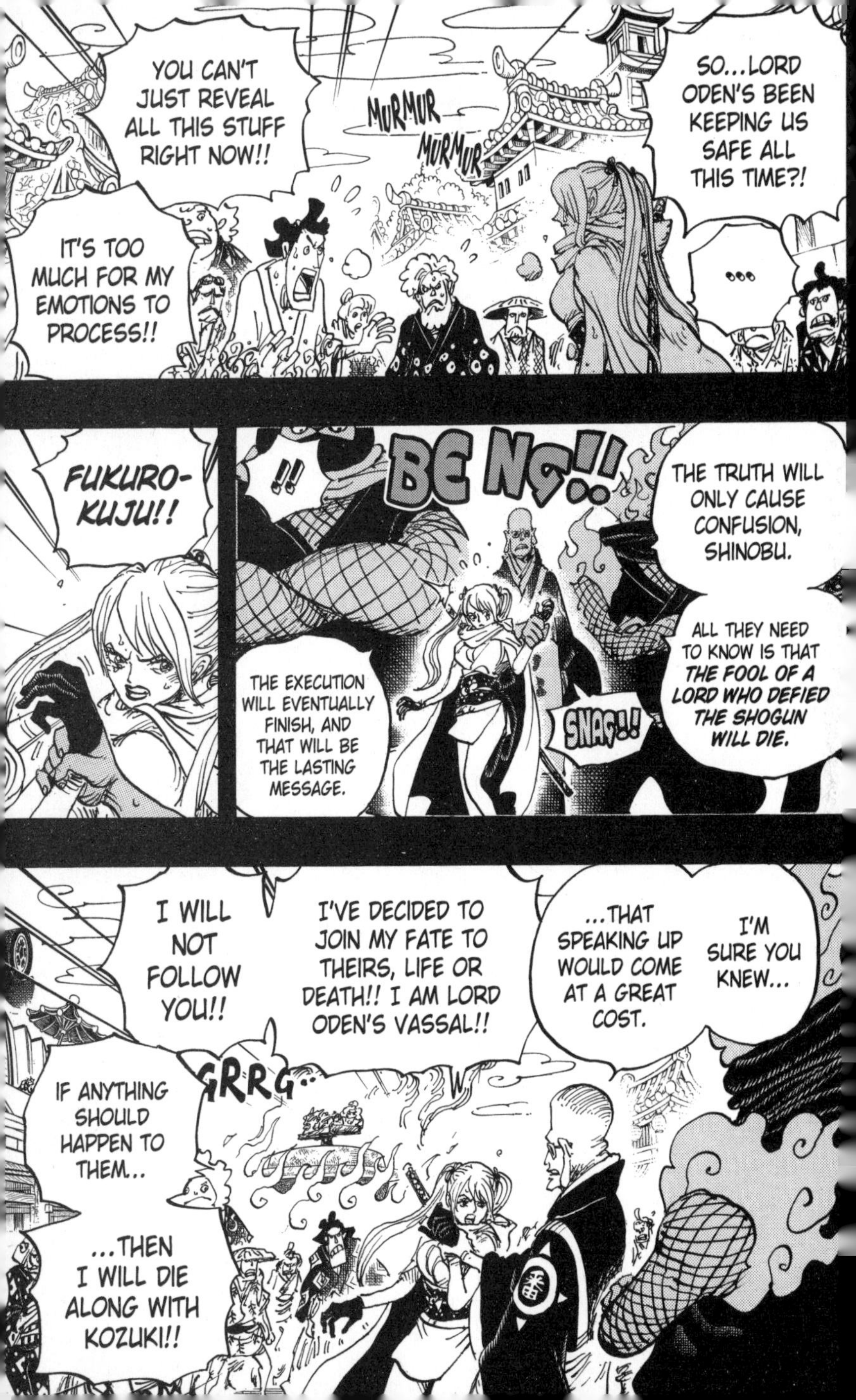
SO...LORD ODEN'S BEEN KEEPING US SAFE ALL THIS TIME?!
...
MURMUR
MURMUR
YOU CAN'T JUST REVEAL ALL THIS STUFF RIGHT NOW!!
IT'S TOO MUCH FOR MY EMOTIONS TO PROCESS!!
BENG!!
!!
THE TRUTH WILL ONLY CAUSE CONFUSION, SHINOBU.
ALL THEY NEED TO KNOW IS THAT *THE FOOL OF A LORD WHO DEFIED THE SHOGUN WILL DIE.*
SNAG!!
THE EXECUTION WILL EVENTUALLY FINISH, AND THAT WILL BE THE LASTING MESSAGE.
FUKURO-KUJU!!
I'M SURE YOU KNEW...
...THAT SPEAKING UP WOULD COME AT A GREAT COST.
I'VE DECIDED TO JOIN MY FATE TO THEIRS, LIFE OR DEATH!! I AM LORD ODEN'S VASSAL!!
I WILL NOT FOLLOW YOU!!
GRRG
IF ANYTHING SHOULD HAPPEN TO THEM...
...THEN I WILL DIE ALONG WITH KOZUKI!!

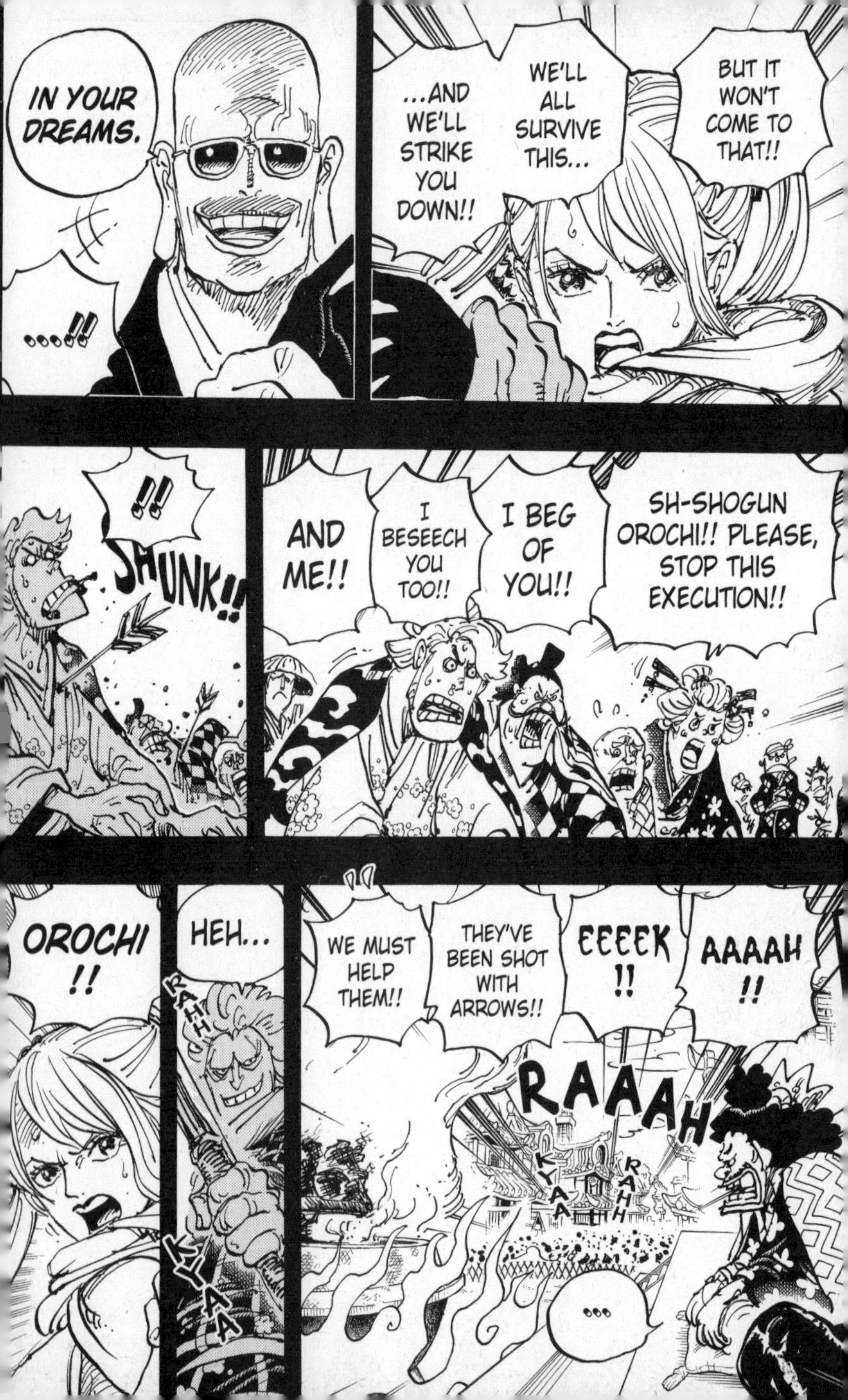
BUT IT WON'T COME TO THAT!!
WE'LL ALL SURVIVE THIS...
...AND WE'LL STRIKE YOU DOWN!!
IN YOUR DREAMS.
...!!
SH-SHOGUN OROCHI!! PLEASE, STOP THIS EXECUTION!!
I BEG OF YOU!!
I BESEECH YOU TOO!!
AND ME!!
!!
SHUNK!!
AAAAH!!
EEEEK!!
THEY'VE BEEN SHOT WITH ARROWS!!
WE MUST HELP THEM!!
RAAAH
KYAA
RAHH
...
HEH...
RAHH
KYAA
OROCHI!!

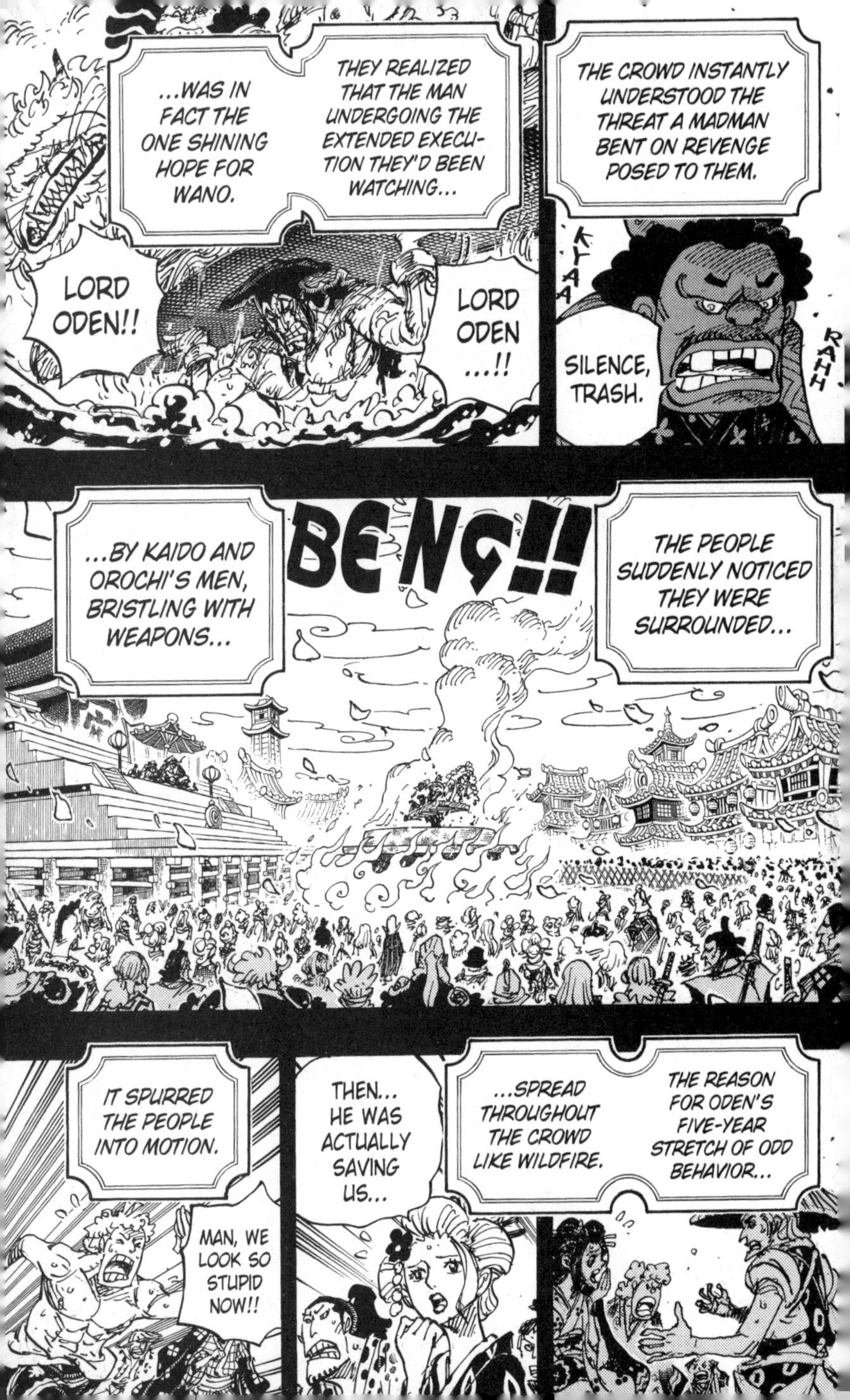
THE CROWD INSTANTLY UNDERSTOOD THE THREAT A MADMAN BENT ON REVENGE POSED TO THEM.
KYAA
RAHH
SILENCE, TRASH.
THEY REALIZED THAT THE MAN UNDERGOING THE EXTENDED EXECU-TION THEY'D BEEN WATCHING...
...WAS IN FACT THE ONE SHINING HOPE FOR WANO.
LORD ODEN ...!!
LORD ODEN!!
THE PEOPLE SUDDENLY NOTICED THEY WERE SURROUNDED...
BENG!!
...BY KAIDO AND OROCHI'S MEN, BRISTLING WITH WEAPONS...
THE REASON FOR ODEN'S FIVE-YEAR STRETCH OF ODD BEHAVIOR...
...SPREAD THROUGHOUT THE CROWD LIKE WILDFIRE.
THEN... HE WAS ACTUALLY SAVING US...
IT SPURRED THE PEOPLE INTO MOTION.
MAN, WE LOOK SO STUPID NOW!!

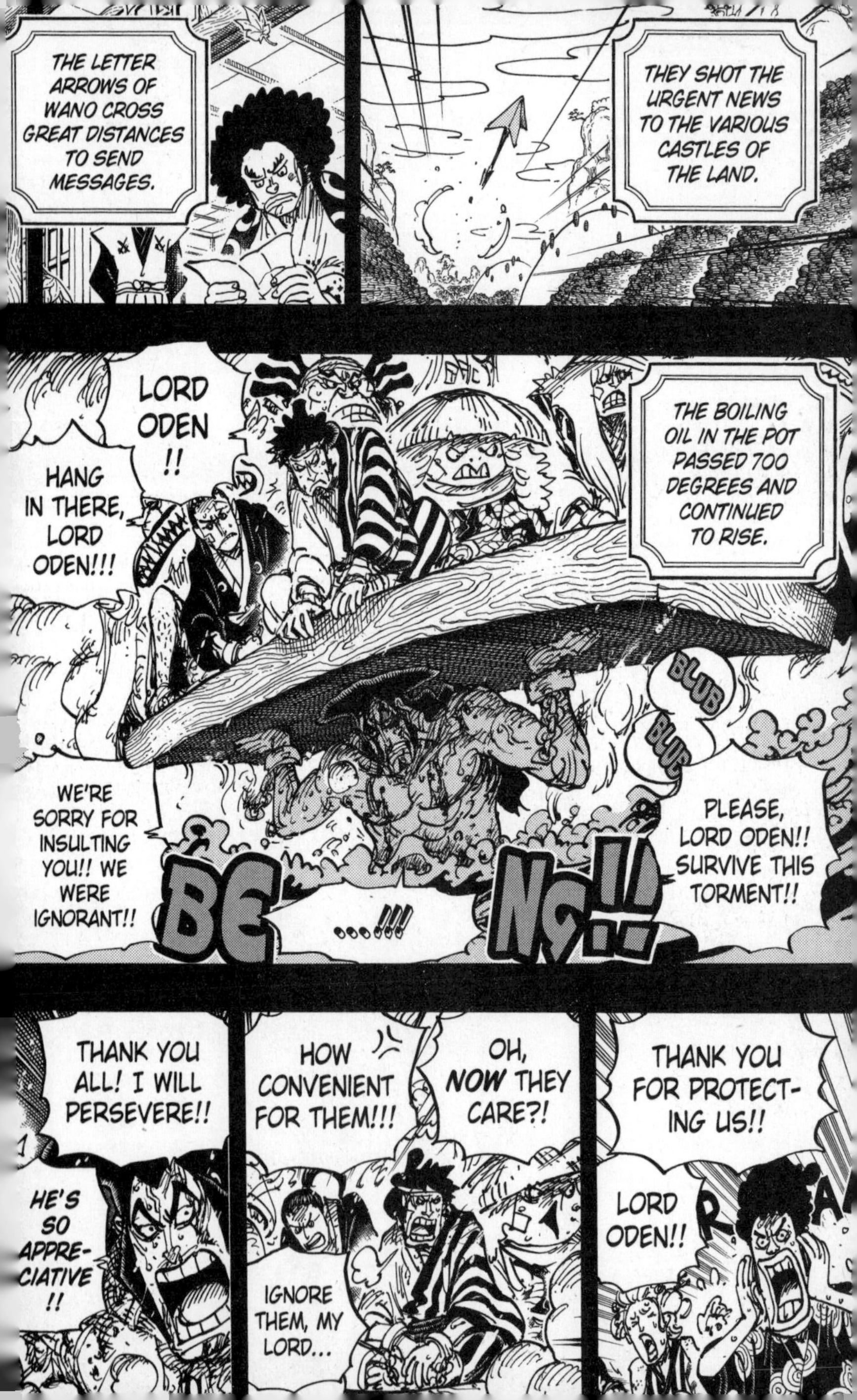
THEY SHOT THE URGENT NEWS TO THE VARIOUS CASTLES OF THE LAND.
THE LETTER ARROWS OF WANO CROSS GREAT DISTANCES TO SEND MESSAGES.
THE BOILING OIL IN THE POT PASSED 700 DEGREES AND CONTINUED TO RISE.
LORD ODEN!!
HANG IN THERE, LORD ODEN!!!
BLUB
BLUB
PLEASE, LORD ODEN!! SURVIVE THIS TORMENT!!
BE ...!!! NG!!
WE'RE SORRY FOR INSULTING YOU!! WE WERE IGNORANT!!
THANK YOU FOR PROTECTING US!!
LORD ODEN!!
OH, NOW THEY CARE?!
HOW CONVENIENT FOR THEM!!!
IGNORE THEM, MY LORD...
THANK YOU ALL! I WILL PERSEVERE!!
HE'S SO APPRECIATIVE!!

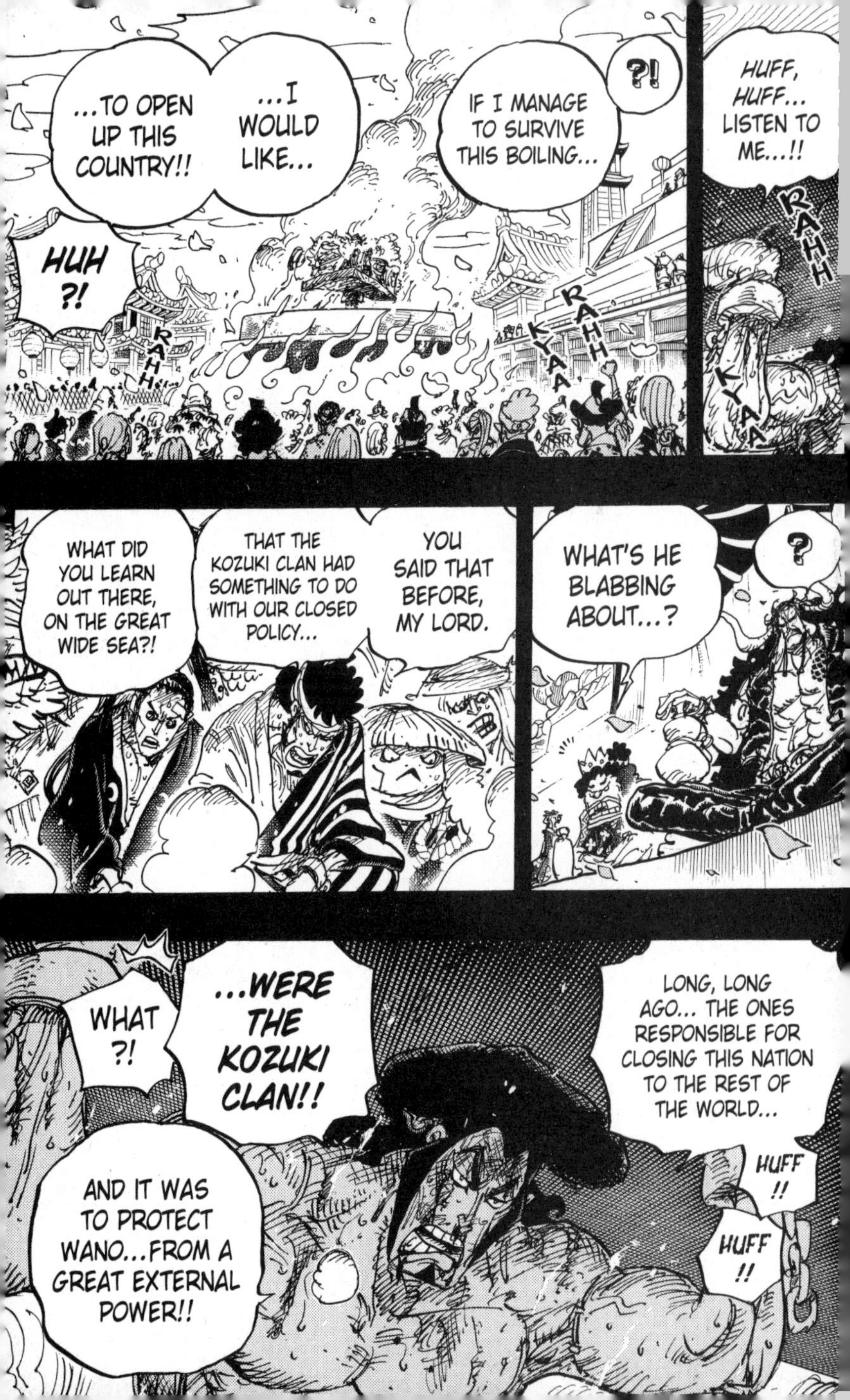
HUFF, HUFF... LISTEN TO ME...!!
RAHH
KYAA
?!
IF I MANAGE TO SURVIVE THIS BOILING...
...I WOULD LIKE...
...TO OPEN UP THIS COUNTRY!!
RAHH
KYAA
HUH ?!
RAHH
?
WHAT'S HE BLABBING ABOUT...?
YOU SAID THAT BEFORE, MY LORD.
THAT THE KOZUKI CLAN HAD SOMETHING TO DO WITH OUR CLOSED POLICY...
WHAT DID YOU LEARN OUT THERE, ON THE GREAT WIDE SEA?!
LONG, LONG AGO... THE ONES RESPONSIBLE FOR CLOSING THIS NATION TO THE REST OF THE WORLD...
HUFF !!
HUFF !!
...WERE THE KOZUKI CLAN!!
WHAT ?!
AND IT WAS TO PROTECT WANO...FROM A GREAT EXTERNAL POWER!!

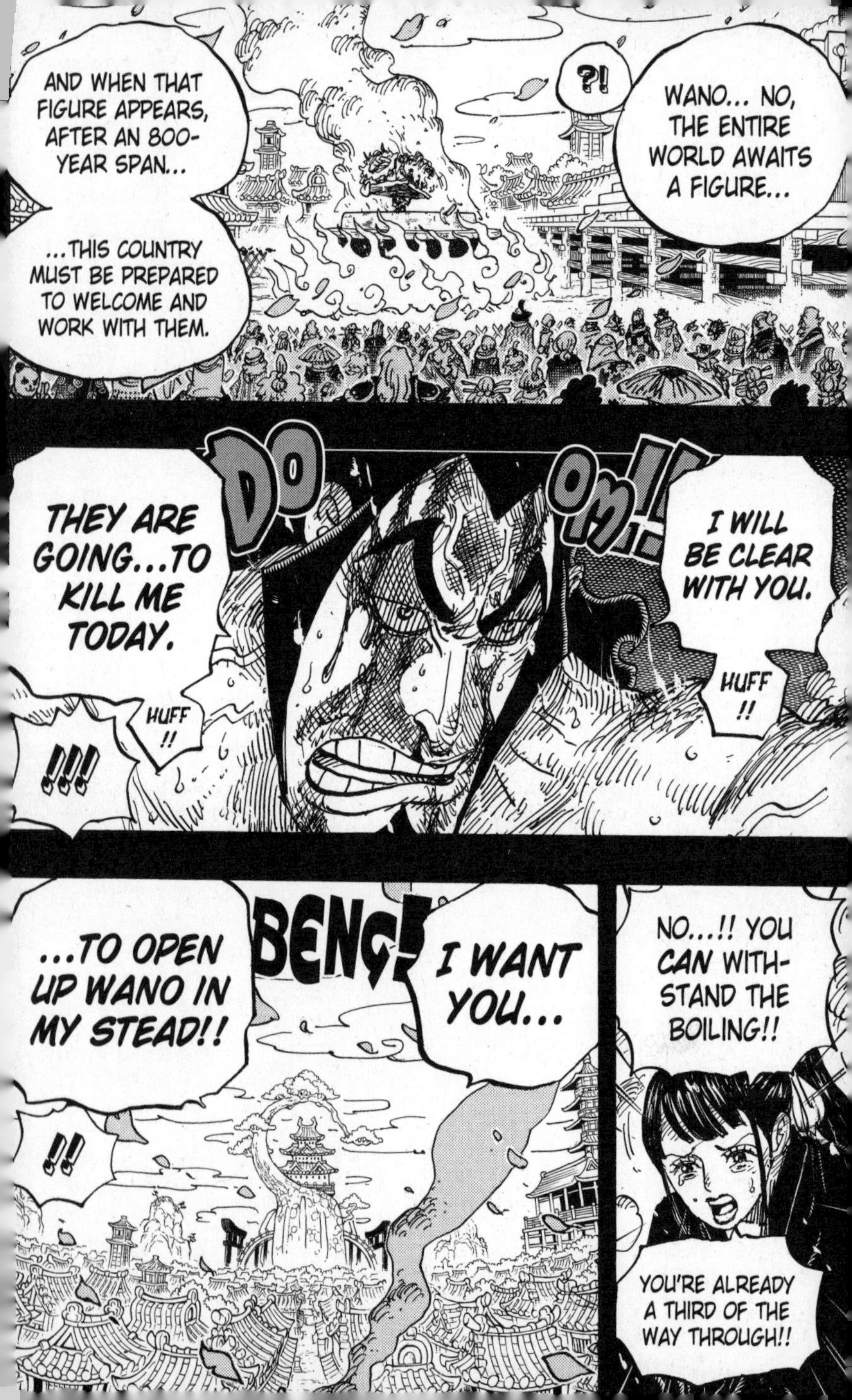
WANO... NO, THE ENTIRE WORLD AWAITS A FIGURE...
?!
AND WHEN THAT FIGURE APPEARS, AFTER AN 800-YEAR SPAN...
...THIS COUNTRY MUST BE PREPARED TO WELCOME AND WORK WITH THEM.
DOOM!!
I WILL BE CLEAR WITH YOU.
HUFF !!
THEY ARE GOING...TO KILL ME TODAY.
HUFF !!
!!!
NO...!! YOU CAN WITH-STAND THE BOILING!!
YOU'RE ALREADY A THIRD OF THE WAY THROUGH!!
BENG!
I WANT YOU...
...TO OPEN UP WANO IN MY STEAD!!
!!

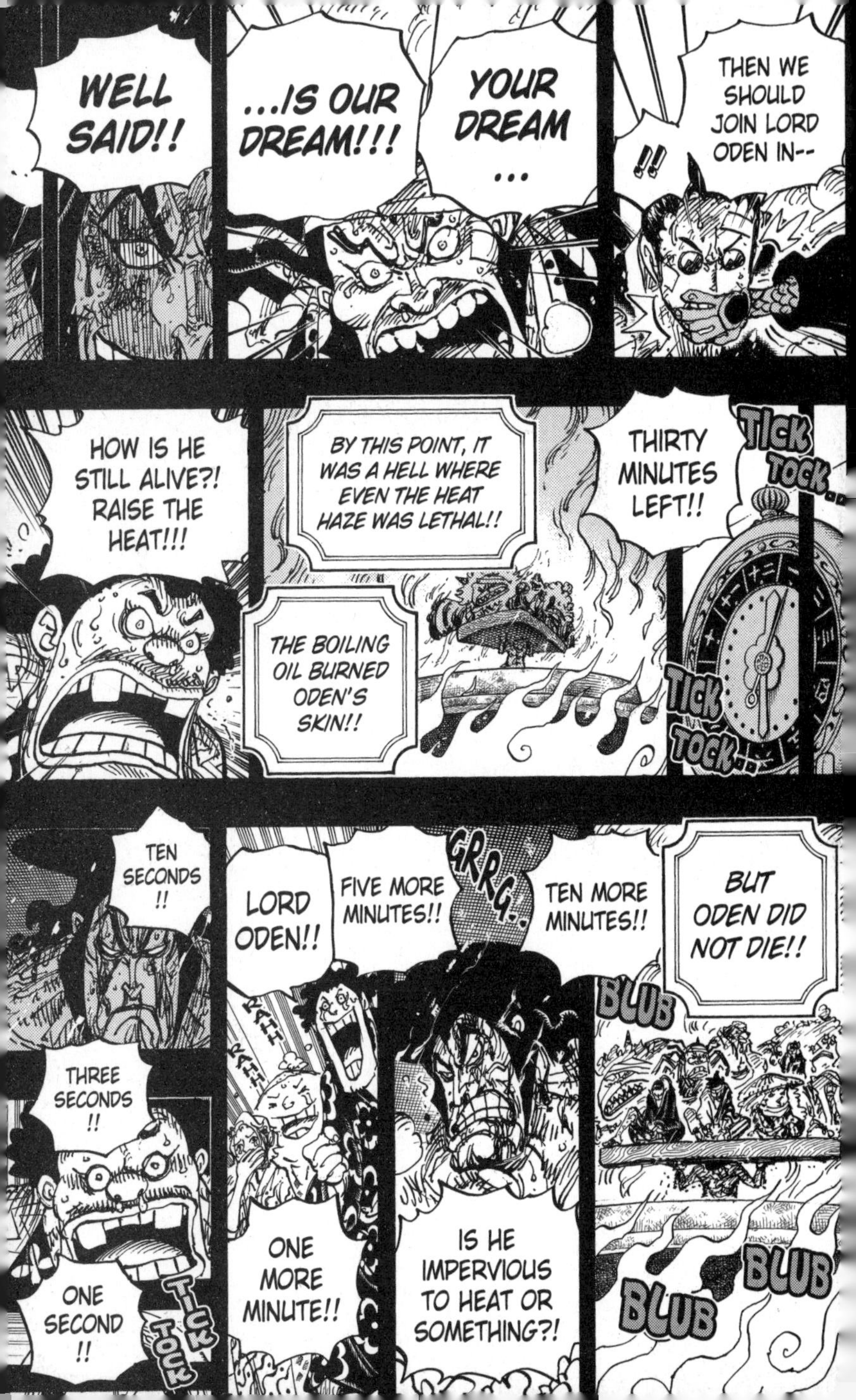
THEN WE SHOULD JOIN LORD ODEN IN--
!!
YOUR DREAM ...
...IS OUR DREAM!!!
WELL SAID!!
TICK TOCK..
THIRTY MINUTES LEFT!!
TICK TOCK..
BY THIS POINT, IT WAS A HELL WHERE EVEN THE HEAT HAZE WAS LETHAL!!
THE BOILING OIL BURNED ODEN'S SKIN!!
HOW IS HE STILL ALIVE?! RAISE THE HEAT!!!
BUT ODEN DID NOT DIE!!
BLUB
BLUB
BLUB
TEN MORE MINUTES!!
GRRG..
FIVE MORE MINUTES!!
LORD ODEN!!
RAHH
RAHH
IS HE IMPERVIOUS TO HEAT OR SOMETHING?!
ONE MORE MINUTE!!
TEN SECONDS !!
THREE SECONDS !!
ONE SECOND !!
TICK TOCK

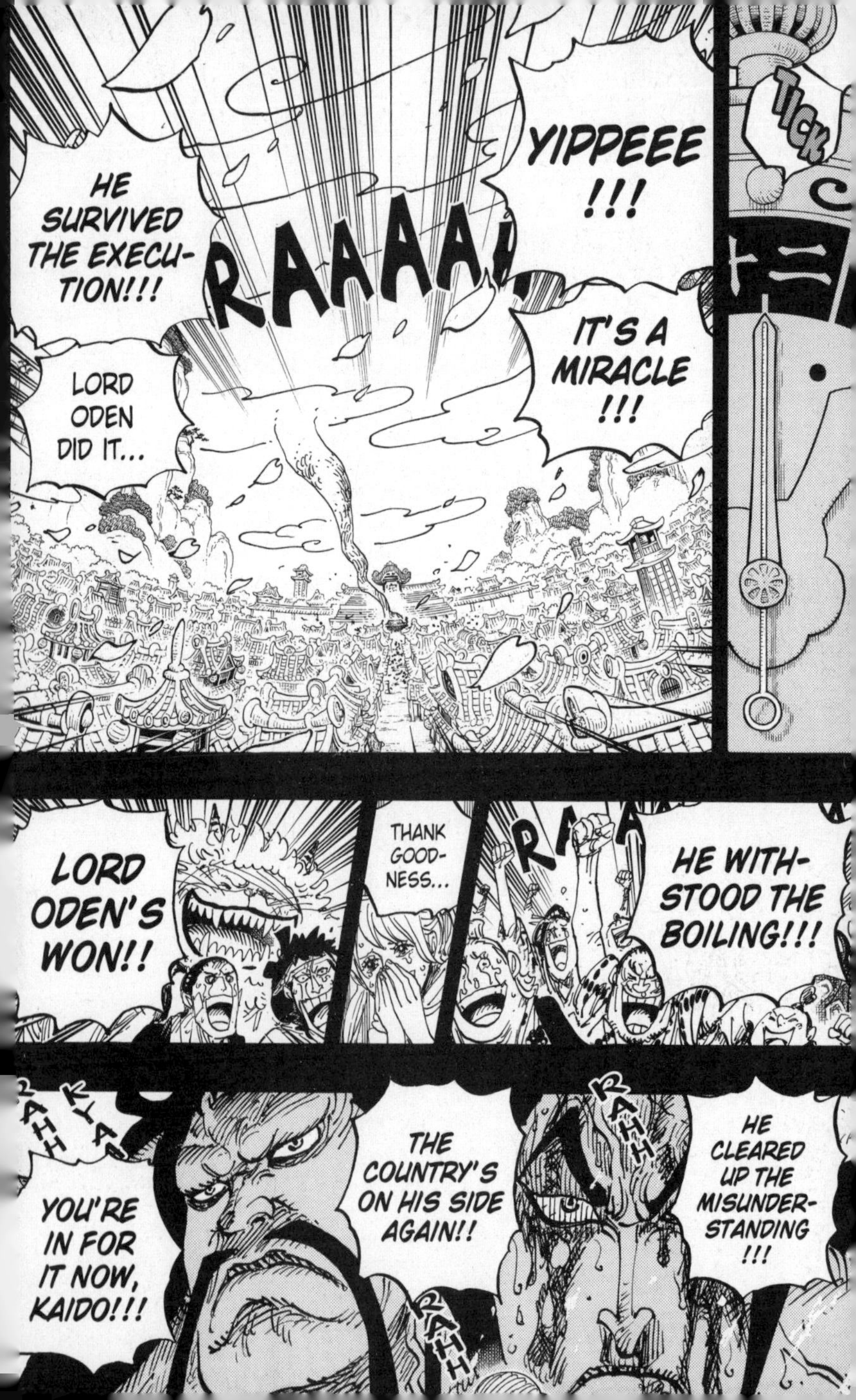
TICK
YIPPEEE!!!
RAAAAH
HE SURVIVED THE EXECUTION!!!
IT'S A MIRACLE!!!
LORD ODEN DID IT...
RA
HE WITHSTOOD THE BOILING!!!
THANK GOODNESS...
LORD ODEN'S WON!!
RAHH
HE CLEARED UP THE MISUNDERSTANDING!!!
THE COUNTRY'S ON HIS SIDE AGAIN!!
RAHH
RAHH
YOU'RE IN FOR IT NOW, KAIDO!!!

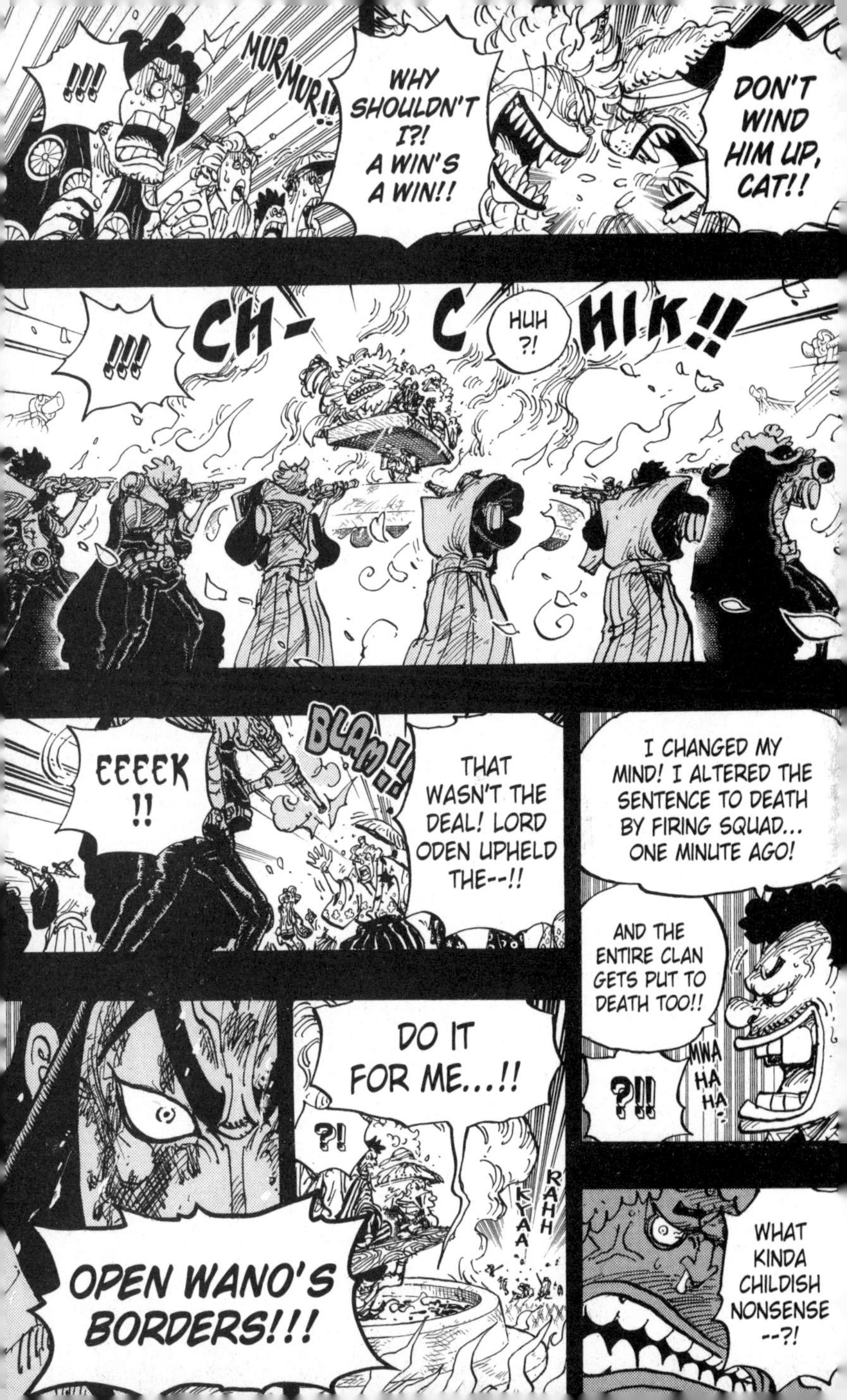
DON'T WIND HIM UP, CAT!!
WHY SHOULDN'T I?! A WIN'S A WIN!!
MURMUR
!!!
CH-CHIK!!
HUH ?!
!!!
I CHANGED MY MIND! I ALTERED THE SENTENCE TO DEATH BY FIRING SQUAD... ONE MINUTE AGO!
AND THE ENTIRE CLAN GETS PUT TO DEATH TOO!!
MWA HA HA
?!!
THAT WASN'T THE DEAL! LORD ODEN UPHELD THE--!!
BLAM!!
EEEEK !!
WHAT KINDA CHILDISH NONSENSE --?!
DO IT FOR ME...!!
RAHH
KYAA
?!
OPEN WANO'S BORDERS!!!

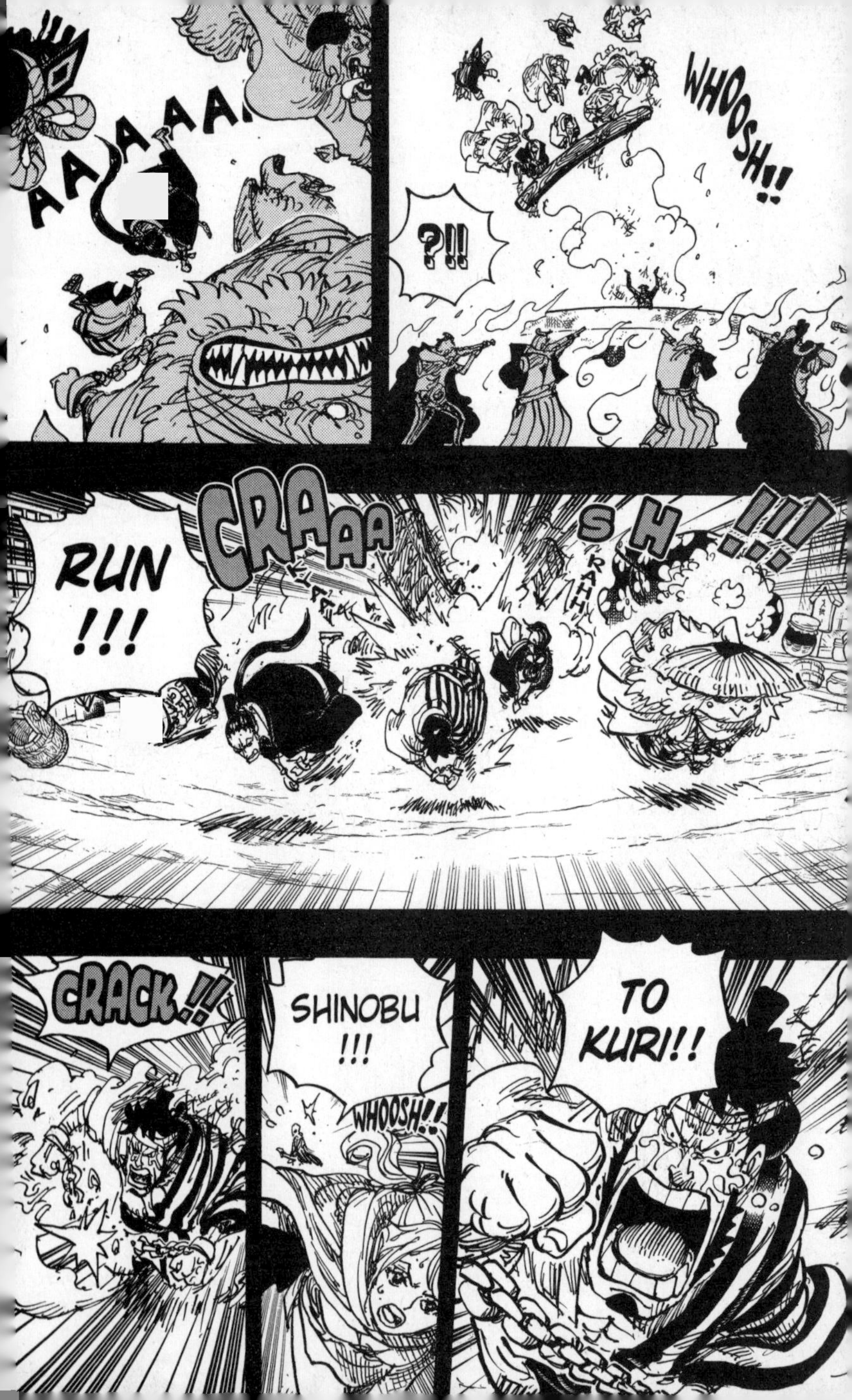
WHOOSH!!
?!!
AAAAAA!!
CRAAASH!!!
RUN !!!
TO KURI!!
SHINOBU !!!
WHOOSH!!
CRACK!!!

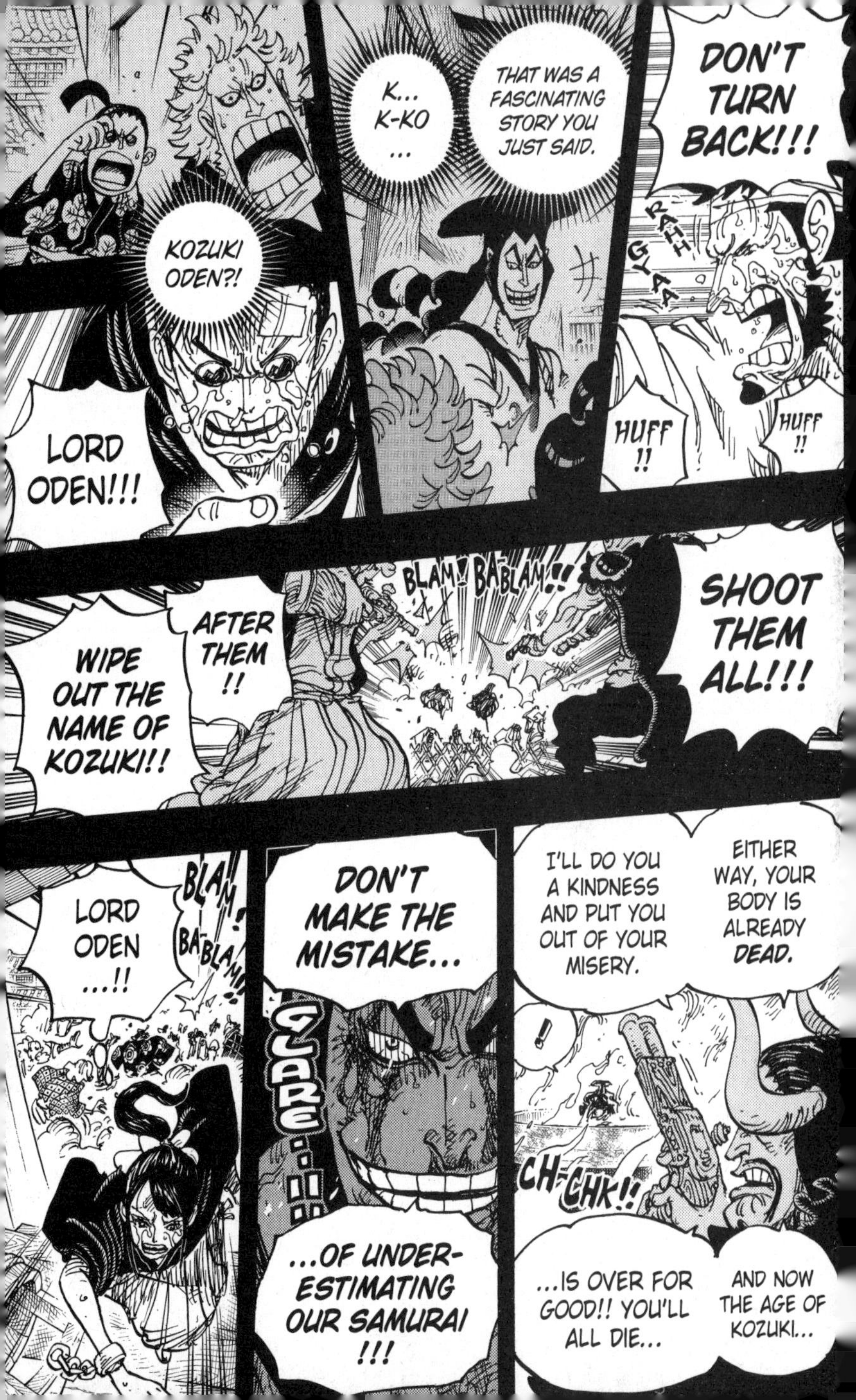
DON'T TURN BACK!!!
GYAA RAHH
HUFF!!
HUFF!!
THAT WAS A FASCINATING STORY YOU JUST SAID.
K... K-KO ...
KOZUKI ODEN?!
LORD ODEN!!!
SHOOT THEM ALL!!!
BLAM! BABLAM!!
AFTER THEM!!
WIPE OUT THE NAME OF KOZUKI!!
EITHER WAY, YOUR BODY IS ALREADY DEAD.
I'LL DO YOU A KINDNESS AND PUT YOU OUT OF YOUR MISERY.
!
CH-CHK!!
AND NOW THE AGE OF KOZUKI...
...IS OVER FOR GOOD!! YOU'LL ALL DIE...
DON'T MAKE THE MISTAKE...
GLARE...!!
...OF UNDER-ESTIMATING OUR SAMURAI!!!
BLAM!
BABLAM!!
LORD ODEN...!!

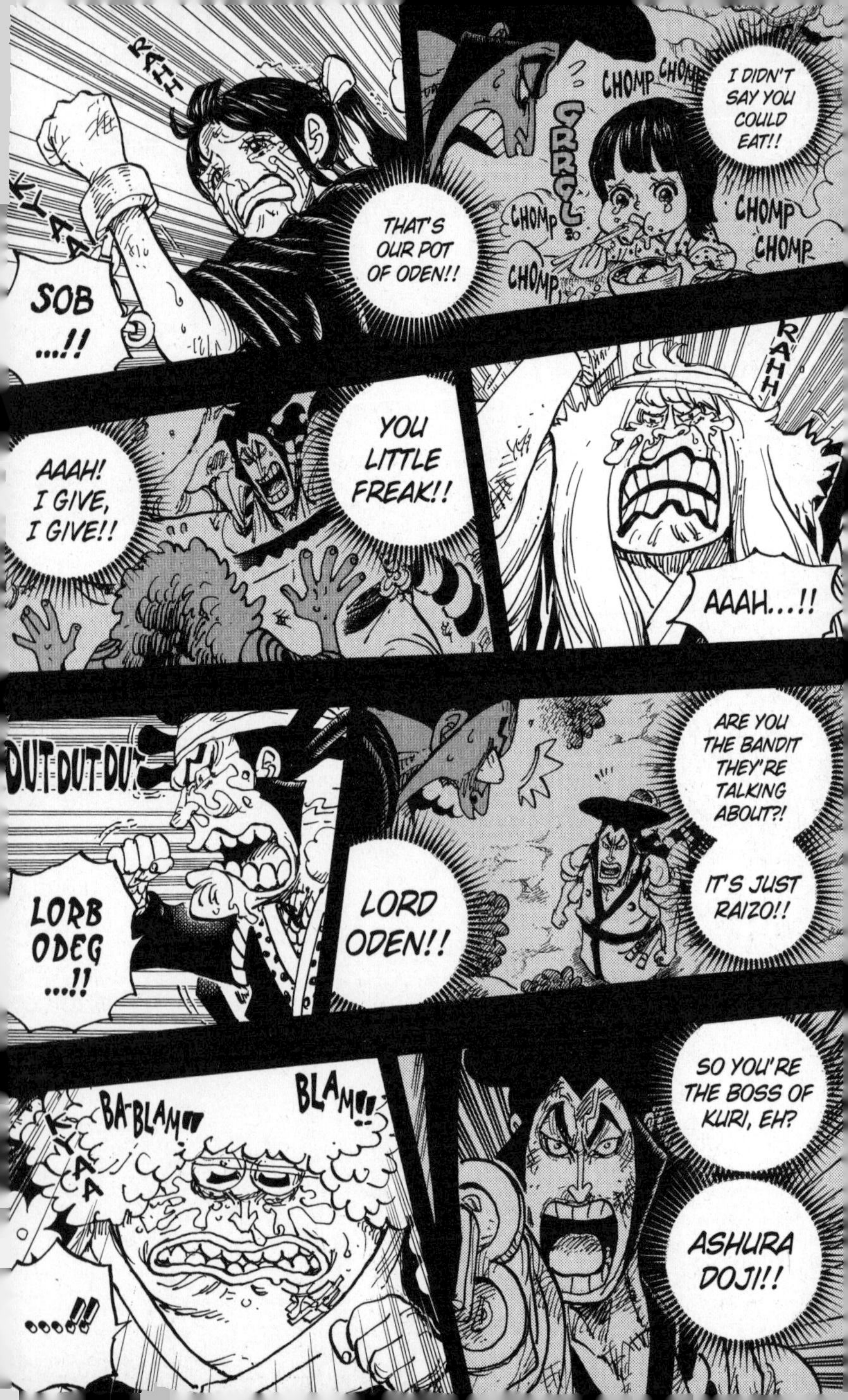
CHOMP CHOMP
I DIDN'T SAY YOU COULD EAT!!
GRRRL
CHOMP CHOMP
CHOMP
CHOMP CHOMP
RAHH
THAT'S OUR POT OF ODEN!!
KYAA
SOB ...!!
RAHH
AAAH...!!
YOU LITTLE FREAK!!
AAAH! I GIVE, I GIVE!!
ARE YOU THE BANDIT THEY'RE TALKING ABOUT?!
IT'S JUST RAIZO!!
LORD ODEN!!
DUT DUT DUT
LORB ODEG ...!!
SO YOU'RE THE BOSS OF KURI, EH?
ASHURA DOJI!!
BLAM!!
BA-BLAM!!
KYAA
....!!

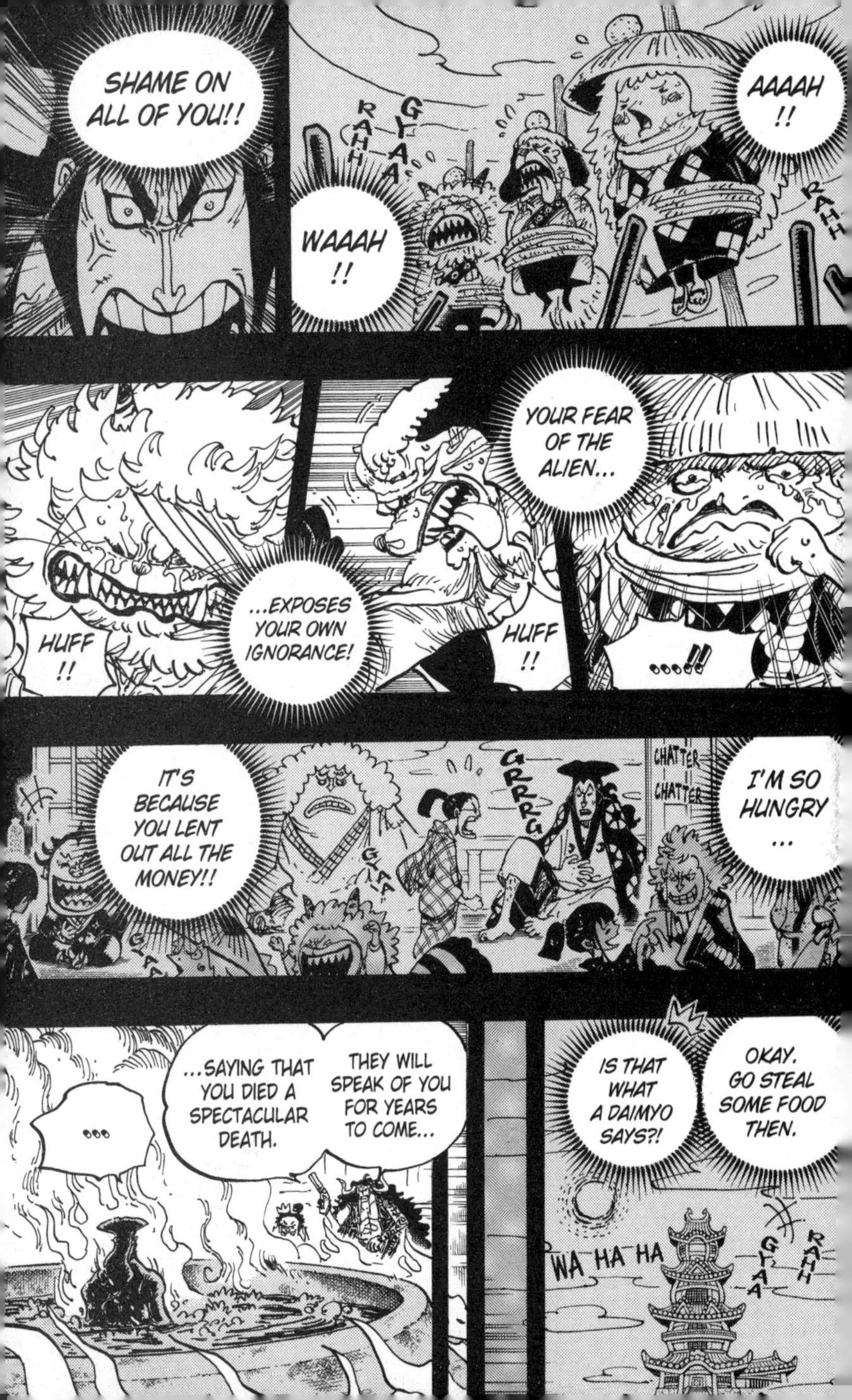
AAAAH !!
RAHH
GYAA
RAHH
WAAAH !!
SHAME ON ALL OF YOU!!
YOUR FEAR OF THE ALIEN...
....!!
HUFF !!
...EXPOSES YOUR OWN IGNORANCE!
HUFF !!
I'M SO HUNGRY ...
CHATTER
CHATTER
GRRRG
GYAA
IT'S BECAUSE YOU LENT OUT ALL THE MONEY!!
GYAA
OKAY. GO STEAL SOME FOOD THEN.
IS THAT WHAT A DAIMYO SAYS?!
RAHH
GYAA
WA HA HA
THEY WILL SPEAK OF YOU FOR YEARS TO COME...
...SAYING THAT YOU DIED A SPECTACULAR DEATH.
...

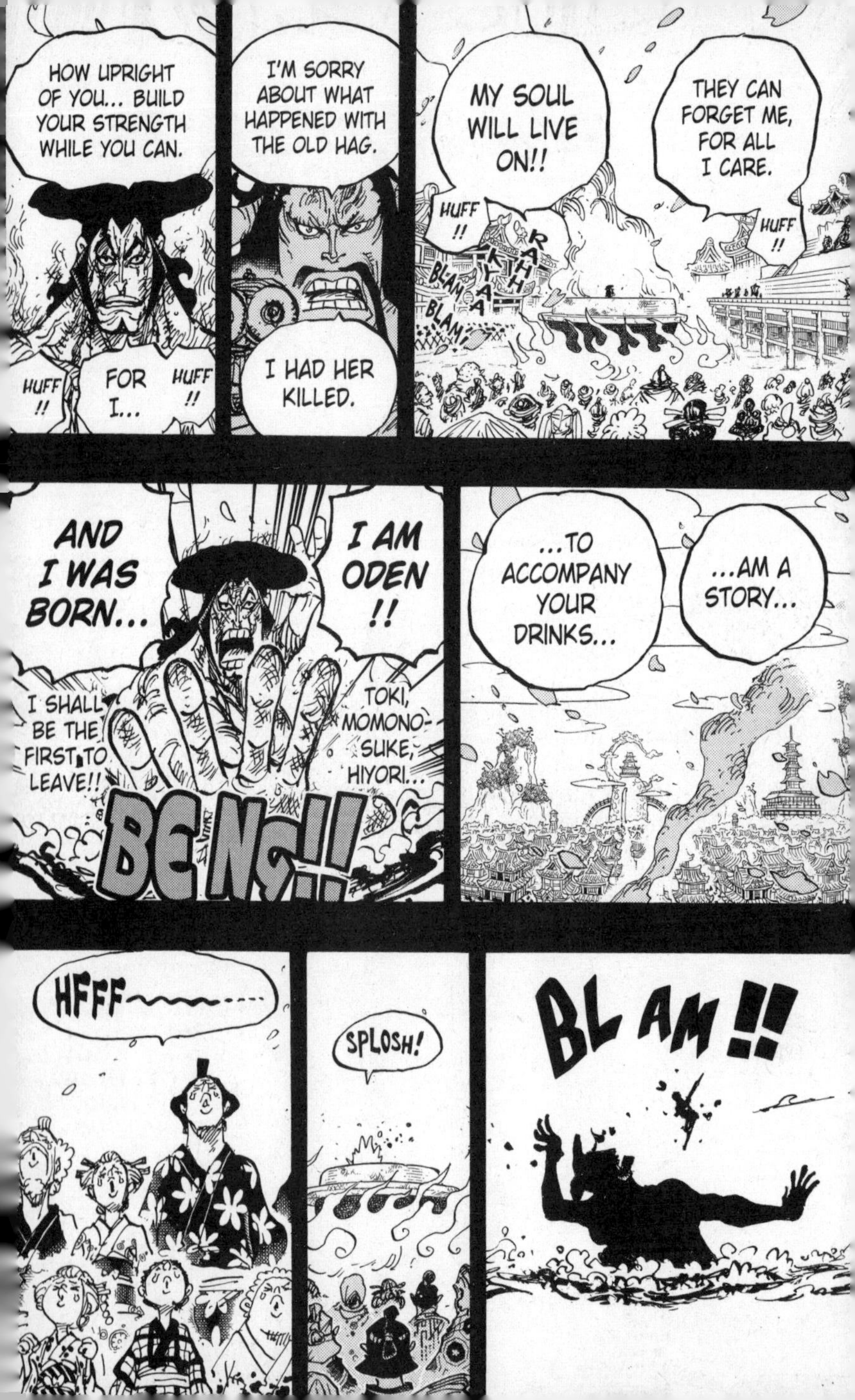
THEY CAN FORGET ME, FOR ALL I CARE.
HUFF !!
MY SOUL WILL LIVE ON!!
HUFF !!
RAHHH
KYAA
BLAM
BLAM
I'M SORRY ABOUT WHAT HAPPENED WITH THE OLD HAG.
I HAD HER KILLED.
HOW UPRIGHT OF YOU... BUILD YOUR STRENGTH WHILE YOU CAN.
HUFF !!
FOR I...
HUFF !!
...AM A STORY...
...TO ACCOMPANY YOUR DRINKS...
I AM ODEN !!
AND I WAS BORN...
TOKI, MOMONOSUKE, HIYORI...
I SHALL BE THE FIRST TO LEAVE!!
BENG!!
BLAM!!
SPLOSH!
HFFF

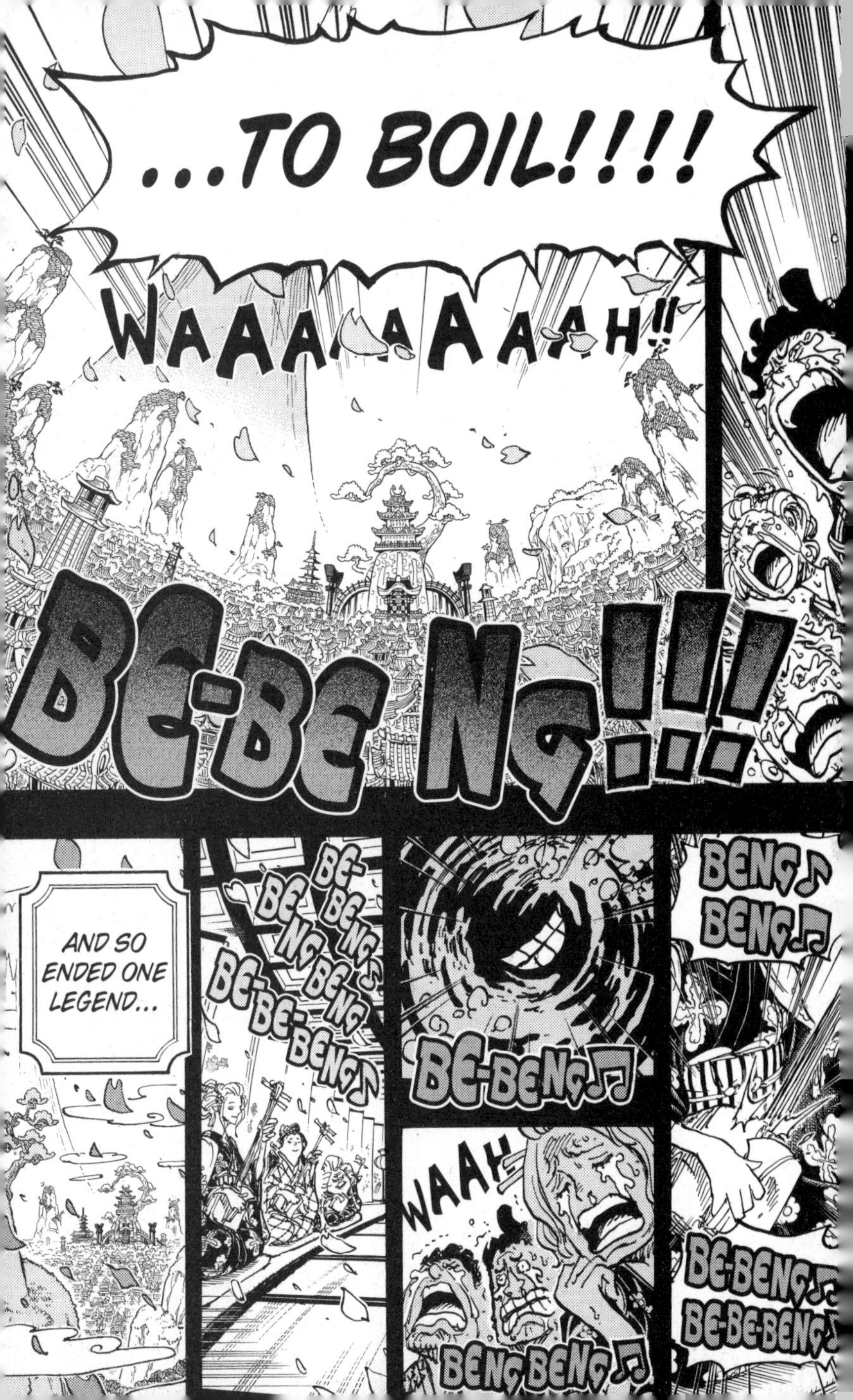
...TO BOIL!!!!
WAAAAAAAAH!!
BE-BENG!!!
BENG♪
BENG♪
BE-BENG♪
BE-BE-BENG♪
BE-BENG♪
WAAH
BENG BENG♪
BE-BENG♪
BE-BENG BE-BENG
BE-BE-BENG♪
AND SO ENDED ONE LEGEND...

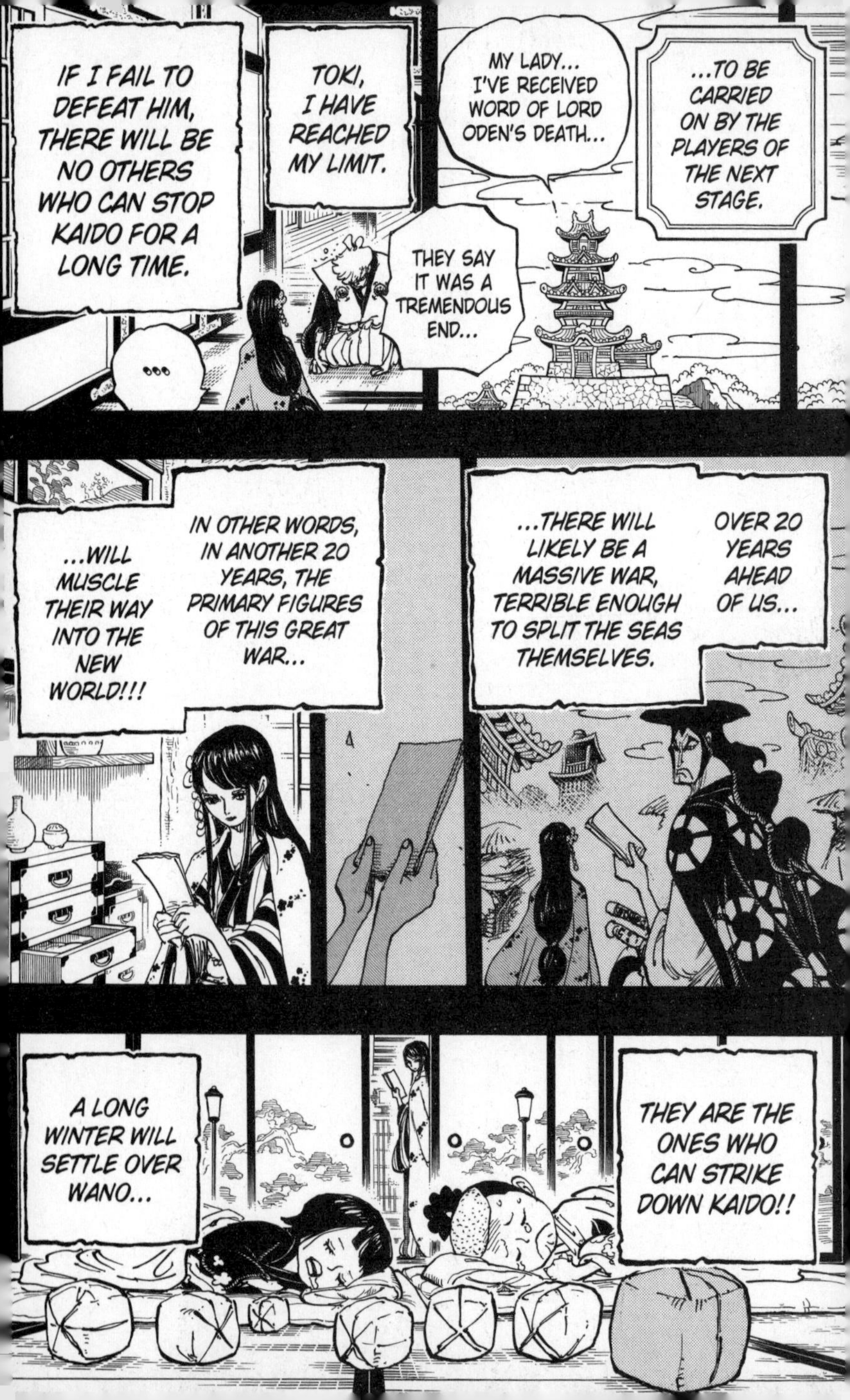
...TO BE CARRIED ON BY THE PLAYERS OF THE NEXT STAGE.
MY LADY... I'VE RECEIVED WORD OF LORD ODEN'S DEATH...
THEY SAY IT WAS A TREMENDOUS END...
TOKI, I HAVE REACHED MY LIMIT.
IF I FAIL TO DEFEAT HIM, THERE WILL BE NO OTHERS WHO CAN STOP KAIDO FOR A LONG TIME.
...
OVER 20 YEARS AHEAD OF US...
...THERE WILL LIKELY BE A MASSIVE WAR, TERRIBLE ENOUGH TO SPLIT THE SEAS THEMSELVES.
IN OTHER WORDS, IN ANOTHER 20 YEARS, THE PRIMARY FIGURES OF THIS GREAT WAR...
...WILL MUSCLE THEIR WAY INTO THE NEW WORLD!!!
THEY ARE THE ONES WHO CAN STRIKE DOWN KAIDO!!
A LONG WINTER WILL SETTLE OVER WANO...

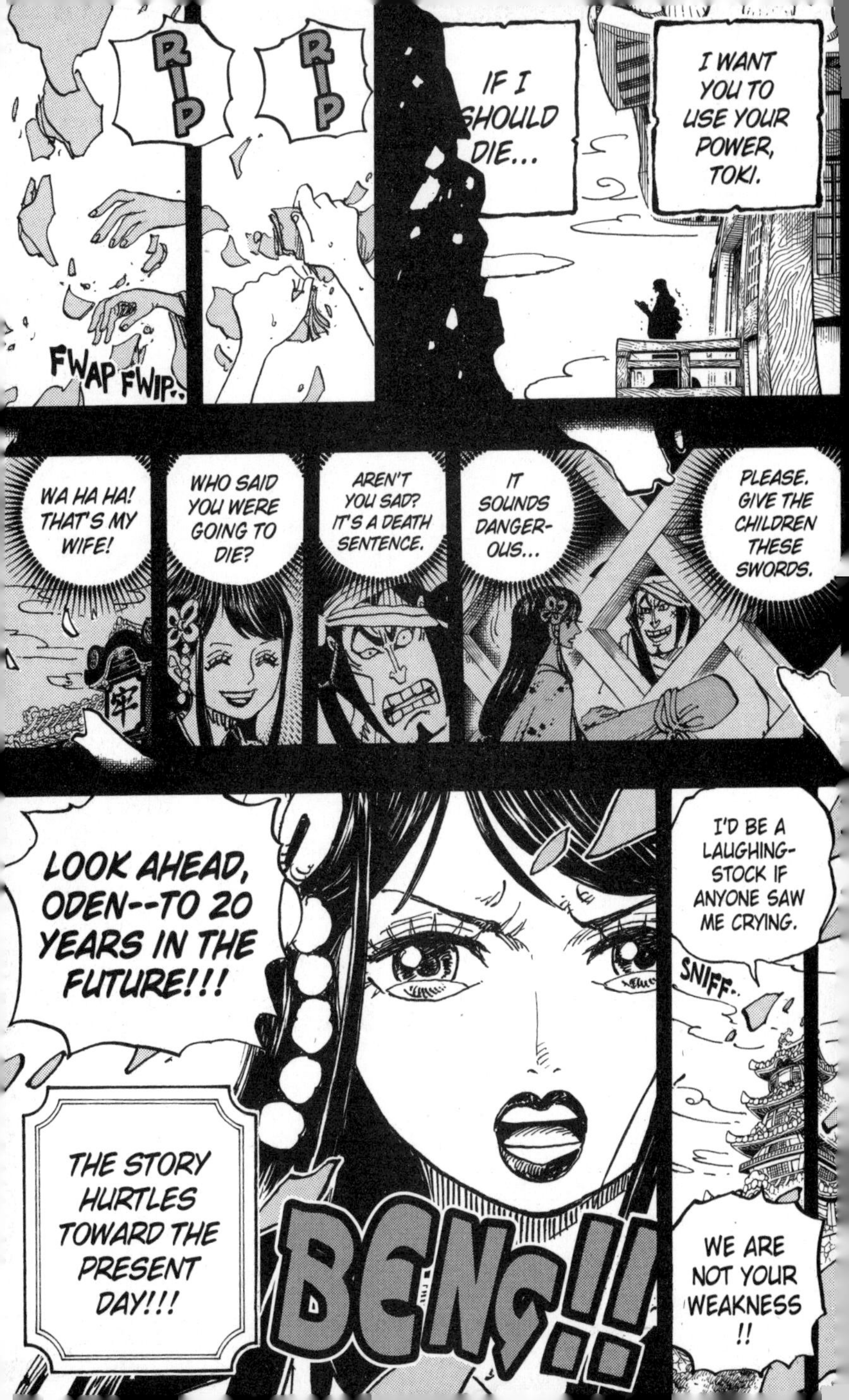
I WANT YOU TO USE YOUR POWER, TOKI.
IF I SHOULD DIE...
RIP
RIP
FWAP FWIP..
PLEASE. GIVE THE CHILDREN THESE SWORDS.
IT SOUNDS DANGER-OUS...
AREN'T YOU SAD? IT'S A DEATH SENTENCE.
WHO SAID YOU WERE GOING TO DIE?
WA HA HA! THAT'S MY WIFE!
I'D BE A LAUGHING-STOCK IF ANYONE SAW ME CRYING.
SNIFF..
WE ARE NOT YOUR WEAKNESS!!
LOOK AHEAD, ODEN--TO 20 YEARS IN THE FUTURE!!!
BENG!!
THE STORY HURTLES TOWARD THE PRESENT DAY!!!

SBS Question Corner

(Takahisa Fujimoto, Nara)

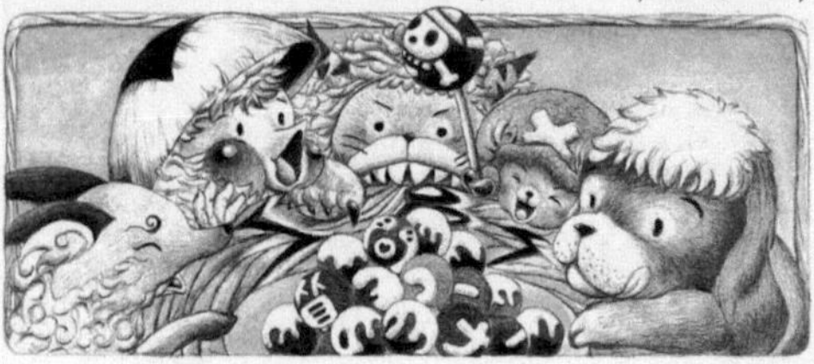

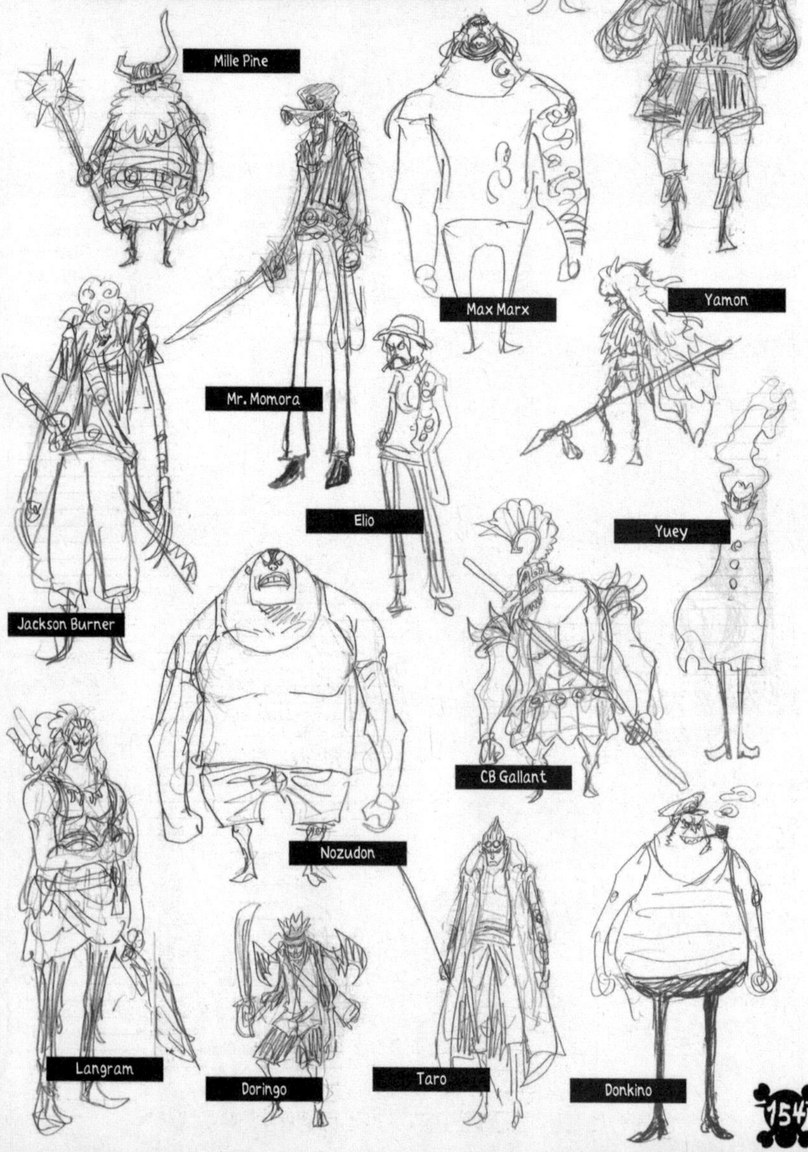
Lowwing
Ganryu
Mille Pine
Max Marx
Mr. Momora
Yamon
Elio
Yuey
Jackson Burner
CB Gallant
Nozudon
Langram
Doringo
Taro
Donkino

Chapter 973:
THE KOZUKI CLAN

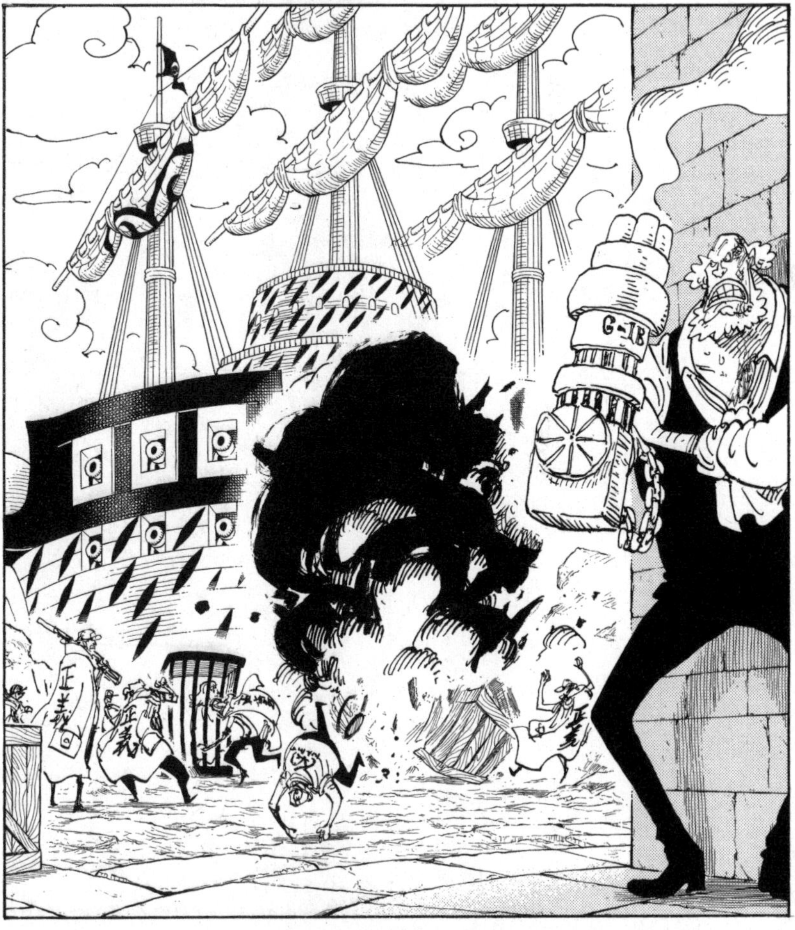
G-1B

GANG BEGE'S OH MY FAMILY
VOL. 21: "GOTTI'S COUNTERATTACK"

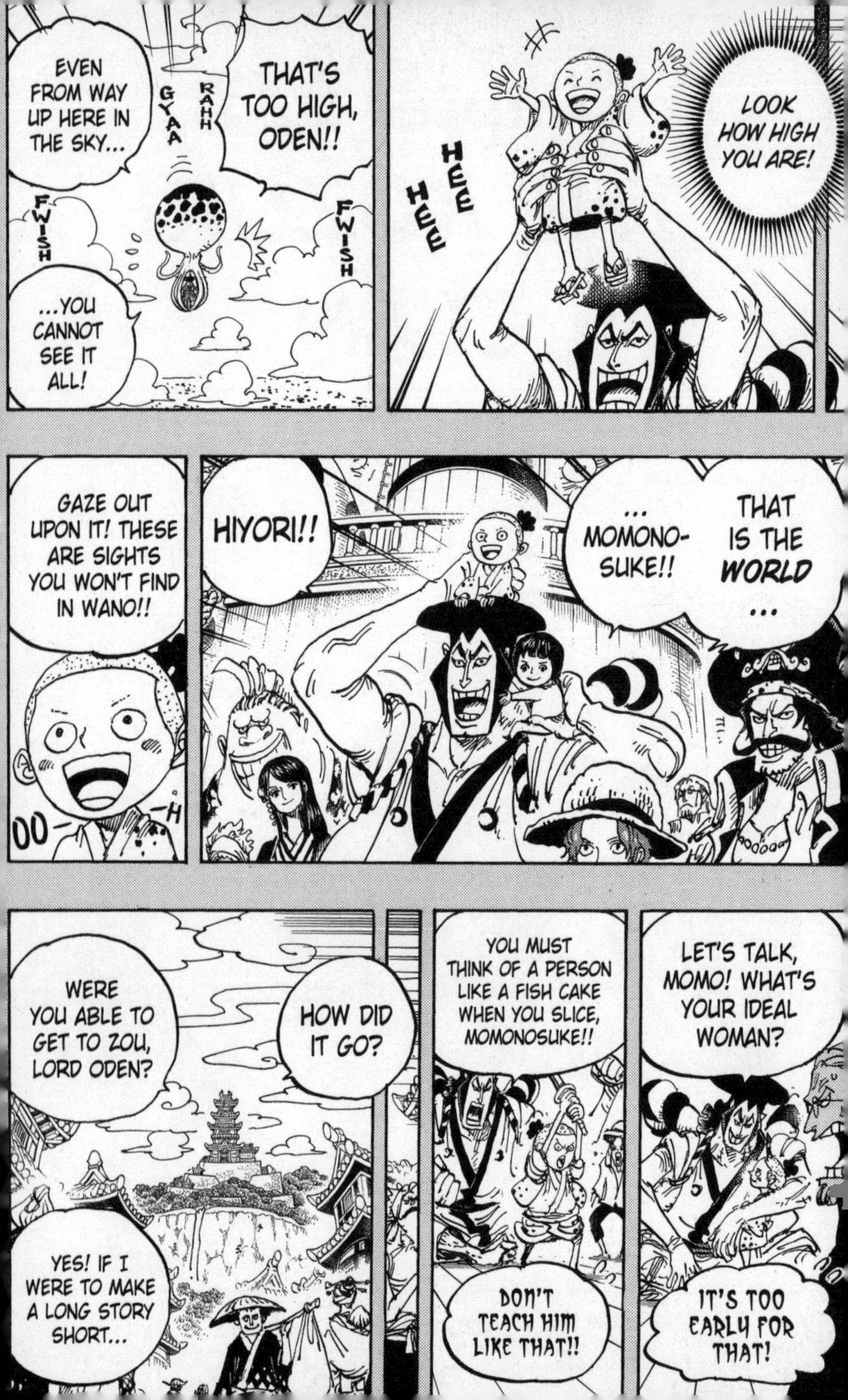
LOOK HOW HIGH YOU ARE!
HEE HEE
THAT'S TOO HIGH, ODEN!!
RAHH
GYAA
EVEN FROM WAY UP HERE IN THE SKY...
FWISH
FWISH
...YOU CANNOT SEE IT ALL!
THAT IS THE WORLD ...
... MOMONO-SUKE!!
HIYORI!!
GAZE OUT UPON IT! THESE ARE SIGHTS YOU WON'T FIND IN WANO!!
OO-H
LET'S TALK, MOMO! WHAT'S YOUR IDEAL WOMAN?
IT'S TOO EARLY FOR THAT!
YOU MUST THINK OF A PERSON LIKE A FISH CAKE WHEN YOU SLICE, MOMONOSUKE!!
DON'T TEACH HIM LIKE THAT!!
HOW DID IT GO?
WERE YOU ABLE TO GET TO ZOU, LORD ODEN?
YES! IF I WERE TO MAKE A LONG STORY SHORT...

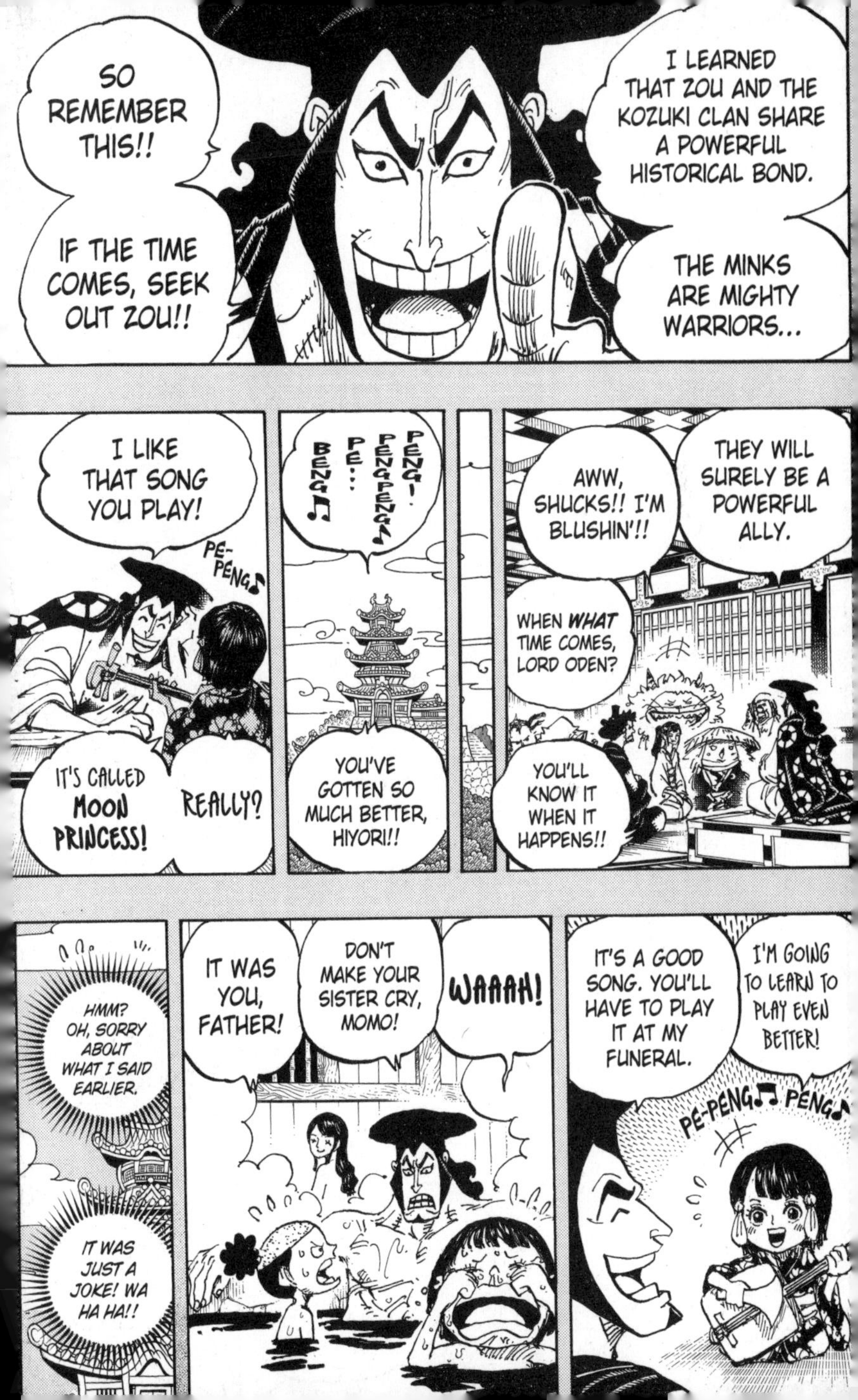
I LEARNED THAT ZOU AND THE KOZUKI CLAN SHARE A POWERFUL HISTORICAL BOND.
THE MINKS ARE MIGHTY WARRIORS...
SO REMEMBER THIS!!
IF THE TIME COMES, SEEK OUT ZOU!!
THEY WILL SURELY BE A POWERFUL ALLY.
AWW, SHUCKS!! I'M BLUSHIN'!!
WHEN WHAT TIME COMES, LORD ODEN?
YOU'LL KNOW IT WHEN IT HAPPENS!!
PENG! PENGPENG♪ PE... BENG♫
YOU'VE GOTTEN SO MUCH BETTER, HIYORI!!
I LIKE THAT SONG YOU PLAY!
PE-PENG♪
REALLY?
IT'S CALLED MOON PRINCESS!
I'M GOING TO LEARN TO PLAY EVEN BETTER!
IT'S A GOOD SONG. YOU'LL HAVE TO PLAY IT AT MY FUNERAL.
PE-PENG♫ PENG♪
WAAAH!
DON'T MAKE YOUR SISTER CRY, MOMO!
IT WAS YOU, FATHER!
HMM? OH, SORRY ABOUT WHAT I SAID EARLIER.
IT WAS JUST A JOKE! WA HA HA!!

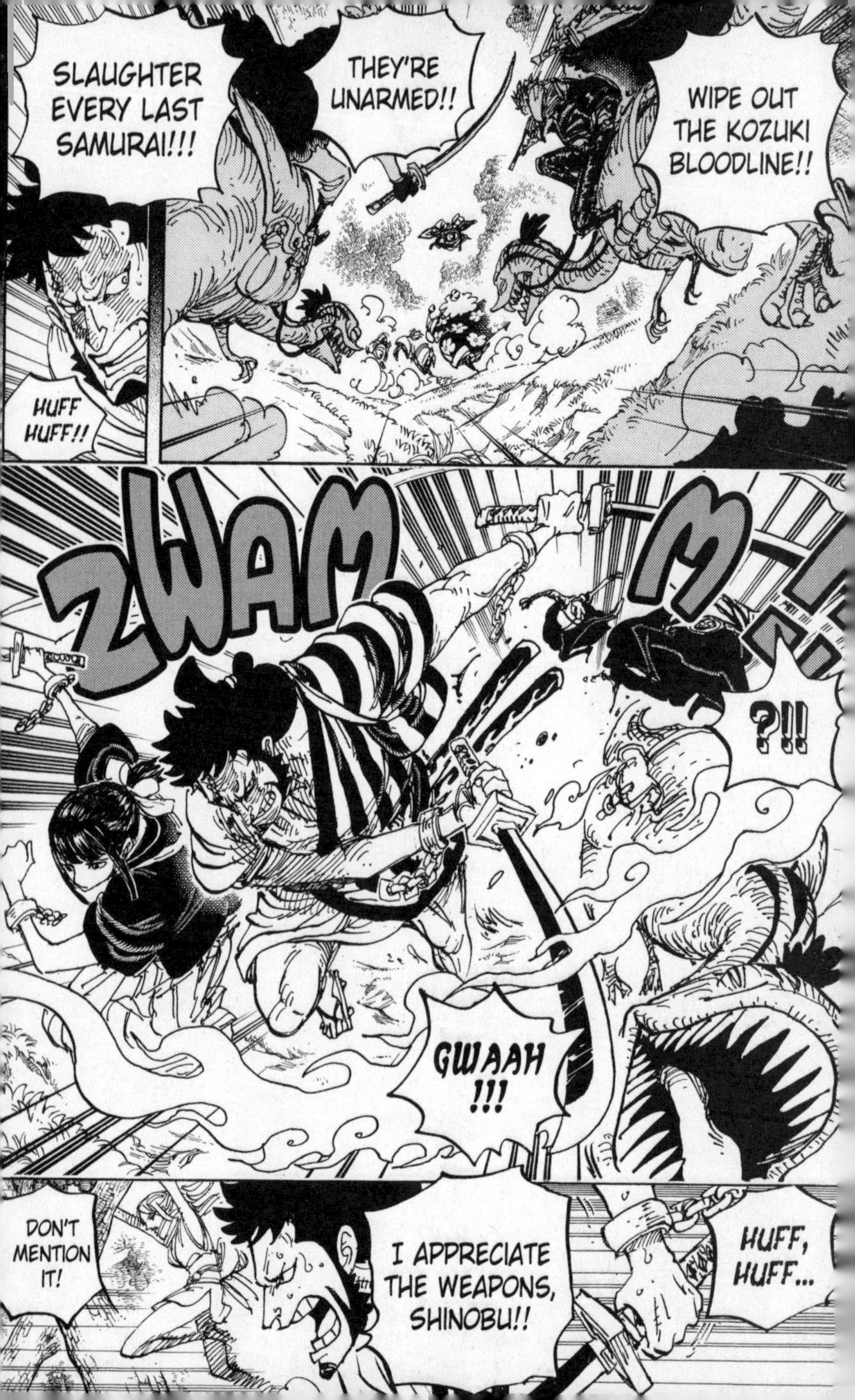
WIPE OUT THE KOZUKI BLOODLINE!!
THEY'RE UNARMED!!
SLAUGHTER EVERY LAST SAMURAI!!!
HUFF HUFF!!
ZWAMM!!
?!!
GWAAH !!!
HUFF, HUFF...
I APPRECIATE THE WEAPONS, SHINOBU!!
DON'T MENTION IT!

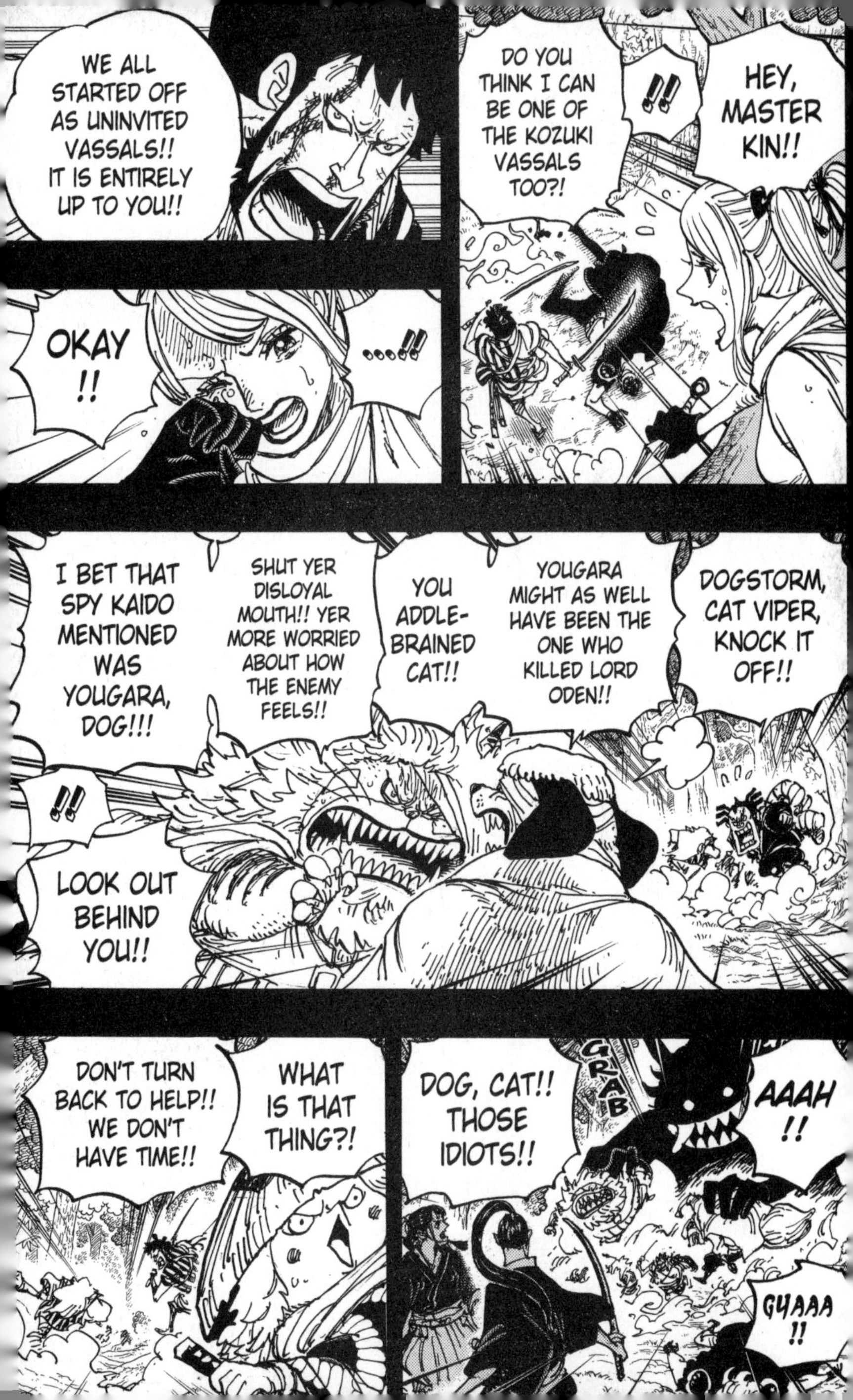

HEY, MASTER KIN!!
!!
DO YOU THINK I CAN BE ONE OF THE KOZUKI VASSALS TOO?!
WE ALL STARTED OFF AS UNINVITED VASSALS!! IT IS ENTIRELY UP TO YOU!!
....!!
OKAY !!
DOGSTORM, CAT VIPER, KNOCK IT OFF!!
YOUGARA MIGHT AS WELL HAVE BEEN THE ONE WHO KILLED LORD ODEN!!
YOU ADDLE-BRAINED CAT!!
SHUT YER DISLOYAL MOUTH!! YER MORE WORRIED ABOUT HOW THE ENEMY FEELS!!
I BET THAT SPY KAIDO MENTIONED WAS YOUGARA, DOG!!!
!!
LOOK OUT BEHIND YOU!!
AAAH !!
GRAB
DOG, CAT!! THOSE IDIOTS!!
GUAAA !!
WHAT IS THAT THING?!
DON'T TURN BACK TO HELP!! WE DON'T HAVE TIME!!

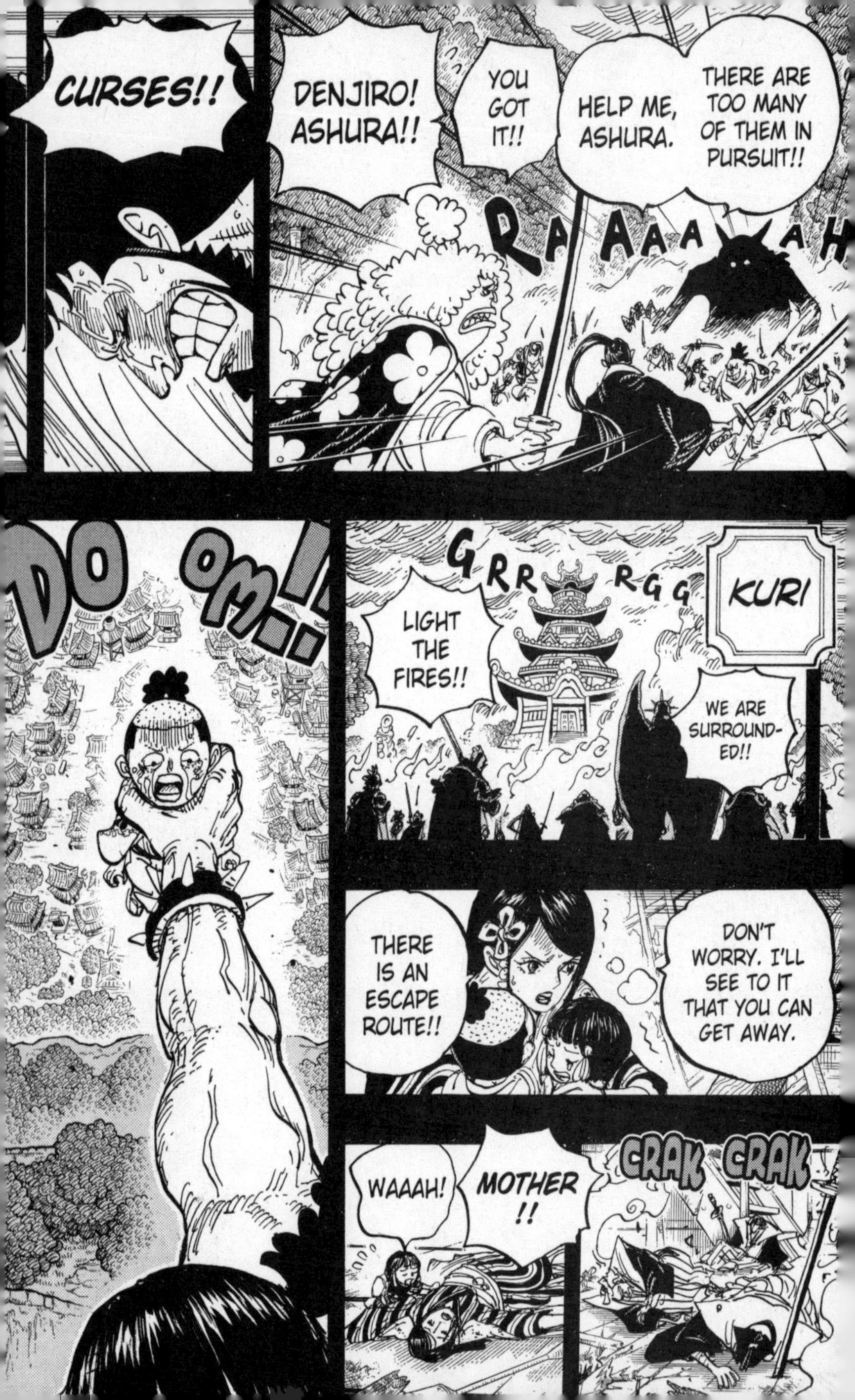
THERE ARE TOO MANY OF THEM IN PURSUIT!!
HELP ME, ASHURA.
YOU GOT IT!!
DENJIRO! ASHURA!!
RAAAAAH
CURSES!!
KURI
GRRRGG
WE ARE SURROUNDED!!
LIGHT THE FIRES!!
DON'T WORRY. I'LL SEE TO IT THAT YOU CAN GET AWAY.
THERE IS AN ESCAPE ROUTE!!
CRAK CRAK
MOTHER!!
WAAAH!
DOOM..!!

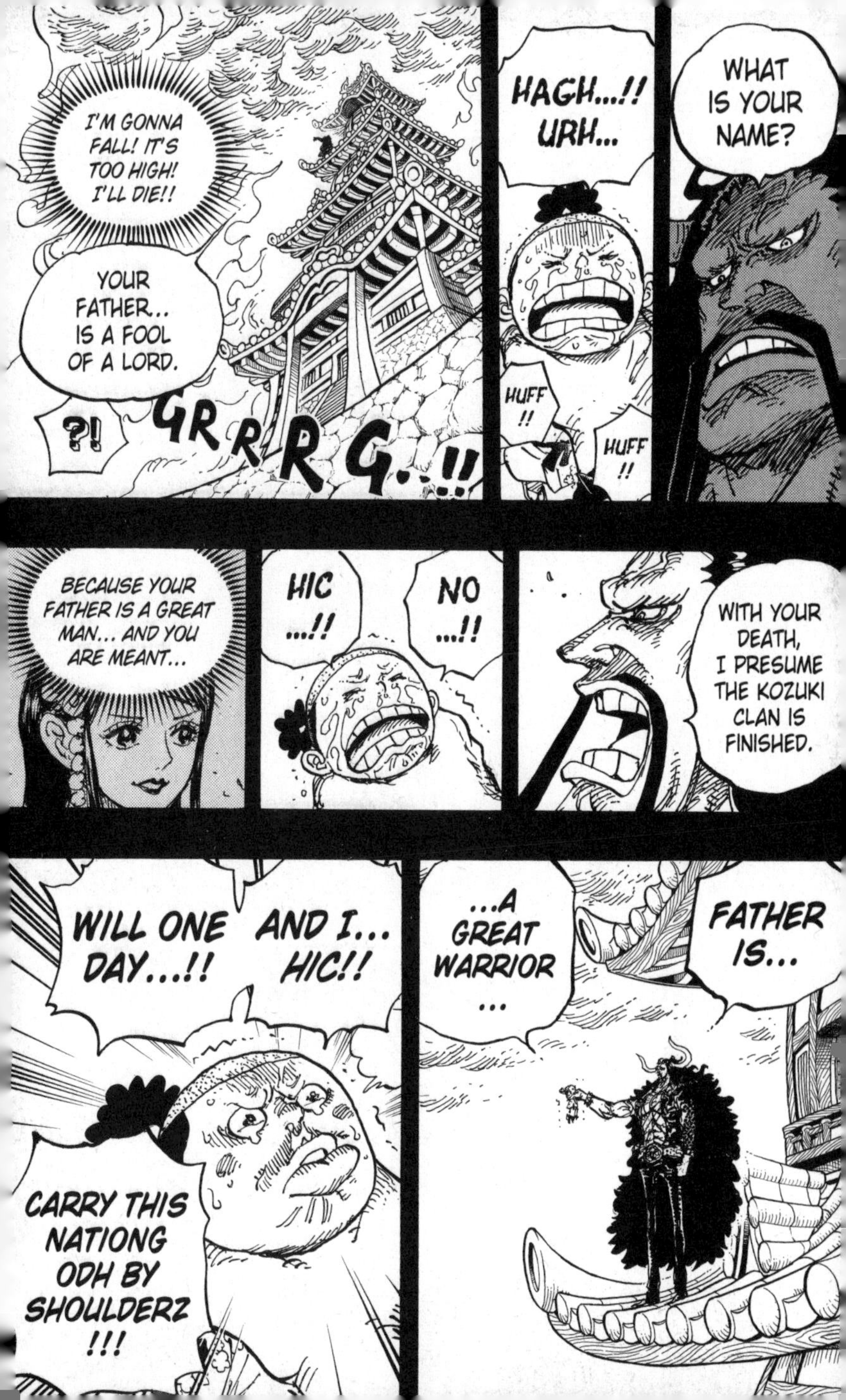
WHAT IS YOUR NAME?
HAGH...!! URH...
HUFF !!
HUFF !!
I'M GONNA FALL! IT'S TOO HIGH! I'LL DIE!!
YOUR FATHER... IS A FOOL OF A LORD.
GRRRRG..!!
?!
WITH YOUR DEATH, I PRESUME THE KOZUKI CLAN IS FINISHED.
NO ...!!
HIC ...!!
BECAUSE YOUR FATHER IS A GREAT MAN... AND YOU ARE MEANT...
FATHER IS...
...A GREAT WARRIOR ...
AND I... HIC!!
WILL ONE DAY...!!
CARRY THIS NATIONG ODH BY SHOULDERZ !!!

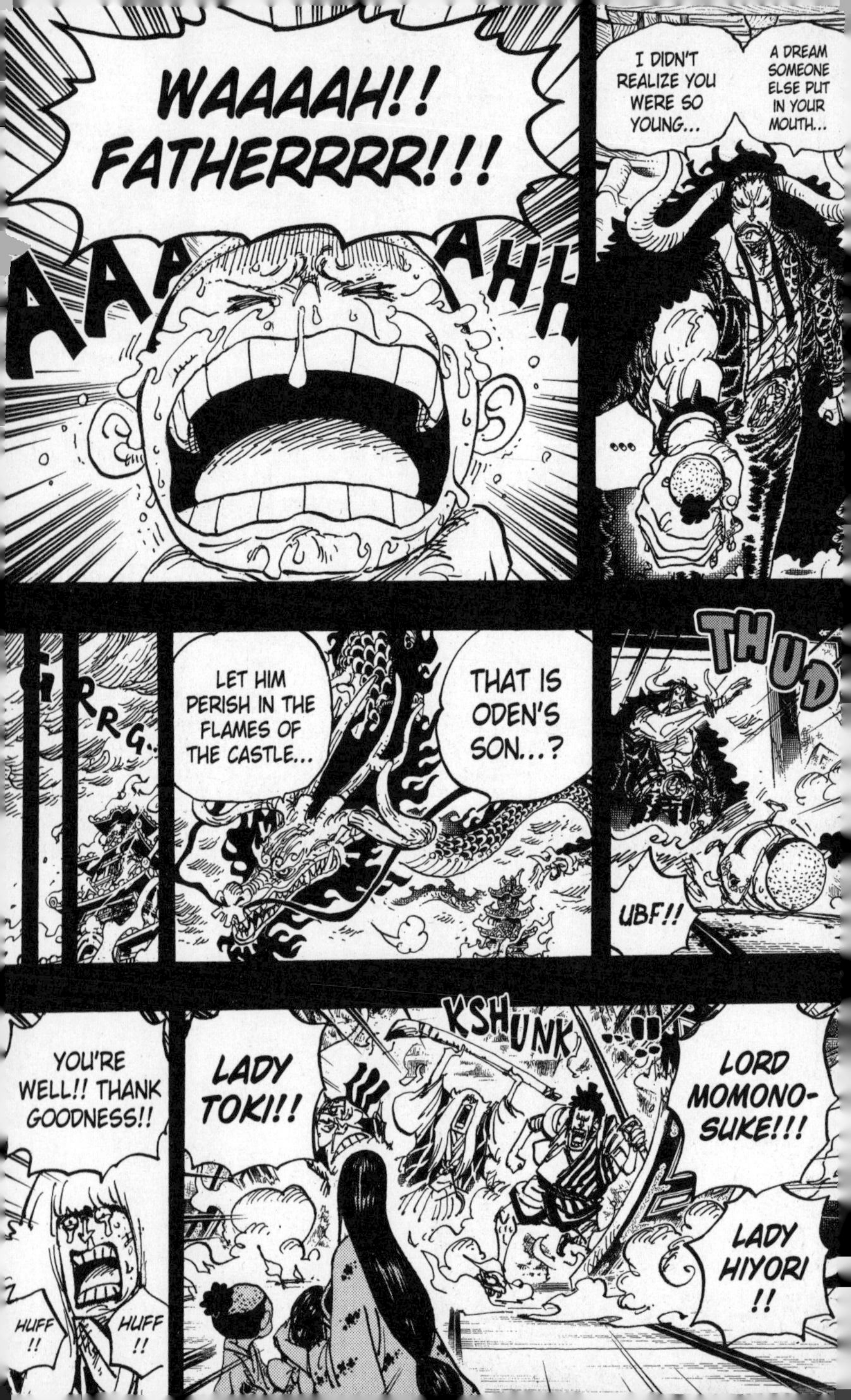
A DREAM SOMEONE ELSE PUT IN YOUR MOUTH...
I DIDN'T REALIZE YOU WERE SO YOUNG...
...
WAAAAH!! FATHERRRR!!!
AAA
AHH
THUD
UBF!!
THAT IS ODEN'S SON...?
LET HIM PERISH IN THE FLAMES OF THE CASTLE...
RRG..
KSHUNK
LORD MOMONOSUKE!!!
LADY HIYORI!!
LADY TOKI!!
YOU'RE WELL!! THANK GOODNESS!!
HUFF!!
HUFF!!

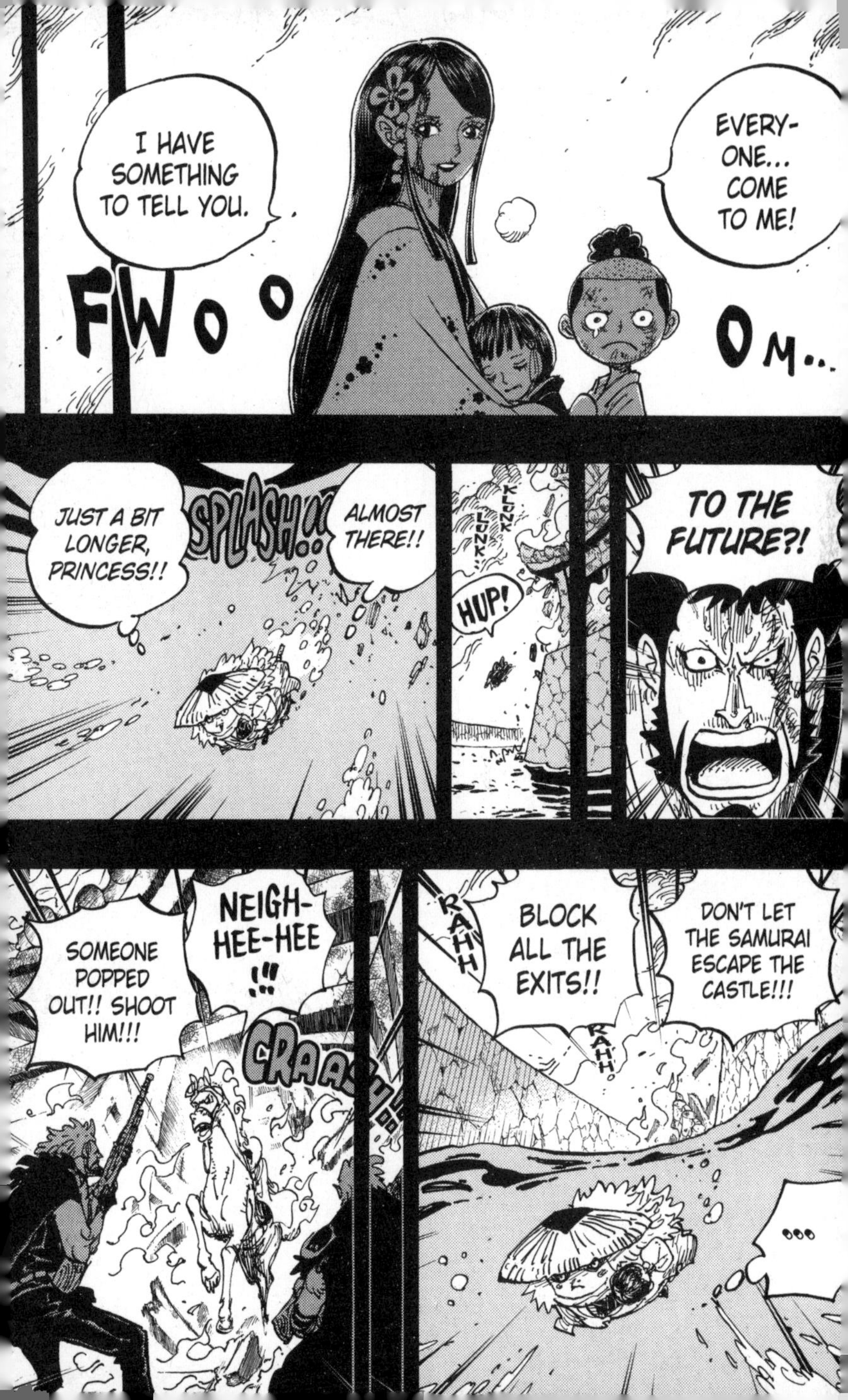
EVERY-ONE... COME TO ME!
I HAVE SOMETHING TO TELL YOU.
FWOO
OM...
TO THE FUTURE?!
KLUNK
KLUNK
HUP!
ALMOST THERE!!
SPLASH!!
JUST A BIT LONGER, PRINCESS!!
DON'T LET THE SAMURAI ESCAPE THE CASTLE!!!
BLOCK ALL THE EXITS!!
RAHH
RAHH
...
NEIGH-HEE-HEE!!!
SOMEONE POPPED OUT!! SHOOT HIM!!!
CRAASH!!

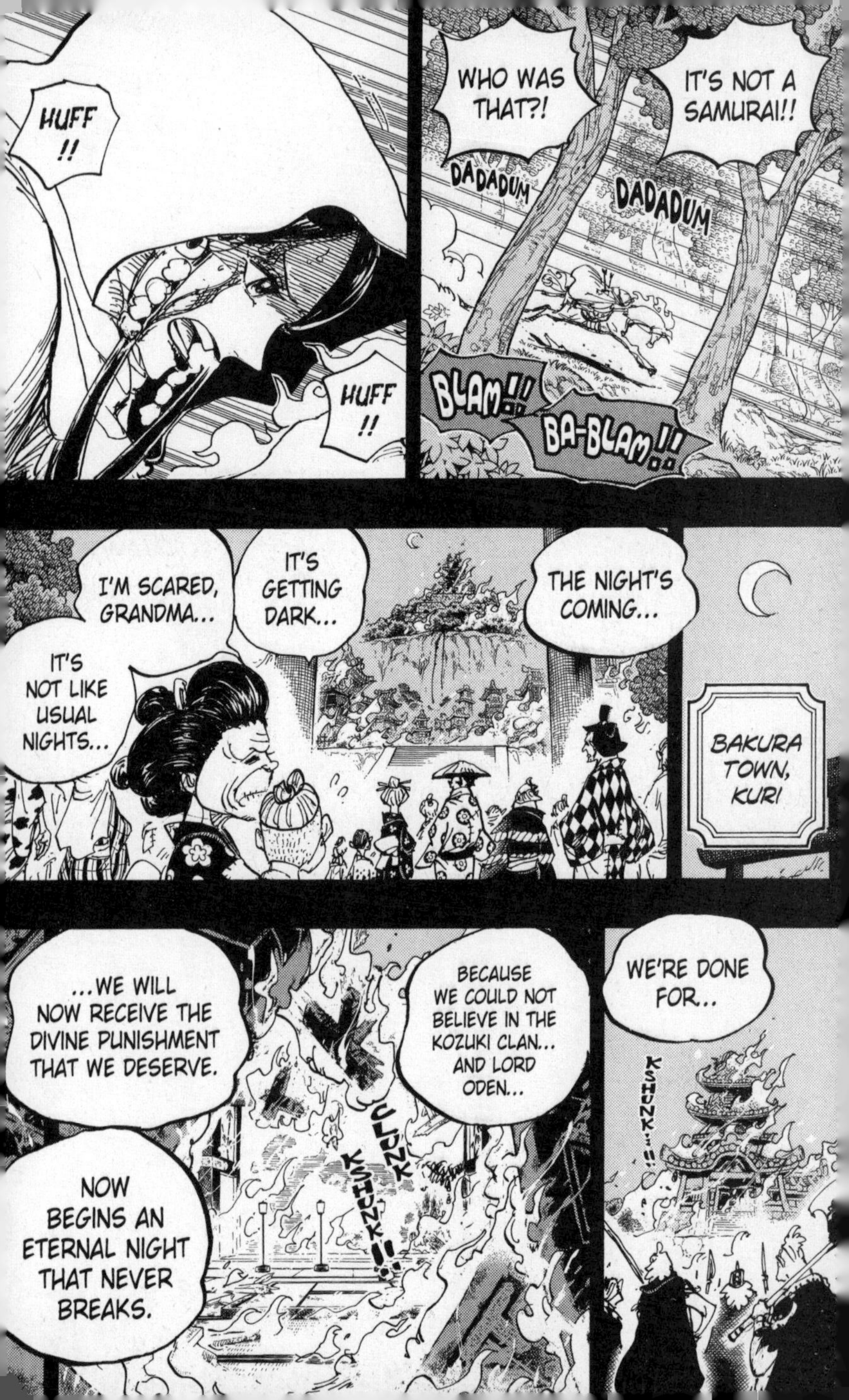
IT'S NOT A SAMURAI!!
WHO WAS THAT?!
DADADUM
DADADUM
BLAM!!
BA-BLAM!!
HUFF!!
HUFF!!
BAKURA TOWN, KURI
THE NIGHT'S COMING...
IT'S GETTING DARK...
I'M SCARED, GRANDMA...
IT'S NOT LIKE USUAL NIGHTS...
WE'RE DONE FOR...
KSHUNK!!
BECAUSE WE COULD NOT BELIEVE IN THE KOZUKI CLAN... AND LORD ODEN...
CLUNK
KSHUNK!!
...WE WILL NOW RECEIVE THE DIVINE PUNISHMENT THAT WE DESERVE.
NOW BEGINS AN ETERNAL NIGHT THAT NEVER BREAKS.

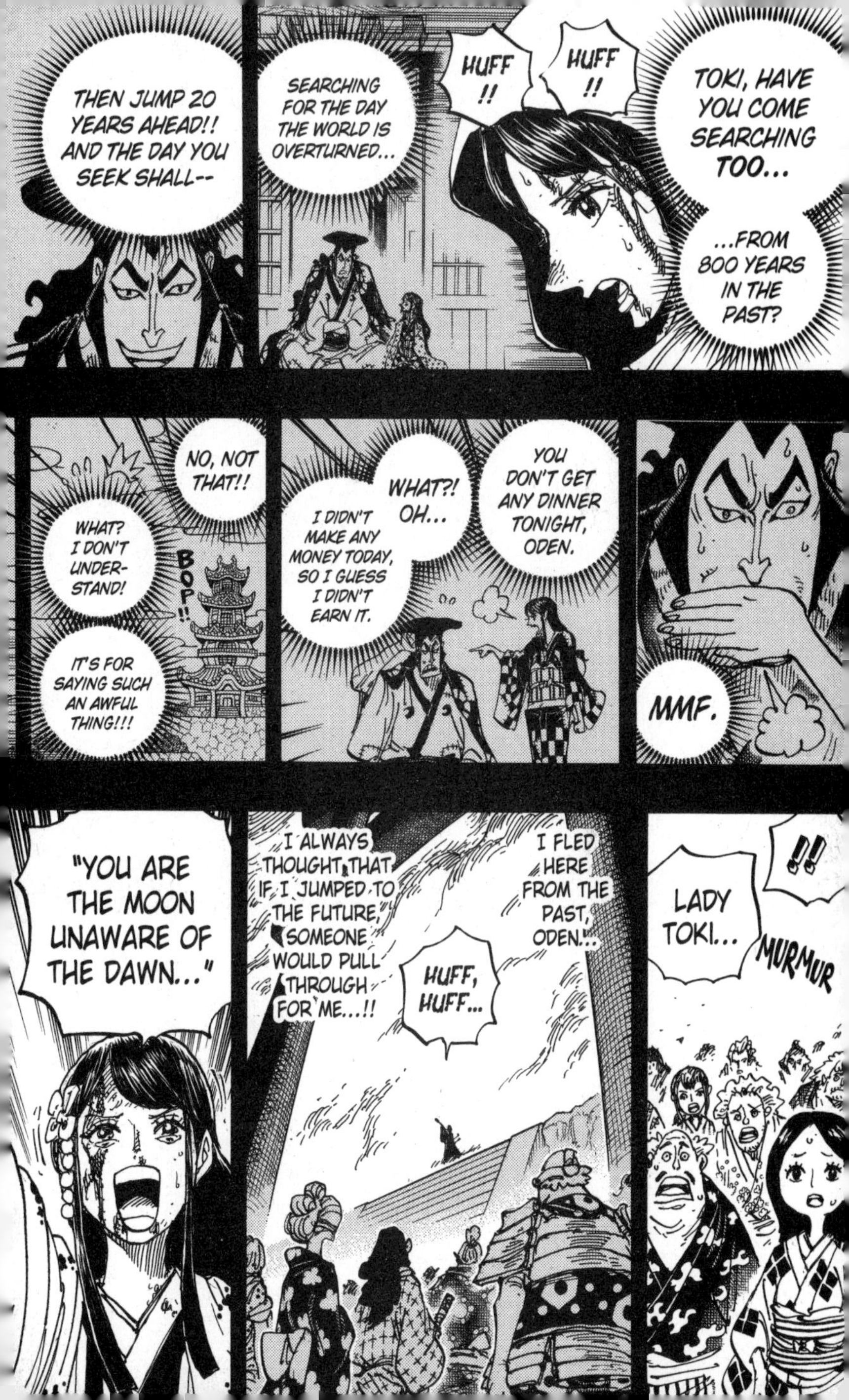
TOKI, HAVE YOU COME SEARCHING TOO...
HUFF !!
HUFF !!
...FROM 800 YEARS IN THE PAST?
SEARCHING FOR THE DAY THE WORLD IS OVERTURNED...
THEN JUMP 20 YEARS AHEAD!! AND THE DAY YOU SEEK SHALL--
MMF.
YOU DON'T GET ANY DINNER TONIGHT, ODEN.
WHAT?! OH...
I DIDN'T MAKE ANY MONEY TODAY, SO I GUESS I DIDN'T EARN IT.
NO, NOT THAT!!
WHAT? I DON'T UNDER-STAND!
BOP!!
IT'S FOR SAYING SUCH AN AWFUL THING!!!
!!
LADY TOKI...
MURMUR
I FLED HERE FROM THE PAST, ODEN...
I ALWAYS THOUGHT THAT IF I JUMPED TO THE FUTURE, SOMEONE WOULD PULL THROUGH FOR ME...!!
HUFF, HUFF...
"YOU ARE THE MOON UNAWARE OF THE DAWN..."

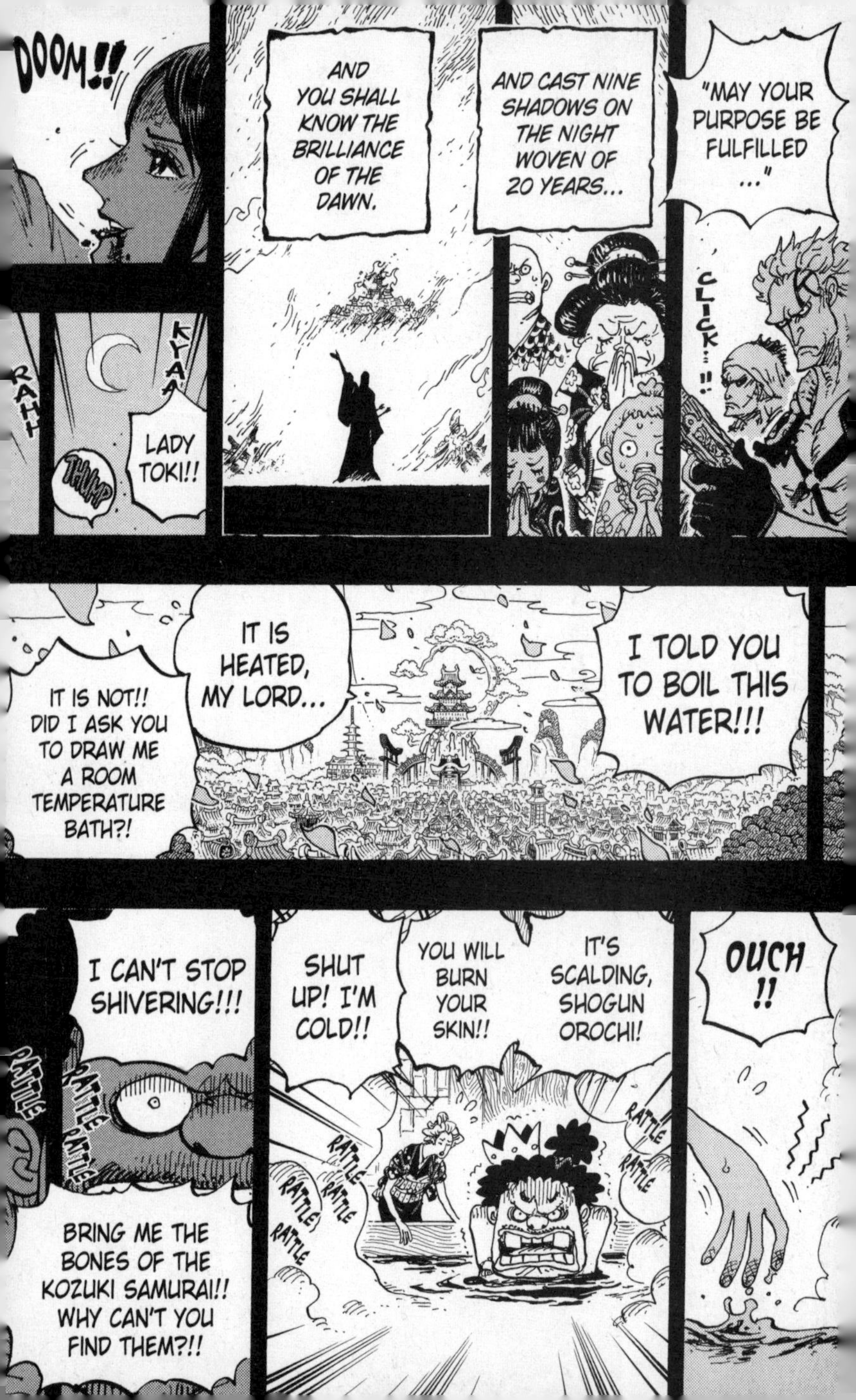
"MAY YOUR PURPOSE BE FULFILLED ..."
CLICK!! !!
AND CAST NINE SHADOWS ON THE NIGHT WOVEN OF 20 YEARS...
AND YOU SHALL KNOW THE BRILLIANCE OF THE DAWN.
DOOM!!!
KYAA
RAHH
LADY TOKI!!
THUMP
I TOLD YOU TO BOIL THIS WATER!!!
IT IS HEATED, MY LORD...
IT IS NOT!! DID I ASK YOU TO DRAW ME A ROOM TEMPERATURE BATH?!
OUCH !!
IT'S SCALDING, SHOGUN OROCHI!
YOU WILL BURN YOUR SKIN!!
SHUT UP! I'M COLD!!
RATTLE RATTLE
RATTLE RATTLE
RATTLE RATTLE
I CAN'T STOP SHIVERING!!!
RATTLE RATTLE RATTLE
BRING ME THE BONES OF THE KOZUKI SAMURAI!! WHY CAN'T YOU FIND THEM?!!

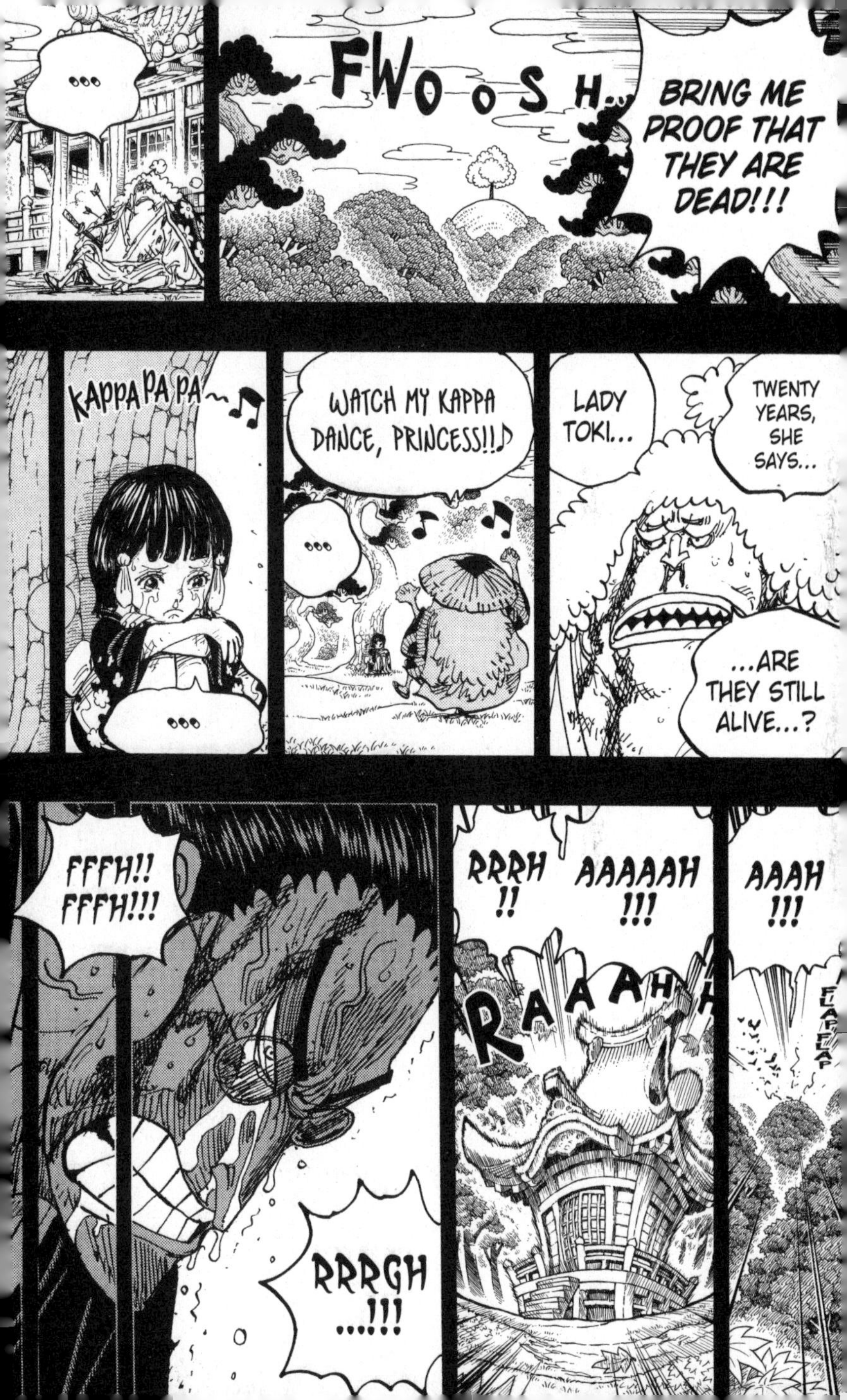
BRING ME PROOF THAT THEY ARE DEAD!!!
FWOOSH
...
TWENTY YEARS, SHE SAYS...
LADY TOKI...
...ARE THEY STILL ALIVE...?
WATCH MY KAPPA DANCE, PRINCESS!!♪
...
KAPPA PA PA~♪
...
AAAH!!!
FLAP FLAP
AAAAAH!!!
RRRH!!
RAAAHH
FFFH!! FFFH!!!
RRRGH...!!!

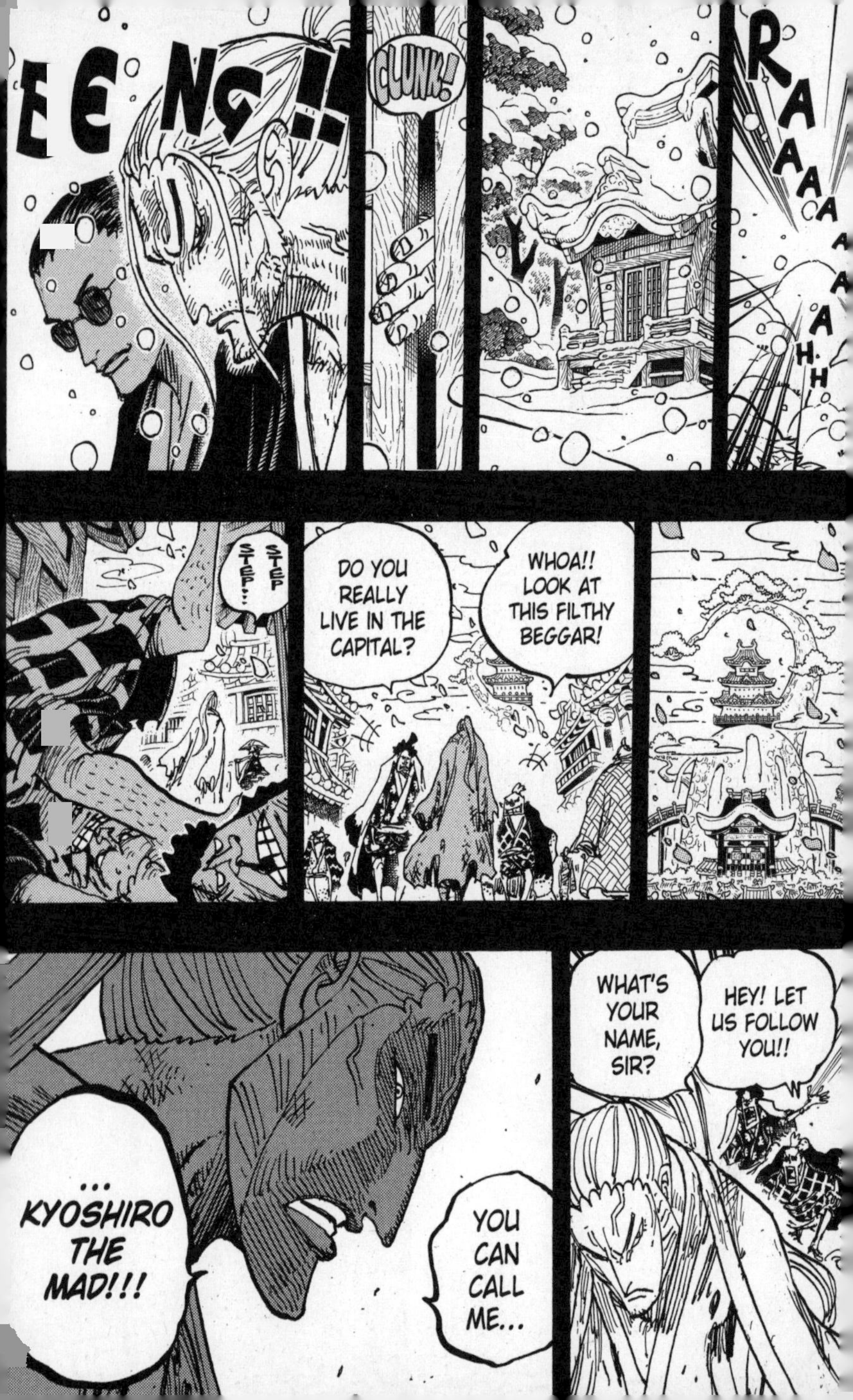
RAAAAAAAHH
CLUNK!
EENG!!
WHOA!! LOOK AT THIS FILTHY BEGGAR!
DO YOU REALLY LIVE IN THE CAPITAL?
STEP STEP...
HEY! LET US FOLLOW YOU!!
WHAT'S YOUR NAME, SIR?
YOU CAN CALL ME...
...KYOSHIRO THE MAD!!!

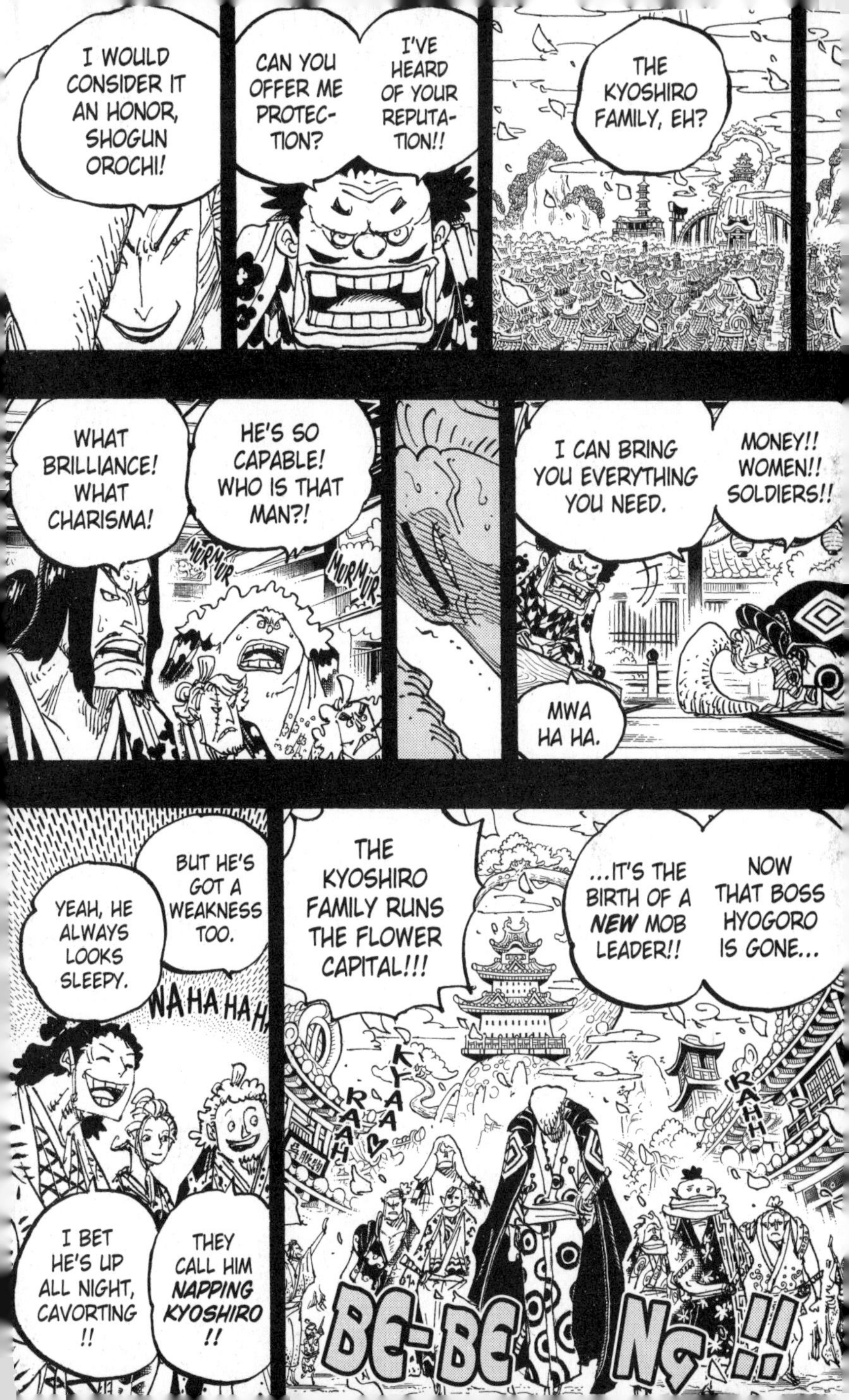
THE KYOSHIRO FAMILY, EH?
I'VE HEARD OF YOUR REPUTATION!!
CAN YOU OFFER ME PROTECTION?
I WOULD CONSIDER IT AN HONOR, SHOGUN OROCHI!
MONEY!! WOMEN!! SOLDIERS!!
I CAN BRING YOU EVERYTHING YOU NEED.
MWA HA HA.
HE'S SO CAPABLE! WHO IS THAT MAN?!
MURMUR
MURMUR
WHAT BRILLIANCE! WHAT CHARISMA!
NOW THAT BOSS HYOGORO IS GONE...
...IT'S THE BIRTH OF A *NEW* MOB LEADER!!
THE KYOSHIRO FAMILY RUNS THE FLOWER CAPITAL!!!
RAHH
KYAA
RAAAH
BE-BENG!!
BUT HE'S GOT A WEAKNESS TOO.
YEAH, HE ALWAYS LOOKS SLEEPY.
WAHAHAHA
THEY CALL HIM *NAPPING KYOSHIRO*!!
I BET HE'S UP ALL NIGHT, CAVORTING!!

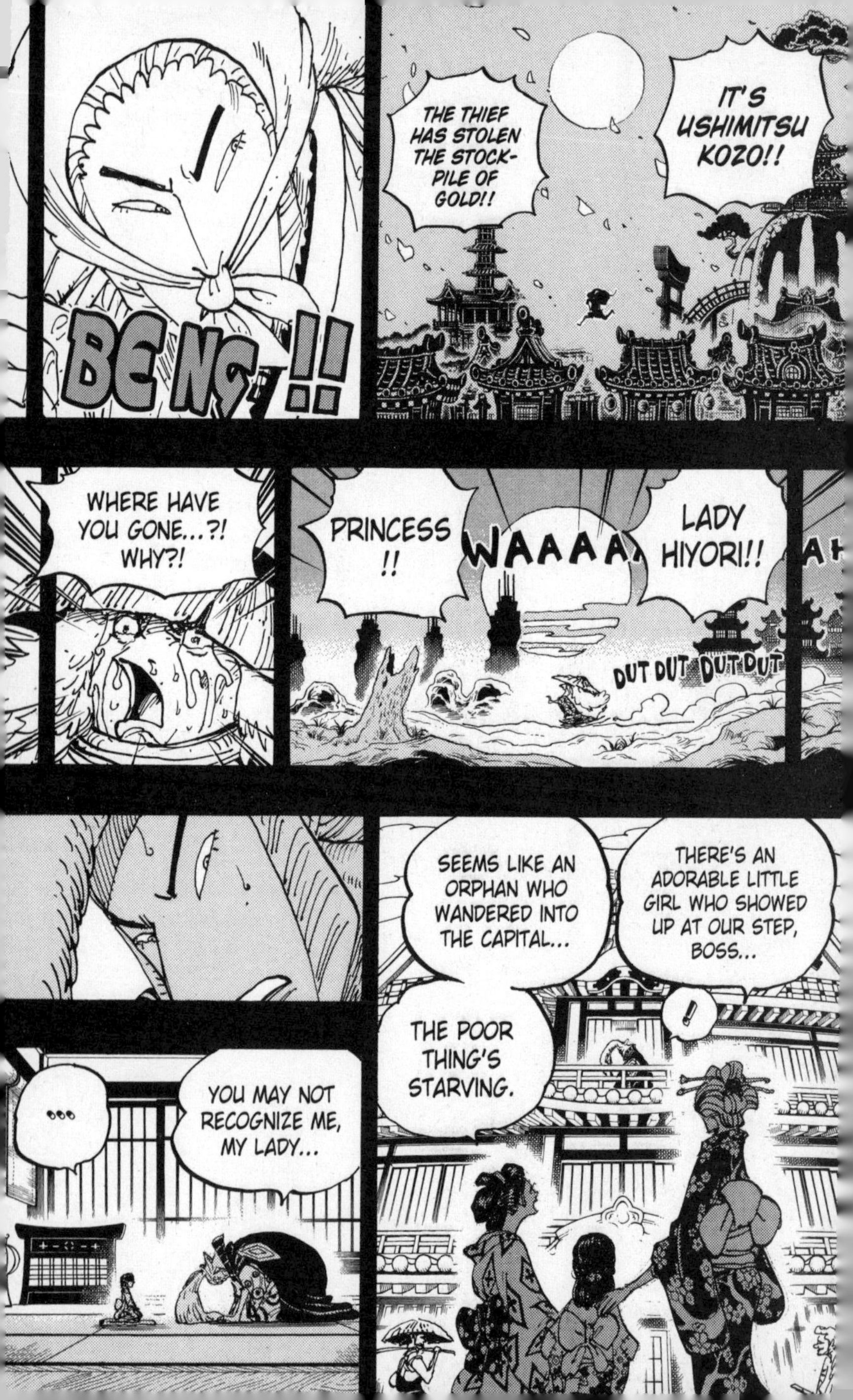
IT'S USHIMITSU KOZO!!
THE THIEF HAS STOLEN THE STOCKPILE OF GOLD!!
BENG!!
LADY HIYORI!!
WAAAA
PRINCESS!!
DUT DUT DUT DUT
WHERE HAVE YOU GONE...?! WHY?!
THERE'S AN ADORABLE LITTLE GIRL WHO SHOWED UP AT OUR STEP, BOSS...
!
SEEMS LIKE AN ORPHAN WHO WANDERED INTO THE CAPITAL...
THE POOR THING'S STARVING.
YOU MAY NOT RECOGNIZE ME, MY LADY...
...

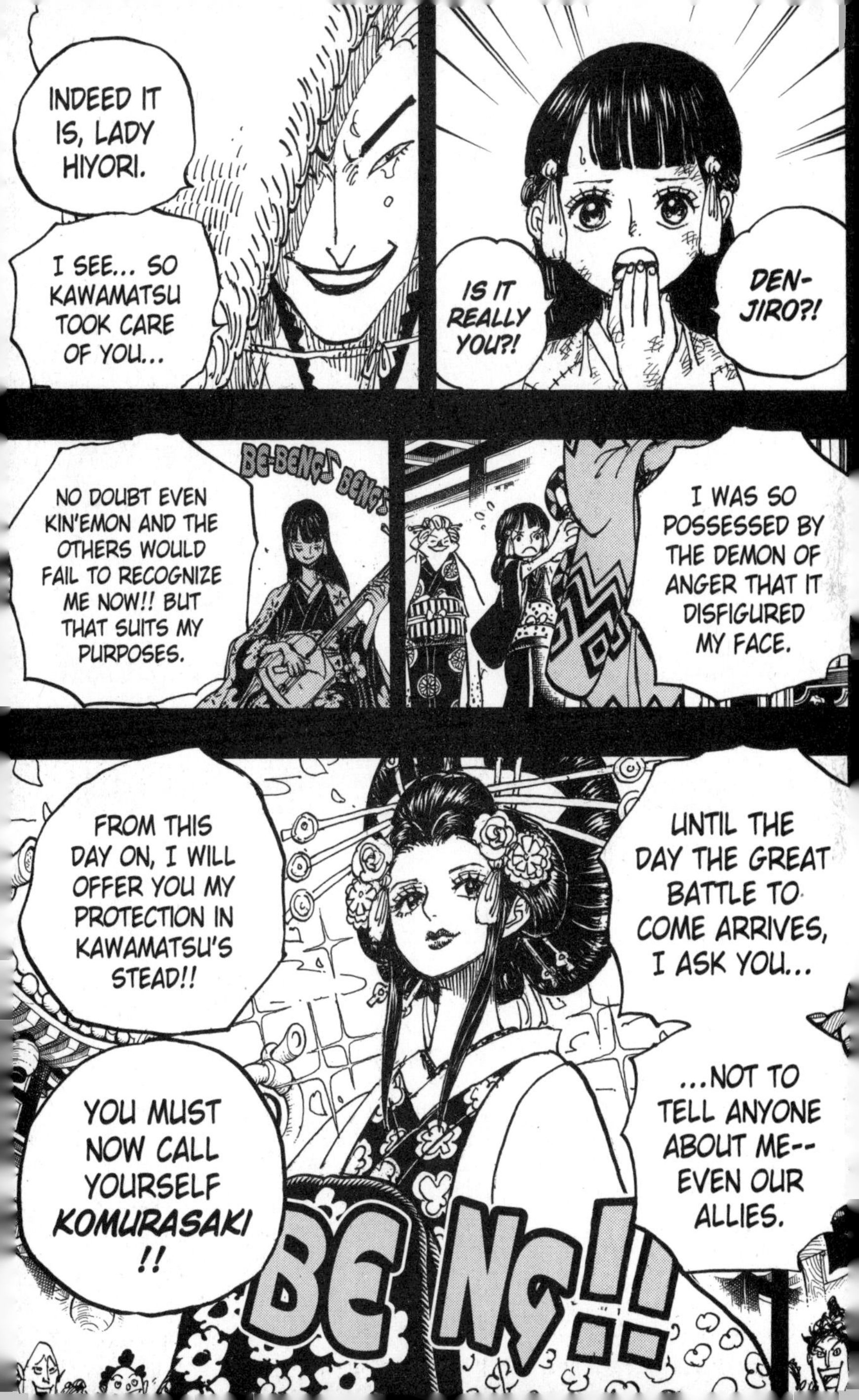
DEN-JIRO?!
IS IT REALLY YOU?!
INDEED IT IS, LADY HIYORI.
I SEE... SO KAWAMATSU TOOK CARE OF YOU...
I WAS SO POSSESSED BY THE DEMON OF ANGER THAT IT DISFIGURED MY FACE.
BE-BENG♪ BENG♪
NO DOUBT EVEN KIN'EMON AND THE OTHERS WOULD FAIL TO RECOGNIZE ME NOW!! BUT THAT SUITS MY PURPOSES.
UNTIL THE DAY THE GREAT BATTLE TO COME ARRIVES, I ASK YOU...
...NOT TO TELL ANYONE ABOUT ME-- EVEN OUR ALLIES.
FROM THIS DAY ON, I WILL OFFER YOU MY PROTECTION IN KAWAMATSU'S STEAD!!
YOU MUST NOW CALL YOURSELF KOMURASAKI!!
BE NG!!

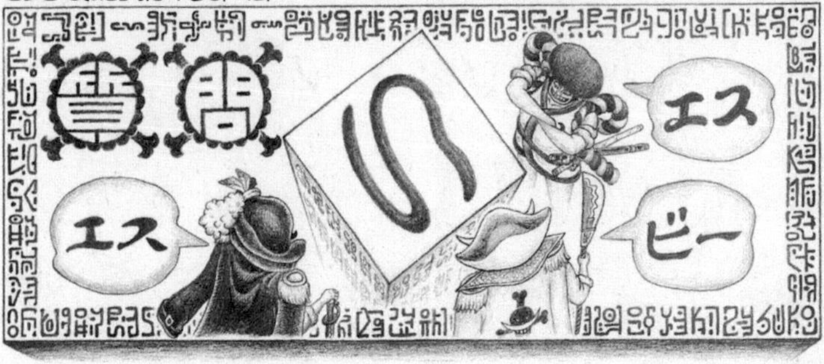
エス
エス
ビー

(Sun Wukong Sensei, China)

Q: Oda Sensei!! I think Boss Kyoshiro looks really cool!! I love his design!! I want a figure and everything!! The fact that this character exists has brought great joy to my life. I'd love to know his height and his favorite food!!

--Majo

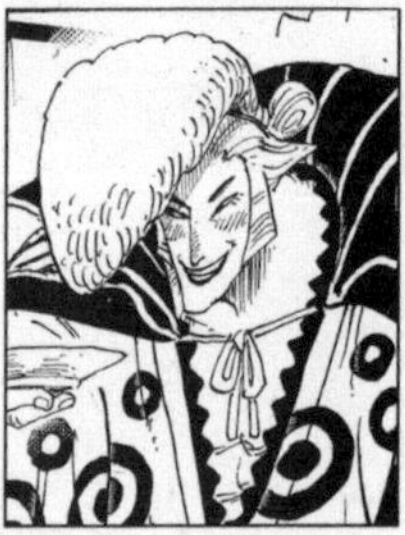

A: Kyoshiro! He's awesome, right? I was very proud of this character design!! I've gotten a lot of questions about the Akazaya Nine as a whole, so I'll give you the height and favorite food for all of them together, and I'll throw in Shinobu and Izo just for good measure.

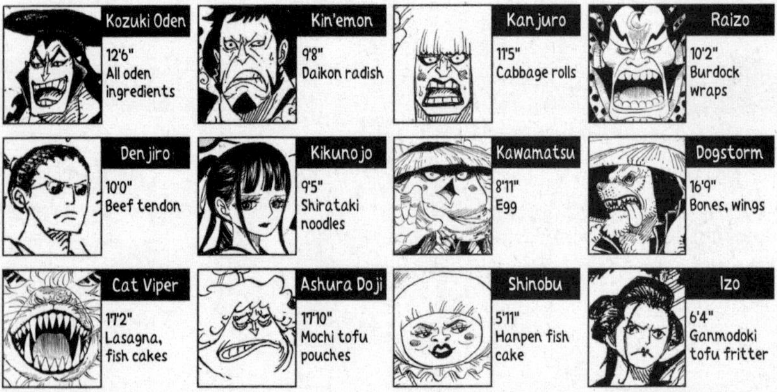
Kozuki Oden
12'6"
All oden ingredients
Kin'emon
9'8"
Daikon radish
Kanjuro
11'5"
Cabbage rolls
Raizo
10'2"
Burdock wraps
Denjiro
10'0"
Beef tendon
Kikunojo
9'5"
Shirataki noodles
Kawamatsu
8'11"
Egg
Dogstorm
16'9"
Bones, wings
Cat Viper
17'2"
Lasagna, fish cakes
Ashura Doji
17'10"
Mochi tofu pouches
Shinobu
5'11"
Hanpen fish cake
Izo
6'4"
Ganmodoki tofu fritter

There. As you can see, they basically all love various ingredients found in an oden hot pot.

Q: Hi, Oda Sensei! In volume 93, Queen sang his catchphrase, "If I get any thinner, I'll steal all your hearts, so I choose the way I am, I stay **FUNKY!!**"♫
So I'm wondering, what would he actually look like if he were skinny? Would he, in fact, steal our hearts?

--Morimori Man

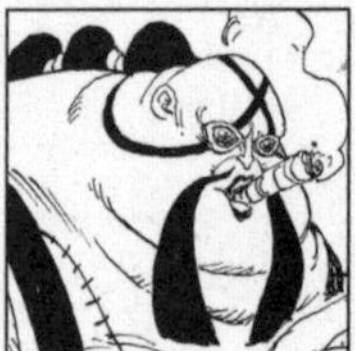

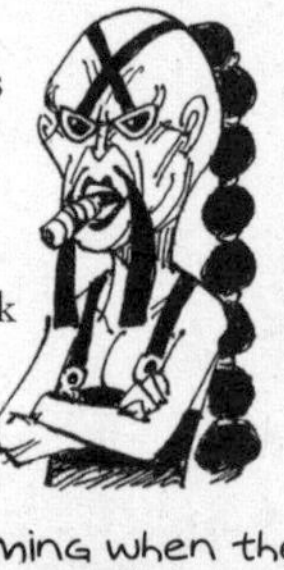

A: Here. Some people are just more charming when they're chubby! That's all for this SBS! See you next volume!!

Chapter 974:
ONWARD TO ONIGASHIMA!!

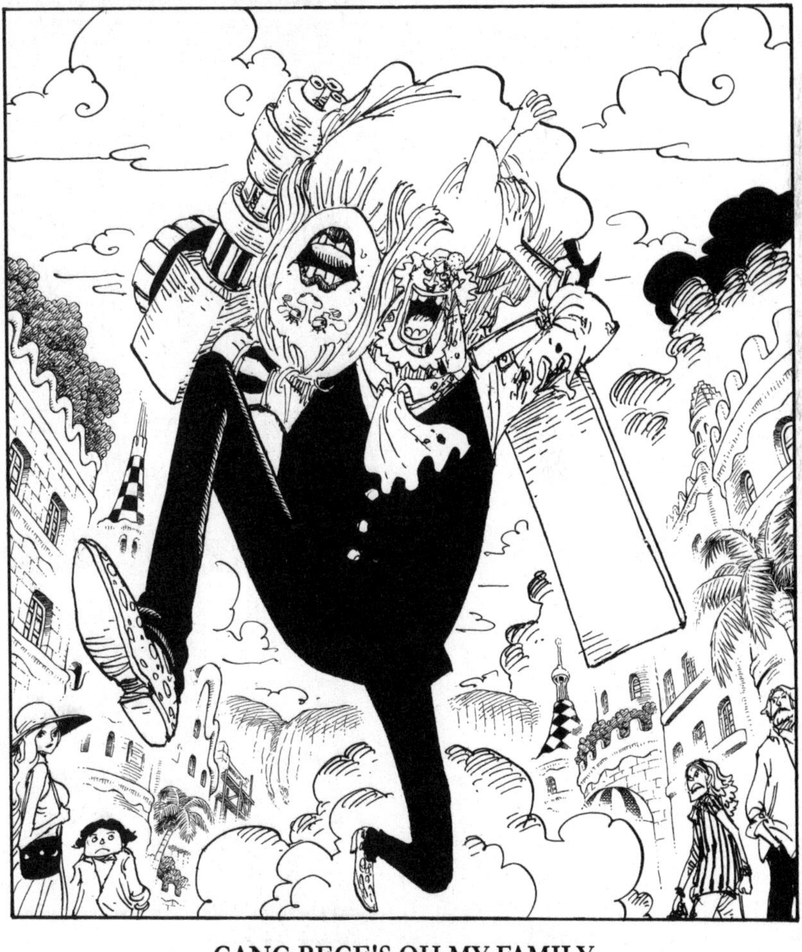

GANG BEGE'S OH MY FAMILY
VOL. 22: "SAVED THE GODFATHER'S WIFE!!"

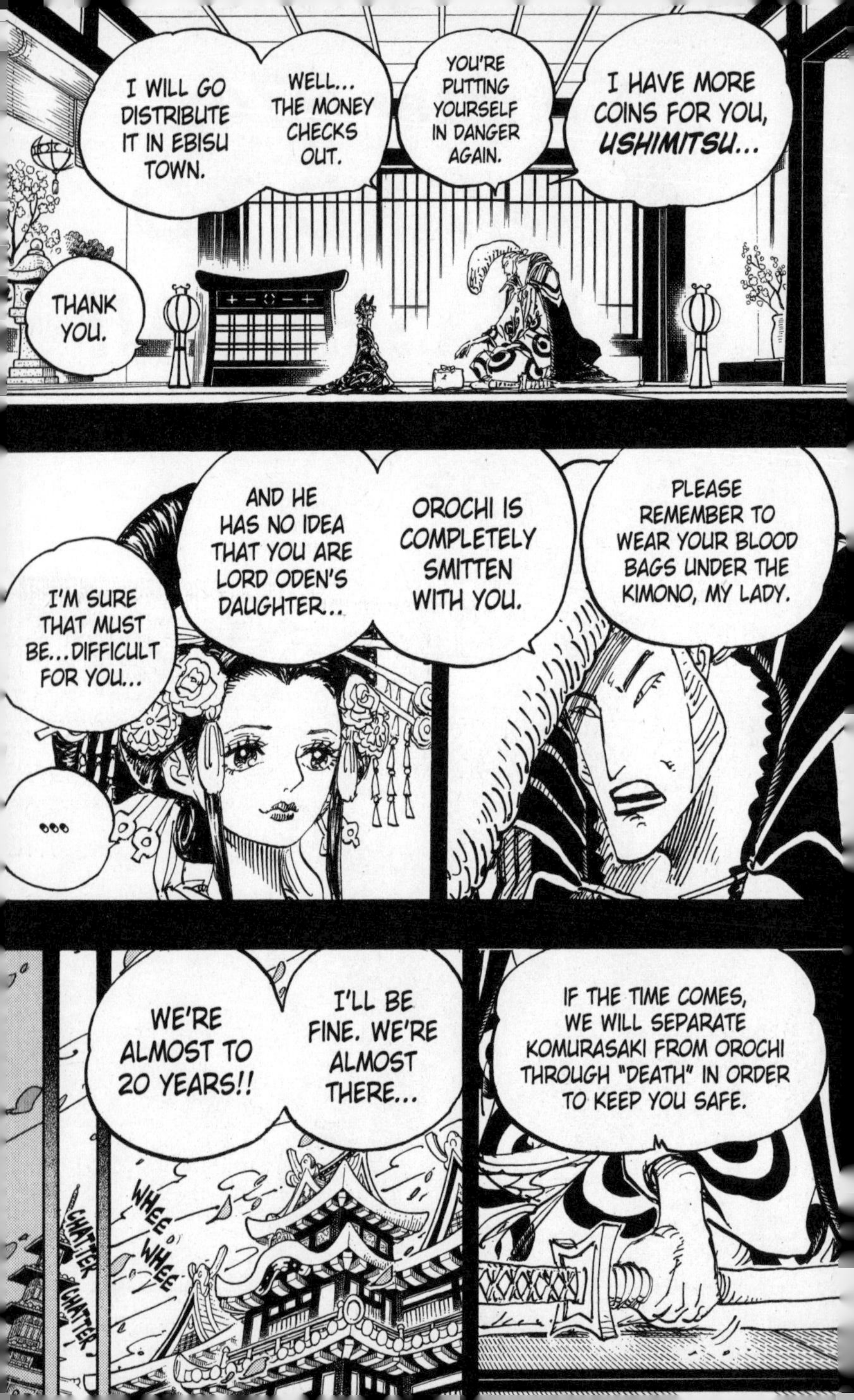
I HAVE MORE COINS FOR YOU, ***USHIMITSU...***
YOU'RE PUTTING YOURSELF IN DANGER AGAIN.
WELL... THE MONEY CHECKS OUT.
I WILL GO DISTRIBUTE IT IN EBISU TOWN.
THANK YOU.
PLEASE REMEMBER TO WEAR YOUR BLOOD BAGS UNDER THE KIMONO, MY LADY.
OROCHI IS COMPLETELY SMITTEN WITH YOU.
AND HE HAS NO IDEA THAT YOU ARE LORD ODEN'S DAUGHTER...
I'M SURE THAT MUST BE...DIFFICULT FOR YOU...
...
IF THE TIME COMES, WE WILL SEPARATE KOMURASAKI FROM OROCHI THROUGH "DEATH" IN ORDER TO KEEP YOU SAFE.
I'LL BE FINE. WE'RE ALMOST THERE...
WE'RE ALMOST TO 20 YEARS!!
WHEE WHEE
CHATTER CHATTER

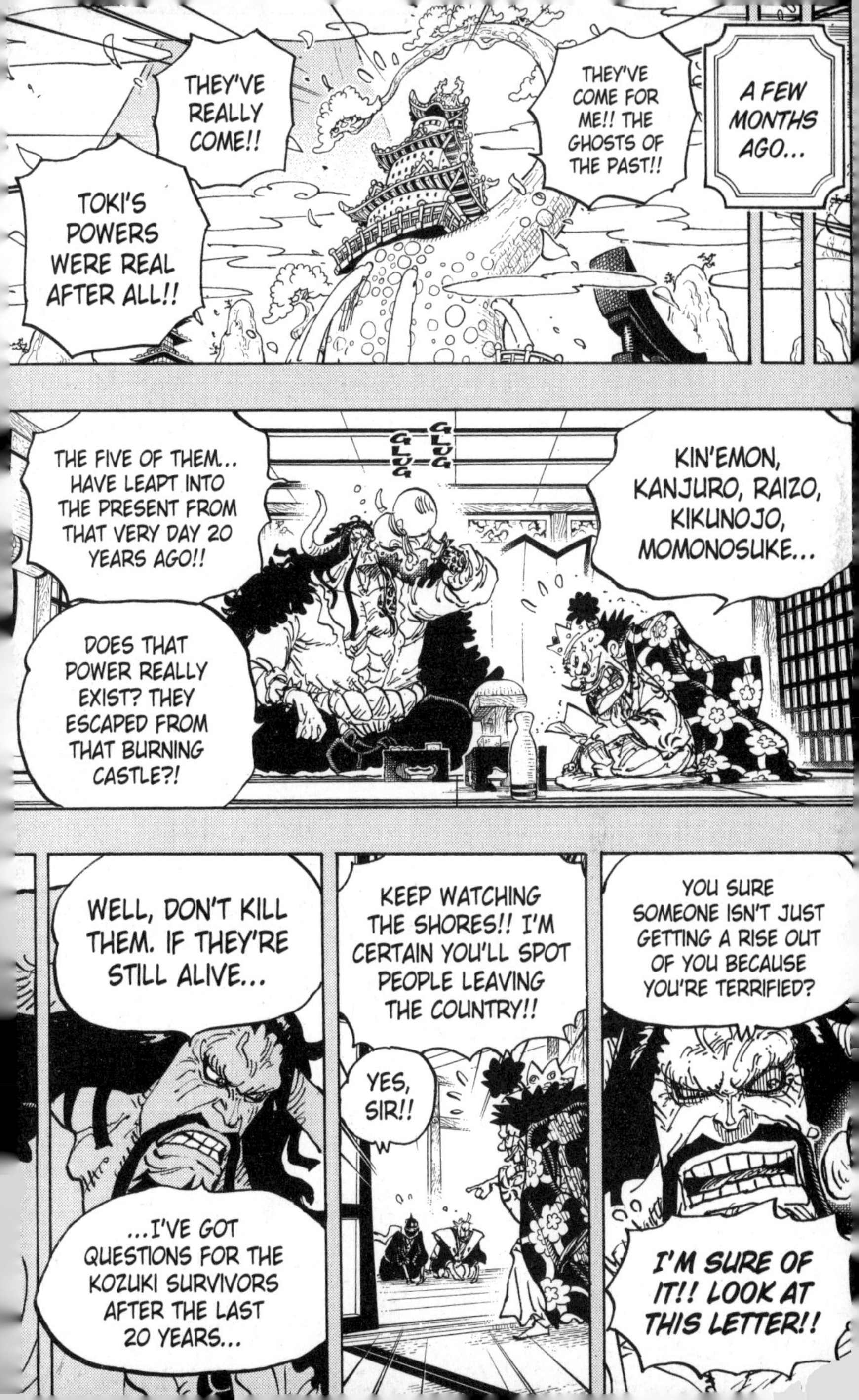
A FEW MONTHS AGO...
THEY'VE COME FOR ME!! THE GHOSTS OF THE PAST!!
THEY'VE REALLY COME!!
TOKI'S POWERS WERE REAL AFTER ALL!!
KIN'EMON, KANJURO, RAIZO, KIKUNOJO, MOMONOSUKE...
GLUG GLUG
THE FIVE OF THEM... HAVE LEAPT INTO THE PRESENT FROM THAT VERY DAY 20 YEARS AGO!!
DOES THAT POWER REALLY EXIST? THEY ESCAPED FROM THAT BURNING CASTLE?!
YOU SURE SOMEONE ISN'T JUST GETTING A RISE OUT OF YOU BECAUSE YOU'RE TERRIFIED?
I'M SURE OF IT!! LOOK AT THIS LETTER!!
KEEP WATCHING THE SHORES!! I'M CERTAIN YOU'LL SPOT PEOPLE LEAVING THE COUNTRY!!
YES, SIR!!
WELL, DON'T KILL THEM. IF THEY'RE STILL ALIVE...
...I'VE GOT QUESTIONS FOR THE KOZUKI SURVIVORS AFTER THE LAST 20 YEARS...

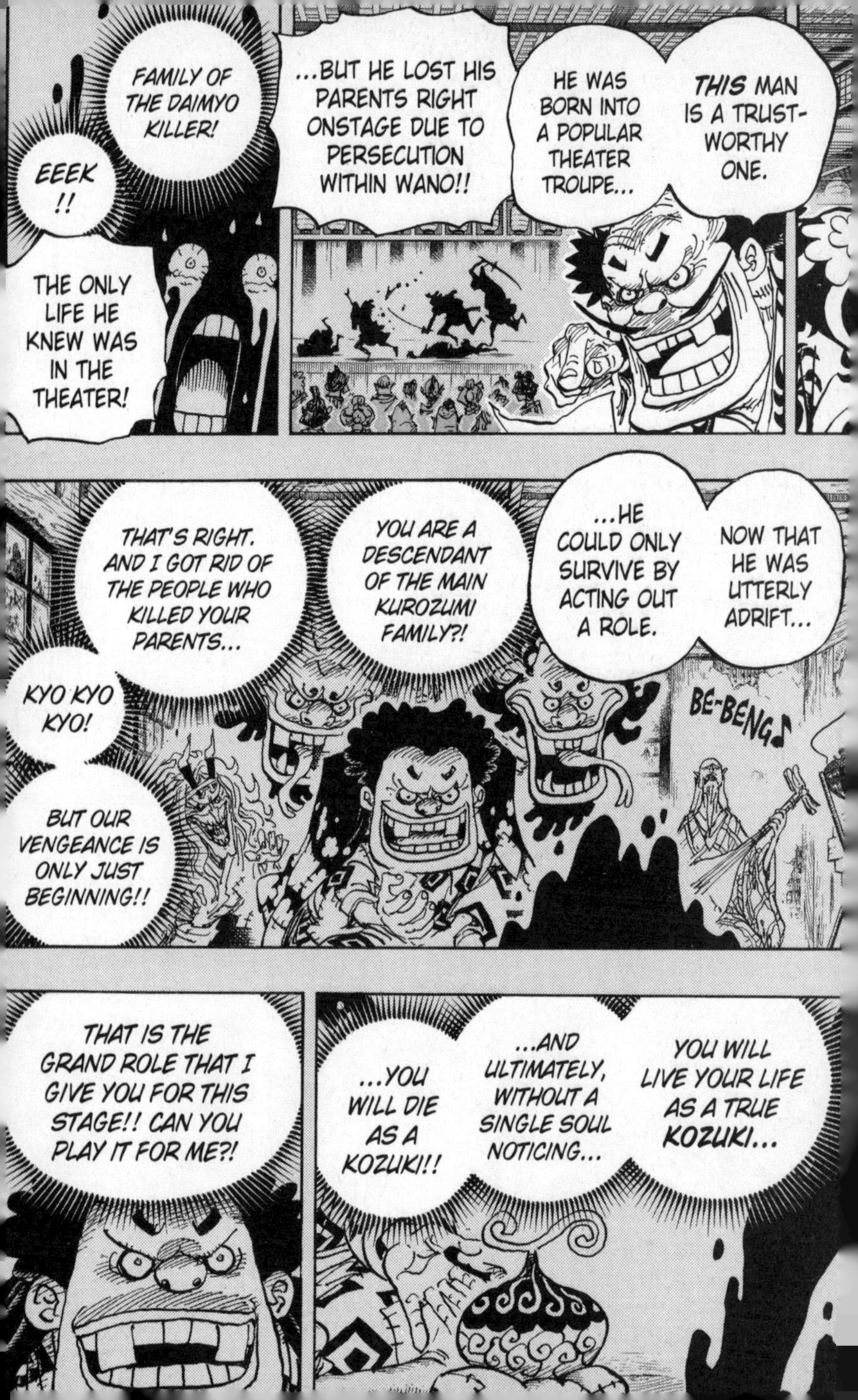

THIS MAN IS A TRUST-WORTHY ONE.
HE WAS BORN INTO A POPULAR THEATER TROUPE...
...BUT HE LOST HIS PARENTS RIGHT ONSTAGE DUE TO PERSECUTION WITHIN WANO!!
FAMILY OF THE DAIMYO KILLER!
EEEK!!
THE ONLY LIFE HE KNEW WAS IN THE THEATER!
NOW THAT HE WAS UTTERLY ADRIFT...
...HE COULD ONLY SURVIVE BY ACTING OUT A ROLE.
BE-BENG♪
YOU ARE A DESCENDANT OF THE MAIN KUROZUMI FAMILY?!
THAT'S RIGHT. AND I GOT RID OF THE PEOPLE WHO KILLED YOUR PARENTS...
KYO KYO KYO!
BUT OUR VENGEANCE IS ONLY JUST BEGINNING!!
YOU WILL LIVE YOUR LIFE AS A TRUE KOZUKI...
...AND ULTIMATELY, WITHOUT A SINGLE SOUL NOTICING...
...YOU WILL DIE AS A KOZUKI!!
THAT IS THE GRAND ROLE THAT I GIVE YOU FOR THIS STAGE!! CAN YOU PLAY IT FOR ME?!

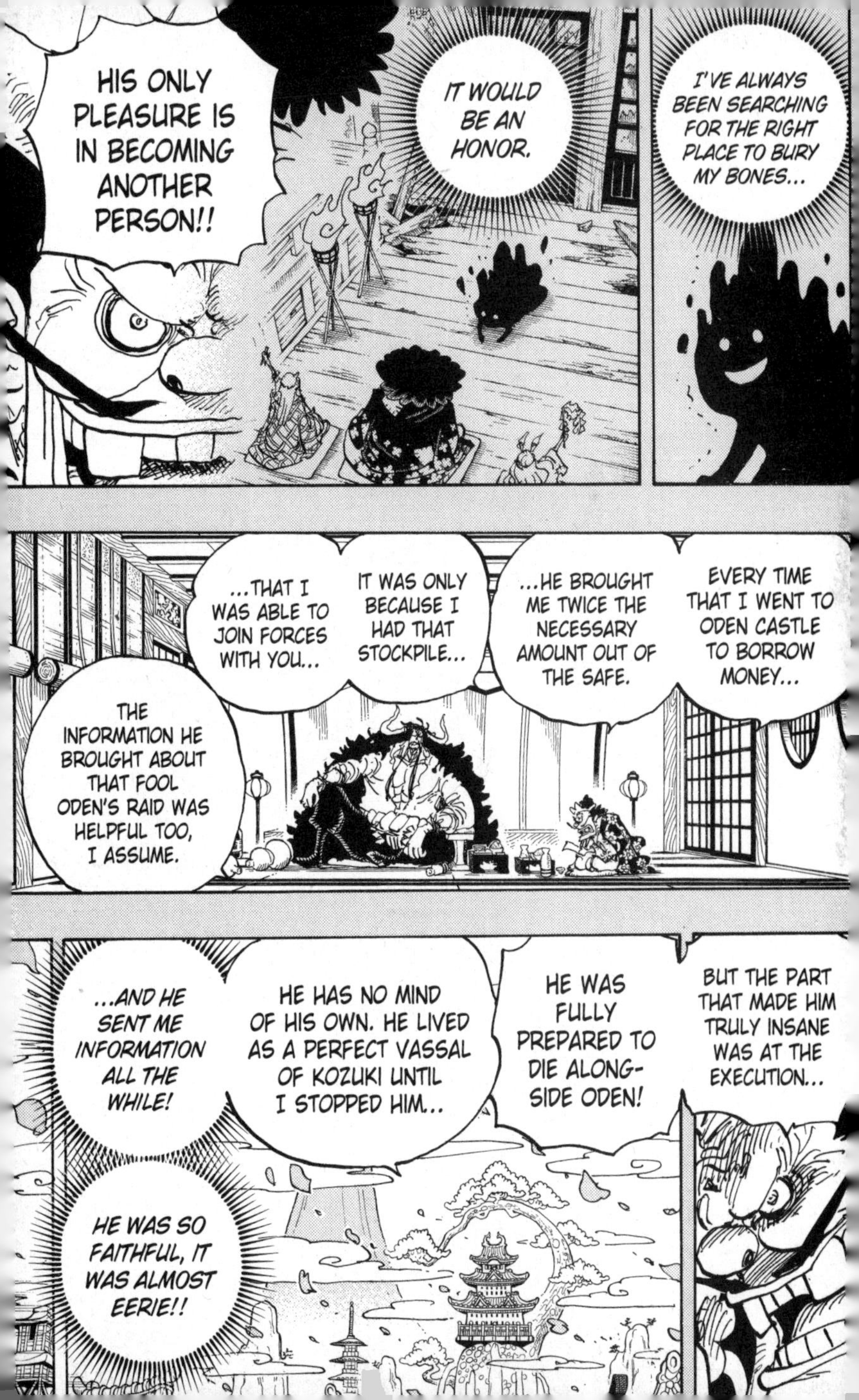
I'VE ALWAYS BEEN SEARCHING FOR THE RIGHT PLACE TO BURY MY BONES...
IT WOULD BE AN HONOR.
HIS ONLY PLEASURE IS IN BECOMING ANOTHER PERSON!!
EVERY TIME THAT I WENT TO ODEN CASTLE TO BORROW MONEY...
...HE BROUGHT ME TWICE THE NECESSARY AMOUNT OUT OF THE SAFE.
IT WAS ONLY BECAUSE I HAD THAT STOCKPILE...
...THAT I WAS ABLE TO JOIN FORCES WITH YOU...
THE INFORMATION HE BROUGHT ABOUT THAT FOOL ODEN'S RAID WAS HELPFUL TOO, I ASSUME.
BUT THE PART THAT MADE HIM TRULY INSANE WAS AT THE EXECUTION...
HE WAS FULLY PREPARED TO DIE ALONG-SIDE ODEN!
HE HAS NO MIND OF HIS OWN. HE LIVED AS A PERFECT VASSAL OF KOZUKI UNTIL I STOPPED HIM...
...AND HE SENT ME INFORMATION ALL THE WHILE!
HE WAS SO FAITHFUL, IT WAS ALMOST EERIE!!

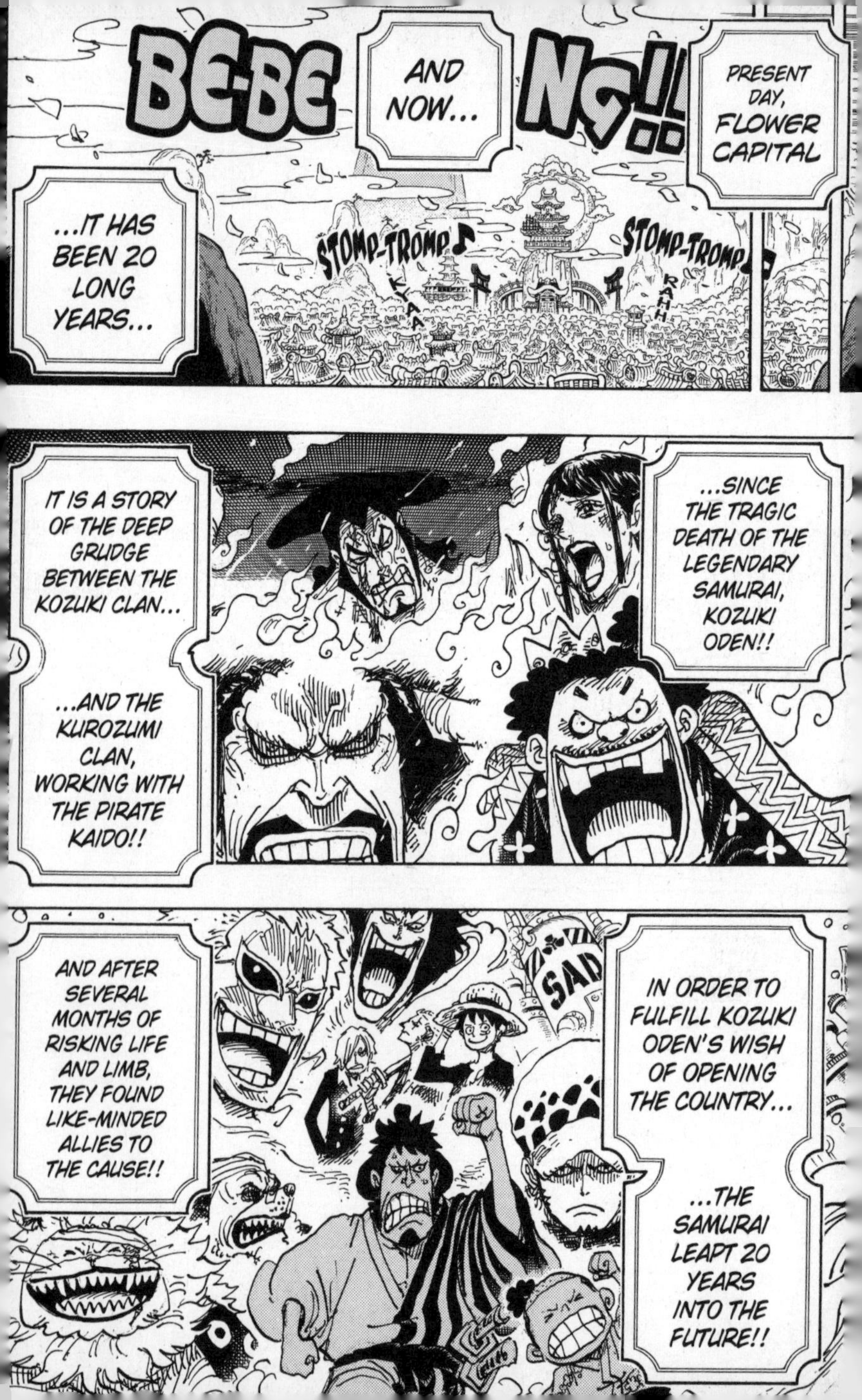
PRESENT DAY, FLOWER CAPITAL
BE-BE NG!!
AND NOW...
...IT HAS BEEN 20 LONG YEARS...
STOMP-TROMP♪
RAHH
STOMP-TROMP♪
KYAA
...SINCE THE TRAGIC DEATH OF THE LEGENDARY SAMURAI, KOZUKI ODEN!!
IT IS A STORY OF THE DEEP GRUDGE BETWEEN THE KOZUKI CLAN...
...AND THE KUROZUMI CLAN, WORKING WITH THE PIRATE KAIDO!!
IN ORDER TO FULFILL KOZUKI ODEN'S WISH OF OPENING THE COUNTRY...
...THE SAMURAI LEAPT 20 YEARS INTO THE FUTURE!!
SAD
AND AFTER SEVERAL MONTHS OF RISKING LIFE AND LIMB, THEY FOUND LIKE-MINDED ALLIES TO THE CAUSE!!

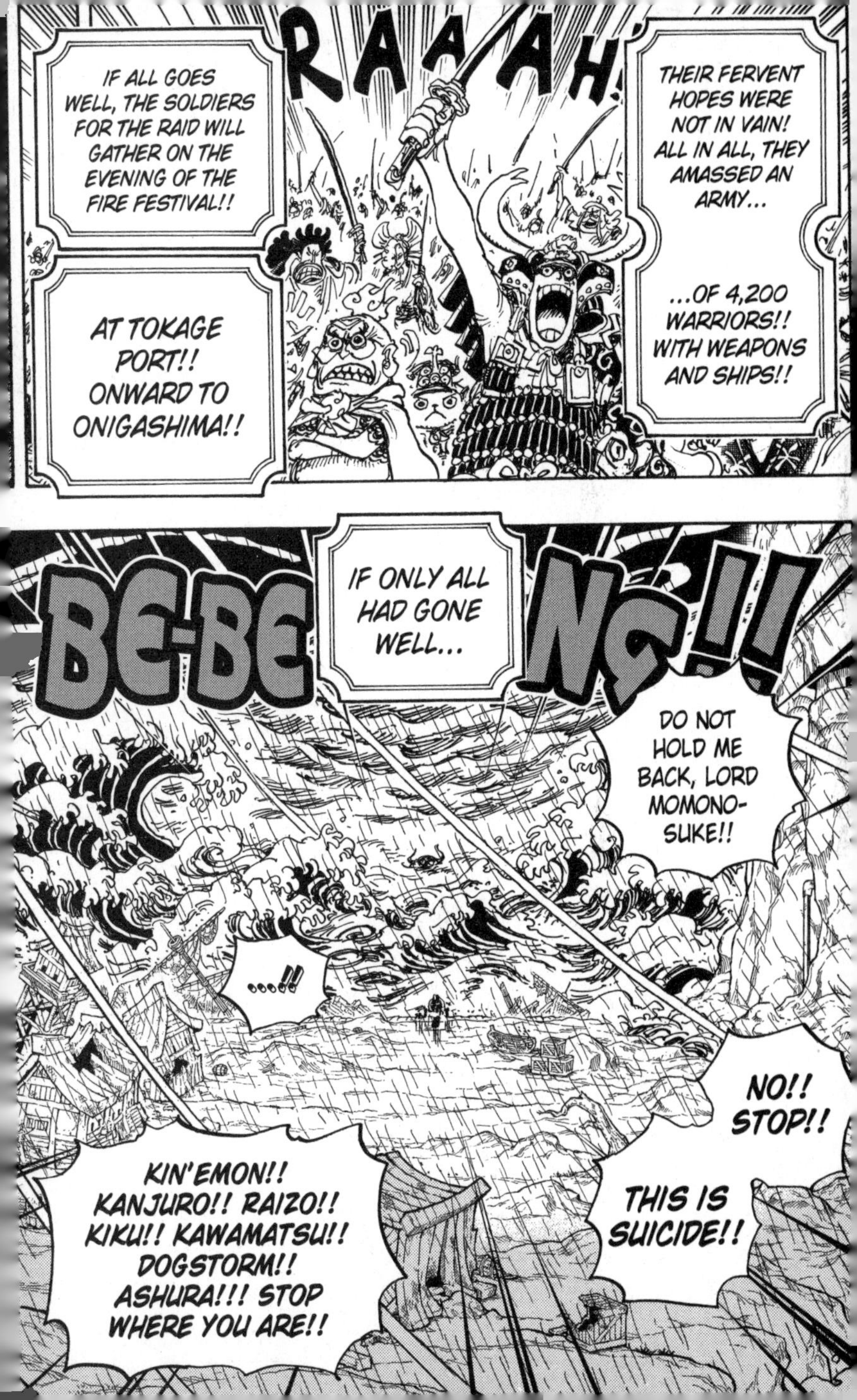
THEIR FERVENT HOPES WERE NOT IN VAIN! ALL IN ALL, THEY AMASSED AN ARMY...
...OF 4,200 WARRIORS!! WITH WEAPONS AND SHIPS!!
RAAAH!
IF ALL GOES WELL, THE SOLDIERS FOR THE RAID WILL GATHER ON THE EVENING OF THE FIRE FESTIVAL!!
AT TOKAGE PORT!! ONWARD TO ONIGASHIMA!!
BE-BENG!!
IF ONLY ALL HAD GONE WELL...
DO NOT HOLD ME BACK, LORD MOMONO-SUKE!!
...!!
NO!! STOP!!
THIS IS SUICIDE!!
KIN'EMON!! KANJURO!! RAIZO!! KIKU!! KAWAMATSU!! DOGSTORM!! ASHURA!!! STOP WHERE YOU ARE!!

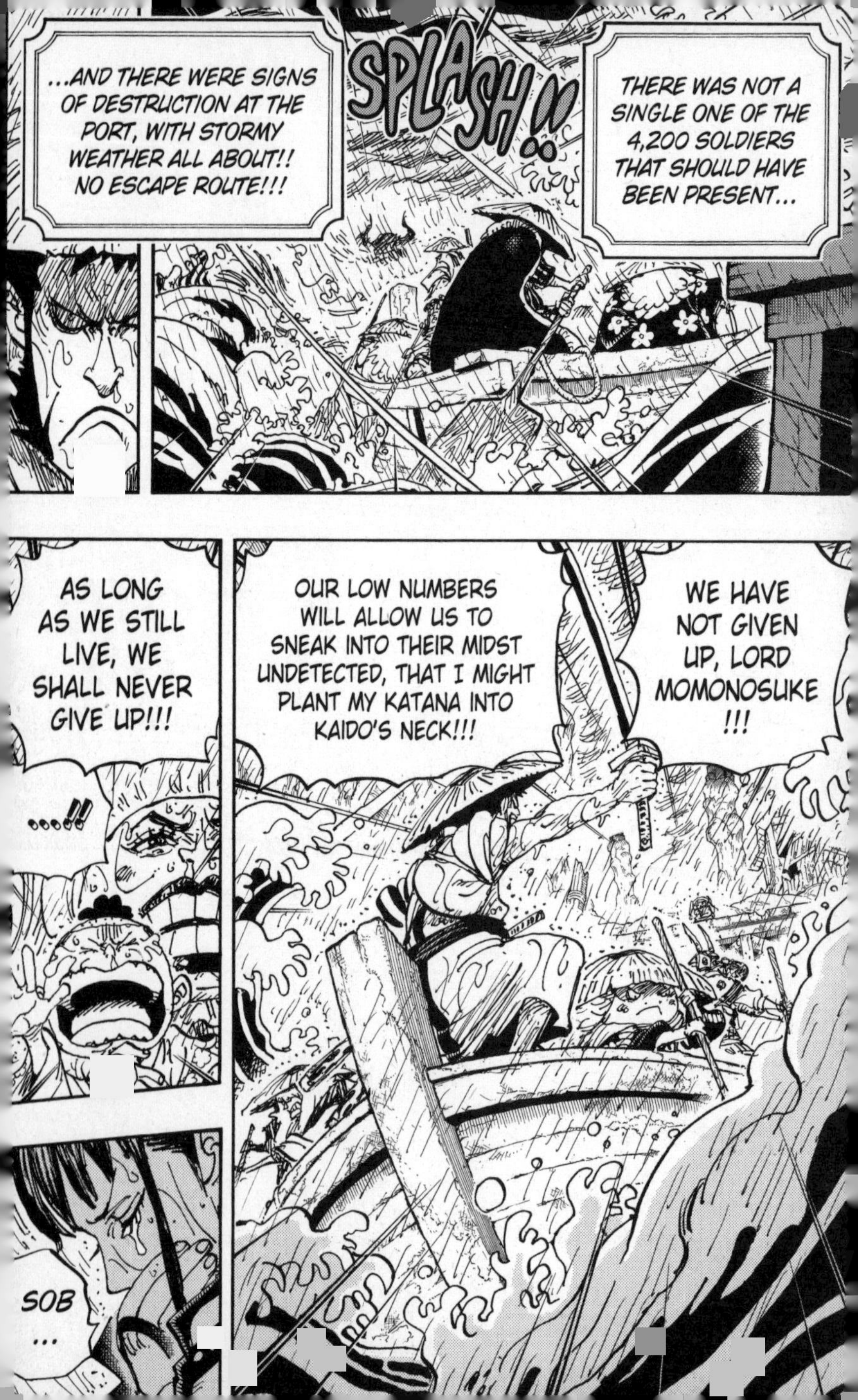
THERE WAS NOT A SINGLE ONE OF THE 4,200 SOLDIERS THAT SHOULD HAVE BEEN PRESENT...
SPLASH!!
...AND THERE WERE SIGNS OF DESTRUCTION AT THE PORT, WITH STORMY WEATHER ALL ABOUT!! NO ESCAPE ROUTE!!!
WE HAVE NOT GIVEN UP, LORD MOMONOSUKE!!!
OUR LOW NUMBERS WILL ALLOW US TO SNEAK INTO THEIR MIDST UNDETECTED, THAT I MIGHT PLANT MY KATANA INTO KAIDO'S NECK!!!
AS LONG AS WE STILL LIVE, WE SHALL NEVER GIVE UP!!!
.....!!
SOB ...

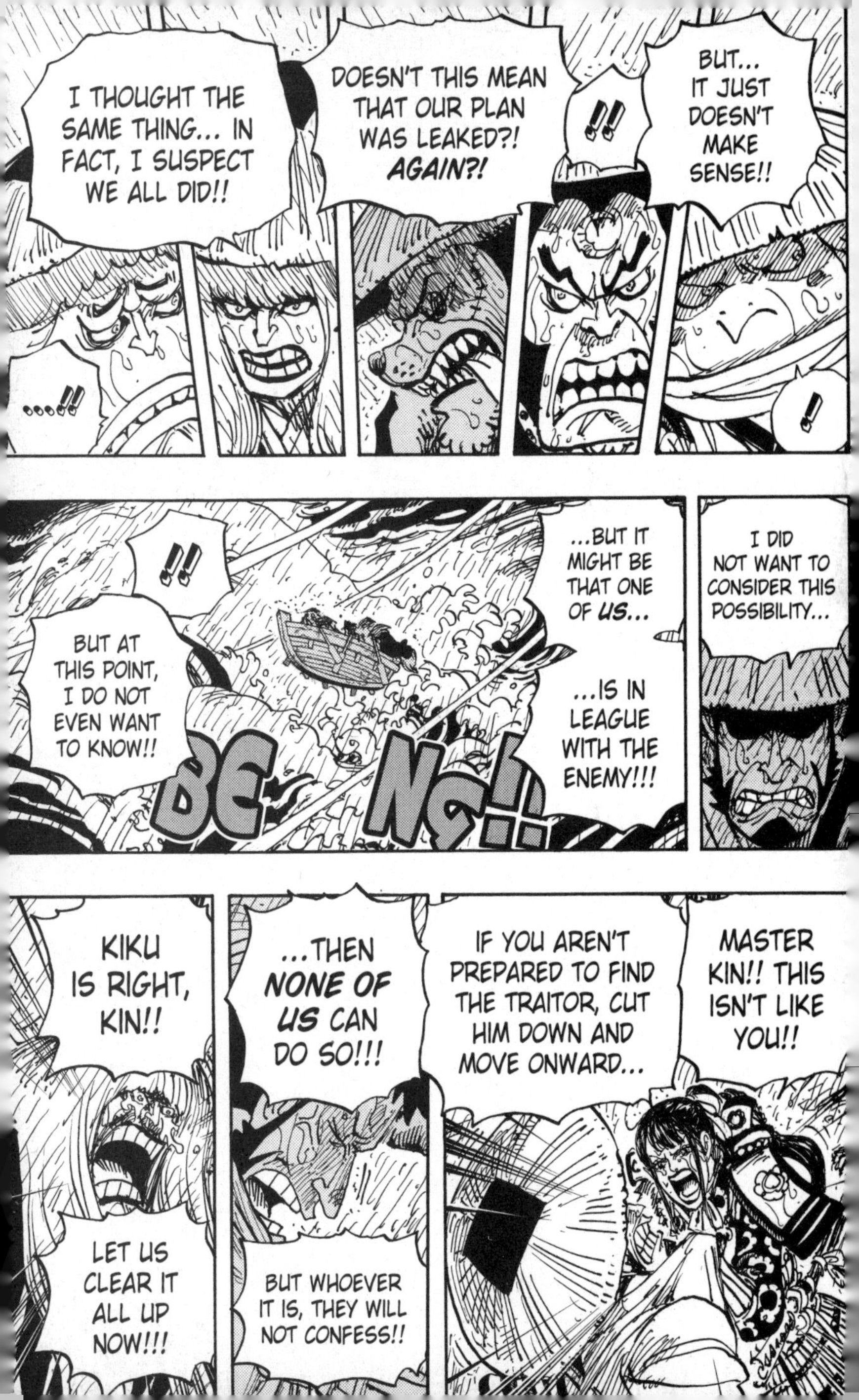
BUT... IT JUST DOESN'T MAKE SENSE!!
!!
DOESN'T THIS MEAN THAT OUR PLAN WAS LEAKED?! *AGAIN?!*
I THOUGHT THE SAME THING... IN FACT, I SUSPECT WE ALL DID!!
!
....!!
I DID NOT WANT TO CONSIDER THIS POSSIBILITY...
...BUT IT MIGHT BE THAT ONE OF *US*...
...IS IN LEAGUE WITH THE ENEMY!!!
!!
BUT AT THIS POINT, I DO NOT EVEN WANT TO KNOW!!
BENG!!
MASTER KIN!! THIS ISN'T LIKE YOU!!
IF YOU AREN'T PREPARED TO FIND THE TRAITOR, CUT HIM DOWN AND MOVE ONWARD...
...THEN *NONE OF US* CAN DO SO!!!
BUT WHOEVER IT IS, THEY WILL NOT CONFESS!!
KIKU IS RIGHT, KIN!!
LET US CLEAR IT ALL UP NOW!!!

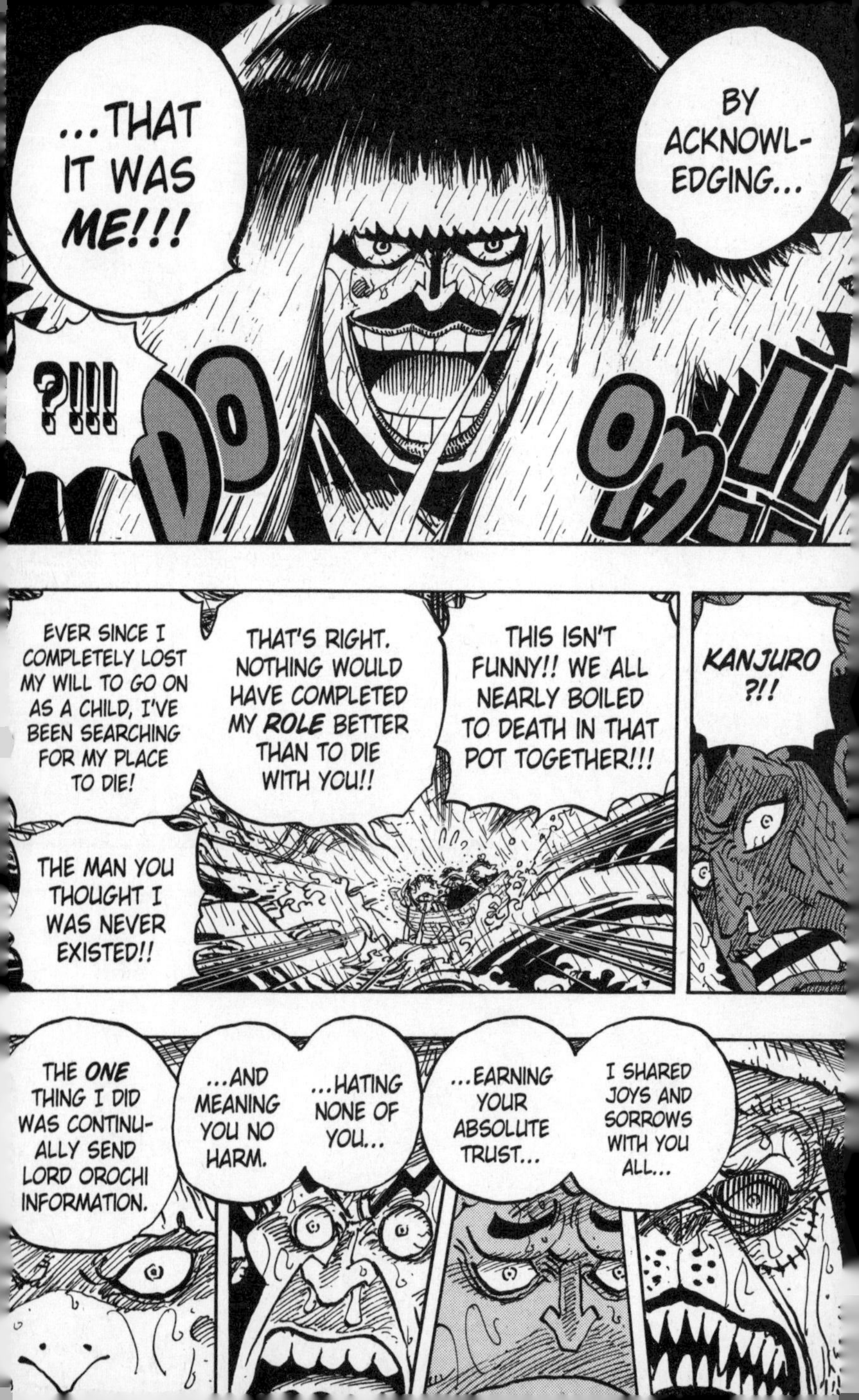
BY ACKNOWL-EDGING...
...THAT IT WAS ME!!!
?!!!
DOOM!!
KANJURO ?!!
THIS ISN'T FUNNY!! WE ALL NEARLY BOILED TO DEATH IN THAT POT TOGETHER!!!
THAT'S RIGHT. NOTHING WOULD HAVE COMPLETED MY ROLE BETTER THAN TO DIE WITH YOU!!
EVER SINCE I COMPLETELY LOST MY WILL TO GO ON AS A CHILD, I'VE BEEN SEARCHING FOR MY PLACE TO DIE!
THE MAN YOU THOUGHT I WAS NEVER EXISTED!!
I SHARED JOYS AND SORROWS WITH YOU ALL...
...EARNING YOUR ABSOLUTE TRUST...
...HATING NONE OF YOU...
...AND MEANING YOU NO HARM.
THE ONE THING I DID WAS CONTINU-ALLY SEND LORD OROCHI INFORMATION.

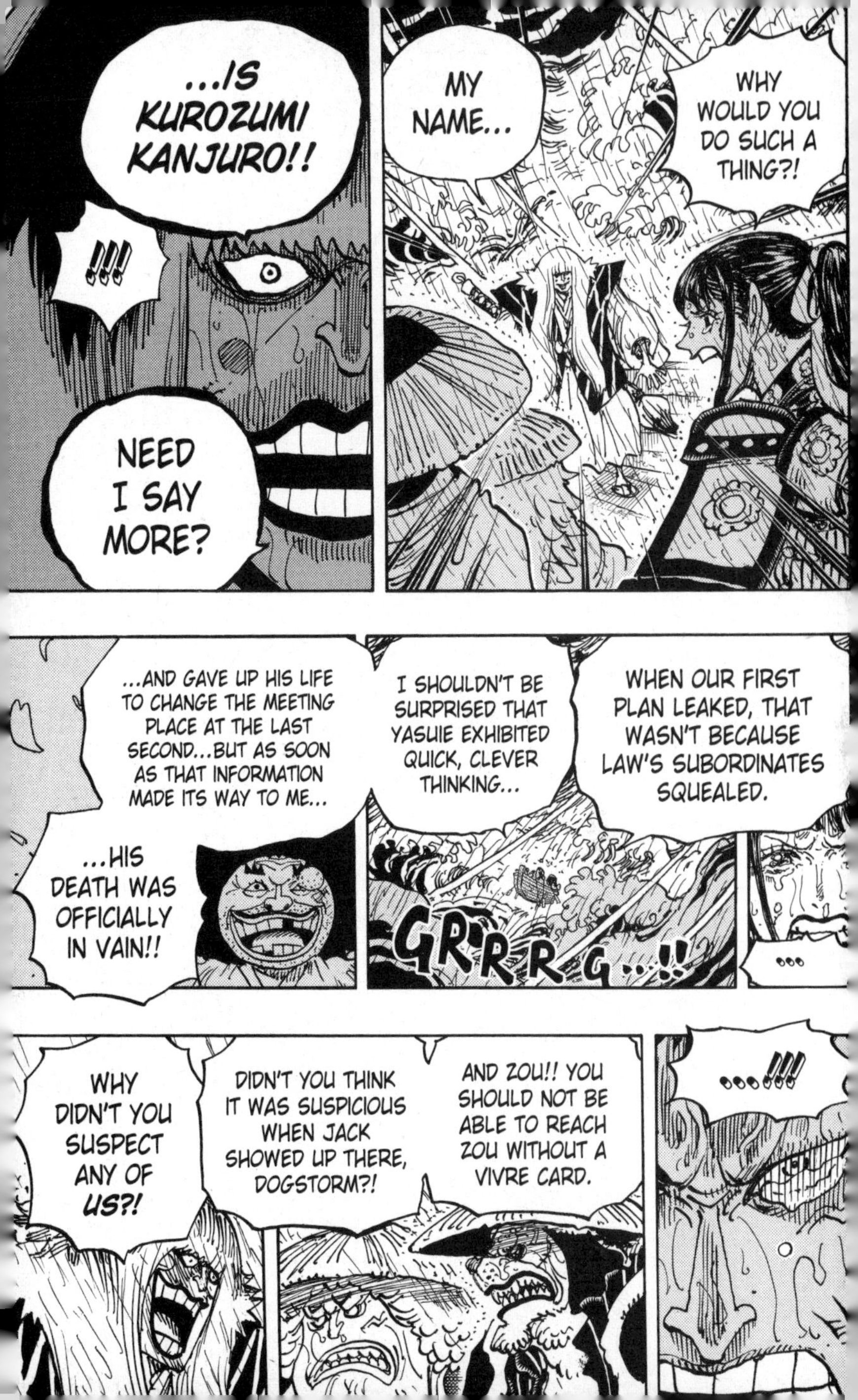
WHY WOULD YOU DO SUCH A THING?!
MY NAME...
...IS KUROZUMI KANJURO!!
!!!
NEED I SAY MORE?
WHEN OUR FIRST PLAN LEAKED, THAT WASN'T BECAUSE LAW'S SUBORDINATES SQUEALED.
...
I SHOULDN'T BE SURPRISED THAT YASUIE EXHIBITED QUICK, CLEVER THINKING...
GRRRG...!!
...AND GAVE UP HIS LIFE TO CHANGE THE MEETING PLACE AT THE LAST SECOND...BUT AS SOON AS THAT INFORMATION MADE ITS WAY TO ME...
...HIS DEATH WAS OFFICIALLY IN VAIN!!
...!!!
AND ZOU!! YOU SHOULD NOT BE ABLE TO REACH ZOU WITHOUT A VIVRE CARD.
DIDN'T YOU THINK IT WAS SUSPICIOUS WHEN JACK SHOWED UP THERE, DOGSTORM?!
WHY DIDN'T YOU SUSPECT ANY OF US?!

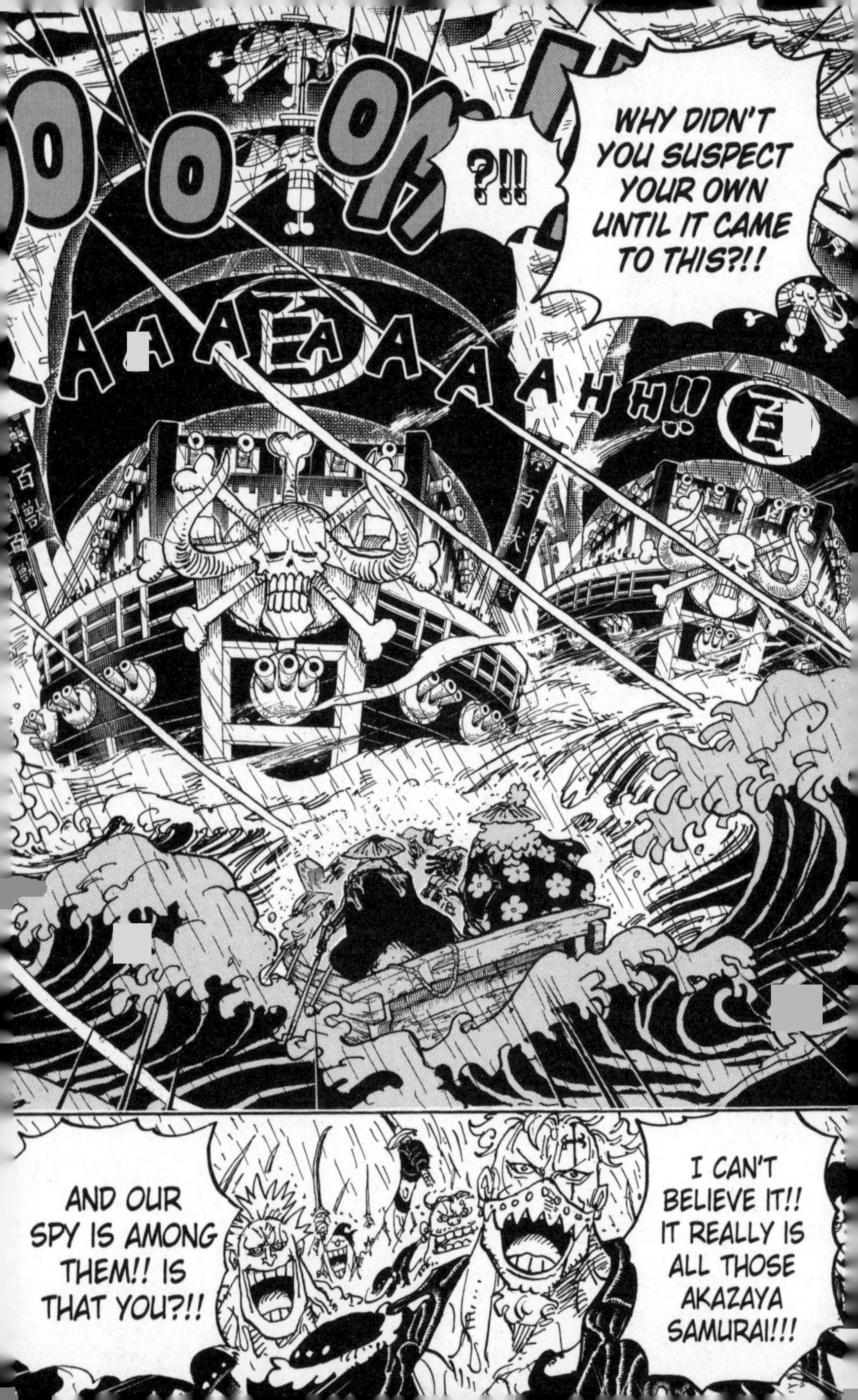
WHY DIDN'T YOU SUSPECT YOUR OWN UNTIL IT CAME TO THIS?!!
OOOOH ?!!
AAAAAAAAAHH!!
I CAN'T BELIEVE IT!! IT REALLY IS ALL THOSE AKAZAYA SAMURAI!!!
AND OUR SPY IS AMONG THEM!! IS THAT YOU?!!

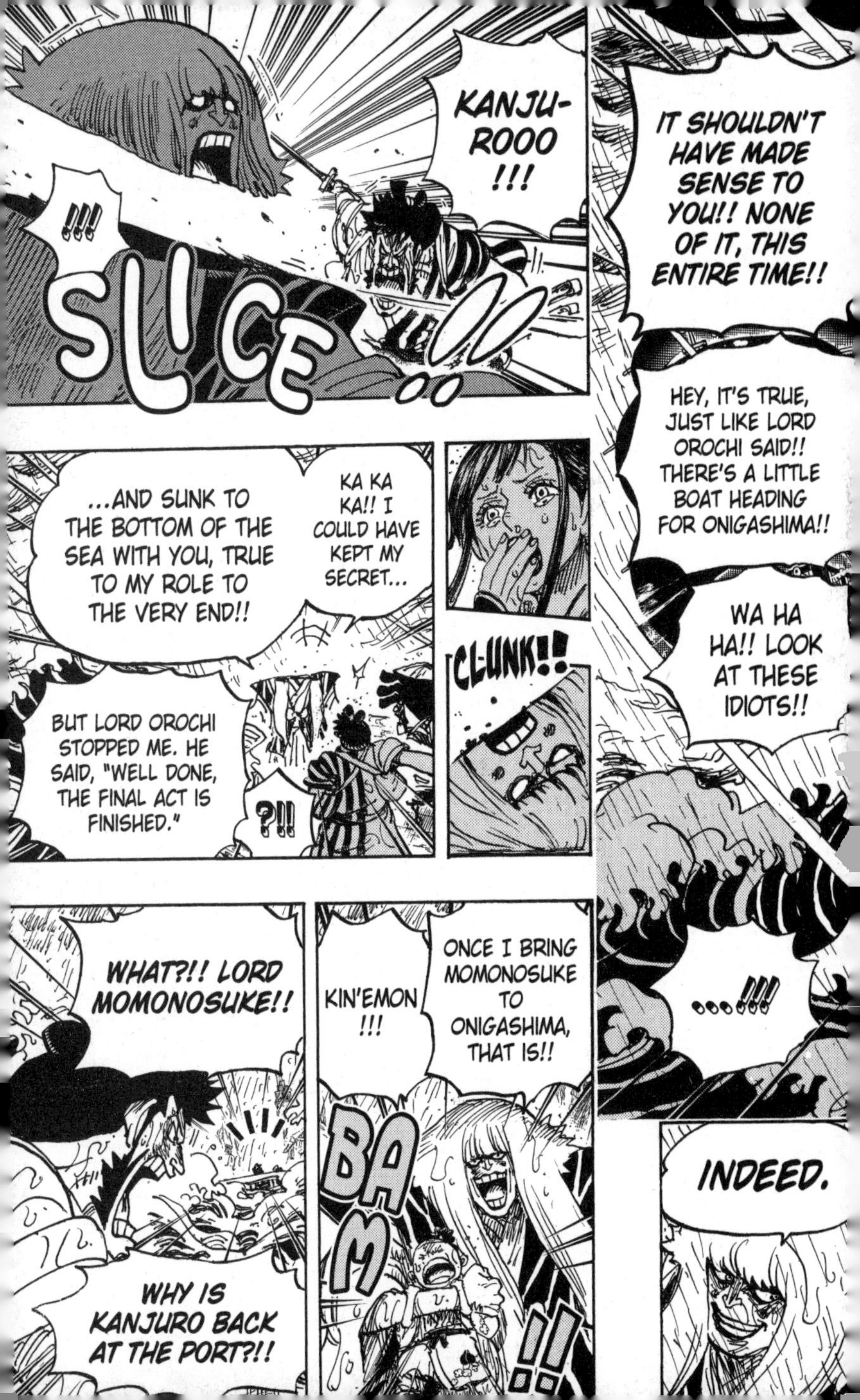
IT SHOULDN'T HAVE MADE SENSE TO YOU!! NONE OF IT, THIS ENTIRE TIME!!
HEY, IT'S TRUE, JUST LIKE LORD OROCHI SAID!! THERE'S A LITTLE BOAT HEADING FOR ONIGASHIMA!!
WA HA HA!! LOOK AT THESE IDIOTS!!
...!!!
INDEED.
KANJU-ROOO !!!
!!!
SLICE
CLUNK!!
KA KA KA!! I COULD HAVE KEPT MY SECRET...
...AND SUNK TO THE BOTTOM OF THE SEA WITH YOU, TRUE TO MY ROLE TO THE VERY END!!
BUT LORD OROCHI STOPPED ME. HE SAID, "WELL DONE, THE FINAL ACT IS FINISHED."
?!!
ONCE I BRING MOMONOSUKE TO ONIGASHIMA, THAT IS!!
KIN'EMON !!!
BAM
!!
WHAT?!! LORD MOMONOSUKE!!
WHY IS KANJURO BACK AT THE PORT?!!

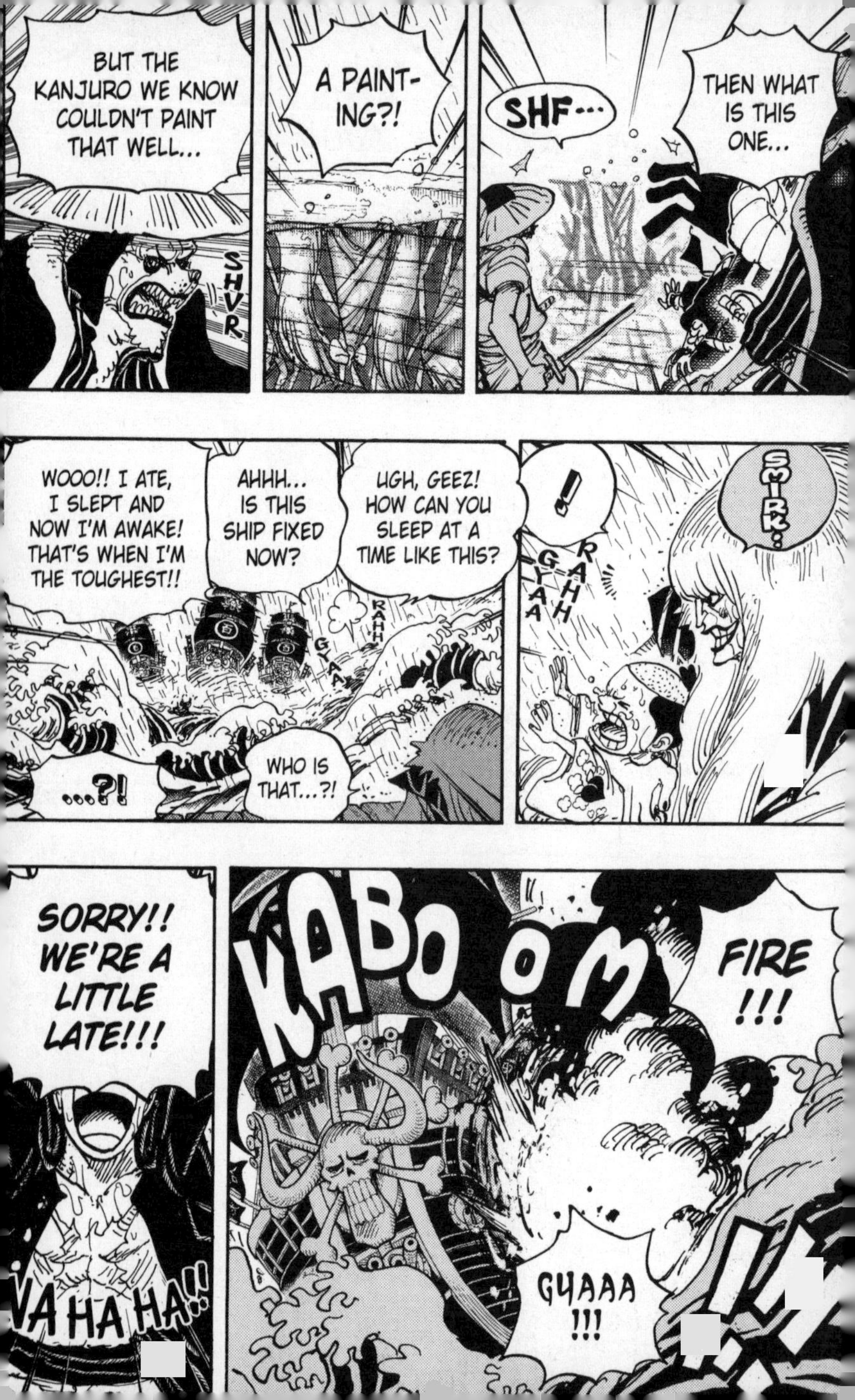
THEN WHAT IS THIS ONE...
SHF...
A PAINT-ING?!
BUT THE KANJURO WE KNOW COULDN'T PAINT THAT WELL...
SHVR
SMIRK
!
RAHH
GYAA
UGH, GEEZ! HOW CAN YOU SLEEP AT A TIME LIKE THIS?
AHHH... IS THIS SHIP FIXED NOW?
WOOO!! I ATE, I SLEPT AND NOW I'M AWAKE! THAT'S WHEN I'M THE TOUGHEST!!
RAHH
GYAA
WHO IS THAT...?!
...?!
FIRE!!!
KABOOM
GUAAA!!!
SORRY!! WE'RE A LITTLE LATE!!!
WA HA HA!!

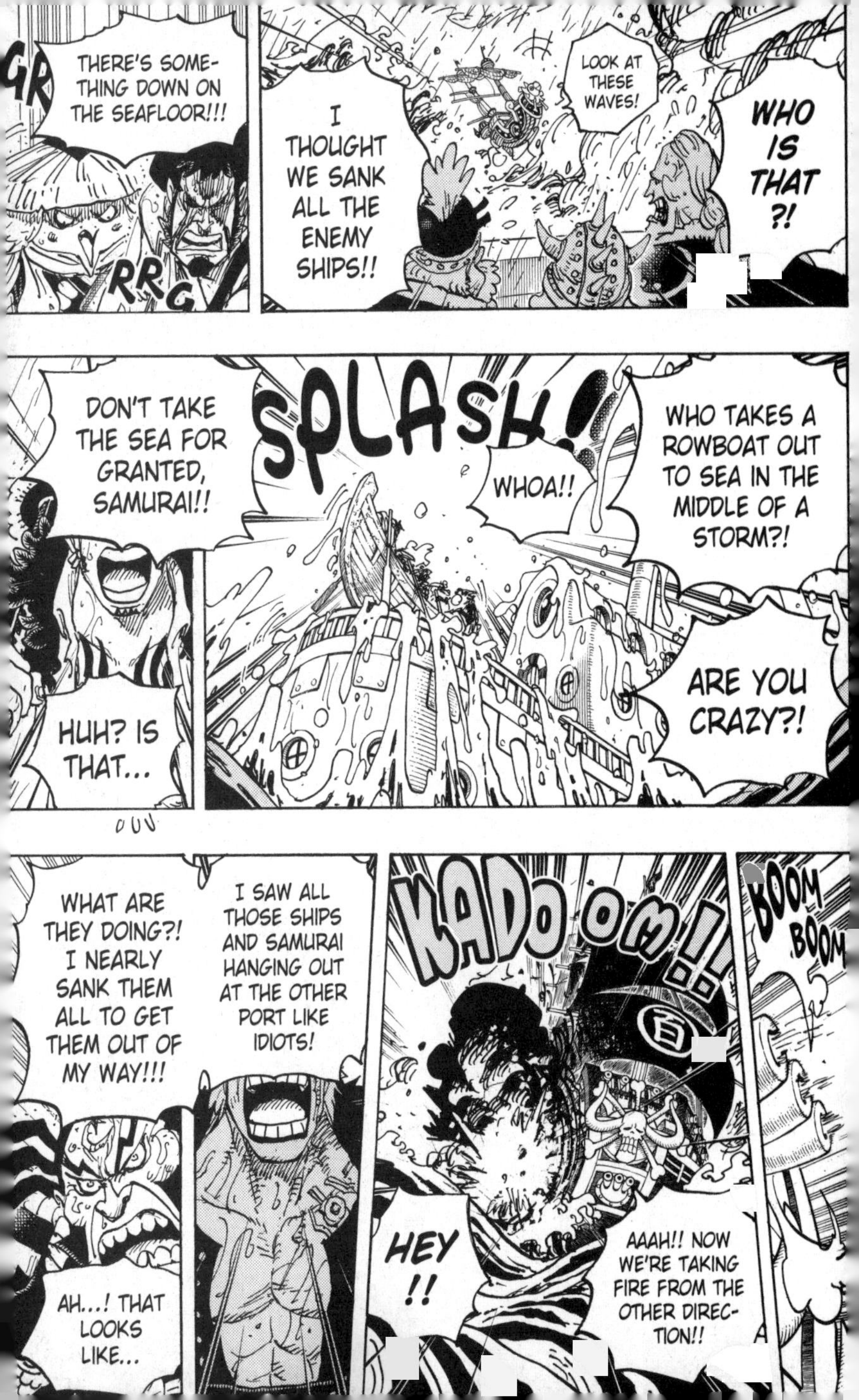
WHO IS THAT?!
LOOK AT THESE WAVES!
I THOUGHT WE SANK ALL THE ENEMY SHIPS!!
GR
THERE'S SOMETHING DOWN ON THE SEAFLOOR!!!
RRRG
WHO TAKES A ROWBOAT OUT TO SEA IN THE MIDDLE OF A STORM?!
SPLASH!!
WHOA!!
ARE YOU CRAZY?!
DON'T TAKE THE SEA FOR GRANTED, SAMURAI!!
HUH? IS THAT...
BOOM BOOM
KADOOM!!
AAAH!! NOW WE'RE TAKING FIRE FROM THE OTHER DIRECTION!!
HEY!!
I SAW ALL THOSE SHIPS AND SAMURAI HANGING OUT AT THE OTHER PORT LIKE IDIOTS!
WHAT ARE THEY DOING?! I NEARLY SANK THEM ALL TO GET THEM OUT OF MY WAY!!!
AH...! THAT LOOKS LIKE...

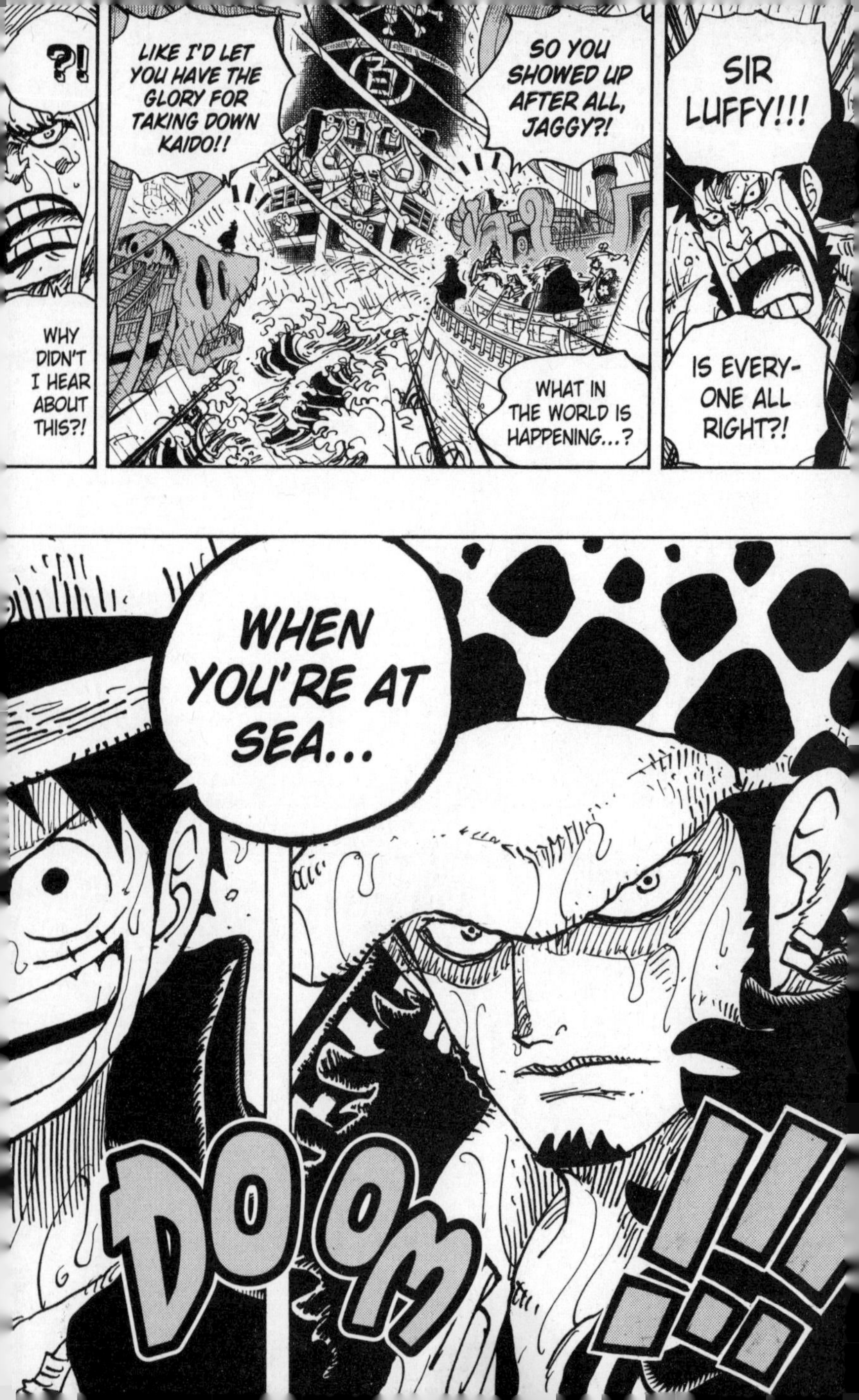

SIR LUFFY!!!
IS EVERY-ONE ALL RIGHT?!
SO YOU SHOWED UP AFTER ALL, JAGGY?!
LIKE I'D LET YOU HAVE THE GLORY FOR TAKING DOWN KAIDO!!
WHAT IN THE WORLD IS HAPPENING...?
?!
WHY DIDN'T I HEAR ABOUT THIS?!
WHEN YOU'RE AT SEA...
DOOM!!!!

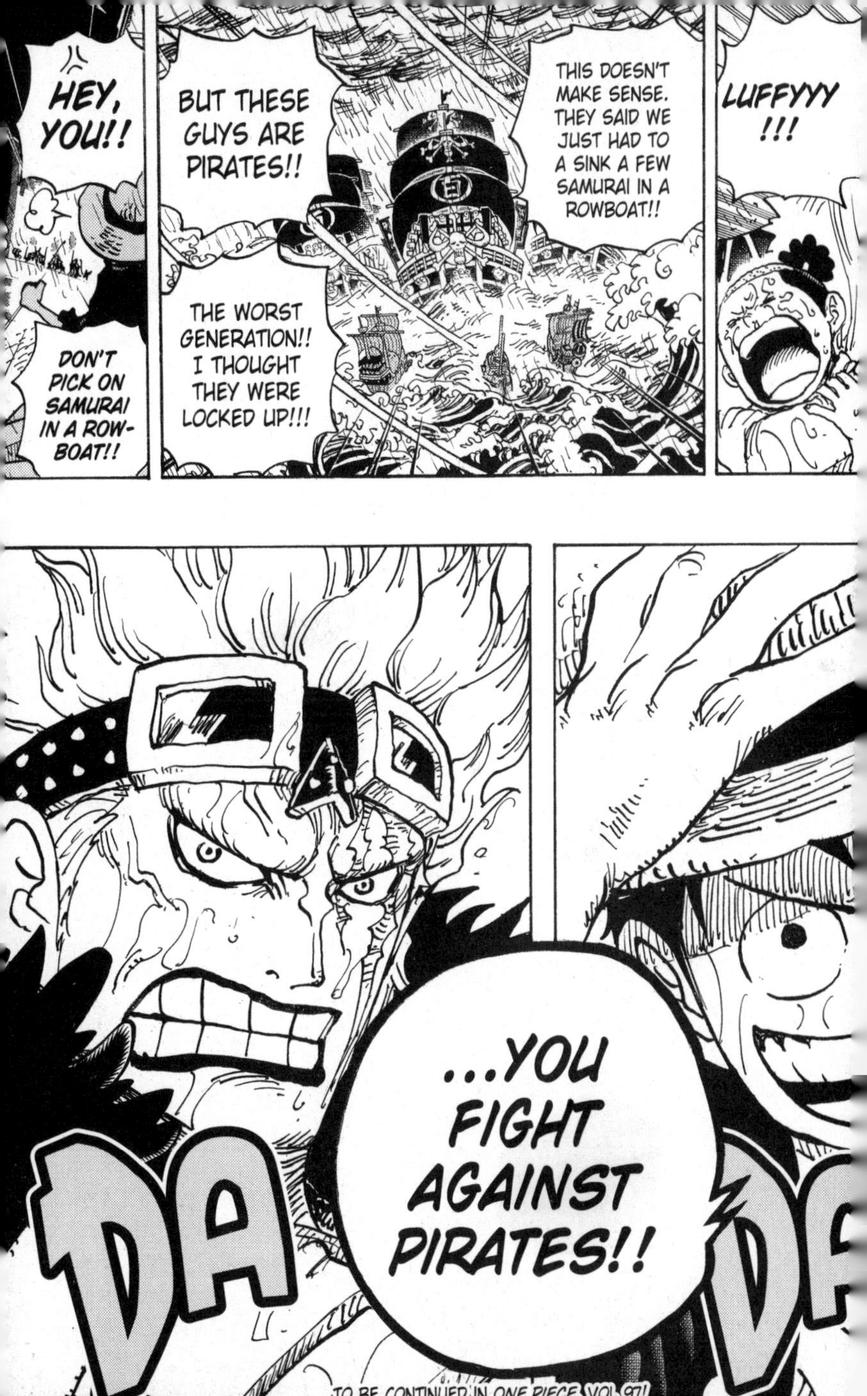

LUFFYYY !!!
THIS DOESN'T MAKE SENSE. THEY SAID WE JUST HAD TO A SINK A FEW SAMURAI IN A ROWBOAT!!
BUT THESE GUYS ARE PIRATES!!
THE WORST GENERATION!! I THOUGHT THEY WERE LOCKED UP!!!
HEY, YOU!!
DON'T PICK ON SAMURAI IN A ROW-BOAT!!
...YOU FIGHT AGAINST PIRATES!!
DA
DA

TO BE CONTINUED IN ONE PIECE, VOL 97!

COMING NEXT VOLUME:

...THE BIGGEST AND BEST PARTY YET!!!

LET'S WIN THIS FIGHT!! AND THEN WE'LL HAVE...

The Straw Hats and their comrades have been betrayed by a former ally and are surrounded on all sides by some of the fiercest pirates in the world. Even Momonosuke has been taken hostage. Time to panic? No, time to party!

ON SALE AUGUST 2021!

尾田栄一郎

Volume 96!!
If you turn it upside down, it's volume 69!!
Wait, never mind, it still says 96!!
But no matter how you flip this, there's no
turning back when the volume 100 party is
so close!! Enjoy volume 96!!

-Eiichiro Oda, 2020

Eiichiro Oda began his manga career at the age of 17, when his one-shot cowboy manga **Wanted!** won second place in the coveted Tezuka manga awards. Oda went on to work as an assistant to some of the biggest manga artists in the industry, including Nobuhiro Watsuki, before winning the Hop Step Award for new artists. His pirate adventure **One Piece**, which debuted in **Weekly Shonen Jump** in 1997, quickly became one of the most popular manga in Japan.

ONE PIECE VOL. 96
WANO PART 7

SHONEN JUMP Manga Edition

STORY AND ART BY EIICHIRO ODA

Translation/Stephen Paul
Touch-up Art & Lettering/Vanessa Satone
Design/Yukiko Whitley
Editor/Alexis Kirsch

Printed in the U.S.A.

Published by VIZ Media, LLC
P.O. Box 77010
San Francisco, CA 94107

10 9 8 7 6 5 4 3 2 1
First printing, April 2021

viz.com

PARENTAL ADVISORY
ONE PIECE is rated T for Teen and is recommended for ages 13 and up. This volume contains fantasy violence and tobacco usage.

ratings.viz.com

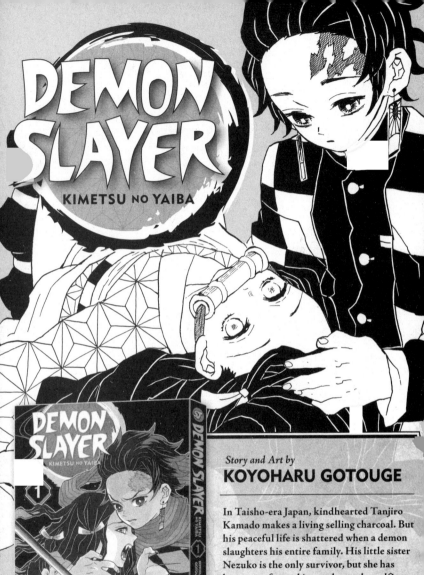

Story and Art by

KOYOHARU GOTOUGE

In Taisho-era Japan, kindhearted Tanjiro Kamado makes a living selling charcoal. But his peaceful life is shattered when a demon slaughters his entire family. His little sister Nezuko is the only survivor, but she has been transformed into a demon herself! Tanjiro sets out on a dangerous journey to find a way to return his sister to normal and destroy the demon who ruined his life.

BORUTO
=NARUTO NEXT GENERATIONS=

CREATOR/SUPERVISOR **Masashi Kishimoto**
ART BY **Mikio Ikemoto** SCRIPT BY **Ukyo Kodachi**

A NEW GENERATION OF NINJA IS HERE!

Naruto was a young shinobi with an incorrigible knack for mischief. He achieved his dream to become the greatest ninja in his village, and now his face sits atop the Hokage monument. But this is not his story... A new generation of ninja is ready to take the stage, led by Naruto's own son, Boruto!

SHONEN JUMP

VIZ MEDIA
viz.com

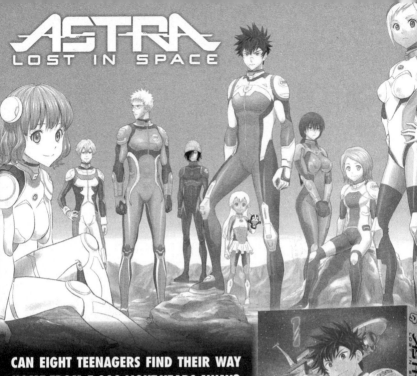

ASTRA LOST IN SPACE

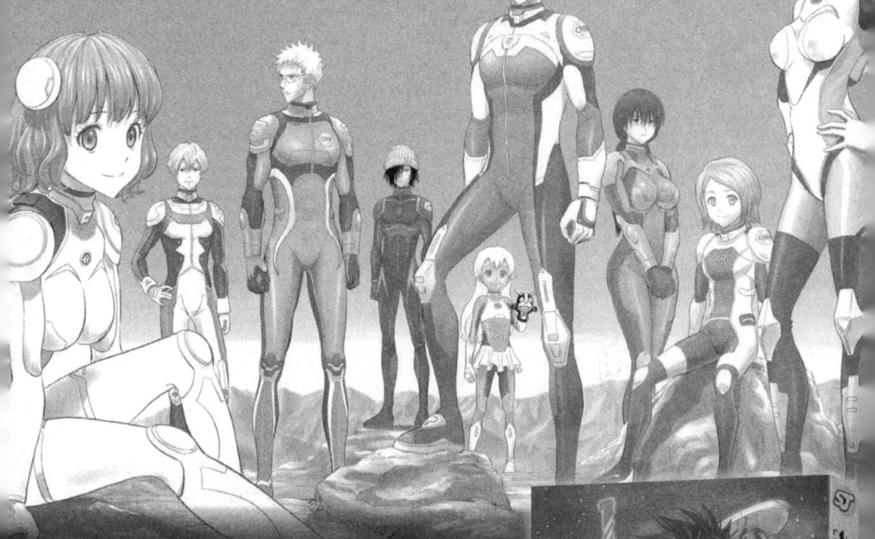

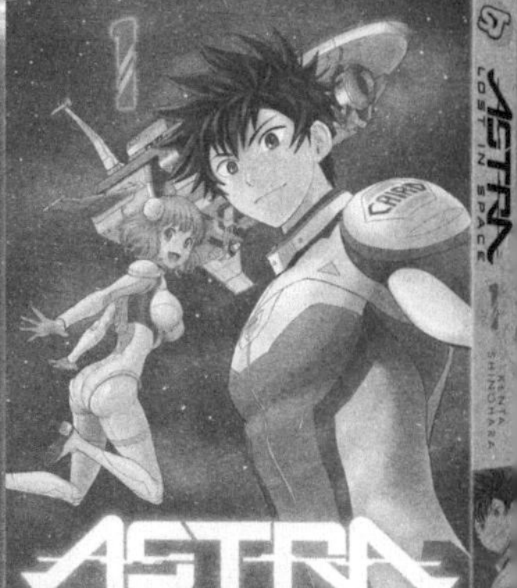
1
ASTRA
LOST IN SPACE
Story and Art by KENTA SHINOHARA
KENTA SHINOHARA
VIZ

CAN EIGHT TEENAGERS FIND THEIR WAY HOME FROM 5,000 LIGHT-YEARS AWAY?

It's the year 2063, and interstellar space travel has become the norm. Eight students from Caird High School and one child set out on a routine planet camp excursion. While there, the students are mysteriously transported 5,000 light-years away to the middle of nowhere! Will they ever make it back home?!

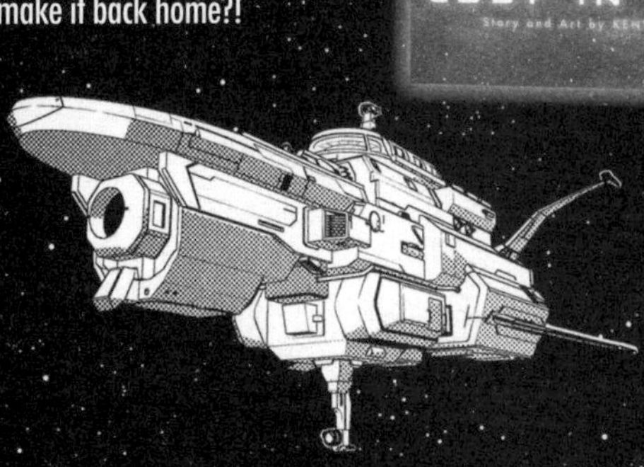

VIZ RATED T TEEN

MY HERO ACADEMIA

IZUKU MIDORIYA WANTS TO BE A HERO MORE THAN ANYTHING, BUT HE HASN'T GOT AN OUNCE OF POWER IN HIM. WITH NO CHANCE OF GETTING INTO THE U.A. HIGH SCHOOL FOR HEROES, HIS LIFE IS LOOKING LIKE A DEAD END. THEN AN ENCOUNTER WITH ALL MIGHT, THE GREATEST HERO OF ALL, GIVES HIM A CHANCE TO CHANGE HIS DESTINY...

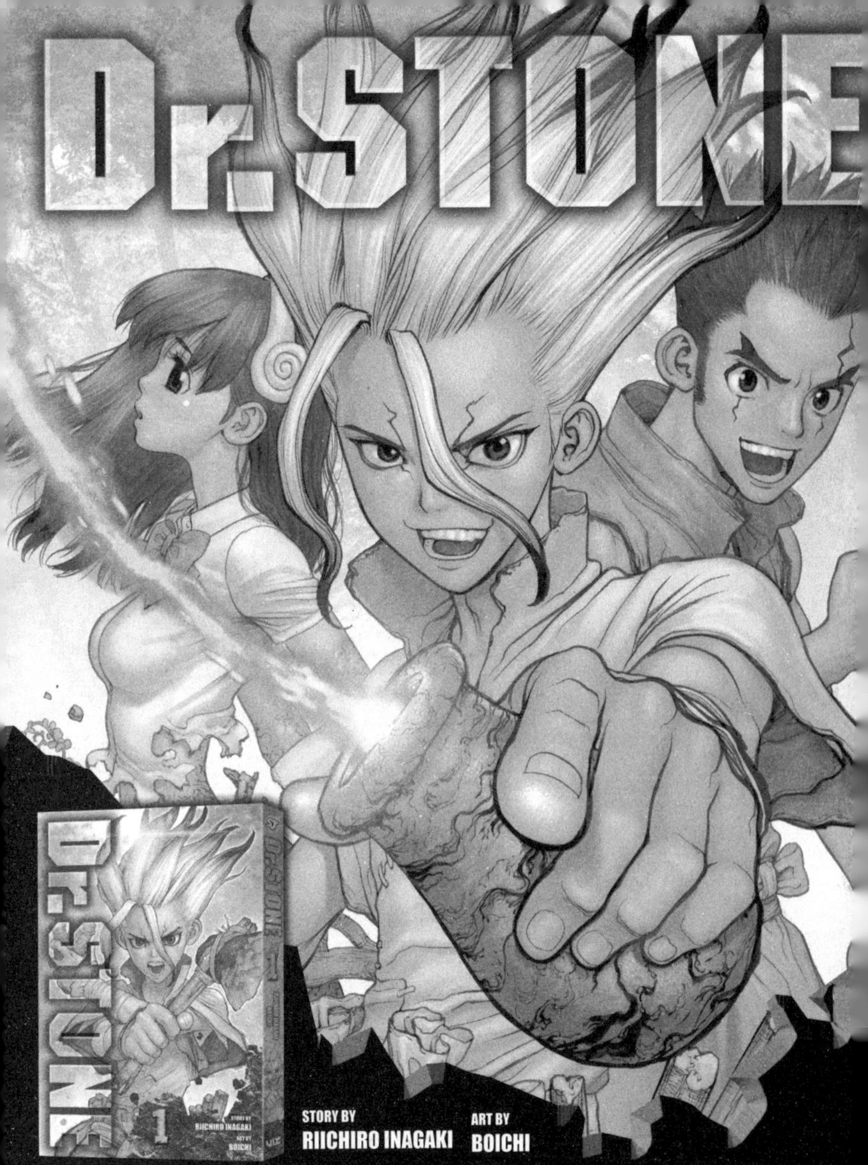

Dr.STONE

STORY BY
RIICHIRO INAGAKI

ART BY
BOICHI

One fateful day, all of humanity turned to stone. Many millenn
later, Taiju frees himself from petrification and finds hims
surrounded by statues. The situation looks grim—until he ru
into his science-loving friend Senku! Together they plan to resta
civilization with the power of science!

THE PROMISED NEVERLAND

STORY BY **KAIU SHIRAI**
ART BY **POSUKA DEMIZU**

Emma, Norman and Ray are the brightest kids at the Grace Field House orphanage. And under the care of the woman they refer to as "Mom," all the kids have enjoyed a comfortable life. Good food, clean clothes and the perfect environment to learn—what more could an orphan ask for? One day, though, Emma and Norman uncover the dark truth of the outside world they are forbidden from seeing.

You're Reading in the Wrong Direction!!

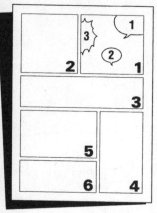

Whoops! Guess what? You're starting at the wrong end of the comic!

...It's true! In keeping with the original Japanese format, **One Piece** is meant to be read from right to left, starting in the upper-right corner.

Unlike English, which is read from left to right, Japanese is read from right to left, meaning that action, sound effects and word-balloon order are completely reversed...something which can make readers unfamiliar with Japanese feel pretty backwards themselves. For this reason, manga or Japanese comics published in the U.S. in English have sometimes been published "flopped"—that is, printed in exact reverse order, as though seen from the other side of a mirror.

By flopping pages, U.S. publishers can avoid confusing readers, but the compromise is not without its downside. For one thing, a character in a flopped manga series who once wore in the original Japanese version a T-shirt emblazoned with "M A Y" (as in "the merry month of") now wears one which reads "Y A M"! Additionally, many manga creators in Japan are themselves unhappy with the process, as some feel the mirror-imaging of their art skews their original intentions.

We are proud to bring you Eiichiro Oda's **One Piece** in the original unflopped format. For now, though, turn to the other side of the book and let the journey begin...!

—Editor

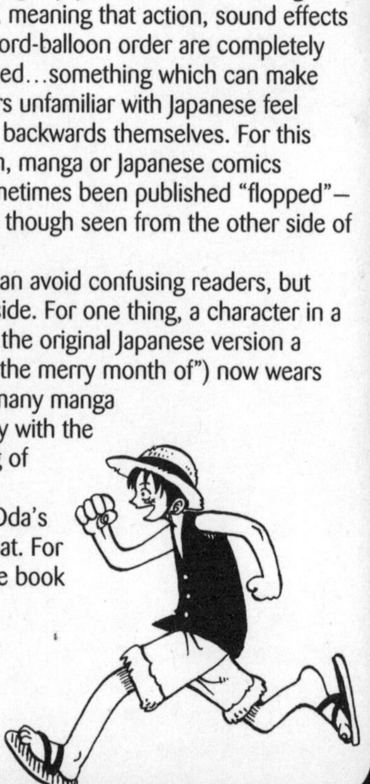